Ambassador *in* ✟Chains

THE APOSTLE PAUL AND REPRESENTING CHRIST IN TRYING TIMES

The Sacred Roots Annual 2015 - 2016

· REVISED COMMON LECTIONARY YEAR C ·

TUMI Press
3701 East Thirteenth Street North
Wichita, Kansas 67208

Ambassador in Chains: The Apostle Paul and Representing Christ in Trying Times, The Sacred Roots Annual 2015-2016
© 2015. The Urban Ministry Institute. All Rights Reserved. Copying, redistribution, and/or sale of these materials, or any unauthorized transmission, except as may be expressly permitted by the 1976 Copyright Act or in writing from the publisher is prohibited. Requests for permission should be addressed in writing to:

The Urban Ministry Institute
3701 East 13th Street
Wichita, KS 67208

ISBN: 978-1-62932-804-1

Published by TUMI Press, a division of World Impact, Inc.
The Urban Ministry Institute is a ministry of World Impact, Inc.

All Scripture quotations, unless otherwise noted, are from The Holy Bible, English Standard Version, © 2001 by Crossway Bible, a division of Good News Publishers. Used by permission. All Rights Reserved.

This Annual is dedicated to

**the 20 Christian Egyptian migrant workers
and 1 African worker
beheaded on a Libyan beach February 15, 2015
by the Islamic State of Iraq**

*who were martyred because of their faith in Jesus Christ,
who were labeled as
"the people of the cross, followers of the hostile Egyptian church,"
who were beheaded on account of their allegiance to the Lord,
whose sacrifice was made in the
same spirit of the martyrs from the beginning,
who refused to deny their Lord,
even if it meant the cost of their own lives,
whose act of courage was acknowledged by the head of the
Coptic Orthodox Church, Pope Tawadros II,
to be commemorated on February 15th of the Gregorian calendar,
of the 20 martyrs who so demonstrated their faith,
that they led 21st martyr, Matthew Ayariga,
who originally was not a believer, but after seeing the 20's faith,
affirmed the Faith of Jesus he saw in them, declaring,
"Their God is my God" . . .*

*To these amazing saints and ambassadors of the Kingdom,
who followed in the same train of the apostles
in giving the extreme sacrifice
of ultimate devotion to Christ with their lives,
to them we dedicate this annual,
with the hope that their courage, steadfastness, and perseverance
might be reproduced in us,
the same virtue shown in the apostle Paul,
the one inspiring our reflections this year.*

"Praying at all times in the Spirit,
with all prayer and supplication.
To that end keep alert with all perseverance,
making supplication for all the saints,
and also for me, that words may be given to me
in opening my mouth boldly
to proclaim the mystery of the gospel,
for which I am an ambassador in chains,
that I may declare it boldly,
as I ought to speak."

~ Ephesians 6.18-20 (ESV)

Our Theme Prayer for 2016

*Almighty God, by whose grace and power thy holy Martyrs
triumphed over suffering, and despised death:
Grant, we beseech thee, that enduring hardness,
and waxing valiant in fight,
we may with the noble army of Martyrs
receive the crown of everlasting life;
through Jesus Christ our Lord.
Amen.*

~ *England Revised Prayer Book.*
In John Wallace Suter, Jr., ed. *The Book of English Collects.*
New York, NY: Harper, 1940. p. 69.

Table of Contents

Preface

"Pray also for me, that whenever I speak, words may be given me so that I will fearlessly make known the mystery of the gospel, for which I am an ambassador in chains. Pray that I may declare it fearlessly, as I should."

~ Ephesians 6.19-20 (ESV)

Shared Spirituality: Sojourning Together as Followers of Christ

All disciples of Jesus worldwide own a common stock, a mutual identity, and a shared destiny. We are saved by grace through faith in the Lord Jesus Christ, all justified by his shed blood on the Cross, and regenerated by the Holy Spirit. We have been born from above, born from Love, united to Christ in his death and resurrection, set free from the Curse and now indwelt by the Holy Spirit. As God's one undivided Church we are growing up into Christ into all things, sharing the same spiritual food, from the same Table of the Lord, baptized in the same name, inspired by the same hope. It is only right, therefore, that we strive to share a common spiritual journey, learning the same lessons, following the same Lord. We are one in the Spirit, and one in Christ Jesus, to the glory of God.

Each year, the TUMI community of missionaries deliberately join hands and hearts to share a spiritual quest and journey, to seek the Lord together in Scripture and sacrament, and to walk together in our efforts to be formed spiritually through the spiritual disciplines. All our practices, services, and activities are integrated together, informed by our commitment to walking the Christ life according to the rhythms of the Church Year. These activities are linked by a commitment to spiritual formation in sync with a biblical theme which we use to intersect and to integrate our diverse lives, numerous tasks, and ministry projects.

As members of World Impact's Religious Missionary Order, the TUMI staff takes seriously our missional identity, and seeks to translate that identity into a lifestyle that reveals us to be followers of Christ even as we seek to train leaders for Christ. We take literally our time-tested adage that *who we are in Christ is more important than what we do*. Actually, we are convinced that who we are fundamentally determines and gives rise to those things we actually represent and do.

Ambassador in Chains: The Sacred Roots Annual 2015-2016
Our guidebook this year is entitled *Ambassador in Chains: The Sacred Roots Annual 2015-2016*. Without question, the Apostle Paul is a person of profound importance in the life of the Church, and as one commentator puts it, "We must never underestimate the unparalleled significance of the Apostle Paul. It is not an exaggeration to say that except for our Lord Jesus Christ, he was surely the most significant and influential man that ever lived." Regardless of one's opinion as to the accuracy of this claim, I do agree with Professor F. F. Bruce's belief that Paul was one of the most significant figures in the history of civilization. His influence in the early Christian movement, his broad impact on the life and thought of the Church throughout the ages, and his evangelical zeal to win the world with the Gospel makes him of special interest to us this upcoming year in our devotion and discipleship to Christ.

Paul became a follower of Jesus after the Lord confronted him on the road to Damascus as he was traveling under priestly orders to persecute Christians there. His journey, ministry, and adventures are chronicled in the book of Acts, which reveal Paul to be perhaps the most influential teacher, herald, and missionary of the Gospel to both Asia Minor and what is known as present day Greece.

This year we will concentrate on Paul's influence after he began his ministry as one of the major contributors to the religious movement that would become Christianity. He was one of the Jews dispersed across the Roman empire, as a part of the Jewish Diaspora, a Pharisee, whom the Lord confronted, converted, and called to be his apostle to the Gentiles. His ministry would be fruitful, taking him throughout the eastern Roman Empire, spreading the Gospel of Jesus and the upcoming Kingdom of God.

At the end of his amazing ministry, Paul was persecuted by members of the Judaistic faith, those who took his teaching as a repudiation of the Mosaic Law and a threat to their customs and religious practices. Over time, his apostolic and pastoral oversight of the new Christian movement would lead to fourteen letters traditionally assigned to his authorship. Scholarly consensus believes that of these fourteen epistles, seven are without question written by Paul: 1 Thessalonians, Galatians, Philemon, Philippians, 1st and 2nd Corinthians, and the epistle of the Romans. Speculations abound concerning the authorship of the other books, with a commonly held view that asserts that they were written by one of Paul's disciples who used Paul's name for authority's sake. In this setting, we will hold to the traditional view of Pauline authorship, i.e., the epistles carrying his name were more than likely written by him.

Paul's life was characterized by constant, unbroken, and taxing rejection and persecution, which would ultimately land him in prison on account of the name of Christ, and ultimately his death as a martyr of Christ. 2 Corinthians 11.16-29 offers a snapshot into the intense opposition Paul encountered throughout the course of his service for Christ:

> I repeat, let no one think me foolish. But even if you do, accept me as a fool, so that I too may boast a little. What I am saying with this boastful confidence, I say not as the Lord would but as a fool. Since many boast according to the flesh, I too will boast. For you gladly bear with fools, being wise yourselves! For you bear it if someone makes slaves of you, or devours you, or takes advantage of you, or puts on airs, or strikes you in the face. To my shame, I must say, we were too weak for that! But whatever anyone else dares to boast of – I am speaking as a fool – I also dare to boast of that. Are they Hebrews? So am I. Are they Israelites? So am I. Are they offspring of Abraham? So am I. Are they servants of Christ? I am a better one – I am talking like a madman – with far greater labors, far more imprisonments, with countless beatings, and often near death. Five times I received at the hands of the Jews the forty lashes less one. Three times I was beaten with rods. Once I was stoned. Three times I was shipwrecked; a night and a day I was adrift at sea; on frequent journeys, in danger from rivers, danger from robbers, danger from my own people, danger from Gentiles, danger in the city, danger in the wilderness, danger at sea, danger from false brothers; in toil and hardship, through many a sleepless night, in hunger and thirst, often without food, in cold and exposure. And, apart from other things, there is the daily pressure on me of my anxiety for all the churches. Who is weak, and I am not weak? Who is made to fall, and I am not indignant?

This amazing catalogue of suffering displays the heart of Christian devotion at its core. Paul's journeys as Christ's ambassador reveal a side of Christian representation that must be both acknowledged and welcomed if we intend on bearing fruit today, representing the Kingdom of Jesus, living as his disciple in a hostile and dying world, and willing to place our lives in jeopardy. No one can live in Christ with godliness and holiness and not suffer profoundly because of it (2 Tim. 3.12). If we commit to be Christ's agents in our personal worlds, we must embrace the real likelihood that we will be falsely accused, deliberately misunderstood, and painfully persecuted because of his name. This year, we will strive to discover the truth of this teaching through our meditation on the life of the apostle Paul and the writings that are traditionally ascribed to his time while in prison.

Ordinary Time Series: The Apostle Paul and the Prison Epistles
During the second, extended period of Ordinary time during the Season after Pentecost we will study together the books of the Pauline corpus traditionally referred to as the Prison Epistles: Ephesians, Philippians, Colossians, and Philemon.

These resources reveal much of the majesty of the Christian life, and the heart and mind of an apostle who writes dramatic letters of freedom and life while himself being a prisoner of Rome. This year, I will be joined by my fine colleagues who with me will be teaching through these letters, whose teachings will be available online at www.tumi.org. Dr. Hank Voss (World Impact's National Church Planting Director) and Rev. Don Allsman (TUMI's Satellite Executive Director) will both teach through the book of Ephesians, and Brian Luke, our Executive Director of Operations will teach through the book of Philippians. I will close our teaching cycle with the books of Colossians and Philemon.

Here is a listing of the teaching sessions in their order of appearance, beginning the week after the celebration of Trinity Sunday:

- Introduction: Ambassador in Chains, Eph. 6.19-20
- Life in Christ, Eph. 1.1-2

- The Purpose of the Church, Eph. 1.3-14
- God's Poetry, Eph. 2.8-10
- A Prisoner's Prayer, Eph. 3.14-21
- The Constitution of the Church, Eph. 4.1-6
- The Fulness of Christ, Eph. 4.11-16
- The Wisdom of Christ, Eph. 5.15-21
- Stand Firm in Christ, Eph. 6.10-20
- Imprisoned with Purpose, Phil. 1.1-30
- Every Knee Will Bow, Every Tongue Confess, Phil. 2.1-18
- For the Work of Christ, Phil. 2.19-30
- True Citizenship, Phil. 3.1-21
- The Lord Is at Hand, Phil. 4.1-9
- Trust in God, Phil. 4.10-23
- The Preeminence of Christ, Col. 1.15-23
- So Walk in Him, Col. 2.1-7
- The Shadow and the Substance, Col. 2.8-23
- Seek the Things That Are Above, Col. 3.1-11
- Let the Peace of Christ Rule, Col. 3.12-4.1
- The Final Instructions, Col. 4.2-6
- Paul's Remembrance of Philemon, Philem. 1-7
- Paul's Request for Onesimus, Philem. 8-25

Our hope is that this reflection on Paul's writings while he was in prison may greatly facilitate in us an understanding of what it means to live victoriously in the midst of trying and difficult times. We are confident that he will lead us, and instruct us together in the way of discipleship.

Our 2015-2016 Church Year Calendar:
The Majestic Splendor of God

We also invite you to use our Annual in association with our Church Year Calendar for 2015-16, *The Majestic Splendor of God*. While the notion of creation continues to be a controversial subject in both academy and human society, nothing has changed the Bible's fundamental affirmation of the source of all things. The LORD, our triune God, is the creator of all things, revealing his majestic splendor in the created universe. This calendar displays photographic snippets of the wonders of God's beautiful creation. In it we affirm a central creedal doctrine of the Faith: The heavens are the LORD's (Ps. 115.16), made by his word and by the breath of his mouth (Ps. 33.6). Each panel follows the natural seasons of creation, given with an association with the themes of the appropriate spiritual journey of the year.

As always, this calendar follows the order of the traditional Christian Year, from Advent to the Reign of Christ the King. Included are the weekly texts of Revised Common Lectionary Year C, along with major Christian feast days. This calendar will make a marvelous companion to the annual; they are coordinated together, to be read in conjunction with one another, practicing the real-time lived story of Christ as outlined in the Scriptures. Both the Annual and the Calendar affirm the same central truth regarding our triune God: the Creator who made the heavens and earth is the same Lord who called, equipped, and sent out the great apostle to the Gentiles, Paul of Tarsus. The God of creation of the heavens and the earth is also the same God of salvation.

Live as an Ambassador for Christ
Paul told the Corinthians that he and the other apostles analogically served as ambassadors, representing a different realm and government, with its own Prince and King, its own law and truths, and its own citizenship and pledge (2 Cor. 5.20). Our genuine desire is that this year's 2015-16 annual, Ambassador In Chains, will move you to think how you can better represent our Lord Christ in the place where he has called you. In your circle of relationships – family, friends, associates, and contacts – you indeed are an ambassador for Jesus and his Kingdom, called to stand in his stead, speaking and living on behalf of the Age to Come in this present age. Our prayer for you and ourselves is that the Spirit would use these texts, images, prayers, reflections, and readings to

move you to heroic representation of the King, allowing you to serve him with honor regardless of the cost, wherever he may lead.

So, join us as we use employ this year's Sacred Roots Annual to meditate on the life and thought of the great apostle who laid down everything for his Lord, whose great hope was to know the fellowship of the Lord's sufferings, being made conformable to the King's death on the Cross. We can learn what it means to be Christ's ambassador by observing him together. If we do it to his glory, we will better honor the One whom we represent, the soon-coming King of the Kingdom, the Lord Jesus Christ. Let all honor be to him alone.

Striving to Represent the King,
Rev. Dr. Don L. Davis

Great Is the Lord Most High

Great is the Lord Most High!
In splendor You dwell, so glorious,
Reigning forever victorious,
God of the earth and sky!
Great is the Lord Most High!
Beholding You, Lord, we stand amazed;
Rock of the Ages, and Ancient of Days,
Great is the Lord Most High!

Great is the Lord Most High!
Creator and King of the universe,
Redeeming creation from chaos and curse,
Savior and El Shaddai!
Great is the Lord Most High!
Your Name is majestic in all the earth,
And we stand in awe of Your fine handiwork.
Great is the Lord Most High!

Great is the Lord Most High!
Your holy dominion shall now endure;
Your covenant promise is certain and sure;
We lift up your name on high!
Great is the Lord Most High!
Forever the kingdom belongs to you;
You're near to all those who will stand on Your truth;
Great is the Lord Most High!

How to Use This Book

The *Sacred Roots Annual* represents the devotional and liturgical structure for the Religious Missionary Order (RMO) community for TUMI International. As members of World Impact's RMO, we center our spiritual formation upon the Church Year, and share individually and corporately in the various readings, prayers, practices, and disciplines associated with it. We invite you to share this common liturgical journey with us, which is connected to the sojourn of the visible Church in the world. This wonderful spiritual trek tracks the events of biblical history with a focus on the life and ministry of Jesus. These devotions, events, emphases, and practices are designed to enhance your personal, family, small group, and congregational journeys through the living of the Christ life with the Christian calendar. Our sincere hope is that you will be greatly enriched and encouraged as you walk with us as we follow Christ.

In order to take full advantage of the *Annual's* various resources, we offer below our explanations of its critical parts, and how they are intended to function in your own spiritual formation.

Following Christ through the Church Year

As you will notice immediately, the *Sacred Roots Annual* is organized around the "Church Year." Informed by the person of Christ from his first coming to his coming in glory, the

Church Year celebrates observances, feasts, and services that allow believers all across the world to think "Christianly" about their life and times.

As a way of both worship and discipleship, the Church Year can help us put the events of our everyday lives in the context of what scholars and liturgists call the "Christ event," those promises, manifestations, and historical moments of God's saving work in the person of Jesus of Nazareth. We form our spiritual practice and discipline on our following of the Church Year, and we can attest to its ability to center worshipers and disciples on the person of Christ, and help to shape discipleship in light of the Scripture's testimony regarding his life and ministry in the world, and the hope of his return.

Shaped By the Story:
Journeying with Jesus through the Church Year Calendar
This year's Sacred Roots devotional is called *Ambassador in Chains: The Sacred Roots Annual 2015-2016*. It follows the episodes and reflections of the Apostle Paul, who refers to himself in Ephesians as an "ambassador in chains" (Eph. 6.20). The Apostle Paul's profound influence on the theology, practice, and mission of the Church makes him someone who deserves our attention, respect, and allegiance.

Our complimentary Church Year calendar, *The Majestic Splendor of God*, compliments the Annual, following the same order of the traditional Christian Year, from Advent to the Reign of Christ the King. Both the Annual and the Calendar refer to the weekly texts of *Revised Common Lectionary Year C*, citing also the major Christian feast days and festivals.

These two resources, the Sacred Roots Annual and the Church Year Calendar, provide the local congregation, pastor, and growing disciple with a clear road map for both worship and reflection through the Church Year 2015-16. The Annual will challenge us on what it means to serve as an ambassador of Christ and his Kingdom in a hostile world, and the Calendar will reveal to us the majestic splendor of God in all his created works. Together, the Annual and Calendar, affirm a single, dominant truth: the God of creation is the God of covenant grace in Christ. The God who made the worlds (Church Year calendar) is also the God who saved it in the finished work of Christ (The Annual).

Again, both the Annual and the calendar follow the traditional Church Year (also called the *Liturgical Year*, or *Christian Calendar*) services and observances, accompanied by references from the *Revised Common Lectionary Year C* readings. Similarly, the Sacred Roots Annual and calendar interact and coordinate well with one another, with both allowing you to enrich your spiritual journey as you imagine, relive, and retell the events of Jesus in real time, re-embracing the hope of Christ, i.e., that he will soon return and transform a restored creation under God's reign.

For the Annual's art, Tim Ladwig illustrated the cover for our *Ambassador in Chains* signature painting, laying out in his own fruitful and sanctified imagination his creative depiction of Paul in chains under the soldier's watchcare. This piece captures the flavor of Paul's prison letters – the reality of being under armed guard, and the zeal of the Church's most productive apostle, ever sharing the Gospel of salvation to all who would listen.

In connection to the Calendar, Carolyn Hennings, our Graphic and Curriculum Designer whose design brilliance seems to have no limit, selected our wonderful array of photographs for this year's calendar. Carolyn's quiet grace gives way to her extraordinary sense of both artistic beauty and spiritual depth, a combination that shows up, literally, in every piece she designs. This extraordinary calendar reflects pictures of the Lord's majestic splendor in his creation which Carolyn, our own gifted missionary designer and artist, compiled and arranged.

Of course, you can obtain additional copies of this year's *Annual* as well as our Church Year Calendar, from *www.tumi.org/annual*. Additionally, here at this website you will also find an abundance of other theological, biblical, and spiritual formation resources, for both personal and small group use.

Meaning of "Proper" in the Church Year

As you follow through the Church Year Calendar, you will notice that during the Season after Pentecost (also referred to as *Ordinary Time* or *Kingdomtide*) the weeks are referred to as "Proper," followed by a particular number. This term (*Proper*) is used for all the weeks during this extended period, except special days (e.g., *Trinity Sunday*, *Reformation Day, All Saints Day*, and *Reign of Christ the King*). The Propers of the Church Year refer to how some church traditions assign appointed prayers (called *collects*) for specific services, along with particular Psalms and Lessons (i.e., lectionary texts) for a given week or special day. For instance, the Anglican and Episcopal traditions (among others) use these Proper references to conduct their worship services in conjunction with their books of order and books of common prayer. These are merely terms to help indicate what prayers, Scriptures, and lessons may be used during that specific week of worship.

Theme for the Week

Usually, we follow the Church Year as the guide for our weekly themes and preaching texts, drawn normally from reference outlines in the *Revised Common Lectionary*. The lectionary is a comprehensive Bible reading program drafted specifically in order to help congregations read through the major sections and stories of the Scriptures over a three-year period. The Years A, B, and C refer to the Gospel readings according to the evangelists: *Year A* referring to *Matthew*, *Year B* to *Mark*, and *Year C* to *Luke*. During these separate years, which cycle the one after the other, the Gospel readings will coincide with these books. The Gospel of John is included in each of the Years A, B, and C, and is referred to liberally at various times and seasons throughout the Church Year.

The majority of this year's Gospel citations will be taken from the Gospel of Luke, the Gospel designation of *Church Year C*. For most of the year, our weekly service themes are based on texts taken directly from the Lectionary, and our times of retreat, prayer, and spiritual discipline are also informed by those Scriptures as well. Within the *Annual*, you will find that our weekly themes are provided for you, along with a descriptive statement that highlights its meaning for us that week. Please check our website *www.tumi.org/annual* for an at-a-glance chart of our entire year's lectionary texts and themes.

An online version of the *Annual* is posted for you to take advantage of during those times when your soft-cover *Annual* is not available. You may find the appropriate week of devotional and liturgical reading and observance at *www.tumi.org/annual*.

Daily Devotional Guide

As a way to "pile drive" the truth of the weekly theme into our individual and corporate minds, we ponder it daily in devotional readings, meditation, and prayer. Set aside time, either in the morning or evening or both, to spend time with the Lord, reflecting on the truths learned from the text in sermon and discussion.

Structure as Servant to Spontaneity

We are convinced that the best prerequisite needed to display skill in a spontaneous environment is prolonged practice and application. Only after you follow the daily regimen of the disciplines can you be enriched in your ongoing walk and devotion to Christ. Please take note of both the order and sequence of our devotional guide, which mirrors the traditional liturgy of the Church in significant ways. First, each day is structured similarly, with a connected sequence:

Preparing Our Hearts
Invocation: Our Prayer of Acclamation
Call to Worship

Praising Our God
Te Deum Laudamus
Praise and Thanksgiving
Gloria Patri

Listening to His Voice
Chronological Bible Reading
Lectionary Readings
Reflection: Silence and/or Journaling

Responding in Faith
Recitation of the Apostles' Creed
Prayers of Confession
Assurance of Pardon
Petitions and Supplications
The Doxology

Departing to Serve
Benediction: Our Prayer of Acknowledgment
Affirmation from the Psalms
Pray without Ceasing – Flash Prayer for the Day

We do not suggest that conformity to service order is demanded in the NT for the worshiper, nor that one gets "brownie points" for following this structure. As a regimen, this is not meant to be empty and formalistic. Rather, we seek to "discipline ourselves for the purpose of godliness" (1 Tim. 4.6-7). This kind of daily focus and repetition is done, not to create mindless repetition and familiarity, but to deliberately build within us the habit of coming to God in shared process and approach.

As a worshiping, serving, and witnessing community, we have found it especially refreshing and helpful over the years to employ together the same guide – reading the same Scripture, reciting the same creed and prayers, and seeking as one body the same grace from the same Lord. We seek the Lord in our own individual ways, but strive to do so from a common prayer, devotion, and practice. Our motto in this is simple: we seek the Lord, alone together. We strive to share a spiritual journey and language with one another so we can better encourage and enrich one another.

We firmly believe that only the Holy Spirit can energize and develop true spirituality. He is our Lord and Life-giver (as the Nicene Creed suggests), and only he can make Christ real to us in our times in the various disciplines of spiritual formation. We seek to daily give ourselves to him in this structure in order to open ourselves to his leading and teaching. The Holy Spirit is neither limited nor hindered by such a structure (notice the Jewish sacred year and its annual rhythms of Passover, Unleavened Bread, the Feast of Weeks, the Feast of Trumpets, the Day of Atonement, and the Feast of Tabernacles). Our Lord's custom was to go both to the synagogue on the Sabbath and to the great feasts in Jerusalem, and all we desire here is to be open to him in all we do.

As you employ the *Annual's* devotional order, it may be helpful to have an explanation of its parts, and what we seek to do during the various stages of our approach and indwelling of the presence of God.

Preparing Our Hearts

Invocation: Our Prayer of Acclamation

Our "Preparing Our Hearts" section begins with Invocation prayers. These are opening prayers tied directly to our weekly themes in the calendar. These are prayers of invitation (seeking the Lord's presence and blessing for our time of worship and praise), as well as prayers of acclamation (affirming the truth of God's goodness and awesome deeds on our behalf). These prayers ask the Lord to speak to us about the theme at hand through our time in praise and worship, reading, prayer, and meditation.

Call to Worship

This affirmation, taken directly from the common liturgy of the main communions of the Church, declares God as the Sovereign Lord of all creation, the receiver of our praise and worship, and acknowledges him as the sole recipient of our praise, faith, and adoration.

Praising Our God

Te Deum Laudamus: We Praise Thee, O God

We open our praise section with a familiar prayer employed now for centuries in many traditions within their morning devotional regimen, the *Te Deum Laudamus*, or translated from the Latin, "We praise Thee, O God." This prayer is an early chant of the Western Church beginning, "We praise Thee, O God, we acknowledge Thee to be the Lord." In the legend of the Church, this prayer is ascribed to an "ecstatic outburst" of St. Ambrose when he baptized St. Augustine. The prayer is now widely attributed to Bishop Nicetas of Dacia (c. 335-414). As mentioned above, the prayer is sung at morning prayer in Anglican churches and at matins in the Roman office. (It is associated with one of the order of services, Rite II, in the classic devotional guide *The Book of Common Prayer.*)

By the way, if you are not accustomed to reading your prayers of devotion and intercession, know that you are not alone! You should not be too squeamish about *reading* or *reciting* a prayer. Recall, for instance, that the Psalms are simply songs and written prayers (as are many hymns of the Church) which have been read and recited in worship for centuries. Furthermore, Christ Jesus himself told us to repeat a prayer he gave us with the Lord's prayer, and often in prayer circles the prayers of Paul, Nehemiah, Daniel, or Jehoshaphat or others are used in our supplications.

Prayer is about authentic heart conversation to God; the question is whether we are reverent, humble, and open in our address to the Lord, not whether we recite or read a prayer, or use someone else's words. Make sure your heart is right with God, and communicate through the words your own heart's desire. Focus on real prayer, not on whether you're reciting the prayers or not!

Praise and Thanksgiving
We should open our approach to God with worship, praise, song, and acclamation. God is great and greatly to be praised! Recall the words of the psalmist, "Make a joyful noise to the LORD, all the earth! Serve the LORD with gladness! Come into his presence with singing! Know that the LORD, he is God! It is he who made us, and we are his; we are his people, and the sheep of his pasture. Enter his gates with thanksgiving, and his courts with praise! Give thanks to him; bless his name!" (Ps. 110.1-4).

Feel free to bring a chorus book or hymnal to your time, and always come prepared to sing and play songs, hymns, and spiritual songs to the Lord. As members of the royal priesthood of God, remember worship of our God is both a privilege and a duty (1 Pet. 2.8-9).

Gloria Patri
> *Glory be to the Father,*
> *And to the Son and to the Holy Spirit:*
> *As it was in the beginning,*
> *Is now, and ever shall be,*
> *World without end. Amen, amen.*

This worship interlude is familiar in many traditions of the Church, and is used in a variety of services and places. For instance, Anglicans mainly use the *Gloria Patri* (Latin, "Glory to the Father") to conclude the singing or recitation of psalms and canticles at the Daily Offices (Devotions) of Morning and Evening Prayer. Lutherans historically have added it after the recitation or chanting of the Psalm during the Service of the Word and at various times in the Daily Office. Evangelical Presbyterian churches and Methodists frequently sing it to conclude the "responsive reading" at the end of the psalm readings.

In this devotional, we have placed the *Gloria Patri* at the end of our time of praise and thanksgiving, serving as a fitting closing affirmation of our triune God as the only Lord worthy of all praise, honor, and glory. In this setting it is meant to highlight our worship to the Lord, Father, Son, and Holy Spirit, as the solitary author of all life and salvation, and therefore alone worthy of our highest and best praise.

Listening to His Voice
Chronological Reading for the Day

The essential rhythm of New Testament worship is word and sacrament. Concentrating on the Word of God, listening to his voice, should be a priority in all our devotional moments in God's presence. Each year we read through the Scriptures together chronologically, gaining greater insight on the entire biblical Story of God, tracking the events of God's covenant promise in their historical order. Included in the *Sacred Roots*

Annual are the texts associated with this through-the-Bible-in-one-year chronological reading process.

You can also pick up a paper guide that includes the references in brochure form. This handy guide is convenient, allowing you to place it in your favorite reading Bible. We highlight the Seasons of the Church Year in attractive colors, and key the sections to the emphases of the Church Year's time schedule. You can obtain this from our website (*www.tumistore.org*).

Reading through the Scriptures chronologically helps you see the underlying plot of the Scriptures: the salvation of God in the person of Jesus of Nazareth, the Christ. This reading provides not only richer insight into the events of Scripture, but also a greater comprehension of the whole story's meaning and movement – a story which climaxes in the Christ event; his birth, his life, his death, burial, resurrection, ascension, and return.

Lectionary Readings

As mentioned before, our reading guide is the *Revised Common Lectionary*, a Bible reading program drafted to help congregations in their public reading of Scripture. It is crafted in such a way that the vast majority of Scripture can be read together over a three-year period. It is the lectionary texts that we use to organize our worship and sermon preparation. The Years A, B, and C refer to the Gospel readings according to the evangelists: Year A referring to Matthew, Year B to Mark, and Year C to Luke's Gospel. During these separate years the Gospel readings will coincide with these books. The Gospel of John is included in each of the Years A, B, and C, and is referred to liberally at various times and seasons throughout the Church Year.

Note: In the *Annual*, the Old Testament lectionary texts are abbreviated with *OT*, and the New Testament are abbreviated with *NT*.

Reflection: Silence and/or Journaling

After hearing from God in his Word, we then respond to the voice of God with meditation, reflection, and silence. Here we would recommend that you take time to silently reflect on the meaning of the personal charge that God has spoken to you through his Word, whether a promise, a command, a teaching, or an insight. Wait in the presence of God, and be silent and patient; allow the Spirit to highlight, pinpoint, or address whatever issues and truths he wishes as you wait before the Lord.

Responding in Faith

The Apostles' Creed

In the tradition of the Church, it has been customary to follow the hearing of God's Word with the affirmation of the historic orthodox faith, in creedal form. Our daily devotional guide includes the confession of the Apostles' Creed, the basic creed of the Reformed churches, and a significant statement still used commonly in baptism. The Apostles' Creed was used as a confessional statement at the baptism of new converts centuries ago and is still used today in that format. Reciting it each day reminds us of our "cruciform life," i.e., our baptismal covenant of allegiance to Christ, and our commitment to share his death and risen life in our daily discipleship.

The Apostles' Creed is one of the most basic statements of early Christian confession, dating from perhaps a half century or so from the time the New Testament was written. It is widely used by many denominations for both worship and Christian education purposes, its use is most prevalent in Western churches. While affirming the classic outline of the Christian faith, it does not address some Christological issues which would be later addressed in other creeds, including our oft-used "Nicene Creed" (i.e., Nicene-Constantinople Creed of CE 381).

Still, the Apostles' Creed represents one of the oldest, clearest, and most authoritative summaries of the faith of the ancient, undivided Church. Please note: the reference in the Creed to "catholic" refers to the universal nature of the Church's membership and makeup, i.e., the Church of all members through all ages and times, of all languages and peoples. It refers to no particular tradition or denominational expression, and does not refer in particular to the Roman Catholic expression of the Church.

Prayers of Confession
Following the traditional liturgy, we include a special moment of confession and cleansing before the Lord. This response of seeking the Lord's forgiveness is an integral element in our walking with God, and maintaining an acceptable communion in Christ. It is an important part of our faith response to the Lord. John says in his first epistle, "This is the message we have heard from him and proclaim to you, that God is light, and in him is no darkness at all. If we say we have fellowship with him while we walk in darkness, we lie and do not practice the truth. But if we walk in the light, as he is in the light, we have fellowship with one another, and the blood of Jesus his Son cleanses us from all sin. If we say we have no sin, we deceive ourselves, and the truth is not in us. If we confess our sins, he is faithful and just to forgive us our sins and to cleanse us from all unrighteousness" (1 John 1.5-9).

Assurance of Pardon
Once we have acknowledged and renounced our sins before the Lord, asking for his cleansing and forgiveness, we can know that we have been forgiven. His Word is clear: if we confess our sins, he is both faithful and just in Christ to

forgive us and to cleanse us. We believe his Word, and affirm and receive his wonderful provision of daily cleansing. Be assured of your pardon today.

Petitions and Supplications Ending with the Lord's Prayer
Take time to offer prayers to God: prayers of adoration, confessions, thanks, and supplications for yourself and others. Recite the Lord's prayer or bring a prayer book and read prayers to God. Be open to the Holy Spirit as you petition the Lord, seeking his aid, grace, and help in your time of need (Heb. 4.16).

Doxology
As a part of our daily devotions we sing the *Doxology*, that wonderful, ancient, and beautiful anthem of praise to God used throughout the Church in the world. Praise the triune God for his glory and grace! (The *Doxology's* copyright is in the Public Domain [available for public usage].)

Departing to Serve
Benediction: Our Prayer of Acknowledgment
We encourage you to formally close your time of meditation, prayer, and worship with God with a formal benediction. These prayers are expressions of our understanding and devotion to God in light of the truths he has imprinted upon us during our time with him. They are short prayers that acknowledge God as our Source and life, that ask him for his aid to make his truth our own, and that focus on God's person and work. They often summarize the theme of the Scripture for the week or the special day of commemoration, and usually close our communion with God with a specific request to him tied directly to our weekly theme. In all things we desire the Lord to be acknowledged for who he truly is: the true and living God, and God and Father of our Lord Jesus Christ.

Of course, as with all the prayers of the *Sacred Roots Annual*, these need not be tied merely to your time alone or together with God. These prayers (invocations, benedictions) may also be recited throughout the day, encouraging us to seek God's favor on a particular request we received through the Spirit's teaching from the Word.

Affirmation from the Psalms

Each devotional session ends with an affirmation from the Psalms which can also be used as "flash prayers" to focus our minds and hearts upon the Lord, who is the aim and goal of all our devotion and service in our spiritual formation disciplines. Let us obey James where he instructs us to pray and praise for spiritual edification: "Is anyone among you suffering? Let him pray. Is anyone cheerful? Let him sing praise" (James 5.13). In everything, too, let us give thanks to God through Christ: "And whatever you do, in word or deed, do everything in the name of the Lord Jesus, giving thanks to God the Father through him" (Col. 3.17).

Pray without Ceasing

This prayer is also another "flash prayer," as Frank Laubach called it, to be used whenever and wherever throughout the day and for the week. We encourage you to stay focused on the theme of the week each day. Concentrating on a single main idea each day throughout the entire week can enable us to bring together our various meditations, prayers, and dialogues, helping us stay focused on one big idea. This prayer encourages you to recall the theme as often as you can. Repeat this short prayer throughout your day to help you stay attuned to the meaning of our weekly theme.

For Your Weekly Journey

In addition to the daily devotional guide, we also provide weekly practices associated with our theme. Other disciplines we share come into play here: additional readings, Scripture memorization, times of retreat, fasting, and prayer, and readings of select books also connect to our themes. Such a rich listing of observances and disciplines requires much adjustment; some weeks, for instance, we find our disciplines easier to accomplish than others! In all things we seek to follow the mind of the Spirit in the rhythm of our lives. Find your own group's unique capacity and availability, and strive to walk together focused on the same spiritual themes and practices. Such a shared walk will strengthen you together in your corporate journey in faith.

Prayer, Fasting, Solitude and Silence Days

As believers committed to living and serving in community, we seek to share our spiritual journeys together in prayer, fasting, silence, and retreat. Set aside time regularly to decompress your life, to give the Lord extended periods of focus and time. Below are some ways you might follow us as we practice these disciplines both alone and together each quarter.

Intercessory Prayer Concerts: Let God Arise! Prayer Movement

We employ our Let God Arise! prayer guide to pray for the urban church and the great cities of the world. You can obtain many resources connected with this movement from our website (*www.tumi.org/LetGodArise*), including our *Let God Arise! Prayer Booklet* which leads through the seven A's of effective prayer concerts in the church. Also, watch each Church Year season on our website for our *Let God Arise!* devotional materials and videos.

Fasting, Solitude, and Silence

In obedience to the biblical injunction to fast, we set aside regular times together to fast and pray each quarter, fasting from food for 1-3 meals, and spending time in prayer during the fast period. We also set aside time alone with the Lord in isolation and in silence, for the purpose of listening to him and opening ourselves up to his Word and his Spirit. We seek neither to be wooden nor legalistic in our practice of these disciplines. Our sole desire is to see and touch the Lord during these times of spiritual seeking. We vary these times (e.g., spending time together or alone, adjust how long they are or how often) depending on our schedule, or our shared sense for retreat with the Lord.

Celebrations and Observances: Special Days of the Church Year
In regard to special days for spiritual purposes, Paul affirmed our freedom in Christ to use observances of days as a means of enhancing our walk with him. Look at his counsel to the Romans on this issue (Rom. 14.5-7):

> *One person esteems one day as better than another, while another esteems all days alike. Each one should be fully convinced in his own mind. [6] The one who observes the day, observes it in honor of the Lord. The one who eats, eats in honor of the Lord, since he gives thanks to God, while the one who abstains, abstains in honor of the Lord and gives thanks to God. [7] For none of us lives to himself, and none of us dies to himself.*

Paul went on to instruct us that if we live or die we are the Lord's, and should do all things with his glory and honor in mind.

Led, counseled, and disciplined by this freedom in Christ, we employ the Church Year. Of course, we also recognize that there is neither merit nor righteousness imputed in the keeping of the Christian calendar! Righteousness is from God through faith in our Lord Jesus Christ (Phil. 3.9). Nevertheless, we observe the Christ journey of the Church Year with its seasons and special days not as days which are sacred in and of themselves, but as a helpful means by which we can remember and reflect on the mystery and wonder of Christ's work in the world, and his soon and coming Kingdom.

As those committed to following and being conformed to the person of Christ, we find the Church Year invaluable. It allows us to follow the life of Jesus in real time in our worship and discipleship context. For us, it is about our commitment, adoration, and delight in the person of Christ and our desire to be identified with his life, death, and resurrection.

So, as we celebrate the Church Year together, we begin with the promise and fulfillment of the incarnation of Christ (*Advent* to *Epiphany*). Next, in our worship and reflection we focus on the revelation of Christ's mission to the world (*Epiphany* and *Transfiguration*). We then journey with our Lord to his Passion, being reminded through the Church Year that Jesus set his face toward Jerusalem and the cross (*Ash Wednesday* and *Lent*). We follow the historical events of Christ's work as it climaxes in his final week – his entry into Jerusalem, his confrontation with his enemies, his Supper with his disciples, his sham trial, his crucifixion, his burial (*Holy Week*), and his resurrection (*Easter*). We affirm in celebration his ascension to the Father's right hand in glory (*Ascension Day*), and remember the birth of his Church through the outpouring of his Spirit on the people (*Pentecost*). We continue our observances as we acknowledge his active presence in the Church, remembering his headship, his mandate to the harvest, and the hope of his Church through-out the ages (*Season after Pentecost*). On October 31 we commemorate the protestant reformation of the Church (*Reformation Day*), and on November 1 we anticipate the gathering of all believers together at his throne, while remem-bering his martyrs and generations gone by (*All Saints Day*). Finally, we anticipate and await his return, and acknowledge in worship and service that Christ will soon reign supreme as Lord and King over all (*Reign of Christ the King*).

In our celebrations, we notice the "rhythms" of worship and doctrine in the Church Year. Advent both ends the cycle and begins it again. It looks forward to his Second

Coming as the conclusion of the Church Year but also prepares to remember again his First Coming and thus starts the Church Year afresh.

The Church Year is our reflection, participation, enactment, and embodiment of the Christ story in the midst of our personal and community lives. Join us as we walk afresh through the major milestones of our Lord's life and ministry, seeking to become like him in his incarnation, death, and resurrection!

Feast Day Invocation and Benediction Prayers

We have included select ancient believers' prayers on each special day and commemoration of the Church Year. As those who deeply cherish the communion of all Christians throughout all the ages we believe it is important to affirm our union with the Church through the ages, whose legacy we defend and follow. Through their prayers we can identify with their longings, and, in them, see our own for the coming of our Lord's Kingdom.

Bibliographic Information for Prayers of the Saints

Bright, William. *Ancient Collects and Other Prayers: Selected for Devotional Use from Various Rituals*, 8th ed. Oxford and London: James Parker, 1908.

Conference of Bishops, ELCA. *Bread for the Day 2008: Daily Bible Readings and Prayers*. Minneapolis, MN: Augsburg Fortress, 2007.

Ferguson, James and Charles L. Wallis, eds. *Prayers for Public Worship: A Service Book of Morning and Evening Prayers Following the Course of the Christian Year*. New York, NY: Harper & Brothers, 1958.

Fox, Selina Fitzherbert. *A Chain of Prayer across the Ages: Forty Centuries of Prayer from 2000 BC-AD 1916*. New York, NY: E. P. Dutton, 1943.

Geffen, Roger. *The Handbook of Public Prayer*. New York, NY: The Macmillan Company, 1963.

Lindemann, Fred H. *The Sermon and the Propers: Volume I, Advent and Epiphany*. St. Louis, MO: Concordia Publishing House, 1958.

Murray, Scott R. *A Year with the Church Fathers: Meditations for Each Day of the Church Year*. St. Louis, MO: Concordia Publishing House, 2011.

Oden, Thomas C. *Ancient Christian Devotional*. Downers Grove, IL: IVP Books, 2007.

Storey, William G. *A Prayer Book of Catholic Devotions: Praying the Seasons and Feasts of the Church Year*. Chicago, IL: Loyola Press, 2004.

Suter, John Wallace, Jr., ed. *The Book of English Collects*. New York, NY: Harper, 1940.

Tittle, Ernest Fremont. *A Book of Pastoral Prayers*. New York, NY: Abington-Cokesbury Press, 1946.

Book Reading

Each year our missionary community reads and discusses several books that integrate and illumine our Annual theme. This years topic, the life, theology, and ministry of the apostle Paul, offered us a vast library of potential texts to draw from. Paul's influence and importance to our shared Christian tradition ensured a lengthy and rich list of texts on the nature of his thought and the meaning of his life. The volumes below represent the texts we will explore together throughout the year, books that highlight facets of his rich theological perspective and give clear data and interpretation of his conversion, ministry, imprisonment and martyrdom.

Gleaning from the oceanic treasures of Paul's thinking and example should provide us with a rich and edifying experience in our own discipleship, our own faithful fulfillment of our call to live and serve as ambassadors of Jesus where we live and work. Please, join us in reflecting on Paul's amazing perspective and practice in our shared spiritual and intellectual journey of discovery. A listing of their bibliographic information is below:

Allen, Roland. *Missionary Methods: St Paul's or Ours?* Grand Rapids, MI: Wm. B. Eerdmans Pub., 1962.

Hamilton, Adam. *The Call: The Life and Message of the Apostle Paul.* Nashville, TN: Abingdon Press, 2015.

Bruce, F. F. *Paul, Apostle of the Heart Set Free.* Exeter: Paternoster, 1977.

Ramsay, William Mitchell, Mark W. Wilson, and William Mitchell Ramsay. *St. Paul: The Traveler and Roman Citizen.* Grand Rapids, MI: Kregel Publications, 2001.

On-Line Sacred Roots Annual

As an added benefit, the devotional content from this year's *Sacred Roots Annual* is also available online for your perusal and use. In addition to these rich spiritual devotional guides you will find many other helpful materials designed to help you grow spiritually in Christ, formed through the Church Year. Visit *www.tumi.org/annual*, and click the *Online Annual* link to find the *Sacred Roots Annual's* devotional content as well as convenient links to Dr. Davis's teaching and outlines for each week's theme. We have also linked you to the ESV Bible's audio recording of the Daily Chronological Reading Guide, which we follow each year. Click on the specific "Week" link to view its devotional guide and resources!

The Sacred Roots Annual: A Swiss Army Knife of Spiritual Formation

Nothing is more powerful in times of preparation, crisis, and opportunity than having the right tool for the right job at the right moment.

The *Sacred Roots Annual* is intended to be such a tool, one that can serve us at every phase or stage of our spiritual formation, as member or minister, whether in devotion, discipleship, or pastoral care. Like a Swiss Army knife, an implement filled with assorted tools for particular tasks, we are convinced that the *Sacred Roots Annual* is appropriate for various levels of spiritual growth and in a variety of venues. We believe it can be a great resource for the Christian seeker, the discipler, and the pastor alike. Over the years, we have entertained and answered numerous questions on the issue of who is best suited for the *Annual* – individuals, small groups, or congregations. Our answers to these questions have become ever more simple and clear: we believe that the *Sacred Roots Annual* can be used by a wide range of people and groups, and that it is a great tool for small groups and congregations interested in sharing a spiritual journey together!

Suitable for the Individual, Family, or Small Group
The *Sacred Roots Annual* is designed for multiple users: individuals wanting to grow in Christ, families hoping to

start regular times of seeking God, or cells or small groups desiring to track with one another in spiritual formation.

Individuals will benefit from a disciplined approach to spiritual formation with Christ at the center. Its clear focus on personal devotion and personal walk makes it an ideal choice for anyone interested in beginning a structured yet flexible regimen of the spiritual disciplines for spiritual growth. Likewise, the exercises, readings, and suggestions of the *Sacred Roots Annual* are also easily employed within a group context. You can practice the disciplines together, or do them separately alone, and come together to share your insights, questions, and ideas. A threefold cord is not easily broken, nor is a tight-knit spiritual formation cell likely to fail in its quest to grow in Christ. We recommend that you practice the disciplines both *alone* and *together with others*. The rhythm of a personal journey and shared spirituality will provide you with greater richness and insight into the wonder and mystery that Christ Jesus is to you, his disciple, and to us, his people.

On this note, the journey and walk motif we use throughout the *Sacred Roots Annual* is done deliberately. Having sought God together rigorously as a community for years now, we understand how powerful and meaningful that shared spirituality can be when we devote ourselves together to mature in Christ. Our hope is that whether you use the *Annual* as an individual, as a family, or as a small group you will begin to practice the disciplines *regularly* and *together*, that you will strive to walk in community in spiritual formation sharing a spirituality, and learning of Christ and his ways as a group.

A Strategic Tool for the Teacher, Discipler, Spiritual Director, or Pastor

Perhaps the greatest added benefit of the *Sacred Roots Annual* is the help it can provide to those who are in roles of spiritual direction and discipling others. If you are a pastor, shepherding others, or if you are responsible for others' spiritually, i.e., the "care of souls," the *Sacred Roots Annual* allows you a wonderful and efficient way to organize your shared journey with those you lead. If you embrace the *Annual's* "spiritual logic," that is, if you determine that following the Christ life through the Church Year has merit, you can structure your preaching, teaching, Christian education, and service and missions projects all in conjunction with the schedule within the *Annual.*

For instance, for you as a busy pastor, seeing Christ formed in you and your congregation can readily occur if you embrace the Church Year as your overall worship and discipleship structure. With a clear, deliberate focus on Christ Jesus in all dimensions of your life together, it is both profitable and effective to order your services, your preaching and teaching, your Christian education (at various levels), and your service and outreach in connection to the themes included. Know too that, if you choose this discipline and regimen, you will certainly not be alone! Literally, hundreds of thousands of congregations order their spiritual formation around the celebration of the Christ life in the Church Year, and the resources for preaching, teaching, and Christian education are voluminous for those who use it. There are a number of practical ideas for you to apply the insights of the *Sacred Roots Annual* to your strategy of spiritual formation:

- Use the *Revised Common Lectionary (RCL) to identify specific texts and themes for preaching and teaching series, and themes for worship service.* For instance, the texts provided in the Lectionary Year C readings allows for you to consistently teach and preach from texts being read throughout the churches worldwide. Often, churches and preachers will opt to go through a series, book, or topical focus during the extended Ordinary Time period, which occurs later in the year.

Our guidebook this year is entitled *Ambassador in Chains: The Sacred Roots Annual 2015-16.* Paul's influence on the early Christian movement, his broad impact on the life and thought of the Church throughout the ages, and his evangelical zeal to win the world with the Gospel makes him of special interest to us this upcoming year in our devotion and discipleship to Christ. Our Lectionary Readings will be taken from the Revised Common Lectionary Year C selections. During the second extended Ordinary Time period in the Season after Pentecost we will study the books referred to as the Prison Epistles (Ephesians, Philippians, Colossians, and Philemon), the four traditional epistles associated with Paul's letter writing during his earlier imprisonments. Our reflection on Paul and his theology should enable us to better understand what it means to be an ambassador of Jesus in a hostile and godless environment.

- Use your imagination and freedom during this extended time to concentrate on those areas of need the Holy Spirit leads you to address, for your own sake and/or the sake of those whom you lead. For instance, you may structure your *weekly worship themes in conjunction with the images, stories, and seasons reflected in the Church Year* (many thousands of churches do this, although most evangelical churches are barely acquainted with such applications of the Church Year, celebrating only Christmas and Easter!) The Annual and the Calendar are resources designed to enrich your worship and devotion, not limit them!

- Incorporate select *Scripture readings of the Lectionary to be included in the worship experience* of the church, as responsive readings or separate Bible readings.

- *Highlight the feast days or seasons of the Church Year* for special times of worship, training, celebration, or outreach (Christmas, Easter, Pentecost, Reign of Christ the King).

- Organize your *Christian education and Sunday School programs* around seasons, concentrating on a particular season of Christ's life and ministry. For various seasons or series synchronize all your Sunday School, small group, and pulpit ministry themes together in order to consider a singular integrated theme and direction for the entire church. Although this is not done often, it pays huge dividends, not only in terms of connecting all members of the body to a single theme (enabling us to walk together spiritually more coherently), it also pile drives the theme home by helping families, whatever the members' age or station, center down on one big, significant idea.

- Think through your entire Church Year calendar, *using it to map out your weekly and seasonal themes* for the entire church body for the year. You might choose (as we have done) to *draft an annual theme for your church based on a selected focus you wish to emphasize or highlight for the Church Year* (remember, the Church Year is from December through November!)

- Use the general structure of the Church Year, *highlighting each of the special seasons as focus for a series or emphasis in your worship or spiritual training* (the "Cycle of Light": Advent, Christmas, Epiphany, and the "Cycle of Life": Lent, Easter, Pentecost. For the purpose of thematic focus we break up the single "Season after Pentecost" into select sections of emphasis, *The Coming of the Holy Spirit, A Season of Christ's Headship, A Season of*

> *Christ's Harvest, A Season of Christ's Hope*, and
> *Remembering the Saints/Exalting the King.*)

- *Create your own special series for the two seasons of
  "Ordinary Time" in the calendar* (after Epiphany, and
  after Pentecost). There is great flexibility here, for
  during these weeks there is no special theme
  emphasized in the Church Year.

The possibilities of using the Church Year as a key structural
tool for you as a spiritual leader are endless. Visit our website,
www.tumi.org/annual, to discover more exciting ways to
incorporate and integrate your spiritual formation efforts
with the Church Year.

This *Sacred Roots Annual* is the formal blueprint for our
community's shared spiritual journey, and we invite you to
join us as we read Scripture, seek God's face, and use this
travel log to be conformed to the image of our dear Savior,
Jesus of Nazareth. In seeking him, we desire to walk in his
steps, to share his journey, and to become like him in his
humiliation and exaltation, for the Father's glory. We use
this *Sacred Roots Annual* to tread the same path that has
been traversed by pilgrims, disciples, and followers of Jesus
through the ages – remembering, rehearsing, and reenacting
the greatest Tale ever told or retold.

Since our earliest records, the Church has made it a point to
remember and celebrate the events of Jesus' life, death, burial,
and resurrection, ascension, session, and return. Come along
with us as we share our lives together, walking with our Lord
as he forms his life in us.

The Season of Advent

THE COMING OF CHRIST

Yours is the day, yours also the night;
you have established the heavenly lights and the sun.
You have fixed all the boundaries of the earth;
you have made summer and winter.

PSALM 74.16-17

THE SEASON OF ADVENT: THE COMING OF CHRIST
NOVEMBER 29 - DECEMBER 23, 2015

Advent is a season of anticipation and repentance which focuses on the First and Second Comings of Christ. The dual focus means that Advent both begins and ends the Christian Year (Isa. 9.1-7, 11.1-16; Mark 1.1-8).

The Coming of Christ
Advent anticipates the First and Second Comings of our Lord. God's prophets foretold his Coming, and angels announced his birth to Mary and the shepherds. We affirm God's promise fulfilled in the arrival of Messiah in Bethlehem.

Week 1: Anticipation
The Advent wreath reminds us of God's eternal love, without a beginning, without an end. The candles remind us of Christ's light coming into the world. We light the first candle looking forward to the coming of the Messiah, Immanuel, God-with-us.

Week 2: Annunciation
We light the second candle to announce the birth of the Savior King, as the angel Gabriel announced to Mary, and the angels announced to the shepherds.

Week 3: Affirmation
We light the third candle recognizing the fulfillment of God's promise of our salvation.

Week 4: Arrival
We light the fourth candle in celebration of the arrival of the baby, born in a stable at Bethlehem, whose name is Immanuel, God-with-us.

Celebrating Advent

Advent season is the start of the Church Year calendar. By observing the Church Year, we remind ourselves that we do not belong to this world but operate in the earth as a peculiar people whose citizenship is in the New Jerusalem. The word Advent means "coming" or "arrival" and the season has a dual focus of remembering the first coming of Christ and looking forward to his second coming.

Theologically speaking, the season of Advent signifies a time of both preparation and hope. Therefore, preaching during Advent has traditionally emphasized both repentance and joy.

Like other seasons in the Church Year, at Advent we use colors to remind us of theological truths. The primary color of Advent is purple (the color of royalty) which is used to remind us that we are awaiting the coming of a king. The secondary color of Advent is green (the color of life) used to remind us that God is sending the One who will make all things new.

The Advent candles consist of five candles: three purple, one pink, and one white candle. The purple candles (lit on the Sundays of week one, two, and four) remind us that we are awaiting royalty, and the sole pink candle (which is lit on the third week), affirms God's intent to eliminate all fear and restore creation through the coming Messiah. The final white center candle (called the Christ Candle), is lit on Christmas Day, and calls us to rejoice in the incarnation of the Son of God into the world. The greenery around the candle reminds us that we are proclaiming the promise of new life that Messiah brings. The flames of the candles remind us that Jesus is the light of the world who shines in the darkness and that the darkness cannot overcome the light. By lighting one new candle each week we remind ourselves that God is doing something in the world and that more is yet to come.

- The first candle is the Anticipation candle which remembers the prophecies made about the Messiah who was to come.

- The second candle is the Annunciation (i.e. announcement) candle which remembers the announcement made by Gabriel to Mary and by the angels to the shepherds.

- The third candle is the Affirmation candle which recognizes that by sending the Messiah, God has affirmed and fulfilled the promises that he made to humanity.

- The fourth candle is the Arrival candle which celebrates the birth of Christ.

- The center white candle, called the Christ Candle, is lit on Christmas Day – "Joy to the world, the Lord is come!"

Come, Thou Long Expected Jesus!

Let us all with one voice join together with Charles Wesley (1744) and Rowland Hugh Prichard (1855) in singing:

Come, thou long expected Jesus, born to set Thy people free.
From our fears and sins release us; let us find our rest in Thee.
Israel's strength and consolation, hope of all the earth Thou art;
Dear Desire of ev'ry nation, joy of ev'ry longing heart.

Born Thy people to deliver, born a Child and yet a King.
Born to reign in us forever, now Thy gracious kingdom bring.
By Thine own eternal Spirit, rule in all our hearts alone;
By Thine all-sufficient merit, raise us to Thy glorious throne.

WEEK 1

First Sunday of Advent: Anticipation
November 29 - December 5, 2015

Advent joyously affirms the First and Second comings of our Lord. Through the prophets, God foretold the Messiah's appearing to his people, Israel. Through the angels, he announced his birth to Zechariah, Mary, and the shepherds. Let us reverently ponder the sure promise of God – the Deliverer will come and ransom captive Israel and the world.

THIS WEEK'S THEME
Your Redemption Is Drawing Near, Luke 21.25-36

The coming of Jesus Christ will be accompanied by signs that will terrify, cosmic manifestations among the sun, moon, and stars, and in the earth and among the nations. In the middle of these signs, the Son of Man will appear to receive his Kingdom – his followers will lift up their heads (a symbol of redemption and hope) because at that time their redemption (i.e., their safety, rescue, and blessing) will be drawing near. In the same way you can detect that summer is near by looking at the fig leaves sprouting in late spring, so when these signs occur, the people of God will know that the Kingdom of God is close at hand.

Daily Devotional Guide

PREPARING OUR HEARTS

Invocation: Our Prayer of Acclamation

God of grace, ever faithful to your promises, the earth rejoices in hope of our Savior's coming and looks forward with longing to his return at the end of time. Prepare our hearts to receive him when he comes, for he is Lord forever and ever. Amen.

~ *Supplemental Liturgical Resource 5*
The Theological and Worship Ministry Unit, p. 167.

Call to Worship

Blessed are you, O God: Father, Son, and Holy Spirit. And blessed is your Kingdom, both now and forever, amen.

PRAISING OUR GOD

Te Deum Laudamus

You are God: we praise you; you are the Lord; we acclaim you; you are the eternal Father: All creation worships you. To you all angels, all the powers of heaven, Cherubim and Seraphim, sing in endless praise: Holy, holy, holy Lord, God of power and might, heaven and earth are full of your glory.

The glorious company of apostles praise you. The noble fellowship of prophets praise you. The white-robed army of martyrs praise you. Throughout the world the holy Church acclaims you; Father, of majesty unbounded, your true and only Son, worthy of all worship, and the Holy Spirit, advocate and guide.

You, Christ, are the king of glory, the eternal Son of the Father. When you became man to set us free you did not shun the Virgin's womb. You overcame the sting of death and opened the kingdom of heaven to all believers. You are seated at God's right hand in glory. We believe that you will come and be our judge. Come then, Lord, and help your people, bought with the price of your own blood, and bring us with your saints to glory everlasting.

Praise and Thanksgiving (Songs and Prayers)

Gloria Patri

Glory be to the Father,
And to the Son and to the Holy Spirit:
As it was in the beginning,
Is now, and ever shall be,
World without end. Amen, amen.

LISTENING TO HIS VOICE

Chronological Reading for the Day
Sunday: Gen. 1-3
Monday: Gen. 4-6; 1 Chron. 1.1-4
Tuesday: Gen. 7-10; 1 Chron. 1.5-23
Wednesday: Gen. 11-14; 1 Chron. 1.24-27
Thursday: Gen. 15-17
Friday: Gen. 18-20
Saturday: Gen. 21-24

Lectionary Readings
Psalm: Ps. 25.1-10   *OT:* Jer. 33.14-16
Gospel: Luke 21.25-36   *NT:* 1 Thess. 3.9-13

Reflection: Silence and/or Journaling

RESPONDING IN FAITH

The Apostles' Creed
*I believe in God, the Father Almighty, Maker of heaven and earth;
and in Jesus Christ, his only Son, our Lord, who was conceived by the
Holy Spirit, born of the Virgin Mary, suffered under Pontius Pilate,
was crucified, dead, and buried; he descended into hell; the third day
he arose again from the dead; he ascended into heaven and sits on
the right hand of God the Father Almighty; from thence he shall come
to judge the quick and the dead.*

I believe in the Holy Spirit, the holy catholic church, the communion
of saints, the forgiveness of sins, the resurrection of the body, and the
life everlasting. Amen.*

* In the Apostles' and Nicene Creeds, the term catholic refers to the Church's
universality, through all ages and times, of all languages and peoples. It refers to no
particular tradition or denominational expression (e.g., as in Roman Catholic).

Prayers of Confession

Let us now confess our sins to God and receive mercy and grace to help in our time of need.

Assurance of Pardon

Having faithfully confessed and renounced your sin, Christ also has been faithful to forgive your sins and to purify you from all unrighteousness. It is certain, that there is One who has spoken to the Father in your defense, Jesus Christ, the Righteous One who is the atoning sacrifice for our sins and for the sins of the whole world. His grace and peace are with you now. Amen.

Petitions and Supplications, Ending with the Lord's Prayer

Our Father which art in heaven, Hallowed be thy name. Thy kingdom come, Thy will be done in earth, as it is in heaven. Give us this day our daily bread. And forgive us our debts, as we forgive our debtors. And lead us not into temptation, but deliver us from evil: For thine is the kingdom, and the power, and the glory, for ever. Amen.

~ Matthew 6.9-13 (KJV)

Doxology (and/or closing song)

Praise God from whom all blessings flow;
Praise Him all creatures here below;
Praise Him above ye heavenly host;
Praise Father, Son and Holy Ghost. Amen.

DEPARTING TO SERVE

Benediction

Stir up our hearts, Lord God, to prepare the way of your only Son. By his coming strengthen us to serve you with purified lives; through Jesus Christ, our Savior and Lord, who lives and reigns with you and the Holy Spirit, one God, now and forever. Amen.

~ Evangelical Lutheran Worship
Conference of Bishops, Evangelical Lutheran Church in America. p. 359.

Affirmation from the Psalms

Let the sea roar, and all that fills it; the world and those who dwell in it!
[8] Let the rivers clap their hands; let the hills sing for joy together
[9] before the Lord, for he comes to judge the earth. He will judge the
world with righteousness, and the peoples with equity.

~ Psalm 98.7-9

Pray without Ceasing – Flash Prayer for the Day

Dear Savior, help us not to miss the signs of your coming, but ever may we be ready for your soon appearing to redeem your people. Amen.

For Your Weekly Journey

Let God Arise! Seasonal Focus

Behold, God Is My Salvation, Isaiah 12.1-6

Book Reading

Allen, *Missionary Methods: St. Paul's or Ours?*

Second Sunday of Advent: Annunciation
December 6 - 12, 2015

Advent joyously affirms the First and Second comings of our Lord. Through the prophets, God foretold the Messiah's appearing to his people, Israel. Through the angels, he announced his birth to Zechariah, Mary, and the shepherds. Let us reverently ponder the sure promise of God – the Deliverer will come and ransom captive Israel and the world.

THIS WEEK'S THEME
The Servant of the Lord, Luke 1.26-38
During the sixth month of Elizabeth's pregnancy with John the Baptizer, God sent the angel Gabriel to Nazareth, a city of Galilee, to a virgin named Mary who was betrothed to Joseph, a man of David's house. After greeting Mary, he told her that she had found favor with God, and that she would conceive and bear a son, and that she would call his name Jesus. This child would be great and be called the Son of the Most High. The Lord God would give him the throne of his father David, he would reign over the house of Jacob forever, with an everlasting Kingdom. When asked how this would happen to her, as a virgin, Gabriel said that the Holy Spirit would come upon her, and that the power of the Most High would overshadow her, and thus, the child born to her would be called holy – the Son of God. He assured her, too, that her relative Elizabeth (who was called barren) had also conceived in her old age, and was in her sixth month. He said, "For nothing will be impossible with God."

In faith and submission, Mary answered Gabriel and said, "Behold, I am the servant of the Lord; let it be to me according to your word." Even in the face of this amazing news, Mary never wavered in her faith and obedience to the Lord. She responded to the divine announcement with conviction and readiness to submit to the will of Lord, even though it was not clear just how it would be done or what it would mean.

Daily Devotional Guide

PREPARING OUR HEARTS

Invocation: Our Prayer of Acclamation

Stir up, we beseech Thee, O Lord, our hearts to prepare the ways of Thine Only-begotten Son; that by His Advent we may be enabled to serve Thee with purified minds; through the same Jesus Christ our Lord. Amen.

~ *Gelasian Sacramentary* (Bright, p. 16)

Call to Worship

Blessed are you, O God: Father, Son, and Holy Spirit. And blessed is your Kingdom, both now and forever, amen.

PRAISING OUR GOD

Te Deum Laudamus

You are God: we praise you; you are the Lord; we acclaim you; you are the eternal Father: All creation worships you. To you all angels, all the powers of heaven, Cherubim and Seraphim, sing in endless praise: Holy, holy, holy Lord, God of power and might, heaven and earth are full of your glory.

The glorious company of apostles praise you. The noble fellowship of prophets praise you. The white-robed army of martyrs praise you. Throughout the world the holy Church acclaims you; Father, of majesty unbounded, your true and only Son, worthy of all worship, and the Holy Spirit, advocate and guide.

You, Christ, are the king of glory, the eternal Son of the Father. When you became man to set us free you did not shun the Virgin's womb. You overcame the sting of death and opened the kingdom of heaven to all believers. You are seated at God's right hand in glory. We believe that you will come and be our judge. Come then, Lord, and help your people, bought with the price of your own blood, and bring us with your saints to glory everlasting.

Praise and Thanksgiving (Songs and Prayers)

Gloria Patri
Glory be to the Father,
And to the Son and to the Holy Spirit:
As it was in the beginning,
Is now, and ever shall be,
World without end. Amen, amen.

LISTENING TO HIS VOICE

Chronological Reading for the Day
Sunday: Gen. 25; 1 Chron. 1.28-34
Monday: Gen. 26-27
Tuesday: Gen. 28-29
Wednesday: Gen. 30-31
Thursday: Gen. 32.1-35.27
Friday: Gen. 36; 1 Chron. 1.35-2.2
Saturday: Gen. 37-39; 1 Chron. 2.3-6, v.8

Lectionary Readings

Psalm: Luke 1.68-79	*OT:* Mal. 3.1-4
Gospel: Luke 3.1-6	*NT:* Phil. 1.3-11

Reflection: Silence and/or Journaling

RESPONDING IN FAITH

The Apostles' Creed
I believe in God, the Father Almighty, Maker of heaven and earth;
and in Jesus Christ, his only Son, our Lord, who was conceived by the
Holy Spirit, born of the Virgin Mary, suffered under Pontius Pilate,
was crucified, dead, and buried; he descended into hell; the third day
he arose again from the dead; he ascended into heaven and sits on
the right hand of God the Father Almighty; from thence he shall come
to judge the quick and the dead.

I believe in the Holy Spirit, the holy catholic* church, the communion of saints, the forgiveness of sins, the resurrection of the body, and the life everlasting. Amen.

* In the Apostles' and Nicene Creeds, the term catholic refers to the Church's universality, through all ages and times, of all languages and peoples. It refers to no particular tradition or denominational expression (e.g., as in Roman Catholic).

Prayers of Confession

Let us now confess our sins to God and receive mercy and grace to help in our time of need.

Assurance of Pardon

Having faithfully confessed and renounced your sin, Christ also has been faithful to forgive your sins and to purify you from all unrighteousness. It is certain, that there is One who has spoken to the Father in your defense, Jesus Christ, the Righteous One who is the atoning sacrifice for our sins and for the sins of the whole world. His grace and peace are with you now. Amen.

Petitions and Supplications, Ending with the Lord's Prayer

Our Father which art in heaven, Hallowed be thy name. Thy kingdom come, Thy will be done in earth, as it is in heaven. Give us this day our daily bread. And forgive us our debts, as we forgive our debtors. And lead us not into temptation, but deliver us from evil: For thine is the kingdom, and the power, and the glory, for ever. Amen.

~ Matthew 6.9-13 (KJV)

Doxology (and/or closing song)

Praise God from whom all blessings flow;
Praise Him all creatures here below;
Praise Him above ye heavenly host;
Praise Father, Son and Holy Ghost. Amen.

DEPARTING TO SERVE

Benediction
Grant, O Almighty God, that as thy blessed Son Jesus Christ at his first advent came to seek and to save that which was lost, so at his second and glorious appearing he may find in us the fruits of the redemption which he wrought; who liveth and reigneth with thee and the Holy Spirit, one God, world without end. Amen.

~ *The Book of English Collects*, 1940 (Geffen, p. 68)

Affirmation from the Psalms
I waited patiently for the Lord; he inclined to me and heard my cry. [2] He drew me up from the pit of destruction, out of the miry bog, and set my feet upon a rock, making my steps secure. [3] He put a new song in my mouth, a song of praise to our God. Many will see and fear, and put their trust in the Lord.

~ Psalm 40.1-3

Pray without Ceasing – Flash Prayer for the Day
Father, give me the heart and soul of Mary, your servant, who responded to the announcement of the angel with conviction and submission. Give me her faith, in Jesus' name, amen.

For Your Weekly Journey

Let God Arise! Seasonal Focus
Behold, God Is My Salvation, Isaiah 12.1-6

Book Reading
Allen, *Missionary Methods: St. Paul's or Ours?*

Our Corporate Disciplines
Fallow Day: Friday, December 11, 2015

WEEK 3

Third Sunday of Advent: Affirmation
December 13 - 19, 2015

Advent joyously affirms the First and Second comings of our Lord. Through the prophets, God foretold the Messiah's appearing to his people, Israel. Through the angels, he announced his birth to Zechariah, Mary, and the shepherds. Let us reverently ponder the sure promise of God – the Deliverer will come and ransom captive Israel and the world.

THIS WEEK'S THEME
Behold, God Is My Salvation, Isaiah 12.2-6

Referring to the time of the appearing of Messiah, when the nation is regathered and the splendor of God's Kingdom is displayed on earth, Isaiah speaks of the remnant's praise offered "in that day." "I will give thanks to you, O Lord, for though you were angry with me, your anger turned away, that you might comfort me. Behold, God is my salvation; I will trust, and will not be afraid; for the Lord God is my strength and my song, and he has become my salvation." He declared that people in that day will draw with joy water from the wells of salvation, and will declare in that day, "Give thanks to the Lord, call upon his name, make known his deeds among the peoples, proclaim that his name is exalted." They will sing praises to the Lord, for he has done gloriously. They will exclaim that this should be made known in all the earth. In that day of redemption and renewal they will shout and sing for joy, all the inhabitants of Zion, for great in their midst will be the Holy One of Israel.

In an act of joyous worship and faith, the prophet declares that we who hope for the Lord's return must affirm his mercy and goodness, and declare that the Lord God is our strength and salvation. Maranatha, even so, come, Lord Jesus!

Daily Devotional Guide

PREPARING OUR HEARTS

Invocation: Our Prayer of Acclamation

We ask you, almighty God, let our souls enjoy this their desire, to be enkindled by your Spirit, that being filled as lamps by your divine gift, we may shine like burning lights before the presence of your Son Christ at his coming; through the same Jesus Christ our Lord. Amen.

~ The Gelasian Sacramentary (Oden, p. 26)

Call to Worship

Blessed are you, O God: Father, Son, and Holy Spirit. And blessed is your Kingdom, both now and forever, amen.

PRAISING OUR GOD

Te Deum Laudamus

You are God: we praise you; you are the Lord; we acclaim you; you are the eternal Father: All creation worships you. To you all angels, all the powers of heaven, Cherubim and Seraphim, sing in endless praise: Holy, holy, holy Lord, God of power and might, heaven and earth are full of your glory.

The glorious company of apostles praise you. The noble fellowship of prophets praise you. The white-robed army of martyrs praise you. Throughout the world the holy Church acclaims you; Father, of majesty unbounded, your true and only Son, worthy of all worship, and the Holy Spirit, advocate and guide.

You, Christ, are the king of glory, the eternal Son of the Father. When you became man to set us free you did not shun the Virgin's womb. You overcame the sting of death and opened the kingdom of heaven to all believers. You are seated at God's right hand in glory. We believe

that you will come and be our judge. Come then, Lord, and help your
people, bought with the price of your own blood, and bring us with
your saints to glory everlasting.

Praise and Thanksgiving (Songs and Prayers)

Gloria Patri
Glory be to the Father,
And to the Son and to the Holy Spirit:
As it was in the beginning,
Is now, and ever shall be,
World without end. Amen, amen.

LISTENING TO HIS VOICE

Chronological Reading for the Day
Sunday: Gen. 35.28-29; ch.40-41
Monday: Gen. 42.1-45.15
Tuesday: Gen. 45.16-47.27
Wednesday: Gen. 47.28-50.26
Thursday: Job 1-4
Friday: Job 5-7
Saturday: Job 8-11

Lectionary Readings
Psalm: Isa. 12.2-6   *OT:* Zeph. 3.14-20
Gospel: Luke 3.7-18   *NT:* Phil. 4.4-7

Reflection: Silence and/or Journaling

RESPONDING IN FAITH

The Apostles' Creed
I believe in God, the Father Almighty, Maker of heaven and earth;
and in Jesus Christ, his only Son, our Lord, who was conceived by the

Holy Spirit, born of the Virgin Mary, suffered under Pontius Pilate, was crucified, dead, and buried; he descended into hell; the third day he arose again from the dead; he ascended into heaven and sits on the right hand of God the Father Almighty; from thence he shall come to judge the quick and the dead.

I believe in the Holy Spirit, the holy catholic* church, the communion of saints, the forgiveness of sins, the resurrection of the body, and the life everlasting. Amen.

* In the Apostles' and Nicene Creeds, the term catholic refers to the Church's universality, through all ages and times, of all languages and peoples. It refers to no particular tradition or denominational expression (e.g., as in Roman Catholic).

Prayers of Confession

Let us now confess our sins to God and receive mercy and grace to help in our time of need.

Assurance of Pardon

Having faithfully confessed and renounced your sin, Christ also has been faithful to forgive your sins and to purify you from all unrighteousness. It is certain, that there is One who has spoken to the Father in your defense, Jesus Christ, the Righteous One who is the atoning sacrifice for our sins and for the sins of the whole world. His grace and peace are with you now. Amen.

Petitions and Supplications, Ending with the Lord's Prayer

Our Father which art in heaven, Hallowed be thy name. Thy kingdom come, Thy will be done in earth, as it is in heaven. Give us this day our daily bread. And forgive us our debts, as we forgive our debtors. And lead us not into temptation, but deliver us from evil: For thine is the kingdom, and the power, and the glory, for ever. Amen.

~ Matthew 6.9-13 (KJV)

Doxology (and/or closing song)

Praise God from whom all blessings flow;
Praise Him all creatures here below;
Praise Him above ye heavenly host;
Praise Father, Son and Holy Ghost. Amen.

DEPARTING TO SERVE

Benediction

Let us then rejoice in this grace, so that our glorying may bear witness
to our good conscience by which we glory, not in ourselves but in the
Lord. That is why Scripture says, "He is my glory, the one who lifts up
my head." For what greater grace could God have made to dawn on
us than to make his only Son become the Son of man, so that human
beings might in their turn become children and heirs of God? Ask if
this were merited; ask for its reason, for its justification and whether
you will find any other answer but sheer grace. Amen.

~ Augustine of Hippo (Oden, 31)

Affirmation from the Psalms

Make a joyful noise to the Lord, all the earth! [2] Serve the Lord with
gladness! Come into his presence with singing! [3] Know that the Lord,
he is God! It is he who made us, and we are his; we are his people, and
the sheep of his pasture.

~ Psalm 100.1-3

Pray without Ceasing – Flash Prayer for the Day

Holy Father, grant to us a spirit of affirmation and rejoicing
as we await the soon return of your Son to earth, his coming
to usher in your reign with glory!

For Your Weekly Journey

Let God Arise! Seasonal Focus

Behold, God Is My Salvation, Isaiah 12.1-6

Book Reading

Allen, *Missionary Methods: St. Paul's or Ours?*

WEEK 4

Fourth Sunday of Advent: Arrival

December 20 - 26, 2015

Advent joyously affirms the First and Second comings of our Lord. Through the prophets, God foretold the Messiah's appearing to his people, Israel. Through the angels, he announced his birth to Zechariah, Mary, and the shepherds. Let us reverently ponder the sure promise of God – the Deliverer will come and ransom captive Israel and the world.

THIS WEEK'S THEME
My Soul Magnifies the Lord, Luke 1.39-55

Shortly after Gabriel's announcement of Mary's giving birth to the Messiah, she went into the hill country of Judah to a town where Zechariah and Elizabeth resided. When Elizabeth heard Mary's greeting, Elizabeth's baby lept in her womb. Elizabeth was filled with the Holy Spirit, she exclaimed with a loud cry, "Blessed are you among women, and blessed is the fruit of your womb! And why is this granted to me that the mother of my Lord should come to me? For behold, when the sound of your greeting came to my ears, the baby in my womb leaped for joy. And blessed is she who believed that there would be a fulfillment of what was spoken to her from the Lord."

On hearing Elizabeth, Mary gave a song of praise which has come to be named in the Church, the Magnificat. It reveals Mary's depth of devotion to God, and her awareness that the events of her day were linked to God's covenant promise to Abraham. Mary said, "My soul magnifies the Lord, and my spirit rejoices in God my Savior, for he has looked on the humble estate of his servant. For behold, from now on all generations will call me blessed; for he who is mighty has done great things for me, and holy is his name. And his mercy is for those who fear him from generation to generation. He has shown strength with his arm; he has scattered the proud in the thoughts of their hearts; he has brought down the mighty from their thrones and exalted those of humble estate; he has filled the hungry with good things, and the rich he has sent away empty. He has helped his servant Israel, in remembrance of his mercy, as he spoke to our fathers, to Abraham and to his offspring forever."

Daily Devotional Guide

PREPARING OUR HEARTS

Invocation: Our Prayer of Acclamation

O eternal God, the creator and preserver of all mankind, who carest for thy human children of every race and nation; make haste, we beseech thee, to help us, for our transgressions have overtaken us; we are compassed about with many and great evils, till we know not where to turn. Look upon us in thy compassion, and come speedily to our aid. Bring us to repentance for the sins which we have all committed against thee, that thou mayest forgive us our sins, and form a right spirit within us, and guide our feet into the way of peace. Put to shame those who would make darkness to be light and light to be darkness. Confound those in whom lust for wealth or power is threatening the world with new disasters. Open the eyes of those who are blinded by ignorance, fear, or prejudice. In thy great mercy bring good tidings to the poor, heal the brokenhearted, set at liberty the oppressed, and fill with rejoicing all workers of good. Let the whole earth be filled with thy praise, O Lord, heavenly Father, almighty and everlasting God; and unto thee be glory and majesty, dominion and power, both now and forever. Amen.

~ Earnest Fremont Tittle (Tittle, p. 52-53)

Call to Worship

Blessed are you, O God: Father, Son, and Holy Spirit. And blessed is your Kingdom, both now and forever, amen.

PRAISING OUR GOD

Te Deum Laudamus

You are God: we praise you; you are the Lord; we acclaim you; you are the eternal Father: All creation worships you. To you all angels, all the powers of heaven, Cherubim and Seraphim, sing in endless praise: Holy, holy, holy Lord, God of power and might, heaven and earth are full of your glory.

The glorious company of apostles praise you. The noble fellowship of prophets praise you. The white-robed army of martyrs praise you. Throughout the world the holy Church acclaims you; Father, of majesty unbounded, your true and only Son, worthy of all worship, and the Holy Spirit, advocate and guide.

You, Christ, are the king of glory, the eternal Son of the Father. When you became man to set us free you did not shun the Virgin's womb. You overcame the sting of death and opened the kingdom of heaven to all believers. You are seated at God's right hand in glory. We believe that you will come and be our judge. Come then, Lord, and help your people, bought with the price of your own blood, and bring us with your saints to glory everlasting.

Praise and Thanksgiving (Songs and Prayers)

Gloria Patri

Glory be to the Father,
And to the Son and to the Holy Spirit:
As it was in the beginning,
Is now, and ever shall be,
World without end. Amen, amen.

LISTENING TO HIS VOICE

Chronological Reading for the Day

Sunday: Job 12-14
Monday: Job 15-18
Tuesday: Job 19-21
Wednesday: Job 22-25

Thursday: Job 26-29
Friday: Job 30-31
Saturday: Job 32-34

Lectionary Readings

Psalm: Ps. 80.1-7
Gospel: Luke 1.39-55

OT: Mic. 5.2-5a
NT: Heb. 10.5-10

Reflection: Silence and/or Journaling

RESPONDING IN FAITH

The Apostles' Creed

I believe in God, the Father Almighty, Maker of heaven and earth; and in Jesus Christ, his only Son, our Lord, who was conceived by the Holy Spirit, born of the Virgin Mary, suffered under Pontius Pilate, was crucified, dead, and buried; he descended into hell; the third day he arose again from the dead; he ascended into heaven and sits on the right hand of God the Father Almighty; from thence he shall come to judge the quick and the dead.

I believe in the Holy Spirit, the holy catholic* church, the communion of saints, the forgiveness of sins, the resurrection of the body, and the life everlasting. Amen.

* In the Apostles' and Nicene Creeds, the term catholic refers to the Church's universality, through all ages and times, of all languages and peoples. It refers to no particular tradition or denominational expression (e.g., as in Roman Catholic).

Prayers of Confession

Let us now confess our sins to God and receive mercy and grace to help in our time of need.

Assurance of Pardon

Having faithfully confessed and renounced your sin, Christ also has been faithful to forgive your sins and to purify you from all unrighteousness. It is certain, that there is One who has spoken to the Father in your defense, Jesus Christ, the Righteous One who is the atoning sacrifice for our sins and for the sins of the whole world. His grace and peace are with you now. Amen.

Petitions and Supplications, Ending with the Lord's Prayer

Our Father which art in heaven, Hallowed be thy name. Thy kingdom come. Thy will be done in earth, as it is in heaven. Give us this day our daily bread. And forgive us our debts, as we forgive our debtors. And lead us not into temptation, but deliver us from evil: For thine is the kingdom, and the power, and the glory, for ever. Amen.

~ Matthew 6.9-13 (KJV)

Doxology (and/or closing song)

Praise God from whom all blessings flow;
Praise Him all creatures here below;
Praise Him above ye heavenly host;
Praise Father, Son and Holy Ghost. Amen.

DEPARTING TO SERVE

Benediction

O LORD, raise up, we pray thee, thy power, and come among us, and with great might succour us; that, whereas through our sins and wickedness we are sore let and hindered in running the race that is set before us, thy bountiful grace and mercy may speedily help and deliver us; through Jesus Christ our Lord, to whom, with thee and the Holy Ghost, be honour and glory world without end. Amen.

~ *Scottish Prayer Book* (Suter, p. 5)

Affirmation from the Psalms

Give ear, O my people, to my teaching; incline your ears to the words of my mouth! [2] I will open my mouth in a parable; I will utter dark sayings from of old, [3] things that we have heard and known, that our fathers have told us. [4] We will not hide them from their children, but tell to the coming generation the glorious deeds of the Lord, and his might, and the wonders that he has done.

~ Psalm 78.1-4

Pray without Ceasing – Flash Prayer for the Day

My soul magnifies the Lord, and my spirit rejoices in God my Savior, for he has looked on the humble estate of his servant.

For Your Weekly Journey

Let God Arise! Seasonal Focus

Behold, God Is My Salvation, Isaiah 12.1-6

Book Reading

Allen, *Missionary Methods: St. Paul's or Ours?*

Special Church Year Services

Christmas Eve: Thursday, December 24, 2015
Christmas Day: Friday, December 25, 2015

The Celebration of Christmas

THE BIRTH OF CHRIST

"For as the rain and the snow come down from heaven
and do not return there but water the earth,
making it bring forth and sprout,
giving seed to the sower and bread to the eater,
so shall my word be that goes out from my mouth;
it shall not return to me empty,
but it shall accomplish that which I purpose,
and shall succeed in the thing for which I sent it."

ISAIAH 55.10-11

Christmas is a celebration of the mystery of the incarnation of the Son of God, the Word made flesh in the world. It celebrates the birth of Christ.

In those days a decree went out from Caesar Augustus that all the world should be registered. [2] This was the first registration when Quirinius was governor of Syria. [3] And all went to be registered, each to his own town. [4] And Joseph also went up from Galilee, from the town of Nazareth, to Judea, to the city of David, which is called Bethlehem, because he was of the house and lineage of David, [5] to be registered with Mary, his betrothed, who was with child.

[6] And while they were there, the time came for her to give birth. [7] And she gave birth to her firstborn son and wrapped him in swaddling cloths and laid him in a manger, because there was no place for them in the inn. [8] And in the same region there were shepherds out in the field, keeping watch over their flock by night. [9] And an angel of the Lord appeared to them, and the glory of the Lord shone around them, and they were filled with fear. [10] And the angel said to them, "Fear not, for behold, I bring you good news of a great joy that will be for all the people. [11] For unto you is born this day in the city of David a Savior, who is Christ the Lord. [12] And this will be a sign for you: you will find a baby wrapped in swaddling cloths and lying in a manger." [13] And suddenly there was with the angel a multitude of the heavenly host praising God and saying, [14] "Glory to God in the highest, and on earth peace among those with whom he is pleased!" [15] When the angels went away from them into heaven, the shepherds said to one another, "Let us go over to Bethlehem and see this thing that has happened, which the Lord has made known to us."

[16] And they went with haste and found Mary and Joseph, and the baby lying in a manger. [17] And when they saw it, they made known the saying that had been told them concerning this child. [18] And all who heard it wondered at what the shepherds told them. [19] But Mary treasured up all these things, pondering them in her heart. [20] And the shepherds returned, glorifying and praising God for all they had heard and seen, as it had been told them.

~ Luke 2.1-20 (ESV)

Christmas celebrates the mystery of the incarnation of the Son of God, the Word made flesh. He enters the world to reveal the Father's love to humankind, to destroy the devil's work, and to redeem his people from their sins. Although the highest Christological reflection has sought to plumb the depths of this mystery, only faith, awe, and worship can draw near to its richness. In order to redeem humankind from its waywardness, to reconcile creation that was cursed at the Fall, to destroy the enemies of God, and to reveal the Father's glory to the world, the eternal Word became a human being. The One through whom the Father created trillions of galaxies by his omnipotent, creative Word, was joined to human likeness, and entered the world as a baby boy. And all this for love and grace.

This grand celebration and time of remembrance is an invitation to wonder, to meditate upon a truth that can easily be recited in the dry theological language of the schools, but can never be fathomed fully. Who can possibly grasp the total meaning of the Christ-child, the One sent and anointed by God to reign forever after he conquered sin and death through his passion? As Christians, we join the shepherds and the Magi at the foot of the baby boy, and quietly, reverently bow with Mary and Joseph under the gleam of the star that rested above him who would one day become King of kings and Lord of lords. His coming is soon, and we eagerly wait still for that time when the prophets' foretellings will become true. Yes, the kingdoms of this world will become the kingdoms of our Lord and of this child, and he will reign forever and ever.

At Christmas, believers worldwide celebrate the birth of the Messiah in Bethlehem, the Lord Jesus Christ. Together we affirm that Jesus was – and is – God's only begotten Son, the Word made flesh, and the human son of the Virgin Mary. In him we see the love of God revealed for all humankind. He is God's mystery that causes broken hearts to marvel and rejoice. This little child would fulfill the prophecy of a Savior who, by dying and rising, would conquer humanity's mortal enemy, the devil, free us from sin's bondage and curse, and restore creation under the reign of God. "Joy to the world, the Lord has come! Let earth receive her King!"

Rev. Dr. Don L. Davis

Hark, the Herald Angels Sing

Hark! the herald angels sing, "Glory to the newborn King;
Peace on earth and mercy mild, God and sinners reconciled."
Joyful, all ye nations, rise, join the triumph of the skies;
With th' angelic host proclaim, "Christ is born in Bethlehem!"
Hark! the herald angels sing, "Glory to the newborn King."

Christ, by highest heav'n adored, Christ, the everlasting Lord;
Late in time behold Him come, offspring of a virgin's womb.
Veiled in flesh the Godhead see, hail, the incarnate Deity!
Pleased as man with men to dwell, Jesus our Emmanuel.
Hark! the herald angels sing, "Glory to the newborn King."

Hail the heav'n born Prince of Peace! Hail the Sun of righteousness!
Light and life to all He brings, ris'n with healing in His wings.
Mild He lays His glory by, born that man no more may die.
Born to raise the sons of earth, born to give them second birth.
Hark! the herald angels sing, "Glory to the newborn King!"

Come, Desire of nations, come! Fix in us Thy humble home.
Rise, the woman's conqu'ring seed, bruise in us the serpent's head;
Adam's likeness now efface, stamp Thine image in its place;
Second Adam from above, reinstate us in Thy love.
Hark! the herald angels sing, "Glory to the newborn King."

~ Charles Wesley, Felix Mendelssohn. © Public Domain.

Christmas Eve

December 24, 2015

Christmas celebrates the birth of Messiah, Jesus, who is the incarnation of the Son of God, Mary's child. He is the Word made flesh, the conqueror who enters this fallen world to reveal to us the Father's love, to destroy the devil's work, and to redeem his people from their sins.

TODAY'S THEME

Glory to God in the Highest, Luke 2.1-20

In the days of Elizabeth's and Mary's pregnacies, a decree went out from Caesar Augustus that all the world should be registered (which was the first registration when Quirinius was governor of Syria). Everyone went to be registered in their ancestral home. Joseph went up from Nazareth of Galilee, to Judea to the city of David, Bethlehem, for he was of David's lineage. He went to be registered with Mary, his betrothed, who was pregnant. While they were there, Mary went into labor, and gave birth to her firstborn son, and wrapped him in swaddling cloths and laid him in a manger (for there was no place for them in the inn).

In that region shepherds were out in the field, keeping watch over their flock by night. An angel of the Lord appeared to them, and the Lord's glory shone around them. The shepherds were filled with great fear, but the angel spoke to them and said, "Fear not, for behold, I bring you good news of great joy that will be for all the people. For unto you is born this day in the city of David a Savior, who is Christ the Lord. For this will be a sign for you: you will find a baby wrapped in swaddling cloths and lying in a manger." After this, suddenly there was with the angel a multitude of the heavenly host praising God and saying, "Glory to God in the highest, and on earth peace among those with whom he is pleased!" After the angels departed from them into heaven, the shepherds determined to go over to Bethlehem to see this thing that happened, which the Lord had made known to them. They hurried and found Mary and Joseph, along with the baby, lying in a manger.

The angels' declaration of Messiah's birth was Good News for all people, the kind that should bring praise and glory to the Father, whose love gave to us the gift of his only Son for our deliverance and salvation.

Daily Devotional Guide

PREPARING OUR HEARTS

Invocation: Our Prayer of Acclamation
May God Almighty, Who by the Incarnation of His only begotten Son drove away the darkness of the world, and by His glorious Birth enlightened this day, drive away from us the darkness of sins and enlighten our hearts with the light of Christian graces. And may He who willed that the great day of His most holy Birth should be told to the shepherds by and angel, pour upon us the refreshing shower of His blessing, and guide us, Himself being our Shepherd, to the pastures of everlasting joy. And may He, Who through His Incarnation united earthly things with heavenly, fill us with the sweetness of inward peace and goodwill, and make us partakers with the heavenly host; for the glory of His great Name. Amen.

~ Treasury of Devotion, 1869 (Fox, p 213)

Call to Worship
Blessed are you, O God: Father, Son, and Holy Spirit. And blessed is your Kingdom, both now and forever, amen.

PRAISING OUR GOD

Te Deum Laudamus

You are God: we praise you; you are the Lord; we acclaim you; you are the eternal Father: All creation worships you. To you all angels, all the powers of heaven, Cherubim and Seraphim, sing in endless praise: Holy, holy, holy Lord, God of power and might, heaven and earth are full of your glory.

The glorious company of apostles praise you. The noble fellowship of prophets praise you. The white-robed army of martyrs praise you. Throughout the world the holy Church acclaims you; Father, of majesty unbounded, your true and only Son, worthy of all worship, and the Holy Spirit, advocate and guide.

You, Christ, are the king of glory, the eternal Son of the Father. When you became man to set us free you did not shun the Virgin's womb. You overcame the sting of death and opened the kingdom of heaven to all believers. You are seated at God's right hand in glory. We believe that you will come and be our judge. Come then, Lord, and help your people, bought with the price of your own blood, and bring us with your saints to glory everlasting.

Praise and Thanksgiving (Songs and Prayers)

Gloria Patri

Glory be to the Father,
And to the Son and to the Holy Spirit:
As it was in the beginning,
Is now, and ever shall be,
World without end. Amen, amen.

LISTENING TO HIS VOICE

Chronological Reading for the Day
Job 26-29

Lectionary Readings
Psalm: Ps. 97   *OT:* Isa. 62.6-12
Gospel: Luke 2.1-20   *NT:* Titus 3.4-7

Reflection: Silence and/or Journaling

RESPONDING IN FAITH

The Apostles' Creed
*I believe in God, the Father Almighty, Maker of heaven and earth;
and in Jesus Christ, his only Son, our Lord, who was conceived by the
Holy Spirit, born of the Virgin Mary, suffered under Pontius Pilate,
was crucified, dead, and buried; he descended into hell; the third day
he arose again from the dead; he ascended into heaven and sits on
the right hand of God the Father Almighty; from thence he shall come
to judge the quick and the dead.*

I believe in the Holy Spirit, the holy catholic church, the communion
of saints, the forgiveness of sins, the resurrection of the body, and the
life everlasting. Amen.*

* In the Apostles' and Nicene Creeds, the term catholic refers to the Church's
universality, through all ages and times, of all languages and peoples. It refers to no
particular tradition or denominational expression (e.g., as in Roman Catholic).

Prayers of Confession
Let us now confess our sins to God and receive mercy and
grace to help in our time of need.

Assurance of Pardon

Having faithfully confessed and renounced your sin, Christ also has been faithful to forgive your sins and to purify you from all unrighteousness. It is certain, that there is One who has spoken to the Father in your defense, Jesus Christ, the Righteous One who is the atoning sacrifice for our sins and for the sins of the whole world. His grace and peace are with you now. Amen.

Petitions and Supplications, Ending with the Lord's Prayer

Our Father which art in heaven, Hallowed be thy name. Thy kingdom come, Thy will be done in earth, as it is in heaven. Give us this day our daily bread. And forgive us our debts, as we forgive our debtors. And lead us not into temptation, but deliver us from evil: For thine is the kingdom, and the power, and the glory, for ever. Amen.

~ Matthew 6.9-13 (KJV)

Doxology (and/or closing song)

Praise God from whom all blessings flow;
Praise Him all creatures here below;
Praise Him above ye heavenly host;
Praise Father, Son and Holy Ghost. Amen.

DEPARTING TO SERVE

Benediction

Almighty God, you made this holy night shine with the brightness of the true Light. Grant that here on earth we may walk in the light of Jesus' presence and in the last day wake to the brightness of his glory; through your Son, Jesus Christ our Lord, who lives and reigns with you and the Holy Spirit, one God, now and forever. Amen.

~ *Evangelical Lutheran Worship*
(Conference of Bishops, Evangelical Lutheran Church in America, p. 376)

Affirmation from the Psalms

You who fear the Lord, praise him! All you offspring of Jacob, glorify him, and stand in awe of him, all you offspring of Israel! [24] For he has not despised or abhorred the affliction of the afflicted, and he has not hidden his face from him, but has heard, when he cried to him. [25] From you comes my praise in the great congregation; my vows I will perform before those who fear him. [26] The afflicted shall eat and be satisfied; those who seek him shall praise the Lord! May your hearts live forever!

~ Psalm 22.23-26

Pray without Ceasing – Flash Prayer for the Day

"Glory to God in the highest, and on earth peace among those with whom he is pleased!"

For Your Weekly Journey

Let God Arise! Seasonal Focus

The Name above All Names, Philippians 2.5-11

Book Reading

Allen, *Missionary Methods: St. Paul's or Ours?*

Christmas Day: Nativity of the Lord

December 25, 2015

Christmas celebrates the birth of Messiah, Jesus, who is the incarnation of the Son of God, Mary's child. He is the Word made flesh, the conqueror who enters this fallen world to reveal to us the Father's love, to destroy the devil's work, and to redeem his people from their sins.

TODAY'S THEME
The Word Became Flesh, John 1.1-14

John begins his Gospel in a way different than the Synoptic Gospels [i.e., Matthew, Mark, and Luke]. Rather than starting with Jesus' genealogical lineage, John speaks of the Lord in his pre-existent state: in the beginning was the Word, and the Word was with God, and the Word was God. The Lord was in the beginning with God. All things were made through him, and in him alone was life, the light of all humankind. It is a light that shines in the darkness, which the darkness can never overcome.

John speaks of God sending John who came as a witness and to bear witness about the light, that the world might believe in the Lord. John was not that light, but the witness about the light. The Lord Jesus is the true light, who gives light to everyone, who came into the world at that time. Although he came to the world, which he created, the world nevertheless did not know him. Further, he came to his very own people, but they did not receive him as Messiah. However, all who do receive him (who believe in his name) he gives to them the right to become God's own children, born neither of blood nor of the will of the flesh nor of human will, but from God Godself.

In a clear and beautiful statement John affirms that the Word became flesh and dwelt among us, and testified that he and others had seen his glory, the very glory as of the only Son from the Father, full of grace and truth. In the coming of Jesus into the world, God's divine Son entered into our earth, was incarnated as a human being, and borne witness to by John and the apostles. From the fullness of the divine Word we all have received, grace upon grace, for the law was given through Moses, but the grace and truth of God came through Jesus Christ. John testifies that no one has ever seen God, yet the only God, who is at the Father's side, Jesus, the Son of God, has in fact now made God known to us.

Daily Devotional Guide

PREPARING OUR HEARTS

Invocation: Our Prayer of Acclamation
Almighty God, you gave us your only Son to take on our human nature and to illumine the world with your light. By your grace adopt us as your children and enlighten us with your Spirit, through Jesus Christ, our Redeemer and Lord, who lives and reigns with you and the Holy Spirit, one God, now and forever. Amen.

~ Evangelical Lutheran Worship
(Conference of Bishops, Evangelical Lutheran Church in America, p. 377)

Call to Worship
Blessed are you, O God: Father, Son, and Holy Spirit. And blessed is your Kingdom, both now and forever, amen.

PRAISING OUR GOD

Te Deum Laudamus
You are God: we praise you; you are the Lord; we acclaim you; you are the eternal Father: All creation worships you. To you all angels, all the powers of heaven, Cherubim and Seraphim, sing in endless praise: Holy, holy, holy Lord, God of power and might, heaven and earth are full of your glory.

The glorious company of apostles praise you. The noble fellowship of prophets praise you. The white-robed army of martyrs praise you. Throughout the world the holy Church acclaims you; Father, of majesty unbounded, your true and only Son, worthy of all worship, and the Holy Spirit, advocate and guide.

You, Christ, are the king of glory, the eternal Son of the Father. When you became man to set us free you did not shun the Virgin's womb. You overcame the sting of death and opened the kingdom of heaven to all believers. You are seated at God's right hand in glory. We believe that you will come and be our judge. Come then, Lord, and help your people, bought with the price of your own blood, and bring us with your saints to glory everlasting.

Praise and Thanksgiving (Songs and Prayers)

Gloria Patri
Glory be to the Father,
And to the Son and to the Holy Spirit:
As it was in the beginning,
Is now, and ever shall be,
World without end. Amen, amen.

LISTENING TO HIS VOICE

Chronological Reading for the Day
Job 30-31

Lectionary Readings
Psalm: Ps. 98   *OT:* Isa. 52.7-10
Gospel: John 1.1-14   *NT:* Heb. 1.1-12

Reflection: Silence and/or Journaling

RESPONDING IN FAITH

The Apostles' Creed
I believe in God, the Father Almighty, Maker of heaven and earth; and in Jesus Christ, his only Son, our Lord, who was conceived by the Holy Spirit, born of the Virgin Mary, suffered under Pontius Pilate, was crucified, dead, and buried; he descended into hell; the third day he arose again from the dead; he ascended into heaven and sits on the right hand of God the Father Almighty; from thence he shall come to judge the quick and the dead.

I believe in the Holy Spirit, the holy catholic* church, the communion of saints, the forgiveness of sins, the resurrection of the body, and the life everlasting. Amen.

* In the Apostles' and Nicene Creeds, the term catholic refers to the Church's universality, through all ages and times, of all languages and peoples. It refers to no particular tradition or denominational expression (e.g., as in Roman Catholic).

Prayers of Confession
Let us now confess our sins to God and receive mercy and grace to help in our time of need.

Assurance of Pardon
Having faithfully confessed and renounced your sin, Christ also has been faithful to forgive your sins and to purify you from all unrighteousness. It is certain, that there is One who has spoken to the Father in your defense, Jesus Christ, the Righteous One who is the atoning sacrifice for our sins and for the sins of the whole world. His grace and peace are with you now. Amen.

Petitions and Supplications, Ending with the Lord's Prayer
Our Father which art in heaven, Hallowed be thy name. Thy kingdom come, Thy will be done in earth, as it is in heaven. Give us this day our daily bread. And forgive us our debts, as we forgive our debtors. And

lead us not into temptation, but deliver us from evil: For thine is the
kingdom, and the power, and the glory, for ever. Amen.

~ Matthew 6.9-13 (KJV)

Doxology (and/or closing song)

Praise God from whom all blessings flow;
Praise Him all creatures here below;
Praise Him above ye heavenly host;
Praise Father, Son and Holy Ghost. Amen.

DEPARTING TO SERVE

Benediction

Dearly beloved, today our Savior is born; let us rejoice. Sadness should
have no place on the birthday of life. The fear of death has been
swallowed up; life brings us joy with the promise of eternal happiness.
No one is shut out from this joy, all share the same reason for rejoicing.
Our Lord, victor over sin and death, finding no one free from sin, came
to free us all. Amen.

~ Leo the Great (Oden, p. 36)

Affirmation from the Psalms

I will extol you, O Lord, for you have drawn me up and have not let my
foes rejoice over me. [2] O Lord my God, I cried to you for help, and you
have healed me. [3] O Lord, you have brought up my soul from Sheol;
you restored me to life from among those who go down to the pit.

~ Psalm 30.1-3

Pray without Ceasing – Flash Prayer for the Day

Thank you Father, that the Word became flesh and has dwelt
among us, and we know that he has displayed his glory, the
very glory as of the only Son from the Father, full of grace
and truth.

For Your Weekly Journey

Let God Arise! Seasonal Focus
The Name above All Names, Philippians 2.5-11

Book Reading
Allen, *Missionary Methods: St. Paul's or Ours?*

First Sunday after Christmas Day

December 27, 2015 - January 2, 2016

Christmas celebrates the birth of Messiah, Jesus, who is the incarnation of the Son of God, Mary's child. He is the Word made flesh, the conqueror who enters this fallen world to reveal to us the Father's love, to destroy the devil's work, and to redeem his people from their sins.

THIS WEEK'S THEME
My Father's House, Luke 2.41-52

Joseph and Mary were devout worshipers, going up to Jerusalem every year at the Feast of the Passover. When Jesus was twelve years old, they went up as was their custom, and when the week-long feast was ended, as they were returning, Jesus stayed behind in Jerusalem (though his folks did not know it). They thought he was in their traveling group during a day's journey on the road, but when they searched for him among their relatives and acquaintances, he was not there. They returned to Jerusalem, searching for him.

After three days they finally found the boy Jesus in the temple, sitting among the teachers, listening to them and asking them questions. Those who heard Jesus were amazed at both his understanding and his answers. Astonished at him, his mother said to him, "Son, why have you treated us so? Behold, your father and I have been searching for you in great distress." Jesus said to his parents, "Why were you looking for me? Did you not know that I must be in my Father's house?" Neither understood his saying to them. Afterwards, he went down with them and back to Nazareth, submitting to them. Mary treasured up all these things in her heart, and the Lord Jesus increased in wisdom and in stature, growing in favor with God and man.

Daily Devotional Guide

PREPARING OUR HEARTS

Invocation: Our Prayer of Acclamation

God and Father of our Lord Jesus Christ, thank you for the gift of your Son. Thank you that even as a young child he understood his mission on this earth. His entire existence was based on obeying your will and bringing you glory, which he did in all that he did and said. Thank you for the pattern that he has set for us, his people. May his lowliness and humility be fulfilled in us, even as he sought to be about your business, serving you in your house. Be glorified in and through us, for Christ's sake, amen.

Call to Worship

Blessed are you, O God: Father, Son, and Holy Spirit. And blessed is your Kingdom, both now and forever, amen.

PRAISING OUR GOD

Te Deum Laudamus

You are God: we praise you; you are the Lord; we acclaim you; you are the eternal Father: All creation worships you. To you all angels, all the powers of heaven, Cherubim and Seraphim, sing in endless praise: Holy, holy, holy Lord, God of power and might, heaven and earth are full of your glory.

The glorious company of apostles praise you. The noble fellowship of prophets praise you. The white-robed army of martyrs praise you. Throughout the world the holy Church acclaims you; Father, of majesty unbounded, your true and only Son, worthy of all worship, and the Holy Spirit, advocate and guide.

You, Christ, are the king of glory, the eternal Son of the Father. When you became man to set us free you did not shun the Virgin's womb. You overcame the sting of death and opened the kingdom of heaven to all believers. You are seated at God's right hand in glory. We believe that you will come and be our judge. Come then, Lord, and help your people, bought with the price of your own blood, and bring us with your saints to glory everlasting.

Praise and Thanksgiving (Songs and Prayers)

Gloria Patri
Glory be to the Father,
And to the Son and to the Holy Spirit:
As it was in the beginning,
Is now, and ever shall be,
World without end. Amen, amen.

LISTENING TO HIS VOICE

Chronological Reading for the Day
Sunday: Job 35-37
Monday: Job 38-39
Tuesday: Job 40-42
Wednesday: Exod. 1-4; 1 Chron. 6.1-3a
Thursday: Exod. 5-7
Friday: Exod. 8-9
Saturday: Exod. 10-12

Lectionary Readings
Psalm: Ps. 148   *OT:* 1 Sam. 2.18-20, 26
Gospel: Luke 2.41-52   *NT:* Col. 3.12-17

Reflection: Silence and/or Journaling

RESPONDING IN FAITH

The Apostles' Creed
I believe in God, the Father Almighty, Maker of heaven and earth; and in Jesus Christ, his only Son, our Lord, who was conceived by the Holy Spirit, born of the Virgin Mary, suffered under Pontius Pilate,

was crucified, dead, and buried; he descended into hell; the third day he arose again from the dead; he ascended into heaven and sits on the right hand of God the Father Almighty; from thence he shall come to judge the quick and the dead.

I believe in the Holy Spirit, the holy catholic* church, the communion of saints, the forgiveness of sins, the resurrection of the body, and the life everlasting. Amen.

* In the Apostles' and Nicene Creeds, the term catholic refers to the Church's universality, through all ages and times, of all languages and peoples. It refers to no particular tradition or denominational expression (e.g., as in Roman Catholic).

Prayers of Confession
Let us now confess our sins to God and receive mercy and grace to help in our time of need.

Assurance of Pardon
Having faithfully confessed and renounced your sin, Christ also has been faithful to forgive your sins and to purify you from all unrighteousness. It is certain, that there is One who has spoken to the Father in your defense, Jesus Christ, the Righteous One who is the atoning sacrifice for our sins and for the sins of the whole world. His grace and peace are with you now. Amen.

Petitions and Supplications, Ending with the Lord's Prayer
Our Father which art in heaven, Hallowed be thy name. Thy kingdom come, Thy will be done in earth, as it is in heaven. Give us this day our daily bread. And forgive us our debts, as we forgive our debtors. And lead us not into temptation, but deliver us from evil: For thine is the kingdom, and the power, and the glory, for ever. Amen.

~ Matthew 6.9-13 (KJV)

Doxology (and/or closing song)
Praise God from whom all blessings flow;
Praise Him all creatures here below;
Praise Him above ye heavenly host;
Praise Father, Son and Holy Ghost. Amen.

DEPARTING TO SERVE

Benediction
Holy Savior, even by the time you were twelve years old, you understood your calling and mission on this earth. You loved your Father, and obeyed his will fully, maintaining throughout your life a zeal for his house. Thank you for your example, and for your Spirit who alone can reproduce your love and life within us. Make us like you in all things. In your name we pray, amen.

Affirmation from the Psalms
In sacrifice and offering you have not delighted, but you have given me an open ear. Burnt offering and sin offering you have not required. [7] Then I said, "Behold, I have come; in the scroll of the book it is written of me: [8] I delight to do your will, O my God; your law is within my heart."

~ Psalm 40.6-8

Pray without Ceasing – Flash Prayer for the Day
Give to us, O Lord, a mind like your Son, who from an early age desired to be about your business in his Father's house.

For Your Weekly Journey

Let God Arise! Seasonal Focus
The Name above All Names, Philippians 2.5-11

Book Reading
Allen, *Missionary Methods: St. Paul's or Ours?*

Special Church Year Service
Holy Name of Jesus/New Year's Day: Friday, January 1, 2016

Holy Name of Jesus/New Year's Day

January 1, 2016

Christmas celebrates the birth of Messiah, Jesus, who is the incarnation of the Son of God, Mary's child. He is the Word made flesh, the conqueror who enters this fallen world to reveal to us the Father's love, to destroy the devil's work, and to redeem his people from their sins.

TODAY'S THEME

The Name above All Names, Philippians 2.5-11

Paul the apostle, in writing to the Philippians, exhorts the believers to have this mind among themselves, a mind which was theirs in Christ Jesus. Although the Lord Jesus was in the form of God, he did not count equality with God a thing that had to be grasped (something he needed to hold onto). Rather, he emptied himself, taking on the form of a servant, and was born in the likeness of men. Then, found in human form, he humbled himself by becoming obedient to the point of death, even death on a cross.

This divine humility and lowliness was rewarded by God, who, therefore highly exalted him and bestowed on him the name that is above every name. Now, at the name of Jesus every knee should bow, in heaven and on earth and under the earth, and every tongue will one day confess that Jesus Christ is Lord, to the glory of God the Father. The name of Jesus is the highest name of all, the only name under heaven given to humankind whereby they can be saved from sin and brought into the favor of the Lord.

Daily Devotional Guide

PREPARING OUR HEARTS

Invocation: Our Prayer of Acclamation
Christ with me, Christ before me, Christ behind me, Christ within me, Christ beneath me, Christ above me, Christ on my right, Christ on my left...Christ on the heart of everyone who thinks of me, Christ in the mouth of everyone who speaks to me, Christ in every eye that sees me, Christ in every ear that hears me. Amen.

· The Canticle of St. Patrick (Oden, 90)

Call to Worship
Blessed are you, O God: Father, Son, and Holy Spirit. And blessed is your Kingdom, both now and forever, amen.

PRAISING OUR GOD

Te Deum Laudamus
You are God: we praise you; you are the Lord; we acclaim you; you are the eternal Father: All creation worships you. To you all angels, all the powers of heaven, Cherubim and Seraphim, sing in endless praise: Holy, holy, holy Lord, God of power and might, heaven and earth are full of your glory.

The glorious company of apostles praise you. The noble fellowship of prophets praise you. The white-robed army of martyrs praise you. Throughout the world the holy Church acclaims you; Father, of majesty unbounded, your true and only Son, worthy of all worship, and the Holy Spirit, advocate and guide.

You, Christ, are the king of glory, the eternal Son of the Father. When you became man to set us free you did not shun the Virgin's womb. You overcame the sting of death and opened the kingdom of heaven to all believers. You are seated at God's right hand in glory. We believe that you will come and be our judge. Come then, Lord, and help your

people, bought with the price of your own blood, and bring us with
your saints to glory everlasting.

Praise and Thanksgiving (Songs and Prayers)

Gloria Patri
Glory be to the Father,
And to the Son and to the Holy Spirit:
As it was in the beginning,
Is now, and ever shall be,
World without end. Amen, amen.

LISTENING TO HIS VOICE

Chronological Reading for the Day
Exod. 8-9

Lectionary Readings for *Holy Name of Jesus*
Psalm: Ps. 8   *OT:* Num. 6.22-27
Gospel: Luke 2.15-21   *NT:* Phil. 2.5-11

Lectionary Readings for *New Year's Day*
Psalm: Ps. 8   *OT:* Eccles. 3.1-13
Gospel: Matt. 25.31-46   *NT:* Rev. 21.1-6a

Reflection: Silence and/or Journaling

RESPONDING IN FAITH

The Apostles' Creed
I believe in God, the Father Almighty, Maker of heaven and earth;
and in Jesus Christ, his only Son, our Lord, who was conceived by the
Holy Spirit, born of the Virgin Mary, suffered under Pontius Pilate,
was crucified, dead, and buried; he descended into hell; the third day
he arose again from the dead; he ascended into heaven and sits on
the right hand of God the Father Almighty; from thence he shall come
to judge the quick and the dead.

I believe in the Holy Spirit, the holy catholic* church, the communion of saints, the forgiveness of sins, the resurrection of the body, and the life everlasting. Amen.

* In the Apostles' and Nicene Creeds, the term catholic refers to the Church's universality, through all ages and times, of all languages and peoples. It refers to no particular tradition or denominational expression (e.g., as in Roman Catholic).

Prayers of Confession

Let us now confess our sins to God and receive mercy and grace to help in our time of need.

Assurance of Pardon

Having faithfully confessed and renounced your sin, Christ also has been faithful to forgive your sins and to purify you from all unrighteousness. It is certain, that there is One who has spoken to the Father in your defense, Jesus Christ, the Righteous One who is the atoning sacrifice for our sins and for the sins of the whole world. His grace and peace are with you now. Amen.

Petitions and Supplications, Ending with the Lord's Prayer

Our Father which art in heaven, Hallowed be thy name. Thy kingdom come, Thy will be done in earth, as it is in heaven. Give us this day our daily bread. And forgive us our debts, as we forgive our debtors. And lead us not into temptation, but deliver us from evil: For thine is the kingdom, and the power, and the glory, for ever. Amen.

~ Matthew 6.9-13 (KJV)

Doxology (and/or closing song)

Praise God from whom all blessings flow;
Praise Him all creatures here below;
Praise Him above ye heavenly host;
Praise Father, Son and Holy Ghost. Amen.

DEPARTING TO SERVE

Benediction
Make us glad, O God, in recounting your mercies and adoring your holiness, and let it be our chief joy to glorify your holy name. Almighty and everlasting God, the brightness of faithful souls, who brought the Gentiles to your light and made known to them him who is the true Light and the bright and morning Star: fill, we ask, the world with your glory, and show yourself by the radiance of your light to all nations. Amen.

~ *The Gregorian Sacramentary* (Oden, p. 41)

Affirmation from the Psalms
In Judah God is known; his name is great in Israel. [2] His abode has been established in Salem, his dwelling place in Zion. [3] There he broke the flashing arrows, the shield, the sword, and the weapons of war. Selah.

~ Psalm 76.1-3

Pray without Ceasing – Flash Prayer for the Day
Receive our submission to the name of Jesus, for we bow our knees to his name and confess with our tongues that Jesus Christ is Lord, to your glory, O glorious Father and God.

For Your Weekly Journey

Let God Arise! Seasonal Focus
The Name above All Names, Philippians 2.5-11

Book Reading
Allen, *Missionary Methods: St. Paul's or Ours?*

Second Sunday after Christmas Day

WEEK 6

January 3 - 9, 2016

Christmas celebrates the birth of Messiah, Jesus, who is the incarnation of the Son of God, Mary's child. He is the Word made flesh, the conqueror who enters this fallen world to reveal to us the Father's love, to destroy the devil's work, and to redeem his people from their sins.

THIS WEEK'S THEME

To the Praise of His Glorious Grace, Ephesians 1.3-14

In Ephesians Paul provides us with a moving discussion of the reason why God the Father of our Lord Jesus Christ is to be praised for his glorious salvation. He has blessed us by giving us every spiritual blessing in the heavenlies. Even before the world was created, God had already chosen us to be his own through our union with Christ, ensuring that we would be holy and without fault before him. He adopted us because of his love, having already decided that through Jesus he would make us his children, which was his divine purpose. We ought to praise him for this glorious grace, this free gift given to us in his Son, whose blood set us free and provided forgiveness.

His amazing grace moved him to work in all wisdom and insight to perform precisely what he had purposed, making known his secret plan what he had determined to do through Christ. This great plan, which will be fulfilled in God's own time, will be to bring creation together and gather everything in heaven and on earth under its true head, even our Lord Jesus Christ. All this will be done according to God's plan and decision, who chose us to be in union with Christ as his own from the very beginning. Paul challenged the Ephesians, then, they who were among the first to hope in Christ, to praise God's glory! For they heard the true message of God's salvation, the Good News that brings salvation, believed it, and as a result God sealed them with the stamp of ownership of his promised Holy Spirit. His Spirit is the guarantee, the down payment and pledge, that we shall also receive all that God has promised, and that we will come into his freedom as those who belong to him will do. And for all these things, we should live to the praise of his glorious grace!

Daily Devotional Guide

PREPARING OUR HEARTS

Invocation: Our Prayer of Acclamation
Holy Father and God, your sovereign grace has been displayed in your mighty works of salvation on behalf of those who believe the Good News concerning your Son. Thank you for your generosity, kindness, and grace, given to us through your Son, and the pledge of the full inheritance made in the gift of your Holy Spirit. We praise your name, and want to live to the praise of your glorious grace. Receive our praise, in Jesus name, amen.

Call to Worship
Blessed are you, O God: Father, Son, and Holy Spirit. And blessed is your Kingdom, both now and forever, amen.

PRAISING OUR GOD

Te Deum Laudamus
You are God: we praise you; you are the Lord; we acclaim you; you are the eternal Father: All creation worships you. To you all angels, all the powers of heaven, Cherubim and Seraphim, sing in endless praise: Holy, holy, holy Lord, God of power and might, heaven and earth are full of your glory.

The glorious company of apostles praise you. The noble fellowship of prophets praise you. The white-robed army of martyrs praise you.

Throughout the world the holy Church acclaims you; Father, of majesty unbounded, your true and only Son, worthy of all worship, and the Holy Spirit, advocate and guide.

You, Christ, are the king of glory, the eternal Son of the Father. When you became man to set us free you did not shun the Virgin's womb. You overcame the sting of death and opened the kingdom of heaven to all believers. You are seated at God's right hand in glory. We believe that you will come and be our judge. Come then, Lord, and help your people, bought with the price of your own blood, and bring us with your saints to glory everlasting.

Praise and Thanksgiving (Songs and Prayers)

Gloria Patri
Glory be to the Father,
And to the Son and to the Holy Spirit:
As it was in the beginning,
Is now, and ever shall be,
World without end. Amen, amen.

LISTENING TO HIS VOICE

Chronological Reading for the Day
Sunday: Exod. 13-15
Monday: Exod. 16-19
Tuesday: Exod. 20-21
Wednesday: Exod. 22-24

Thursday: Exod. 25-28
Friday: Exod. 29-31
Saturday: Exod. 32-34

Lectionary Readings
Psalm: Ps. 147.12-20
Gospel: John 1.1-18

OT: Jer. 31.7-14
NT: Eph. 1.3-14

Reflection: Silence and/or Journaling

RESPONDING IN FAITH

The Apostles' Creed

*I believe in God, the Father Almighty, Maker of heaven and earth;
and in Jesus Christ, his only Son, our Lord, who was conceived by the
Holy Spirit, born of the Virgin Mary, suffered under Pontius Pilate,
was crucified, dead, and buried; he descended into hell; the third day
he arose again from the dead; he ascended into heaven and sits on
the right hand of God the Father Almighty; from thence he shall come
to judge the quick and the dead.*

I believe in the Holy Spirit, the holy catholic church, the communion
of saints, the forgiveness of sins, the resurrection of the body, and the
life everlasting. Amen.*

* In the Apostles' and Nicene Creeds, the term catholic refers to the Church's
universality, through all ages and times, of all languages and peoples. It refers to no
particular tradition or denominational expression (e.g., as in Roman Catholic).

Prayers of Confession

Let us now confess our sins to God and receive mercy and
grace to help in our time of need.

Assurance of Pardon

Having faithfully confessed and renounced your sin, Christ
also has been faithful to forgive your sins and to purify you
from all unrighteousness. It is certain, that there is One who
has spoken to the Father in your defense, Jesus Christ, the
Righteous One who is the atoning sacrifice for our sins and
for the sins of the whole world. His grace and peace are with
you now. Amen.

Petitions and Supplications, Ending with the Lord's Prayer
Our Father which art in heaven, Hallowed be thy name. Thy kingdom come, Thy will be done in earth, as it is in heaven. Give us this day our daily bread. And forgive us our debts, as we forgive our debtors. And lead us not into temptation, but deliver us from evil: For thine is the kingdom, and the power, and the glory, for ever. Amen.

~ Matthew 6.9-13 (KJV)

Doxology (and/or closing song)
Praise God from whom all blessings flow;
Praise Him all creatures here below;
Praise Him above ye heavenly host;
Praise Father, Son and Holy Ghost. Amen.

DEPARTING TO SERVE

Benediction
Words will never suffice, dear Savior, to express to you how amazed, how touched, and how blessed we are at the fullness of the Father's grace through the gift of your life for us. We worship you and bless you, and pray that you receive our lives as a living sacrifice of gratitude for the marvelous works you have done for us. We love you, Jesus, in your name we say it, amen.

Affirmation from the Psalms
Because the Lord is righteous and good, he teaches sinners the path they should follow. [9] He leads the humble in the right way and teaches them his will. [10] With faithfulness and love he leads all who keep his covenant and obey his commands.

~ Psalm 25.8-10

Pray without Ceasing – Flash Prayer for the Day
We have heard the true message of your salvation, the Good News that brings life, and we believe it, and know you have sealed us with the stamp of ownership of your promised Holy Spirit.

For Your Weekly Journey

Let God Arise! Seasonal Focus
The Name above All Names, Philippians 2.5-11

Book Reading
Allen, *Missionary Methods: St. Paul's or Ours?*

Special Church Year Service
The Epiphany of the Lord: Wednesday, January 6, 2016

Our Corporate Disciplines
Book Discussion: Monday, January 4, 2016
Day of Solitude: Thursday, January 7, 2016

The Season after Epiphany

THE MANIFESTATION OF CHRIST

By awesome deeds you answer us with righteousness,
O God of our salvation,
the hope of all the ends of the earth and of the farthest seas;
the one who by his strength established the mountains,
being girded with might; who stills the roaring of the seas,
the roaring of their waves, the tumult of the peoples,
so that those who dwell at the ends of the earth
are in awe at your signs. You make the going out
of the morning and the evening to shout for joy.

PSALM 65.5-8

THE SEASON AFTER EPIPHANY: THE MANIFESTATION OF CHRIST
JANUARY 6 - FEBRUARY 9, 2016

The *Feast of Epiphany* on January 6 commemorates the coming of the Magi which reveals Christ's mission to the world. The entire season of Epiphany then emphasizes the way in which Christ revealed himself to the world as the Son of God (Luke 2.32; Matt. 17.1-6; John 12.32).

Again, *Epiphany* remembers the Magi's arrival, those remarkable seekers who followed the star in search of the Christ child. The season emphasizes Christ's mission to and for the entire world, including the Gentile nations. The light of God's salvation is revealed to all peoples in the person of Jesus, the Son of God.

The Season after Epiphany begins with the celebration of the *Epiphany of the Lord* on January 6 each year, and is celebrated until the Lenten season begins on *Ash Wednesday*.

Epiphany means "manifestation" and teaches us that God revealed himself in Christ Jesus.

We celebrate *Epiphany* remembering our Lord Jesus Christ as light to the Gentiles, who was revealed to the non-Jewish Magi (wise ones) who themselves symbolize that God's salvation is available to all people.

The "Season after Epiphany" is the time between *Epiphany* and *Transfiguration Day* in which we remember how Christ was revealed as God in the world.

How was Christ revealed as God? Through the Magi, through his presentation at the Temple, through John the Baptist's testimony, through the Voice at his baptism, through the miracle at Cana, through his healings, through Peter's confession, and through the Transfiguration.

Epiphany is known as the season of light because we remember the words of the prophet: "The people walking in darkness have seen a great light; on those living in the land of the shadow of death a light has dawned" (Isa. 9.2, Isa. 2.5, John 1.5).

- The *Baptism of the Lord* (the first Sunday after the *Epiphany of the Lord*): This special day commemorates the baptism of the Lord. On it we reflect on and remember Jesus' baptism by John the Baptizer at the beginning of his public ministry. Jesus' true identity as Messiah and Lord was revealed by the Holy Spirit's descent upon him in the form of a dove, and the Father's testimony concerning him, "This is my beloved Son, with whom I am well pleased" (Matt. 3.17).

- The *Presentation of the Lord*: The Presentation at the Temple is a feast celebrated forty days after Christmas. The event is described in Luke 2.22-40 where Mary and Joseph presented Jesus as their firstborn to God, as required by the Law. All firstborn males were required not only to be circumcised on the eighth day following their birth (Lev. 12.3), but also to be presented to God thirty-three days later, along with an offering for the mother's purification after childbirth (Lev. 12.1-8; Exod. 13.2, 12). Upon bringing Jesus to the Temple, they met godly Simeon, who had been promised by the LORD that he would not die till he saw the Lord's Messiah (Luke 2.26). Simeon's prayer prophesied regarding the ministry of Jesus, who would become a light to the nations, and the glory of Israel (Luke 2.29-32). Anna, an elderly widow and prophetess, also acknowledged the baby Jesus' upcoming role in the salvation of Israel (Luke 2.36-38).

- *Transfiguration Sunday*: This feast day "recalls the Transfiguration of Christ on the last Sunday of Epiphany (which is the Sunday before *Ash Wednesday*, the beginning of our Lenten journey)" [Robert Webber]. The glory of Christ manifest in this world – to us and through us.

The first period of Ordinary Time (meaning *ordinal* [*numbered*] *time*, not *plain* or *common time*) begins in many Western liturgical settings on the day after the feast of the *Baptism of the Lord* (which normally falls on the Sunday after Epiphany). This period continues to the Season of Lent, which begins on *Ash Wednesday*. While there is some variation among traditions as to when the *Baptism of the Lord* is celebrated, this first cycle of Ordinary Time begins in many Western churches on the day after the *Epiphany of the Lord*.

In a spiritual sense, the Church Year's weeks are "numbered," counted in anticipation (in the first cycle) toward our journey to the Cross, and in the second period of Ordinary Time, from the coming of the Holy Spirit to the return of Christ in glory.

The Epiphany of the Lord
January 6, 2016

Epiphany commemorates the coming of the Magi, the wise men from the East who followed the star in search of the Christ child. This season emphasizes Christ's mission to the Gentiles and his claim of salvation for the world.

TODAY'S THEME
The King of the Jews, Matthew 2.1-12

Our Lord Jesus was born in Bethlehem of Judea when Herod was king. Soon afterward, Magi came from the East to Jerusalem, and asked "Where is the baby born to be the king of the Jews? We saw his star when it came up in the east, and we have come to worship him." When Herod heard their question, he became very upset, as did all those who lived in Jerusalem.

Herod called the chief priests and the teachers of the Law together, and asked them where the Messiah would be born. They answered, "In the town of Bethlehem in Judea, for this is what the prophet wrote: 'Bethlehem in the land of Judah, you are by no means the least of the leading cities of Judah; for from you will come a leader who will guide my people Israel.'"

Herod again called the Magi, inquiring as to the exact time they had seen the star appear. He then sent them to Bethlehem, asking them to go and make a careful search for the child. He said when they found him, they should then let him know, that he might go and worship him, too. On this, the Magi left, and again saw the same star, which made them tremendously joyous. The star went before them and finally stopped over the place where the child was. The Magi went to the house, saw the child with his mother Mary, and knelt down, worshiping him. They offered to him their gifts of gold, frankincense, and myrrh, and later returned to their country by another route, having been warned in a dream by God not to return to Herod.

Christ Jesus is revealed to us as a king – a lowly child, born to peasant parents, and yet the God-chosen King of the Jews, and King of all the earth. God's revelation to the Magi is correct. The child born to Mary was none other than the King of all kings, and Lord of all lords, deserving of our worship and service.

Daily Devotional Guide

PREPARING OUR HEARTS

Invocation: Our Prayer of Acclamation
Almighty and everlasting God, who has made known the incarnation of your Son by the bright shining of a star, which, when the wise men beheld, they presented costly gifts and adored your majesty; grant that the star of your righteousness may always shine into our hearts; and that, as our treasure, we may give ourselves and all we possess to your service; through Jesus Christ our Lord. Amen.

~ *The Gelasian Sacramentary* (Oden, p. 37)

Call to Worship
Blessed are you, O God: Father, Son, and Holy Spirit. And blessed is your Kingdom, both now and forever, amen.

PRAISING OUR GOD

Te Deum Laudamus
You are God: we praise you; you are the Lord; we acclaim you; you are the eternal Father: All creation worships you. To you all angels, all the powers of heaven, Cherubim and Seraphim, sing in endless praise:

Holy, holy, holy Lord, God of power and might, heaven and earth are full of your glory.

The glorious company of apostles praise you. The noble fellowship of prophets praise you. The white-robed army of martyrs praise you. Throughout the world the holy Church acclaims you; Father, of majesty unbounded, your true and only Son, worthy of all worship, and the Holy Spirit, advocate and guide.

You, Christ, are the king of glory, the eternal Son of the Father. When you became man to set us free you did not shun the Virgin's womb. You overcame the sting of death and opened the kingdom of heaven to all believers. You are seated at God's right hand in glory. We believe that you will come and be our judge. Come then, Lord, and help your people, bought with the price of your own blood, and bring us with your saints to glory everlasting.

Praise and Thanksgiving (Songs and Prayers)

Gloria Patri
Glory be to the Father,
And to the Son and to the Holy Spirit:
As it was in the beginning,
Is now, and ever shall be,
World without end. Amen, amen.

LISTENING TO HIS VOICE

Chronological Reading for the Day
Exod. 22-24

Lectionary Readings
Psalm: Ps. 72.1-7, 10-14   OT: Isa. 60.1-6
Gospel: Matt. 2.1-12   NT: Eph. 3.1-12

Reflection: Silence and/or Journaling

RESPONDING IN FAITH

The Apostles' Creed
I believe in God, the Father Almighty, Maker of heaven and earth; and in Jesus Christ, his only Son, our Lord, who was conceived by the Holy Spirit, born of the Virgin Mary, suffered under Pontius Pilate, was crucified, dead, and buried; he descended into hell; the third day he arose again from the dead; he ascended into heaven and sits on the right hand of God the Father Almighty; from thence he shall come to judge the quick and the dead.

I believe in the Holy Spirit, the holy catholic* church, the communion of saints, the forgiveness of sins, the resurrection of the body, and the life everlasting. Amen.

* In the Apostles' and Nicene Creeds, the term catholic refers to the Church's universality, through all ages and times, of all languages and peoples. It refers to no particular tradition or denominational expression (e.g., as in Roman Catholic).

Prayers of Confession
Let us now confess our sins to God and receive mercy and grace to help in our time of need.

Assurance of Pardon
Having faithfully confessed and renounced your sin, Christ also has been faithful to forgive your sins and to purify you from all unrighteousness. It is certain, that there is One who has spoken to the Father in your defense, Jesus Christ, the Righteous One who is the atoning sacrifice for our sins and for the sins of the whole world. His grace and peace are with you now. Amen.

Petitions and Supplications, Ending with the Lord's Prayer
Our Father which art in heaven, Hallowed be thy name. Thy kingdom come, Thy will be done in earth, as it is in heaven. Give us this day our daily bread. And forgive us our debts, as we forgive our debtors. And lead us not into temptation, but deliver us from evil: For thine is the kingdom, and the power, and the glory, for ever. Amen.

~ Matthew 6.9-13 (KJV)

Doxology (and/or closing song)
Praise God from whom all blessings flow;
Praise Him all creatures here below;
Praise Him above ye heavenly host;
Praise Father, Son and Holy Ghost. Amen.

DEPARTING TO SERVE

Benediction
O God, by whose light men from the east were led into the knowledge of thy blessed Son; send out thy light and thy truth into the east and the west, and into the north and the south; that all men everywhere may behold thy glory in the face of Jesus Christ; and that so thy kingdom may be set forward among the nations and thy peace be established in all the earth; through the same Jesus Christ our Lord. Amen.

~ Earnest Fremont Tittle (Tittle, p. 57)

Affirmation from the Psalms
Clap your hands, all peoples! Shout to God with loud songs of joy! [2] For the Lord, the Most High, is to be feared, a great king over all the earth. [3] He subdued peoples under us, and nations under our feet. [4] He chose our heritage for us, the pride of Jacob whom he loves. Selah.

~ Psalm 47.1-4

Pray without Ceasing – Flash Prayer for the Day
By faith, O Lord and God, we have sought him who was born in Bethlehem, and have found him who is King of the Jews and King of the world. We offer him our lives and our love. Amen.

For Your Weekly Journey

Let God Arise! Seasonal Focus
The Signs of His Glory, John 2.1-11

Book Reading
Allen, *Missionary Methods: St. Paul's or Ours?*

WEEK
7

Baptism of the Lord

First Sunday after the Epiphany • January 10 - 16, 2016

Epiphany commemorates the coming of the Magi, the wise men from the East who followed the star in search of the Christ child. This season emphasizes Christ's mission to the Gentiles and his claim of salvation for the world.

THIS WEEK'S THEME
You Are My Beloved Son, Luke 3.15-17, 21-22

When John the Baptizer proclaimed repentance to the nation of Israel, the people were in great expectation, questioning in their hearts whether or not John himself might be the Messiah of God, the Christ who was to come. John answered them all on this matter, saying "I baptize you with water, but he who is mightier than I is coming, the strap of whose sandals I am not worthy to untie. He will baptize you with the Holy Spirit and fire. His winnowing fork is in his hand, to clear his threshing floor and to gather the wheat into his barn, but the chaff he will burn with unquenchable fire."

Now when all the people had been baptized, then Jesus himself was baptized. When Jesus had been baptized and was praying, the heavens were opened, and the Holy Spirit descended on him in bodily form, like a dove; and a voice came from heaven, "You are my beloved Son; with you I am well pleased."

Jesus of Nazareth was confirmed to be God's Son, the Christ, by John at his baptism. In this sacred moment, the triune God revealed the true identity of Jesus, the one on whom the Spirit rests, and whom the Father testifies to be his beloved Son, the one which pleases him well in all things. Jesus is the Christ, the Son of the living God.

Daily Devotional Guide

PREPARING OUR HEARTS

Invocation: Our Prayer of Acclamation

Holy God, you sent your Son to be baptized among sinners to seek and save the lost. May we, who have been baptized in his name, never turn away from the world, but reach out in love to rescue the wayward; by the mercy of Christ our Lord, who lives and reigns with you and the Holy Spirit, one God, now and forever, Amen.

~ *The Worshipbook: Services*
(The Theological and Worship Ministry Unit, p. 199)

Call to Worship

Blessed are you, O God: Father, Son, and Holy Spirit. And blessed is your Kingdom, both now and forever, amen.

PRAISING OUR GOD

Te Deum Laudamus

You are God: we praise you; you are the Lord; we acclaim you; you are the eternal Father: All creation worships you. To you all angels, all the powers of heaven, Cherubim and Seraphim, sing in endless praise: Holy, holy, holy Lord, God of power and might, heaven and earth are full of your glory.

The glorious company of apostles praise you. The noble fellowship of prophets praise you. The white-robed army of martyrs praise you. Throughout the world the holy Church acclaims you; Father, of majesty unbounded, your true and only Son, worthy of all worship, and the Holy Spirit, advocate and guide.

You, Christ, are the king of glory, the eternal Son of the Father. When you became man to set us free you did not shun the Virgin's womb. You overcame the sting of death and opened the kingdom of heaven to all believers. You are seated at God's right hand in glory. We believe

that you will come and be our judge. Come then, Lord, and help your people, bought with the price of your own blood, and bring us with your saints to glory everlasting.

Praise and Thanksgiving (Songs and Prayers)

Gloria Patri
Glory be to the Father,
And to the Son and to the Holy Spirit:
As it was in the beginning,
Is now, and ever shall be,
World without end. Amen. amen.

LISTENING TO HIS VOICE

Chronological Reading for the Day
Sunday: Exod. 35-36
Monday: Exod. 37-38
Tuesday: Exod. 39-40; Num. 9.15-23
Wednesday: Num. 7
Thursday: Num. 8.1-9.14; Lev. 1-3
Friday: Lev. 4-6
Saturday: Lev. 7-8

Lectionary Readings
Psalm: Ps. 29   *OT:* Isa. 43.1-7
Gospel: Luke 3.15-17, 21-22   *NT:* Acts 8.14-17

Reflection: Silence and/or Journaling

RESPONDING IN FAITH

The Apostles' Creed
I believe in God, the Father Almighty, Maker of heaven and earth; and in Jesus Christ, his only Son, our Lord, who was conceived by the Holy Spirit, born of the Virgin Mary, suffered under Pontius Pilate,

was crucified, dead, and buried; he descended into hell; the third day he arose again from the dead; he ascended into heaven and sits on the right hand of God the Father Almighty; from thence he shall come to judge the quick and the dead.

I believe in the Holy Spirit, the holy catholic* church, the communion of saints, the forgiveness of sins, the resurrection of the body, and the life everlasting. Amen.

* In the Apostles' and Nicene Creeds, the term catholic refers to the Church's universality, through all ages and times, of all languages and peoples. It refers to no particular tradition or denominational expression (e.g., as in Roman Catholic).

Prayers of Confession
Let us now confess our sins to God and receive mercy and grace to help in our time of need.

Assurance of Pardon
Having faithfully confessed and renounced your sin, Christ also has been faithful to forgive your sins and to purify you from all unrighteousness. It is certain, that there is One who has spoken to the Father in your defense, Jesus Christ, the Righteous One who is the atoning sacrifice for our sins and for the sins of the whole world. His grace and peace are with you now. Amen.

Petitions and Supplications, Ending with the Lord's Prayer
Our Father which art in heaven, Hallowed be thy name. Thy kingdom come, Thy will be done in earth, as it is in heaven. Give us this day our daily bread. And forgive us our debts, as we forgive our debtors. And lead us not into temptation, but deliver us from evil: For thine is the kingdom, and the power, and the glory, for ever. Amen.

~ Matthew 6.9-13 (KJV)

Doxology (and/or closing song)

Praise God from whom all blessings flow;
Praise Him all creatures here below;
Praise Him above ye heavenly host;
Praise Father, Son and Holy Ghost. Amen.

DEPARTING TO SERVE

Benediction

O God, Who through Thine Only-begotten Son Jesus Christ our Lord hast endowed the regenerating waters with the grace which halloweth unto eternal salvation; and didst Thyself come upon Him by Thy Spirit, in the descent of the mysterious Dove on His head; grant, we beseech Thee, that there may come upon Thy whole Church a blessing which may keep us all continually safe, may unceasingly bless all classes of Thy servants, may direct the course of those who follow Thee, and open the door of the heavenly kingdom to all who are waiting to enter; through Jesus Christ our Lord. Amen.

~ Gothic Missal (Bright, pp. 29-30)

Affirmation from the Psalms

Your throne, O God, is forever and ever. The scepter of your kingdom is a scepter of uprightness; [7] you have loved righteousness and hated wickedness. Therefore God, your God, has anointed you with the oil of gladness beyond your companions.

~ Psalm 45.6-7

Pray without Ceasing – Flash Prayer for the Day

Lord Jesus, you are God's beloved Son, in whom he is well pleased. We praise your great and awesome name, for you are holy!

For Your Weekly Journey

Let God Arise! Seasonal Focus
The Signs of His Glory, John 2.1-11

Book Reading
Allen, *Missionary Methods: St. Paul's or Ours?*

Our Corporate Disciplines
National Day of Prayer: Monday, January 11, 2016

Second Sunday after the Epiphany
January 17 - 23, 2016

Epiphany commemorates the coming of the Magi, the wise men from the East who followed the star in search of the Christ child. This season emphasizes Christ's mission to the Gentiles and his claim of salvation for the world.

THIS WEEK'S THEME
The Signs of His Glory, John 2.1-11

Early in his ministry, Jesus and his disciples attended a wedding at Cana in Galilee, and his mother was there. When the party ran out of wine, Jesus' mother said to him, "They have no wine." Jesus replied, "Woman, what does this have to do with me? My hour has not yet come." On hearing this, Mary said to the servants, "Do whatever he tells you."

Now, six stone water jars for the Jewish rites of purification, each holding twenty or thirty gallons were there. Jesus said to the servants, "Fill the jars with water," and they filled them up to the brim. Then he said to them, "Now draw some out and take it to the master of the feast." So they took it.

The master of the feast then tasted the water which had become wine, and yet he did not know where it came from (although the servants knew!). Then, the master called the bridegroom and said to him, "Everyone serves the good wine first, and when people have drunk freely, then the poor wine. But you have kept the good wine until now." This extraordinary miracle was the first of his signs, performed at Cana in Galilee, and through it, Jesus manifested his glory. And his disciples believed in him.

In his miracles, exorcisms, healings, teaching, and person Jesus demonstrated himself to be the very Son of God. Through his sign miracles Jesus manifested his divine majesty and glory – and his followers believed in him through them.

Daily Devotional Guide

PREPARING OUR HEARTS

Invocation: Our Prayer of Acclamation
Holy Father, your Son manifested his transforming power by changing 120 gallons of water into matchless, tasting wine! This miracle of transformation reveals our Lord's power to instantly and powerfully infuse our lives with your joy and life. We put our faith in him, and in you, the Giver of this amazing Gift of your Son. Reveal more of him to us, for your glory's sake, amen.

Call to Worship
Blessed are you, O God: Father, Son, and Holy Spirit. And blessed is your Kingdom, both now and forever, amen.

PRAISING OUR GOD

Te Deum Laudamus
You are God: we praise you; you are the Lord; we acclaim you; you are the eternal Father: All creation worships you. To you all angels, all the powers of heaven, Cherubim and Seraphim, sing in endless praise: Holy, holy, holy Lord, God of power and might, heaven and earth are full of your glory.

The glorious company of apostles praise you. The noble fellowship of prophets praise you. The white-robed army of martyrs praise you. Throughout the world the holy Church acclaims you; Father, of majesty unbounded, your true and only Son, worthy of all worship, and the Holy Spirit, advocate and guide.

You, Christ, are the king of glory, the eternal Son of the Father. When you became man to set us free you did not shun the Virgin's womb. You overcame the sting of death and opened the kingdom of heaven to all believers. You are seated at God's right hand in glory. We believe that you will come and be our judge. Come then, Lord, and help your people, bought with the price of your own blood, and bring us with your saints to glory everlasting.

Praise and Thanksgiving (Songs and Prayers)

Gloria Patri
Glory be to the Father,
And to the Son and to the Holy Spirit:
As it was in the beginning,
Is now, and ever shall be,
World without end. Amen, amen.

LISTENING TO HIS VOICE

Chronological Reading for the Day

Sunday: Lev. 9-11	*Thursday:* Lev. 20-22
Monday: Lev. 12-14	*Friday:* Lev. 23-24
Tuesday: Lev. 15-16	*Saturday:* Lev. 25-26
Wednesday: Lev. 17-19	

Lectionary Readings

Psalm: Ps. 36.5-10	*OT:* Isa. 62.1-5
Gospel: John 2.1-11	*NT:* 1 Cor. 12.1-11

Reflection: Silence and/or Journaling

RESPONDING IN FAITH

The Apostles' Creed

*I believe in God, the Father Almighty, Maker of heaven and earth;
and in Jesus Christ, his only Son, our Lord, who was conceived by the
Holy Spirit, born of the Virgin Mary, suffered under Pontius Pilate,
was crucified, dead, and buried; he descended into hell; the third day
he arose again from the dead; he ascended into heaven and sits on
the right hand of God the Father Almighty; from thence he shall come
to judge the quick and the dead.*

I believe in the Holy Spirit, the holy catholic church, the communion
of saints, the forgiveness of sins, the resurrection of the body, and the
life everlasting. Amen.*

* In the Apostles' and Nicene Creeds, the term catholic refers to the Church's
universality, through all ages and times, of all languages and peoples. It refers to no
particular tradition or denominational expression (e.g., as in Roman Catholic).

Prayers of Confession

Let us now confess our sins to God and receive mercy and
grace to help in our time of need.

Assurance of Pardon

Having faithfully confessed and renounced your sin, Christ
also has been faithful to forgive your sins and to purify you
from all unrighteousness. It is certain, that there is One who
has spoken to the Father in your defense, Jesus Christ, the
Righteous One who is the atoning sacrifice for our sins and
for the sins of the whole world. His grace and peace are with
you now. Amen.

Petitions and Supplications, Ending with the Lord's Prayer
Our Father which art in heaven, Hallowed be thy name. Thy kingdom come, Thy will be done in earth, as it is in heaven. Give us this day our daily bread. And forgive us our debts, as we forgive our debtors. And lead us not into temptation, but deliver us from evil: For thine is the kingdom, and the power, and the glory, for ever. Amen.

~ Matthew 6.9-13 (KJV)

Doxology (and/or closing song)
Praise God from whom all blessings flow;
Praise Him all creatures here below;
Praise Him above ye heavenly host;
Praise Father, Son and Holy Ghost. Amen.

DEPARTING TO SERVE

Benediction
Dear Lord Jesus, your gift of wine to the newly wed couple so many centuries ago points to your transforming power, the kind of power you manifested throughout your ministry, and in your leadership of our lives together. Without you, there can be no transformation – no turning of water to wine, no turning of the bland into the beautiful. Work in us still this transforming power, for your sake, amen.

Affirmation from the Psalms
But let all who take refuge in you rejoice; let them ever sing for joy, and spread your protection over them, that those who love your name may exult in you. [12] For you bless the righteous, O Lord; you cover him with favor as with a shield.

~ Psalm 5.11-12

Pray without Ceasing – Flash Prayer for the Day
We exalt you, O Christ of God, for in you alone can our mundane and normal be transformed into the majestic and the magnificent.

For Your Weekly Journey

Let God Arise! Seasonal Focus
The Signs of His Glory, John 2.1-11

Book Reading
Allen, *Missionary Methods: St. Paul's or Ours?*

Our Corporate Disciplines
Book Discussion: Monday, January 18, 2016

Third Sunday after the Epiphany
January 24 - 30, 2016

Epiphany affirms Jesus' presence in the world as hope for all peoples. In him alone, God provides the light of his salvation, making known God's grace to all peoples, even to the farthest corners of the earth.

THIS WEEK'S THEME
Proclaim Liberty to the Captives, Luke 4.14-21

After triumphing over Satan during his temptation in the wilderness, the Lord Jesus returned in the power of the Spirit to Galilee. A report about him went out through all the surrounding country, and Jesus taught in their synagogues, being acknowledged and glorified by all.

During his travels he came to Nazareth, his hometown where he had been brought up. As was the Lord's custom, he went to the synagogue on the Sabbath day, and this time, he stood up to read. The scroll of Isaiah the prophet was given to him, which he unrolled, having found the place where a specific passage was written. He read, "The Spirit of the Lord is upon me, because he has anointed me to proclaim good news to the poor. He has sent me to proclaim liberty to the captives and recovering of sight to the blind, to set at liberty those who are oppressed, to proclaim the year of the Lord's favor."

After reading this passage, Jesus rolled up the scroll, and gave it back to the attendant. Then, he sat down. The eyes of everyone in the synagogue were fixed on him, and Jesus began to say to them, "Today this Scripture has been fulfilled in your hearing."

In reading this Messianic prophetic text and applying it to himself, Jesus publicly and definitively announced to the synagogue audience, there in his hometown, that he was the Christ. That specific text, he declared, had been fulfilled in their hearing. While that audience found it hard to accept,

Jesus of Nazareth, whose report they had heard about, was in fact the Messiah of God and the king of Israel. He is the liberator of the poor, the captive, and the blind, and he continues to free those who believe in his name.

Daily Devotional Guide

Preparing Our Hearts

Invocation: Our Prayer of Acclamation

Eternal God and Father of our Lord Jesus Christ, we praise you for the revelation you gave the synagogue folk that Sabbath day of the true identity of Jesus of Nazareth. We know that he is the Messiah, the liberator, the proclaimer of freedom and liberty, and the one who sets the captives free. How do we know this, O righteous Father? Because he has set us free! Be glorified in us as we worship you in his name, amen.

Call to Worship

Blessed are you, O God: Father, Son, and Holy Spirit. And blessed is your Kingdom, both now and forever, amen.

Praising Our God

Te Deum Laudamus

You are God: we praise you; you are the Lord; we acclaim you; you are the eternal Father: All creation worships you. To you all angels, all the powers of heaven, Cherubim and Seraphim, sing in endless praise: Holy, holy, holy Lord, God of power and might, heaven and earth are full of your glory.

The glorious company of apostles praise you. The noble fellowship of prophets praise you. The white-robed army of martyrs praise you. Throughout the world the holy Church acclaims you; Father, of majesty unbounded, your true and only Son, worthy of all worship, and the Holy Spirit, advocate and guide.

You, Christ, are the king of glory, the eternal Son of the Father. When you became man to set us free you did not shun the Virgin's womb. You overcame the sting of death and opened the kingdom of heaven to all believers. You are seated at God's right hand in glory. We believe that you will come and be our judge. Come then, Lord, and help your people, bought with the price of your own blood, and bring us with your saints to glory everlasting.

Praise and Thanksgiving (Songs and Prayers)

Gloria Patri
Glory be to the Father,
And to the Son and to the Holy Spirit:
As it was in the beginning,
Is now, and ever shall be,
World without end. Amen, amen.

LISTENING TO HIS VOICE

Chronological Reading for the Day
Sunday: Lev. 27; Num. 1
Monday: Num. 2-3
Tuesday: Num. 4-5
Wednesday: Num. 6; 10

Thursday: Num. 11-13
Friday: Num. 14-15
Saturday: Num. 16-18

Lectionary Readings
Psalm: Ps. 19
Gospel: Luke 4.14-21

OT: Neh. 8.1-10
NT: 1 Cor. 12.12-31a

Reflection: Silence and/or Journaling

RESPONDING IN FAITH

The Apostles' Creed
I believe in God, the Father Almighty, Maker of heaven and earth;
and in Jesus Christ, his only Son, our Lord, who was conceived by the

Holy Spirit, born of the Virgin Mary, suffered under Pontius Pilate, was crucified, dead, and buried; he descended into hell; the third day he arose again from the dead; he ascended into heaven and sits on the right hand of God the Father Almighty; from thence he shall come to judge the quick and the dead.

I believe in the Holy Spirit, the holy catholic* church, the communion of saints, the forgiveness of sins, the resurrection of the body, and the life everlasting. Amen.

* In the Apostles' and Nicene Creeds, the term catholic refers to the Church's universality, through all ages and times, of all languages and peoples. It refers to no particular tradition or denominational expression (e.g., as in Roman Catholic).

Prayers of Confession

Let us now confess our sins to God and receive mercy and grace to help in our time of need.

Assurance of Pardon

Having faithfully confessed and renounced your sin, Christ also has been faithful to forgive your sins and to purify you from all unrighteousness. It is certain, that there is One who has spoken to the Father in your defense, Jesus Christ, the Righteous One who is the atoning sacrifice for our sins and for the sins of the whole world. His grace and peace are with you now. Amen.

Petitions and Supplications, Ending with the Lord's Prayer

Our Father which art in heaven, Hallowed be thy name. Thy kingdom come, Thy will be done in earth, as it is in heaven. Give us this day our daily bread. And forgive us our debts, as we forgive our debtors. And lead us not into temptation, but deliver us from evil: For thine is the kingdom, and the power, and the glory, for ever. Amen.

~ Matthew 6.9-13 (KJV)

Doxology (and/or closing song)

Praise God from whom all blessings flow;
Praise Him all creatures here below;
Praise Him above ye heavenly host;
Praise Father, Son and Holy Ghost. Amen.

DEPARTING TO SERVE

Benediction

Lord Jesus, what a surprise it must have been to your friends and neighbors to hear your gracious words that you, in fact, were the fulfillment of that messianic prayer in Isaiah. Though we are Gentiles, we have come to know that you are the liberator, the prophet of righteousness, our Lord and King. Give us grace to represent you in all we are, for you, indeed, are the Messiah of God. In your name we pray, amen.

Affirmation from the Psalms

Out of my distress I called on the Lord; the Lord answered me and set me free. [6] The Lord is on my side; I will not fear. What can man do to me? [7] The Lord is on my side as my helper; I shall look in triumph on those who hate me. [8] It is better to take refuge in the Lord than to trust in man.

~ Psalm 118.5-8

Pray without Ceasing – Flash Prayer for the Day

You, Lord Jesus, fulfill Isaiah's prophecy, for the Spirit of the Lord was upon you, for he anointed you to proclaim good news to the poor, liberty to the captives, and recovering of sight to the blind. You set the oppressed free and declared the year of the Lord's favor, even to us.

For Your Weekly Journey

Let God Arise! Seasonal Focus
The Signs of His Glory, John 2.1-11

Book Reading
Allen, *Missionary Methods: St. Paul's or Ours?*

Fourth Sunday after the Epiphany
January 31 - February 6, 2016

Epiphany affirms Jesus' presence in the world as hope for all peoples. In him alone, God provides the light of his salvation, making known God's grace to all peoples, even to the farthest corners of the earth.

THIS WEEK'S THEME
Jesus Rejected at Nazareth, Luke 4.21-30

During his inaugural homily, and on declaring the messianic text of Isaiah fulfilled in the hearing of his fellow Nazareth worshipers, Jesus made himself known as the Messiah. Immediately, all spoke well of him and marveled at the gracious words that were coming from his mouth. They did, however, acknowledge his familiarity: "Is not this Joseph's son?"

Jesus replied to them, "Doubtless you will quote to me this proverb, 'Physician, heal yourself.' What we have heard you did at Capernaum, do here in your hometown as well." Recognizing their growing skepticism, Jesus said further, "Truly, I say to you, no prophet is acceptable in his hometown. But in truth, I tell you, there were many widows in Israel in the days of Elijah, when the heavens were shut up three years and six months, and a great famine came over all the land, and Elijah was sent to none of them but only to Zarephath, in the land of Sidon, to a woman who was a widow. And there were many lepers in Israel in the time of the prophet Elisha, and none of them was cleansed, but only Naaman the Syrian."

On hearing Jesus' reply to their questions, everyone in the synagogue was filled with wrath. The crowd rose up and drove Jesus out of the town, bringing him to the brow of the hill on which their town was built, with the intent to throw him down the cliff. Jesus, however, passed through their midst, and went away. The people of Nazareth could not bear

Jesus' revelation of himself as the Messiah. Jesus declared plainly that no prophet is acceptable in his own hometown; the thought that they already knew him, their overfamiliarity with him, eclipsed their ability to see him as he truly was.

Daily Devotional Guide

PREPARING OUR HEARTS

Invocation: Our Prayer of Acclamation
Lord, protect us from overfamiliarity with you and your Word, and save us from the tendency to think we understand all we need to know of you and your will. Keep us open to you, in order that you might reveal yourself to us more and more, beyond our so-called knowledge of you. Do this in your Son's name, amen.

Call to Worship
Blessed are you, O God: Father, Son, and Holy Spirit. And blessed is your Kingdom, both now and forever, amen.

PRAISING OUR GOD

Te Deum Laudamus
You are God: we praise you; you are the Lord; we acclaim you; you are the eternal Father: All creation worships you. To you all angels, all the powers of heaven, Cherubim and Seraphim, sing in endless praise: Holy, holy, holy Lord, God of power and might, heaven and earth are full of your glory.

The glorious company of apostles praise you. The noble fellowship of prophets praise you. The white-robed army of martyrs praise you. Throughout the world the holy Church acclaims you; Father, of majesty unbounded, your true and only Son, worthy of all worship, and the Holy Spirit, advocate and guide.

You, Christ, are the king of glory, the eternal Son of the Father. When you became man to set us free you did not shun the Virgin's womb. You overcame the sting of death and opened the kingdom of heaven to all believers. You are seated at God's right hand in glory. We believe that you will come and be our judge. Come then, Lord, and help your people, bought with the price of your own blood, and bring us with your saints to glory everlasting.

Praise and Thanksgiving (Songs and Prayers)

Gloria Patri
Glory be to the Father,
And to the Son and to the Holy Spirit:
As it was in the beginning,
Is now, and ever shall be,
World without end. Amen, amen.

LISTENING TO HIS VOICE

Chronological Reading for the Day
Sunday: Num. 19-21   *Thursday:* Num. 30-31
Monday: Num. 22-24   *Friday:* Num. 32-33
Tuesday: Num. 25-26   *Saturday:* Num. 34-36
Wednesday: Num. 27-29

Lectionary Readings
Psalm: Ps. 71.1-6   *OT:* Jer. 1.4-10
Gospel: Luke 4.21-30   *NT:* 1 Cor. 13.1-13

Reflection: Silence and/or Journaling

RESPONDING IN FAITH

The Apostles' Creed
I believe in God, the Father Almighty, Maker of heaven and earth; and in Jesus Christ, his only Son, our Lord, who was conceived by the

Holy Spirit, born of the Virgin Mary, suffered under Pontius Pilate, was crucified, dead, and buried; he descended into hell; the third day he arose again from the dead; he ascended into heaven and sits on the right hand of God the Father Almighty; from thence he shall come to judge the quick and the dead.

I believe in the Holy Spirit, the holy catholic* church, the communion of saints, the forgiveness of sins, the resurrection of the body, and the life everlasting. Amen.

* In the Apostles' and Nicene Creeds, the term catholic refers to the Church's universality, through all ages and times, of all languages and peoples. It refers to no particular tradition or denominational expression (e.g., as in Roman Catholic).

Prayers of Confession
Let us now confess our sins to God and receive mercy and grace to help in our time of need.

Assurance of Pardon
Having faithfully confessed and renounced your sin, Christ also has been faithful to forgive your sins and to purify you from all unrighteousness. It is certain, that there is One who has spoken to the Father in your defense, Jesus Christ, the Righteous One who is the atoning sacrifice for our sins and for the sins of the whole world. His grace and peace are with you now. Amen.

Petitions and Supplications, Ending with the Lord's Prayer
Our Father which art in heaven, Hallowed be thy name. Thy kingdom come, Thy will be done in earth, as it is in heaven. Give us this day our daily bread. And forgive us our debts, as we forgive our debtors. And lead us not into temptation, but deliver us from evil: For thine is the kingdom, and the power, and the glory, for ever. Amen.

~ Matthew 6.9-13 (KJV)

Doxology (and/or closing song)
Praise God from whom all blessings flow;
Praise Him all creatures here below;
Praise Him above ye heavenly host;
Praise Father, Son and Holy Ghost. Amen.

DEPARTING TO SERVE

Benediction
Lord Jesus, forgive us for the many times we assume that we understand you, and treat you with the disdain of over-familiarity like your hometown neighbors in Nazareth. Free our minds and our spirits to see and hear you afresh, and to be ever ready to receive a new, fresh Word from you for our lives and for others. In your name we pray, amen.

Affirmation from the Psalms
One thing have I asked of the Lord, that will I seek after: that I may dwell in the house of the Lord all the days of my life, to gaze upon the beauty of the Lord and to inquire in his temple. [5] For he will hide me in his shelter in the day of trouble; he will conceal me under the cover of his tent; he will lift me high upon a rock.

~ Psalm 27.4-5

Pray without Ceasing – Flash Prayer for the Day
Open my eyes, O Lord, to see wonderful and new things from your Word for my life.

For Your Weekly Journey

Let God Arise! Seasonal Focus
The Signs of His Glory, John 2.1-11

Book Reading
Allen, *Missionary Methods: St. Paul's or Ours?*

Special Church Year Services
Presentation of the Lord: Tuesday, February 2, 2016

Our Corporate Disciplines
Book Discussion: Monday, February 1, 2016
Day of Prayer and Fasting: Thursday, February 4, 2016

Presentation of the Lord

February 2, 2016

Epiphany affirms Jesus' presence in the world as hope for all peoples. In him alone, God provides the light of his salvation, making known God's grace to all peoples, even to the farthest corners of the earth.

THIS WEEK'S THEME

Our Merciful and Faithful High Priest, Hebrews 2.14-18

The preacher of the sermon of Hebrews declares that since therefore the children shared in flesh and blood, Jesus our Lord himself likewise partook of the very same nature, the very same things, that through death he might actually destroy the one who has the power of death today, that is, the devil. By his sharing of the same nature as we human beings, through the incarnation, Jesus is also able to deliver all those who through fear of death have been subject to lifelong slavery. The preacher argues that for surely it is not angels that Jesus helps, but the offspring of Abraham.

Therefore Jesus had to be made like us, his own people, in every respect, in order that he might become a merciful and faithful high priest in the service of God, to make propitiation (full atonement) on behalf of the sins of the people. Because Jesus suffered when he himself was tempted, he now is able to help those (like us!) who are also being tempted. He understands us and knows us, for he is like us, except he is without sin.

Daily Devotional Guide

PREPARING OUR HEARTS

Invocation: Our Prayer of Acclamation

All-powerful Father, Christ your Son became man for us and was presented in the temple. May he free our hearts from sin and bring us into your presence, where he lives and reigns with you and the Holy Spirit, one God, now and forever. Amen.

~ International Committee on English in the Liturgy (Storey, p. 68)

Call to Worship

Blessed are you, O God: Father, Son, and Holy Spirit. And blessed is your Kingdom, both now and forever, amen.

PRAISING OUR GOD

Te Deum Laudamus

You are God: we praise you; you are the Lord; we acclaim you; you are the eternal Father: All creation worships you. To you all angels, all the powers of heaven, Cherubim and Seraphim, sing in endless praise: Holy, holy, holy Lord, God of power and might, heaven and earth are full of your glory.

The glorious company of apostles praise you. The noble fellowship of prophets praise you. The white-robed army of martyrs praise you. Throughout the world the holy Church acclaims you; Father, of majesty unbounded, your true and only Son, worthy of all worship, and the Holy Spirit, advocate and guide.

You, Christ, are the king of glory, the eternal Son of the Father. When you became man to set us free you did not shun the Virgin's womb. You overcame the sting of death and opened the kingdom of heaven to all believers. You are seated at God's right hand in glory. We believe

*that you will come and be our judge. Come then, Lord, and help your
people, bought with the price of your own blood, and bring us with
your saints to glory everlasting.*

Praise and Thanksgiving (Songs and Prayers)

Gloria Patri
*Glory be to the Father,
And to the Son and to the Holy Spirit:
As it was in the beginning,
Is now, and ever shall be,
World without end. Amen, amen.*

LISTENING TO HIS VOICE

Chronological Reading for the Day
Num. 25-26

Lectionary Readings
Psalm: Ps. 84   *OT:* Mal. 3.1-4
Gospel: Luke 2.22-40   *NT:* Heb. 2.14-18

Reflection: Silence and/or Journaling

RESPONDING IN FAITH

The Apostles' Creed
*I believe in God, the Father Almighty, Maker of heaven and earth;
and in Jesus Christ, his only Son, our Lord, who was conceived by the
Holy Spirit, born of the Virgin Mary, suffered under Pontius Pilate,
was crucified, dead, and buried; he descended into hell; the third day
he arose again from the dead; he ascended into heaven and sits on
the right hand of God the Father Almighty; from thence he shall come
to judge the quick and the dead.*

I believe in the Holy Spirit, the holy catholic* church, the communion of saints, the forgiveness of sins, the resurrection of the body, and the life everlasting. Amen.

* In the Apostles' and Nicene Creeds, the term catholic refers to the Church's universality, through all ages and times, of all languages and peoples. It refers to no particular tradition or denominational expression (e.g., as in Roman Catholic).

Prayers of Confession

Let us now confess our sins to God and receive mercy and grace to help in our time of need.

Assurance of Pardon

Having faithfully confessed and renounced your sin, Christ also has been faithful to forgive your sins and to purify you from all unrighteousness. It is certain, that there is One who has spoken to the Father in your defense, Jesus Christ, the Righteous One who is the atoning sacrifice for our sins and for the sins of the whole world. His grace and peace are with you now. Amen.

Petitions and Supplications, Ending with the Lord's Prayer
Our Father which art in heaven, Hallowed be thy name. Thy kingdom come, Thy will be done in earth, as it is in heaven. Give us this day our daily bread. And forgive us our debts, as we forgive our debtors. And lead us not into temptation, but deliver us from evil: For thine is the kingdom, and the power, and the glory, for ever. Amen.

~ Matthew 6.9-13 (KJV)

Doxology (and/or closing song)
Praise God from whom all blessings flow;
Praise Him all creatures here below;
Praise Him above ye heavenly host;
Praise Father, Son and Holy Ghost. Amen.

DEPARTING TO SERVE

Benediction

Almighty and ever-living God, your only-begotten Son was presented this day in the temple. May we be presented to you with clean and pure hearts by the same Jesus Christ our great high priest, who lives and reigns with you and the Holy Spirit, one God, now and forever. Amen.

~ *Evangelical Lutheran Worship*
(Conference of Bishops, Evangelical Lutheran Church in America, p. 40)

Affirmation from the Psalms

O Lord, how many are my foes! Many are rising against me; [2] many are saying of my soul, there is no salvation for him in God. Selah. [3] But you, O Lord, are a shield about me, my glory, and the lifter of my head. [4] I cried aloud to the Lord, and he answered me from his holy hill. Selah [5] I lay down and slept; I woke again, for the Lord sustained me. [6] I will not be afraid of many thousands of people who have set themselves against me all around.

~ Psalm 3.1-6

Pray without Ceasing – Flash Prayer for the Day

Thank you, Lord Jesus Christ, for being my merciful and faithful high priest, who can help me in my temptations for you were tempted and overcame them in the Father's strength.

For Your Weekly Journey

Let God Arise! Seasonal Focus

The Signs of His Glory, John 2.1-11

Book Reading

Allen, *Missionary Methods: St. Paul's or Ours?*

Transfiguration Sunday

Last Sunday before Lent • February 7 - 13, 2016

Epiphany affirms Jesus' presence in the world as hope for all peoples. In him alone, God provides the light of his salvation, making known God's grace to all peoples, even to the farthest corners of the earth.

THIS WEEK'S THEME
The Chosen One of God, Luke 9.28-43a

Now about eight days after Jesus' teachings on discipleship, he took Peter, John and James with him on the mountain to pray. And, as the Lord was praying, his facial appearance was altered and his clothing became dazzling white as a flash of lightning. Suddenly, two men, Moses and Elijah in glory, were speaking with Jesus of his departure (exodon) soon about to occur in Jerusalem.

Peter and the others were heavy with sleep, but after becoming fully awake, they saw Jesus' glory along with the two men beside him. As the men were parting from the Lord, Peter exclaimed to Jesus, "Master, it is good that we are here. Let us make three tents, one for you and one for Moses and one for Elijah" – not fully comprehending what he was saying. As Peter said these words, a cloud came and overshadowed them, and they were afraid as they entered the cloud. A voice came out of the cloud, saying, "This is my Son, my Chosen One; listen to him!" And when the voice had spoken, Jesus was found alone. And those who witnessed this event kept silent and told no one in those days anything of what they had seen.

On the mount Jesus was transfigured before the Three (Peter, James, and John), being visited by the appearing of Moses and Elijah in glory, speaking with him of his "departure" (exodus) from this world through his death at Jerusalem. Much in the same way that the LORD God delivered Israel in its Exodus from Egypt, so our Lord would in like effect an exodus from Jerusalem. From this time on, our Lord declared that he would go to Jerusalem and save his people through his death and resurrection. The voice in the cloud urged the Three to "listen to him," no doubt a reference to Deuteronomy 18.15 with a prediction of one to whom the people must listen, the Prophet to come. Although they witnessed this manifestation, they did not mention it till later in their ministries (cf. 2 Pet. 2.16-19).

Daily Devotional Guide

PREPARING OUR HEARTS

Invocation: Our Prayer of Acclamation

O God, in the transfiguration of your Son you confirmed the mysteries of the faith by the witness of Moses and Elijah, and in the voice from the bright cloud declaring Jesus your beloved Son, you foreshadowed our adoption as your children. Make us heirs with Christ of your glory, and bring us to enjoy its fullness, through Jesus Christ, our Savior and Lord, who lives and reigns with you and the Holy Spirit, one God, now and forever. Amen.

~ Evangelical Lutheran Worship
(Conference of Bishops, Evangelical Lutheran Church in America, p. 41)

Call to Worship

Blessed are you, O God: Father, Son, and Holy Spirit. And blessed is your Kingdom, both now and forever, amen.

PRAISING OUR GOD

Te Deum Laudamus

You are God: we praise you; you are the Lord; we acclaim you; you are the eternal Father: All creation worships you. To you all angels, all the powers of heaven, Cherubim and Seraphim, sing in endless praise:

Holy, holy, holy Lord, God of power and might, heaven and earth are full of your glory.

The glorious company of apostles praise you. The noble fellowship of prophets praise you. The white-robed army of martyrs praise you. Throughout the world the holy Church acclaims you; Father, of majesty unbounded, your true and only Son, worthy of all worship, and the Holy Spirit, advocate and guide.

You, Christ, are the king of glory, the eternal Son of the Father. When you became man to set us free you did not shun the Virgin's womb. You overcame the sting of death and opened the kingdom of heaven to all believers. You are seated at God's right hand in glory. We believe that you will come and be our judge. Come then, Lord, and help your people, bought with the price of your own blood, and bring us with your saints to glory everlasting.

Praise and Thanksgiving (Songs and Prayers)

Gloria Patri
Glory be to the Father,
And to the Son and to the Holy Spirit:
As it was in the beginning,
Is now, and ever shall be,
World without end. Amen, amen.

LISTENING TO HIS VOICE

Chronological Reading for the Day

Sunday: Deut. 1-3	*Thursday:* Deut. 13-16
Monday: Deut. 4-5	*Friday:* Deut. 17-20
Tuesday: Deut. 6-9	*Saturday:* Deut. 21-25
Wednesday: Deut. 10-12	

Lectionary Readings

Psalm: Ps. 99	*OT:* Exod. 34.29-35
Gospel: Luke 9.28-43a	*NT:* 2 Cor. 3.12-4.2

Reflection: Silence and/or Journaling

RESPONDING IN FAITH

The Apostles' Creed
I believe in God, the Father Almighty, Maker of heaven and earth; and in Jesus Christ, his only Son, our Lord, who was conceived by the Holy Spirit, born of the Virgin Mary, suffered under Pontius Pilate, was crucified, dead, and buried; he descended into hell; the third day he arose again from the dead; he ascended into heaven and sits on the right hand of God the Father Almighty; from thence he shall come to judge the quick and the dead.

I believe in the Holy Spirit, the holy catholic* church, the communion of saints, the forgiveness of sins, the resurrection of the body, and the life everlasting. Amen.

* In the Apostles' and Nicene Creeds, the term catholic refers to the Church's universality, through all ages and times, of all languages and peoples. It refers to no particular tradition or denominational expression (e.g., as in Roman Catholic).

Prayers of Confession
Let us now confess our sins to God and receive mercy and grace to help in our time of need.

Assurance of Pardon
Having faithfully confessed and renounced your sin, Christ also has been faithful to forgive your sins and to purify you from all unrighteousness. It is certain, that there is One who has spoken to the Father in your defense, Jesus Christ, the Righteous One who is the atoning sacrifice for our sins and for the sins of the whole world. His grace and peace are with you now. Amen.

Petitions and Supplications, Ending with the Lord's Prayer
Our Father which art in heaven, Hallowed be thy name. Thy kingdom come, Thy will be done in earth, as it is in heaven. Give us this day our daily bread. And forgive us our debts, as we forgive our debtors. And lead us not into temptation, but deliver us from evil: For thine is the kingdom, and the power, and the glory, for ever. Amen.

~ Matthew 6.9-13 (KJV)

Doxology (and/or closing song)
Praise God from whom all blessings flow;
Praise Him all creatures here below;
Praise Him above ye heavenly host;
Praise Father, Son and Holy Ghost. Amen.

DEPARTING TO SERVE

Benediction
O God, glorious and faithful, to those who seek you with a sincere heart you reveal the beauty of your face. Strengthen us in faith to embrace the mystery of the cross, and open our hearts to its trans-figuring power; that, clinging in love to your will for us, we may walk the path of discipleship as followers of your Son, Jesus Christ our Lord, who lives and reigns with you and the Holy Spirit, one God, forever and ever. Amen.

~ *Messale Romano, The Italian Sacramentary*
(The Theological and Worship Ministry Unit, p. 215)

Affirmation from the Psalms
Lift up your heads, O gates! And be lifted up, O ancient doors, that the King of glory may come in. [8] Who is this King of glory? The Lord, strong and mighty, the Lord, mighty in battle! [9] Lift up your heads, O gates! And lift them up, O ancient doors, that the King of glory may come in. [10] Who is this King of glory? The Lord of hosts, he is the King of glory! Selah.

~ Psalm 24.7-10

Pray without Ceasing – Flash Prayer for the Day
Lord Jesus Christ, you are the Father's beloved Son, and we will listen and obey your voice.

For Your Weekly Journey

Let God Arise! Seasonal Focus
The Signs of His Glory, John 2.1-11

Book Reading
Allen, *Missionary Methods: St. Paul's or Ours?*

Special Church Year Service
Ash Wednesday: Wednesday, February 10, 2016

The Season of Lent

THE LOWLINESS OF CHRIST

A voice cries:
"In the wilderness prepare the way of the LORD;
make straight in the desert a highway for our God.
Every valley shall be lifted up,
and every mountain and hill be made low;
the uneven ground shall become level,
and the rough places a plain.
And the glory of the LORD shall be revealed,
and all flesh shall see it together,
for the mouth of the LORD has spoken."

ISAIAH 40.3-5

The Lenten season is that forty-day period of the Church Year which starts on *Ash Wednesday* and ends on Saturday of Holy Week. It calls the faithful community to reflect on Jesus' suffering, crucifixion, and death. Following our Lord in his preparation for his Passion, we prepare ourselves on the way of the Cross for full obedience to God. The season of Lent is, therefore, as one commentator put it, a season of "preparation, accompaniment, and journey." As followers of Jesus of Nazareth, the Church finds its life in his sacrifice on the Cross, his victory over evil, chaos, sin, and death, and his restoration of all things through his resurrection, his ascension, and soon return.

Beginning with the recognition of *Ash Wednesday*, we accompany our Lord on his journey to the Cross, humbling ourselves before him who gave his all for us in order that we might be set free from sin, Satan, and the grave. *Ash Wednesday* historically has been observed as a day of fasting and repentance that reminds us that as disciples our journey with Jesus ends with him at the Cross (Luke 9.51). *Ash Wednesday* begins the observance of Lent.

Welcoming New Converts, Restoring Backsliders, Strengthening Disciples: Lent in the Ancient Church

Modeling our spiritual passion after the candidates for baptism of the ancient church, so we too strive during our observance of the Lenten season to be faithful with Jesus on our way to the Cross and the Tomb. This is the heart of our participation and witness of the covenant of faith confirmed in our baptism. Even as Jesus died upon the Cross, so we too, by faith, have died with him to sin, and even as he lives forevermore, so too we live in newness of life (Rom. 6.4-6). In all phases of our personal and private worship, in our small groups, our congregational times, and all our disciplined seeking of the Lord, we acknowledge our Lord's lowliness, humiliation, and sacrifice on our behalf, and ask for his grace to become more like him in his death. Only through this humbling, this brokenness, and openness to his Spirit, can we as followers of Jesus come to fully know the freedom and life that he alone can provide.

In the ancient Church, this season was a dedicated time of preparation for those seeking baptism and incorporation into the Church. This was a season of profound soul-searching and preparation. In a striking display of allegiance to Christ and departure from worldliness, candidates for baptism experienced a formal service of exorcism, one final act of supreme separation from the world in preparation for their incorporation into the Church.

After undergoing an extended vigil on holy Saturday, all new converts were welcomed into the Church on Easter morning through their confession at baptism! The Lenten season, too, was a time to reclaim the penitent – it was a time when back-sliders who had returned to the Church were encouraged to join in these observances and ready themselves for a fresh start as re-committed disciples. Over time, the whole Church joined these converts and penitents in this season of readiness, with all believers affirming together their desire to flesh out in tangible and compelling ways their discipleship. Discipleship is not merely for those seeking baptism or to be restored after sin; rather, it is also for all who love the Lord Jesus and who strive to honor him in truth and deed. During this season, we all accompany these seekers and together follow the journey of our Lord as he traveled to the Tree where our redemption was won.

Through God's gracious act of his revelation, Peter acknowledged Jesus of Nazareth as the Messiah and Son of the Living God. Immediately after this, the disciples were warned to tell no one of this truth. It was then that our Lord began to teach the disciples of his impending death, and the resurrection to come. It was then that he challenged them to take up their crosses and follow him. It was then that he revealed God's full plan for his entering into sufferings in order that he might be glorified later:

> *Luke 9.22-26 – saying, "The Son of Man must suffer many things and be rejected by the elders and chief priests and scribes, and be killed, and on the third day be raised." [23] And he said to all, "If anyone would come after me, let him deny himself and take up his cross daily and follow me. [24] For whoever would save his life will lose it, but whoever loses his life for my sake will save it. [25] For what does it profit a man if he gains the whole world and loses or forfeits himself? [26] For whoever is ashamed of me and of my words, of him will the Son of Man be ashamed when he comes in his glory and the glory of the Father and of the holy angels."*

Lent is our resounding "Yes!" to follow our Lord to the Cross. During this season we take up our crosses and follow him. This journey is recognized in different ways by different traditions and churches. Using ashes made of the previous year's palm leaves from *Palm Sunday* celebrations, many congregations start the journey on *Ash Wednesday*, signifying their commitment to brokenness with the mark of ashes on their foreheads on that day. Others begin with special times of discipline, reading, and practice of spiritual and ministry disciplines to show their solidarity with all other believing congregations who spiritually accompany our Lord to the Cross once more during the Lenten season. However you choose to begin your journey and recognize our Lord's humility and availability, stay focused on the challenge and blessing of identifying with our Lord in his death. Let your tradition, context, and situation guide you as you explore ways to tangibly demonstrate your identification with our Lord and his people as they journey to Calvary.

Incorporating Believers into the Church through Baptism: Following the Way of Jesus

Restoring the ancient Church's focus on preparation for incorporation into the Church through baptism can be a wonderful way to renew one's faith and discipleship. The *Revised Common Lectionary* readings emphasize this focus.

Placing the observance of Lent in its ancient and historical context enables us to see how significant this season of the Church Year was for penitents and new converts then, and for our spiritual formation now. This entire season was known as a time of preparation and readiness, climaxing for candidates for baptism in an Easter baptism and celebration of the Lord's Supper. Backsliders who had repented and were coming back to the Church used this season to reorient their lives under the lordship of Christ, and sought to forsake the world and its pollution, and be re-incorporated into the family of God. Through the teaching on the Creed, the cleansings and the rites, and the tutoring and training, the new converts and penitents prepared with the entire congregation for a new level of spiritual life and growth.

Truly, Lent was not merely a time of giving up a few delicacies or habits; rather, Lent became associated with a re-ordering of one's priorities and direction, all under the long-casting shadow of the Cross of Calvary. Jesus' story of submission and humility, then, is offered to us as our own personal journey of transformation as we prepare to die to ourselves in order to live anew with the risen Christ.

Walking the Way of the Cross: Remembering the Passion of Jesus of Nazareth

The Lenten season, then, is a time for reflection on the suffering and death of Jesus. During this time we emphasize our own dying with him, and so, like Jesus, we must prepare ourselves to obey God no matter what sacrifice it involves.

Lenten observance calls for people to fast as a way of affirming this attitude of obedience (Luke 5.35; 1 Cor. 9.27; 2 Tim. 2.4; Heb. 11.1-3). Let us then humble ourselves, inviting one another to new levels of identifying with our Lord in his death through times of fasting, sacrifice, and prayer.

Some traditions challenge their members to engage in tangible acts of "self-denial," in order to visibly make oneself more open to God's leading. Others invite members, couples, and families to deny themselves of things which hinder or distract during this season, and to serve in ways that reflect obedience to God and love to neighbor. As those made free through the shed blood of Christ (Gal. 5.1), we ought to emphasize that, whatever our observances during the season of Lent, we are free in Christ to respond as he leads us. We ought neither to mandate nor insist that we fast during this season; such practice cannot be seen as an emblem of spiritual superiority or uniqueness.

On the contrary, Lenten observance has been viewed as a journey where the Christian community joins its candidates for baptism and reconciled believers in following Christ into a life of repentance and faith. Let us encourage and bless one another in all areas of our responses, and insist only that each follows that which the Holy Spirit has prompted them to do in solidarity with God's people.

However you may specifically reflect and respond to our Lord's suffering and death, let your meditation and practice individually and corporately affirm your participation in the humility of Christ, and your longing together to be one with him in his death and risen life.

Rev. Dr. Don L. Davis

Ash Wednesday

February 10, 2016

The Lenten Season, a forty-day period starting on Ash Wednesday and ending on Holy Saturday of Holy Week, calls us to reflect on Jesus' suffering, crucifixion, and death. As disciples of the humble Nazarene, we embrace his lowliness and humility, seeking to share the mind of him who was obedient to death, even death on a cross.

THIS WEEK'S THEME
Have Mercy on Me, O God, Psalm 51.1-17

On this Ash Wednesday, we begin our journey of lowliness with the Lord Jesus Christ, who set his face to go to Jerusalem, and there offer himself as a sacrifice for the sins of all humankind. As pilgrims together with our Lord, we pledge to walk the next forty days in openness, confession, and in generosity for his name's sake.

Let our hearts cry out as David did, in contrition and humility after being confronted by the prophet Nathan for his sin with Bathsheba in Psalm 51. Let our hearts cry out for mercy to God, according to his steadfast love and abundant mercy. Let us petitition the Lord to blot out our transgressions, to wash us thoroughly from our iniquities, and to cleanse us from our sins. He knows our transgression, and our sins are before us. Against him alone have we sinned and done evil. The Lord is righteous in all his indictments against us.

Let us flatly confess the truth: we were brought forth in error and conceived in sin. The Lord delights in truth in the inward being, the place from where he teaches us wisdom in the secret heart. He can purge us, wash us, and we will be clean, whiter than snow. Let us begin our journey this lenten season with petitions for joy and gladness, that he might hide his face from our sins and blot out our inquities. He alone can create in us a clean heart, and fill us with his Spirit. He alone can deliver, and, if he does, our souls will be set free and our joy will be restored. Finally healed, we can testify to others of the Lord's goodness.

Let us now, then, set forth on this journey with the Lord, carrying our cross, and following him as he leads us. Let us offer to the Lord a broken spirit and a contrite heart. If we offer them, he will not despise them – he will accept them – and transform us.

Daily Devotional Guide

PREPARING OUR HEARTS

Invocation: Our Prayer of Acclamation

O merciful God, who hast promised forgiveness to all those who confess and forsake their sins; make us to be heartily sorry for our misdoings, that thou mayest forgive all our iniquities, and heal all our diseases, and redeem our life from destruction. Put far from us the self-righteousness which has blinded our eyes, so that we do not see ourselves as sinful men in need of thy mercy. Take away the foolish pride and self-concern which make us to hurt one another and to add to the fear and confusion of the world. Mercifully deliver us from inordinate love of self and from every false ambition, and grant us the constant aid of thy Holy Spirit, that we may follow daily the path of righteousness and enter at the last into thy peace; through Jesus Christ our Lord. Amen.

~ Earnest Fremont Tittle (Tittle, pp. 57-58)

Call to Worship

Blessed are you, O God: Father, Son, and Holy Spirit. And blessed is your Kingdom, both now and forever, amen.

PRAISING OUR GOD

Te Deum Laudamus

You are God: we praise you; you are the Lord; we acclaim you; you are the eternal Father: All creation worships you. To you all angels, all the powers of heaven, Cherubim and Seraphim, sing in endless praise: Holy, holy, holy Lord, God of power and might, heaven and earth are full of your glory.

The glorious company of apostles praise you. The noble fellowship of prophets praise you. The white-robed army of martyrs praise you. Throughout the world the holy Church acclaims you: Father, of majesty unbounded, your true and only Son, worthy of all worship, and the Holy Spirit, advocate and guide.

You, Christ, are the king of glory, the eternal Son of the Father. When you became man to set us free you did not shun the Virgin's womb. You overcame the sting of death and opened the kingdom of heaven to all believers. You are seated at God's right hand in glory. We believe that you will come and be our judge. Come then, Lord, and help your people, bought with the price of your own blood, and bring us with your saints to glory everlasting.

Praise and Thanksgiving (Songs and Prayers)

Gloria Patri

Glory be to the Father,
And to the Son and to the Holy Spirit:
As it was in the beginning,
Is now, and ever shall be,
World without end. Amen, amen.

LISTENING TO HIS VOICE

Chronological Reading for the Day

Deut. 10-12

Lectionary Readings
Psalm: Ps. 51.1-17   *OT:* Isa. 58.1-12
Gospel: Matt. 6.1-6, 16-21   *NT:* 2 Cor. 5.20b-6.10

Reflection: Silence and/or Journaling

RESPONDING IN FAITH
___

The Apostles' Creed
*I believe in God, the Father Almighty, Maker of heaven and earth;
and in Jesus Christ, his only Son, our Lord, who was conceived by the
Holy Spirit, born of the Virgin Mary, suffered under Pontius Pilate,
was crucified, dead, and buried; he descended into hell; the third day
he arose again from the dead; he ascended into heaven and sits on
the right hand of God the Father Almighty; from thence he shall come
to judge the quick and the dead.*

I believe in the Holy Spirit, the holy catholic church, the communion
of saints, the forgiveness of sins, the resurrection of the body, and the
life everlasting. Amen.*

* In the Apostles' and Nicene Creeds, the term catholic refers to the Church's
universality, through all ages and times, of all languages and peoples. It refers to no
particular tradition or denominational expression (e.g., as in Roman Catholic).

Prayers of Confession
Let us now confess our sins to God and receive mercy and
grace to help in our time of need.

Assurance of Pardon
Having faithfully confessed and renounced your sin, Christ
also has been faithful to forgive your sins and to purify you
from all unrighteousness. It is certain, that there is One who
has spoken to the Father in your defense, Jesus Christ, the
Righteous One who is the atoning sacrifice for our sins and
for the sins of the whole world. His grace and peace are with
you now. Amen.

Petitions and Supplications, Ending with the Lord's Prayer

Our Father which art in heaven, Hallowed be thy name. Thy kingdom come, Thy will be done in earth, as it is in heaven. Give us this day our daily bread. And forgive us our debts, as we forgive our debtors. And lead us not into temptation, but deliver us from evil: For thine is the kingdom, and the power, and the glory, for ever. Amen.

~ Matthew 6.9-13 (KJV)

Doxology (and/or closing song)

Praise God from whom all blessings flow;
Praise Him all creatures here below;
Praise Him above ye heavenly host;
Praise Father, Son and Holy Ghost. Amen.

DEPARTING TO SERVE

Benediction

We beseech Thee, O Lord, let Thy gracious favour carry us through the fast which we have begun; that as we observe it by bodily discipline, so we may be able to fulfil it with sincerity of mind; through Jesus Christ our Lord. Amen.

~ *Gelasian Sacramentary* (Bright, p. 31)

Affirmation from the Psalms

The eyes of the Lord are toward the righteous and his ears toward their cry. [16] The face of the Lord is against those who do evil, to cut off the memory of them from the earth. [17] When the righteous cry for help, the Lord hears and delivers them out of all their troubles. [18] The Lord is near to the brokenhearted and saves the crushed in spirit. [19] Many are the afflictions of the righteous, but the Lord delivers him out of them all.

~ Psalm 34.15-19

Pray without Ceasing – Flash Prayer for the Day
Have mercy on me, O God, according to your steadfast love, and according to your abundant mercy blot out my transgressions.

For Your Weekly Journey

Let God Arise! Seasonal Focus
That I May Gain Christ, Philippians 3.4b-14

Book Reading
Allen, *Missionary Methods: St. Paul's or Ours?*

First Sunday in Lent

February 14 - 20, 2016

The Lenten Season, a forty-day period starting on Ash Wednesday and ending on Holy Saturday of Holy Week, calls us to reflect on Jesus' suffering, crucifixion, and death. As disciples of the humble Nazarene, we embrace his lowliness and humility, seeking to share the mind of him who was obedient to death, even death on a cross.

THIS WEEK'S THEME
It Is Written, Luke 4.1-13

After his baptism by John in the Jordan, Jesus was full of the Holy Spirit, and was led by the Spirit in the wilderness where he spent forty days, being tempted by the devil. During that time he did not eat anything. When these days were done, the Lord was hungry. The devil said to him, "If you are the Son of God, command this stone to become bread." Jesus answered him, "It is written, 'Man shall not live by bread alone.'"

Then, the devil took him up and showed him all the kingdoms of the world, in a moment of time. The adversary said to him, "To you I will give all this authority and their glory, for it has been delivered to me, and I give it to whom I will. If you, then, will worship me, it will all be yours." Again, Jesus answered him, "It is written, 'You shall worship the Lord your God, and him only shall you serve.'"

Finally, Satan took him to Jerusalem and set him on the pinnacle of the temple. The devil said to him, "If you are the Son of God, throw yourself down from here, for it is written, 'He will command his angels concerning you, to guard you,' and 'On their hands they will bear you up, lest you strike your foot against a stone.'" Again, Jesus answered him, "It is said, 'You shall not put the Lord your God to the test.'" And when the devil had ended every temptation, he then departed from Jesus, until an opportune time would show itself again.

In his recapitulation (reenactment, retracing) of Israel's wanderings and temptations, Jesus withstood the temptations of the devil by quoting as final authority passages from Deuteronomy chapters 6 and 8. These texts suggests that he was thinking about the experience of Israel in their wilderness wanderings. In every case Jesus deferred to the will of God – that we do not live by bread alone but by God's Word (Deut. 8.3), that we worship God alone (Deut. 6.13), and that we never should put the Lord to the test (Deut. 6.16). The devil's efforts to deceive and distract the Lord were not sucessful; Jesus refuted his lies and distractions with the Word of God, "It is written." It remains an effective sword against the enemy's lies (cf. Eph. 6.17).

Daily Devotional Guide

PREPARING OUR HEARTS

Invocation: Our Prayer of Acclamation
Gracious Father, even though the adversary sought to get Jesus to change his mind about your will, to sacrifice both his mission and ministry for selfish gain, our Lord refuted his lies with your Word. Thank you for the "sword of the Spirit," which can search out and destroy the lies and misbeliefs of the enemy, and fortify us to stand true to your will and Word. Make us like your Son; show us how to withstand the devil's temptations and lies with "It is written." In Jesus' name, amen.

Call to Worship
Blessed are you, O God: Father, Son, and Holy Spirit. And blessed is your Kingdom, both now and forever, amen.

PRAISING OUR GOD

Te Deum Laudamus

You are God: we praise you; you are the Lord; we acclaim you; you are the eternal Father: All creation worships you. To you all angels, all the powers of heaven, Cherubim and Seraphim, sing in endless praise: Holy, holy, holy Lord, God of power and might, heaven and earth are full of your glory.

The glorious company of apostles praise you. The noble fellowship of prophets praise you. The white-robed army of martyrs praise you. Throughout the world the holy Church acclaims you; Father, of majesty unbounded, your true and only Son, worthy of all worship, and the Holy Spirit, advocate and guide.

You, Christ, are the king of glory, the eternal Son of the Father. When you became man to set us free you did not shun the Virgin's womb. You overcame the sting of death and opened the kingdom of heaven to all believers. You are seated at God's right hand in glory. We believe that you will come and be our judge. Come then, Lord, and help your people, bought with the price of your own blood, and bring us with your saints to glory everlasting.

Praise and Thanksgiving (Songs and Prayers)

Gloria Patri

Glory be to the Father,
And to the Son and to the Holy Spirit:
As it was in the beginning,
Is now, and ever shall be,
World without end. Amen, amen.

LISTENING TO HIS VOICE

Chronological Reading for the Day
Sunday: Deut. 26-28
Monday: Deut. 29-30
Tuesday: Deut. 31-32; Ps. 90
Wednesday: Deut. 33-34; Josh. 1-2
Thursday: Josh. 3-6
Friday: Josh. 7-9; 1 Chron. 2.7
Saturday: Josh. 10-11

Lectionary Readings
Psalm: Ps. 91.1-2, 9-16   *OT:* Deut. 26.1-11
Gospel: Luke 4.1-13   *NT:* Rom. 10.8b-13

Reflection: Silence and/or Journaling

RESPONDING IN FAITH

The Apostles' Creed
I believe in God, the Father Almighty, Maker of heaven and earth; and in Jesus Christ, his only Son, our Lord, who was conceived by the Holy Spirit, born of the Virgin Mary, suffered under Pontius Pilate, was crucified, dead, and buried; he descended into hell; the third day he arose again from the dead; he ascended into heaven and sits on the right hand of God the Father Almighty; from thence he shall come to judge the quick and the dead.

I believe in the Holy Spirit, the holy catholic* church, the communion of saints, the forgiveness of sins, the resurrection of the body, and the life everlasting. Amen.

* In the Apostles' and Nicene Creeds, the term catholic refers to the Church's universality, through all ages and times, of all languages and peoples. It refers to no particular tradition or denominational expression (e.g., as in Roman Catholic).

Prayers of Confession

Let us now confess our sins to God and receive mercy and grace to help in our time of need.

Assurance of Pardon

Having faithfully confessed and renounced your sin, Christ also has been faithful to forgive your sins and to purify you from all unrighteousness. It is certain, that there is One who has spoken to the Father in your defense, Jesus Christ, the Righteous One who is the atoning sacrifice for our sins and for the sins of the whole world. His grace and peace are with you now. Amen.

Petitions and Supplications, Ending with the Lord's Prayer

Our Father which art in heaven, Hallowed be thy name. Thy kingdom come, Thy will be done in earth, as it is in heaven. Give us this day our daily bread. And forgive us our debts, as we forgive our debtors. And lead us not into temptation, but deliver us from evil: For thine is the kingdom, and the power, and the glory, for ever. Amen.

~ Matthew 6.9-13 (KJV)

Doxology (and/or closing song)

Praise God from whom all blessings flow;
Praise Him all creatures here below;
Praise Him above ye heavenly host;
Praise Father, Son and Holy Ghost. Amen.

DEPARTING TO SERVE

Benediction

Lord Jesus, teach us to wield the sword of the Spirit with the same kind of humility, truth, and commitment that you did when you confronted the enemy in the desolate wilderness of Judea. You overcame the enemy, and triumphed for you quoted God's Word and refused to let the enemy change your mind regarding the structure and intent of your ministry. Train us through the Spirit to do the same. In Jesus' name, amen.

Affirmation from the Psalms

I give you thanks, O Lord, with my whole heart; before the gods I sing your praise; [2] I bow down toward your holy temple and give thanks to your name for your steadfast love and your faithfulness, for you have exalted above all things your name and your word. [3] On the day I called, you answered me; my strength of soul you increased.

~ Psalm 138.1-3

Pray without Ceasing – Flash Prayer for the Day

Lord Jesus Christ, victor over the adversary's lies, set us free as we abide in and confess your truth.

For Your Weekly Journey

Let God Arise! Seasonal Focus
That I May Gain Christ, Philippians 3.4b-14

Book Reading
Allen, *Missionary Methods: St. Paul's or Ours?*

Our Corporate Disciplines
Book Discussion: Monday, February 15, 2016
TUMI Retreat: Friday, February 19, 2016

WEEK 13

Second Sunday in Lent

February 21 - 27, 2016

The Lenten Season, a forty-day period starting on Ash Wednesday and ending on Holy Saturday of Holy Week, calls us to reflect on Jesus' suffering, crucifixion, and death. As disciples of the humble Nazarene, we embrace his lowliness and humility, seeking to share the mind of him who was obedient to death, even death on a cross.

THIS WEEK'S THEME
O Jerusalem, Jerusalem, Luke 13.31-35

At the very hour some Pharisees came to Jesus, warning him to avoid Jerusalem because Herod, who resided there, wanted to kill him. Whatever their motive may have been, Jesus replied to them, "Go and tell that fox, 'Behold, I cast out demons and perform cures today and tomorrow, and the third day I finish my course. Nevertheless, I must go on my way today and tomorrow and the day following, for it cannot be that a prophet should perish away from Jerusalem.'" Rather than be intimidated at the prospect of death, Jesus stated he had a mission to accomplish, and nothing would prevent him from finishing his course. Jesus sent the Pharisees on their own mission; go and tell Herod I am coming, yes, to Jerusalem for "it cannot be that a prophet should perish away from Jerusalem."

Jesus then offers his tragic lament and assessment of the spiritual state of the city of David. "O Jerusalem, Jerusalem, the city that kills the prophets and stones those who are sent to it! How often would I have gathered your children together as a hen gathers her brood under her wings, and you were not willing! Behold, your house is forsaken. And I tell you, you will not see me until you say, 'Blessed is he who comes in the name of the Lord!'"

While he had longed to protect it as a hen gathers her chicks under her wings, the city was not willing. His offer of the Kingdom to the people of God, represented by Israel, had been rejected by them. Rather, they had killed the prophets and stoned those sent to it. Now, they would reject the words of the Son himself, and their house would be left desolate, forsaken, abandoned to itself. The city would not cry Hosanna again until the Son returned the second time to reign as Lord over the entire earth.

Daily Devotional Guide

PREPARING OUR HEARTS

Invocation: Our Prayer of Acclamation
Dear Father, the example of Jerusalem's hardness of heart reveals our need to be ever vigilant about our fitness and readiness to listen to and obey your offers of love and grace. Though you sent prophets and seers to that great city, they refused to hear your word, and ultimately rejected the very presence and word of your own Son. Make us tender and ready always to hear your Word and to respond to you, whenever and however you may address us. In Jesus name, amen.

Call to Worship
Blessed are you, O God: Father, Son, and Holy Spirit. And blessed is your Kingdom, both now and forever, amen.

PRAISING OUR GOD

Te Deum Laudamus
You are God: we praise you; you are the Lord; we acclaim you; you are the eternal Father: All creation worships you. To you all angels, all the powers of heaven, Cherubim and Seraphim, sing in endless praise:

Holy, holy, holy Lord, God of power and might, heaven and earth are full of your glory.

The glorious company of apostles praise you. The noble fellowship of prophets praise you. The white-robed army of martyrs praise you. Throughout the world the holy Church acclaims you; Father, of majesty unbounded, your true and only Son, worthy of all worship, and the Holy Spirit, advocate and guide.

You, Christ, are the king of glory, the eternal Son of the Father. When you became man to set us free you did not shun the Virgin's womb. You overcame the sting of death and opened the kingdom of heaven to all believers. You are seated at God's right hand in glory. We believe that you will come and be our judge. Come then, Lord, and help your people, bought with the price of your own blood, and bring us with your saints to glory everlasting.

Praise and Thanksgiving (Songs and Prayers)

Gloria Patri
Glory be to the Father,
And to the Son and to the Holy Spirit:
As it was in the beginning,
Is now, and ever shall be,
World without end. Amen, amen.

LISTENING TO HIS VOICE

Chronological Reading for the Day
Sunday: Josh. 12-14
Monday: Josh. 15-17
Tuesday: Josh. 18-19
Wednesday: Josh. 20-21; 1 Chron. 6.54-81
Thursday: Josh. 22-24
Friday: Judg. 1-3
Saturday: Judg. 4-6

Lectionary Readings
Psalm: Ps. 27
Gospel: Luke 13.31-35

OT: Gen. 15.1-12, 17-18
NT: Phil. 3.17-4.1

Reflection: Silence and/or Journaling

Responding in Faith

The Apostles' Creed
I believe in God, the Father Almighty, Maker of heaven and earth;
and in Jesus Christ, his only Son, our Lord, who was conceived by the
Holy Spirit, born of the Virgin Mary, suffered under Pontius Pilate,
was crucified, dead, and buried; he descended into hell; the third day
he arose again from the dead; he ascended into heaven and sits on
the right hand of God the Father Almighty; from thence he shall come
to judge the quick and the dead.

I believe in the Holy Spirit, the holy catholic* church, the communion
of saints, the forgiveness of sins, the resurrection of the body, and the
life everlasting. Amen.

* In the Apostles' and Nicene Creeds, the term catholic refers to the Church's
universality, through all ages and times, of all languages and peoples. It refers to no
particular tradition or denominational expression (e.g., as in Roman Catholic).

Prayers of Confession
Let us now confess our sins to God and receive mercy and
grace to help in our time of need.

Assurance of Pardon
Having faithfully confessed and renounced your sin, Christ
also has been faithful to forgive your sins and to purify you
from all unrighteousness. It is certain, that there is One who
has spoken to the Father in your defense, Jesus Christ, the
Righteous One who is the atoning sacrifice for our sins and
for the sins of the whole world. His grace and peace are with
you now. Amen.

Petitions and Supplications, Ending with the Lord's Prayer
Our Father which art in heaven, Hallowed be thy name. Thy kingdom come, Thy will be done in earth, as it is in heaven. Give us this day our daily bread. And forgive us our debts, as we forgive our debtors. And lead us not into temptation, but deliver us from evil: For thine is the kingdom, and the power, and the glory, for ever. Amen.

~ Matthew 6.9-13 (KJV)

Doxology (and/or closing song)
Praise God from whom all blessings flow;
Praise Him all creatures here below;
Praise Him above ye heavenly host;
Praise Father, Son and Holy Ghost. Amen.

DEPARTING TO SERVE

Benediction
Dear Lord Jesus, our sincere heart's desire during this lenten season is to be so open to you that whatever you have for us will be embraced and accepted. Forgive us for the many times we failed to listen to your pleas for change, when we refused to act on your Word to our hearts. We acknowledge our need for you today. Cleanse us, prepare us, and change us, all for your glory. In your name we pray, amen.

Affirmation from the Psalms
Oh come, let us worship and bow down; let us kneel before the Lord, our Maker! [7] For he is our God, and we are the people of his pasture, and the sheep of his hand. Today, if you hear his voice, [8] do not harden your hearts, as at Meribah, as on the day at Massah in the wilderness, [9] when your fathers put me to the test and put me to the proof, though they had seen my work. [10] For forty years I loathed that generation and said, "They are a people who go astray in their heart, and they have not known my ways." [11] Therefore I swore in my wrath, "They shall not enter my rest."

~ Psalm 95.6-11

Pray without Ceasing – Flash Prayer for the Day
Lord Jesus Christ, help us today to hear your voice, to never harden our hearts, and to follow you that we might enter into your rest.

For Your Weekly Journey

Let God Arise! Seasonal Focus
That I May Gain Christ, Philippians 3.4b-14

Book Reading
Allen, *Missionary Methods: St. Paul's or Ours?*

WEEK 14

Third Sunday in Lent

February 28 - March 5, 2016

The Lenten Season, a forty-day period starting on Ash Wednesday and ending on Holy Saturday of Holy Week, calls us to reflect on Jesus' suffering, crucifixion, and death. As disciples of the humble Nazarene, we embrace his lowliness and humility, seeking to share the mind of him who was obedient to death, even death on a cross.

THIS WEEK'S THEME
Repent or Perish, Luke 13.1-9

The question of fate, i.e., those people whose actions somehow condemn them to both tragedy and death, was a common issue Jesus confronted in his interactions with others during his ministry. At one point on his journeys there were some people who told him about some Galileans whose blood Pilate had mingled with their sacrifices. Jesus answered them "Do you think that these Galileans were worse sinners than all the other Galileans, because they suffered in this way? No, I tell you; but unless you repent, you will all likewise perish. Or those eighteen on whom the tower in Siloam fell and killed them: do you think that they were worse offenders than all the others who lived in Jerusalem? No, I tell you; but unless you repent, you will all likewise perish."

The force of our Lord's teaching cannot be missed. It is quite common for people today to speculate on the ways in which others may have earned tragedy or judgment because of their own sinfulness and guilt. Jesus however says that the events which occur appear to suggest that people suffer due to their own culpability and error, say nothing of the need for everyone to repent and believe. Salvation is for everyone; we are all guilty before the Lord. No person or group is exempt from the need to repent and receive God's forgiveness through faith in Jesus Christ. Unless we repent, each one of us, we all will face judgment, and no one can save themselves. The Gospel is truly good news for the world.

Daily Devotional Guide

PREPARING OUR HEARTS

Invocation: Our Prayer of Acclamation

Eternal God our Father, thank you for the amazing grace you have granted us through faith in your Son. We are neither naive nor deceived; without you and the mercy of Jesus on our lives, we know that not a single one of us can stand in your presence. We live only because of your loving heart and steadfast mercy, mercy granted to all peoples everywhere. Thank you for life, thank you for Jesus. In his name we pray, amen.

Call to Worship

Blessed are you, O God: Father, Son, and Holy Spirit. And blessed is your Kingdom, both now and forever, amen.

PRAISING OUR GOD

Te Deum Laudamus

You are God: we praise you; you are the Lord; we acclaim you; you are the eternal Father: All creation worships you. To you all angels, all the powers of heaven, Cherubim and Seraphim, sing in endless praise: Holy, holy, holy Lord, God of power and might, heaven and earth are full of your glory.

The glorious company of apostles praise you. The noble fellowship of prophets praise you. The white-robed army of martyrs praise you. Throughout the world the holy Church acclaims you; Father, of majesty unbounded, your true and only Son, worthy of all worship, and the Holy Spirit, advocate and guide.

*You, Christ, are the king of glory, the eternal Son of the Father. When
you became man to set us free you did not shun the Virgin's womb.
You overcame the sting of death and opened the kingdom of heaven
to all believers. You are seated at God's right hand in glory. We believe
that you will come and be our judge. Come then, Lord, and help your
people, bought with the price of your own blood, and bring us with
your saints to glory everlasting.*

Praise and Thanksgiving (Songs and Prayers)

Gloria Patri
*Glory be to the Father,
And to the Son and to the Holy Spirit:
As it was in the beginning,
Is now, and ever shall be,
World without end. Amen, amen.*

LISTENING TO HIS VOICE

Chronological Reading for the Day
Sunday: Judg. 7-9
Monday: Judg. 10-12
Tuesday: Judg. 13-15
Wednesday: Judg. 16-18
Thursday: Judg. 19-21
Friday: Ruth 1-4
Saturday: 1 Chron. 2.9-55; 4.1-23; 1 Sam. 1

Lectionary Readings
Psalm: Ps. 63.1-8   *OT:* Isa. 55.1-9
Gospel: Luke 13.1-9   *NT:* 1 Cor. 10.1-13

Reflection: Silence and/or Journaling

RESPONDING IN FAITH

The Apostles' Creed
*I believe in God, the Father Almighty, Maker of heaven and earth;
and in Jesus Christ, his only Son, our Lord, who was conceived by the
Holy Spirit, born of the Virgin Mary, suffered under Pontius Pilate,
was crucified, dead, and buried; he descended into hell; the third day
he arose again from the dead; he ascended into heaven and sits on
the right hand of God the Father Almighty; from thence he shall come
to judge the quick and the dead.*

I believe in the Holy Spirit, the holy catholic church, the communion
of saints, the forgiveness of sins, the resurrection of the body, and the
life everlasting. Amen.*

* In the Apostles' and Nicene Creeds, the term catholic refers to the Church's
universality, through all ages and times, of all languages and peoples. It refers to no
particular tradition or denominational expression (e.g., as in Roman Catholic).

Prayers of Confession
Let us now confess our sins to God and receive mercy and
grace to help in our time of need.

Assurance of Pardon
Having faithfully confessed and renounced your sin, Christ
also has been faithful to forgive your sins and to purify you
from all unrighteousness. It is certain, that there is One who
has spoken to the Father in your defense, Jesus Christ, the
Righteous One who is the atoning sacrifice for our sins and
for the sins of the whole world. His grace and peace are with
you now. Amen.

Petitions and Supplications, Ending with the Lord's Prayer

Our Father which art in heaven, Hallowed be thy name. Thy kingdom come, Thy will be done in earth, as it is in heaven. Give us this day our daily bread. And forgive us our debts, as we forgive our debtors. And lead us not into temptation, but deliver us from evil: For thine is the kingdom, and the power, and the glory, for ever. Amen.

~ Matthew 6.9-13 (KJV)

Doxology (and/or closing song)

Praise God from whom all blessings flow;
Praise Him all creatures here below;
Praise Him above ye heavenly host;
Praise Father, Son and Holy Ghost. Amen.

DEPARTING TO SERVE

Benediction

Lord Jesus Christ, grant us the grace to love you more than we do now, more than we have ever loved you. Help us to truly comprehend how lost and broken we are apart from your mercy. Enable us to acknowledge, with love and understanding, the simple truth that apart from the Good News of salvation in your name, not a single soul will survive the judgment. You alone are our source and our life. To you alone be praise, to the glory of the Father. In your name we pray, amen.

Affirmation from the Psalms

Blessed be the Lord, for he has wondrously shown his steadfast love to me when I was in a besieged city. [22] I had said in my alarm, "I am cut off from your sight." But you heard the voice of my pleas for mercy when I cried to you for help. [23] Love the Lord, all you his saints! The Lord preserves the faithful but abundantly repays the one who acts in pride. [24] Be strong, and let your heart take courage, all you who wait for the Lord!

~ Psalm 31.21-24

Pray without Ceasing – Flash Prayer for the Day
Lord Jesus Christ, Son of God, have mercy upon me.

For Your Weekly Journey

Let God Arise! Seasonal Focus
That I May Gain Christ, Philippians 3.4b-14

Book Reading
Allen, *Missionary Methods: St. Paul's or Ours?*

Our Corporate Disciplines
Book Discussion: Monday, February 29, 2016

Fourth Sunday in Lent

March 6 - 12, 2016

The Lenten Season, a forty-day period starting on Ash Wednesday and ending on Holy Saturday of Holy Week, calls us to reflect on Jesus' suffering, crucifixion, and death. As disciples of the humble Nazarene, we embrace his lowliness and humility, seeking to share the mind of him who was obedient to death, even death on a cross.

THIS WEEK'S THEME
More Joy in Heaven, Luke 15.1-3, 11b-32

Jesus' compassionate accessibility to the poor, broken, and sinners was a major irritant to many of the religious leaders of his day. When the tax collectors and sinners were all drawing near to Jesus to listen to his teaching, the Pharisees and the scribes grumbled, saying, "This man receives sinners and eats with them."

Jesus recognized their grumbling and irritation, and so told them the parable of the Prodigal Son. He explained the story of a man who had two sons, with the younger demanding his share of the property, even before his dad had died! So the dad divided his property between him and his older son. Now, not long after this, the younger son gathered his belongings and took a journey into a far country. While he was there, he wasted all his property and resources in reckless living. And, after he had spent everything he had, a severe famine came to that country, and he was in dire need. He hired himself out to one of the citizens of that place, who gave him the job of feeding pigs, an unclean task indeed! He was so hungry that he longed to eat the very pods that the unclean pigs were eating, and no one gave him a thing.

In the midst of this suffering, Jesus said that he "came to himself" and said, "How many of my father's hired servants have more than enough bread, but I perish here with hunger!

I will arise and go to my father, and I will say to him, 'Father, I have sinned against heaven and before you. I am no longer worthy to be called your son. Treat me as one of your hired servants.'"

Broken and humbled, the younger son arose and went back home, to his dad. But, while the son was still a long way off from home, his father happened to see him and felt compassion for him, and ran towards him, met him, and embraced him, and kissed him. The younger son said to him, "Father, I have sinned against heaven and before you. I am no longer worthy to be called your son." The father, however, said to his servants, servants, "Bring quickly the best robe, and put it on him, and put a ring on his hand, and shoes on his feet. And bring the fattened calf and kill it, and let us eat and celebrate. For this my son was dead, and is alive again; he was lost, and is found."And they began to celebrate.

The father's older son was in the field, came up to the house, heard the commotion, and asked what all the music and dancing was about. One of the servants remarked, "Your brother has come, and your father has killed the fattened calf, because he has received him back safe and sound." The older brother, however, was angry and refused to go in! The father came out and entreated him to join the celebration, but the older brother commented that in all the years he had faithfully worked, his dad had never even given him a goat to celebrate with his friends. Yet, when the wasteful, immoral brother who devoured your property with prostitutes returns, you threw him this party! The father reassured the older brother, saying, "Son, you are always with me, and all that is mine is yours. It was fitting to celebrate and be glad, for this your brother was dead, and is alive; he was lost, and is found."

The picture Jesus gives of our father is a compassionate, loving, and gracious dad, who is more than willing to embrace a wayward son who returns to him broken and humble. Our God is a God of grace and boundless love for the repentant.

Daily Devotional Guide

PREPARING OUR HEARTS

Invocation: Our Prayer of Acclamation
Holy Father, the very dad who ran to meet us when we returned to you while we were a long way off, thank you for welcoming us back home. Though we have squandered our inheritance in selfish and foolish ways, you have graciously received us back home, embraced us, kissed us, and thrown a celebration! What can we say to love like this? We will therefore, in gratitude and wonder, give our hearts back to you. Thank you for your grace and mercy to us. In Jesus' name we pray, amen.

Call to Worship
Blessed are you, O God: Father, Son, and Holy Spirit. And blessed is your Kingdom, both now and forever, amen.

PRAISING OUR GOD

Te Deum Laudamus
You are God: we praise you; you are the Lord; we acclaim you; you are the eternal Father: All creation worships you. To you all angels, all the powers of heaven, Cherubim and Seraphim, sing in endless praise: Holy, holy, holy Lord, God of power and might, heaven and earth are full of your glory.

The glorious company of apostles praise you. The noble fellowship of prophets praise you. The white-robed army of martyrs praise you. Throughout the world the holy Church acclaims you; Father, of majesty unbounded, your true and only Son, worthy of all worship, and the Holy Spirit, advocate and guide.

You, Christ, are the king of glory, the eternal Son of the Father. When you became man to set us free you did not shun the Virgin's womb. You overcame the sting of death and opened the kingdom of heaven to all believers. You are seated at God's right hand in glory. We believe that you will come and be our judge. Come then, Lord, and help your people, bought with the price of your own blood, and bring us with your saints to glory everlasting.

Praise and Thanksgiving (Songs and Prayers)

Gloria Patri
Glory be to the Father,
And to the Son and to the Holy Spirit:
As it was in the beginning,
Is now, and ever shall be,
World without end. Amen, amen.

LISTENING TO HIS VOICE

Chronological Reading for the Day
Sunday: 1 Sam. 2-4
Monday: 1 Sam. 5-8
Tuesday: 1 Sam. 9-12
Wednesday: 1 Chron. 9.35-39; 1 Sam. 13-14
Thursday: 1 Sam. 15-17
Friday: 1 Sam. 18-19; Ps. 59
Saturday: 1 Sam. 20-21; Ps. 34

Lectionary Readings
Psalm: Ps. 32   *OT:* Josh. 5.9-12
Gospel: Luke 15.1-3, 11b-32   *NT:* 2 Cor. 5.16-21

Reflection: Silence and/or Journaling

RESPONDING IN FAITH

The Apostles' Creed

I believe in God, the Father Almighty, Maker of heaven and earth; and in Jesus Christ, his only Son, our Lord, who was conceived by the Holy Spirit, born of the Virgin Mary, suffered under Pontius Pilate, was crucified, dead, and buried; he descended into hell; the third day he arose again from the dead; he ascended into heaven and sits on the right hand of God the Father Almighty; from thence he shall come to judge the quick and the dead.

I believe in the Holy Spirit, the holy catholic* church, the communion of saints, the forgiveness of sins, the resurrection of the body, and the life everlasting. Amen.

* In the Apostles' and Nicene Creeds, the term catholic refers to the Church's universality, through all ages and times, of all languages and peoples. It refers to no particular tradition or denominational expression (e.g., as in Roman Catholic).

Prayers of Confession

Let us now confess our sins to God and receive mercy and grace to help in our time of need.

Assurance of Pardon

Having faithfully confessed and renounced your sin, Christ also has been faithful to forgive your sins and to purify you from all unrighteousness. It is certain, that there is One who has spoken to the Father in your defense, Jesus Christ, the Righteous One who is the atoning sacrifice for our sins and for the sins of the whole world. His grace and peace are with you now. Amen.

Petitions and Supplications, Ending with the Lord's Prayer
Our Father which art in heaven, Hallowed be thy name. Thy kingdom come, Thy will be done in earth, as it is in heaven. Give us this day our daily bread. And forgive us our debts, as we forgive our debtors. And lead us not into temptation, but deliver us from evil: For thine is the kingdom, and the power, and the glory, for ever. Amen.

~ Matthew 6.9-13 (KJV)

Doxology (and/or closing song)
Praise God from whom all blessings flow;
Praise Him all creatures here below;
Praise Him above ye heavenly host;
Praise Father, Son and Holy Ghost. Amen.

DEPARTING TO SERVE

Benediction
Lord Jesus, forgive us for how begrudging we are sometimes at how loving and gracious you truly are. It is hard for us to grasp that heaven is more joyful at the prospect of a sinner returning to you than dozens who need no repentance. Form in us your faithful heart of mercy and grace; make us patient and caring to all, for your sake, amen.

Affirmation from the Psalms
Deliver me from sinking in the mire; let me be delivered from my enemies and from the deep waters. [15] Let not the flood sweep over me, or the deep swallow me up, or the pit close its mouth over me. [16] Answer me, O Lord, for your steadfast love is good; according to your abundant mercy, turn to me. [17] Hide not your face from your servant; for I am in distress; make haste to answer me. [18] Draw near to my soul, redeem me; ransom me because of my enemies! [19] You know my reproach, and my shame and my dishonor; my foes are all known to you.

~ Psalm 69.14-19

Pray without Ceasing – Flash Prayer for the Day
Lord Jesus Christ, help me to rejoice and be glad at the repentance of the broken, for you are good to those who return to you.

For Your Weekly Journey

Let God Arise! Seasonal Focus
That I May Gain Christ, Philippians 3.4b-14

Book Reading
Allen, *Missionary Methods: St. Paul's or Ours?*

Fifth Sunday in Lent

March 13 - 19, 2016

The Lenten Season, a forty-day period starting on Ash Wednesday and ending on Holy Saturday of Holy Week, calls us to reflect on Jesus' suffering, crucifixion, and death. As disciples of the humble Nazarene, we embrace his lowliness and humility, seeking to share the mind of him who was obedient to death, even death on a cross.

THIS WEEK'S THEME
That I May Gain Christ, Philippians 3.4b-14

Paul exhorted the Philippians to look out for those "evildoers" who relied on the externals of law keeping to sustain a relationship with God. He told them that they were in fact the true circumcision, those who worship by the Spirit of God, glory in Christ Jesus, and put no confidence at all in the trappings of external righteousness.

He was clear however, that, if he were to play that game, so to speak, he would have greater cause to depend on his own acts of self-righteousness than anyone. He was circumcised on the eighth day, of the people of Israel, of the tribe of Benjamin, a Hebrew of Hebrews, a direct descendant of Abraham's lineage. As to knowing and keeping the law, he was a member of the Pharisees, and as to zeal for the faith of his fathers, he was a persecutor of the Nazarene sect, the church. As to the kind of righteousness you can obtain from being under the law, he was literally blameless.

All of these things however, and whatever position or benefit they held for him, whatever gain he had, he now counted them all as loss for the sake of Christ. Indeed, he now counted everything as loss because of the surpassing worth of knowing Christ Jesus his Lord. Now, for the sake of Jesus he had suffered the loss of all things and counted them as rubbish, in order that he might gain Christ.

Now the apostle Paul's desire was to be found in Jesus alone, not having a righteousness of his own that came from the law, but the kind that comes through faith in Christ, the righteousness from God that depends on faith. His single focus now was to know Christ and the power of his resurrection, to share his sufferings, and to become like him in his death, and by any means possible to attain the resurrection from the dead.

Paul considered himself, however, neither to have obtained this nor to be perfect already. Rather, he pressed on to make this vision his very own, since Christ Jesus had made him his own. He determined to do only one thing alone: he would forget what lay behind and would now strain forward to what lay ahead, pressing toward the goal for the prize of the upward call of God in Christ Jesus. This was his heart, a heart he said all mature believers in Christ share deeply with one another. Our single focus is to gain Christ alone.

Daily Devotional Guide

PREPARING OUR HEARTS

Invocation: Our Prayer of Acclamation

God and Father of our Lord Jesus, thank you for the gift, the unspeakable gracious provision of Jesus to us. Help us to turn our back on all our fleshly accomplishments, on the trappings of fleshly religion and personal attainment. Rather, grant to us a vision to see Jesus as our life, our very source, the only hope of our hearts and the vision of our very lives. He alone is what we need, and all he is will always be enough. Make this so for all of us. In his name we pray, amen.

Call to Worship

Blessed are you, O God: Father, Son, and Holy Spirit. And blessed is your Kingdom, both now and forever, amen.

PRAISING OUR GOD

Te Deum Laudamus

You are God: we praise you; you are the Lord; we acclaim you; you are the eternal Father: All creation worships you. To you all angels, all the powers of heaven, Cherubim and Seraphim, sing in endless praise: Holy, holy, holy Lord, God of power and might, heaven and earth are full of your glory.

The glorious company of apostles praise you. The noble fellowship of prophets praise you. The white-robed army of martyrs praise you. Throughout the world the holy Church acclaims you; Father, of majesty unbounded, your true and only Son, worthy of all worship, and the Holy Spirit, advocate and guide.

You, Christ, are the king of glory, the eternal Son of the Father. When you became man to set us free you did not shun the Virgin's womb. You overcame the sting of death and opened the kingdom of heaven to all believers. You are seated at God's right hand in glory. We believe that you will come and be our judge. Come then, Lord, and help your people, bought with the price of your own blood, and bring us with your saints to glory everlasting.

Praise and Thanksgiving (Songs and Prayers)

Gloria Patri

Glory be to the Father,
And to the Son and to the Holy Spirit:
As it was in the beginning,
Is now, and ever shall be,
World without end. Amen, amen.

LISTENING TO HIS VOICE

Chronological Reading for the Day
Sunday: 1 Sam. 22-23; Pss. 52; 57; 142; 1 Chron. 12.8-18
Monday: 1 Sam. 24-25; Ps. 54
Tuesday: 1 Sam. 26-29; 1 Chron. 12.1-7, v.19; Ps. 56
Wednesday: 1 Sam. 30-31; 1 Chron. 9.40-10.14; 12.20-22;
    2 Sam. 1
Thursday: 2 Sam. 2.1-3.5; 23.8-39; 1 Chron. 3.1-4a; 11.10-47
Friday: 2 Sam. 3.6-4.12
Saturday: 2 Sam. 5.1-13, vv.17-25; 6.1-11; 1 Chron. 3.4b;
    11.1 9; 12.23 14.2; 14.8 17

Chronological Holy Week Readings
Saturday: Matt. 26.6-13; Mark 14.3-9; John 12.1-8

Lectionary Readings
Psalm: Ps. 126   *OT:* Isa. 43.16-21
Gospel: John 12.1-8   *NT:* Phil. 3.4b-14

Reflection: Silence and/or Journaling

RESPONDING IN FAITH

The Apostles' Creed
I believe in God, the Father Almighty, Maker of heaven and earth;
and in Jesus Christ, his only Son, our Lord, who was conceived by the
Holy Spirit, born of the Virgin Mary, suffered under Pontius Pilate,
was crucified, dead, and buried; he descended into hell; the third day
he arose again from the dead; he ascended into heaven and sits on
the right hand of God the Father Almighty; from thence he shall come
to judge the quick and the dead.

I believe in the Holy Spirit, the holy catholic* church, the communion of saints, the forgiveness of sins, the resurrection of the body, and the life everlasting. Amen.

* In the Apostles' and Nicene Creeds, the term catholic refers to the Church's universality, through all ages and times, of all languages and peoples. It refers to no particular tradition or denominational expression (e.g., as in Roman Catholic).

Prayers of Confession

Let us now confess our sins to God and receive mercy and grace to help in our time of need.

Assurance of Pardon

Having faithfully confessed and renounced your sin, Christ also has been faithful to forgive your sins and to purify you from all unrighteousness. It is certain, that there is One who has spoken to the Father in your defense, Jesus Christ, the Righteous One who is the atoning sacrifice for our sins and for the sins of the whole world. His grace and peace are with you now. Amen.

Petitions and Supplications, Ending with the Lord's Prayer

Our Father which art in heaven, Hallowed be thy name. Thy kingdom come, Thy will be done in earth, as it is in heaven. Give us this day our daily bread. And forgive us our debts, as we forgive our debtors. And lead us not into temptation, but deliver us from evil: For thine is the kingdom, and the power, and the glory, for ever. Amen.

~ Matthew 6.9-13 (KJV)

Doxology (and/or closing song)

Praise God from whom all blessings flow;
Praise Him all creatures here below;
Praise Him above ye heavenly host;
Praise Father, Son and Holy Ghost. Amen.

DEPARTING TO SERVE

Benediction

Lord Jesus Christ, we hold onto these promises – that you alone are our righteousness, that faith in you grants life eternal, that one day we will see you with the glory that you had with the Father, that we will one day be like you are, and that we shall sit with you and reign. You are our life and our source. Apart from you we can do nothing. Flow through us by your Spirit. In your name we pray, amen.

Affirmation from the Psalms

Trust in him at all times, O people; pour out your heart before him; God is a refuge for us. Selah [9] Those of low estate are but a breath; those of high estate are a delusion; in the balances they go up; they are together lighter than a breath. [10] Put no trust in extortion; set no vain hopes on robbery; if riches increase, set not your heart on them. [11] Once God has spoken; twice have I heard this: that power belongs to God, [12] and that to you, O Lord, belongs steadfast love. For you will render to a man according to his work.

~ Psalm 62.8-12

Pray without Ceasing – Flash Prayer for the Day

Lord Jesus Christ, we count everything as loss because of the surpassing worth of knowing you alone, our Savior and our Lord.

For Your Weekly Journey

Let God Arise! Seasonal Focus
That I May Gain Christ, Philippians 3.4b-14

Book Reading
Allen, *Missionary Methods: St. Paul's or Ours?*

Our Corporate Disciplines
Book Discussion: Monday, March 14, 2016

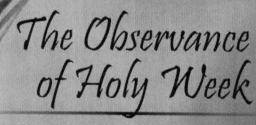

The Observance of Holy Week

THE PASSION OF CHRIST

*Truly, truly, I say to you, unless a grain of wheat
falls into the earth and dies, it remains alone;
but if it dies, it bears much fruit.*

JOHN 12.24

Holy Week: Sharing His Death to Rise with Him

**Palms of Welcome, the Passion of Suffering,
the Pain of Crucifixion, and the Power of Resurrection**
For believers, Christ crucified is both the power and wisdom of God. This is the period where followers of Jesus enter the high point of our spiritual formation in observance of the Church Year: our participation by faith in the Passion of our Lord.

Holy Week is the last week of the Lenten season. Beginning with our *Palm Sunday Celebration*, and through the various activities of the week, we join with believers worldwide to recall and be transformed by the story of Jesus of Nazareth – his trial, suffering, and death which occurred so many centuries ago in Jerusalem. The three days at the end of this week represent the most serious and solemn days of the Church calendar, focusing as they do on the events of Jesus' final hours before his death on the Cross.

> In the ancient church the three days [of the Paschal Triduum] started on Thursday evening and ended with the great Paschal vigil of Saturday night. These services are called the Paschal Triduum [or, the Three Great Days] ... They are the most holy, solemn, and serious days of the entire year. For in these days we experience and encounter our own destiny in the destiny of Christ's ignominious death and burial and in his triumphant resurrection from the dead.
>
> ~ Robert Webber. *Ancient Future Time.*
> Grand Rapids: Baker Books, 2004, p. 125.

During Holy Week we recall the events of our Lord's trial, suffering, and death. We ponder with joy and anticipation his triumphant entry into Jerusalem on *Palm Sunday*, listen to his matchless teaching through the week, and huddle with his disciples in the Upper Room as he gives the new commandment of love on *Maundy Thursday*. We hang our heads in shame and regret as we recall his crucifixion on *Good Friday*, and finally we end the week with the solemn vigil of Saturday night before *Easter Sunday*.

Holy Week Observances

Below is a short description of some of the highlights we observe and celebrate during this upcoming week:

Palm Sunday

The Sunday before Easter which commemorates the Triumphal Entry of Jesus of Nazareth into Jerusalem, his public proclamation of his identity as Messiah and Lord (John 12.12-18).

Maundy Thursday

The Thursday before Easter which commemorates the giving of the New Commandment and the Lord's Supper prior to Christ's Death (Mark 14.12-26; John 13). [From the Latin *mandatum novarum* which means "new commandment" (John 13.34).]

Good Friday

The Friday before Easter which commemorates the crucifixion of Christ (John 18-19).

Holy Saturday

The day before Easter which commemorates the burial of Jesus before his resurrection on Sunday (John 18-19).

Again, *Holy Week* is Lent's final week. As a season, Lent starts on *Ash Wednesday* and ends Saturday of Holy Week, with the vigil on *Holy Saturday*. As a time of soul-searching and preparation in the ancient Church, so today we ought to let this week be our own personal journey to the Cross, spending time reflecting on the lowliness and humiliation of our Lord. Here we clearly see the meaning of our baptism in Christ – being united with him in his suffering, death, burial, and resurrection from the dead.

When We Survey the Wondrous Cross: Pondering the Passion of Jesus Christ

During Holy Week we invite you to join with us and the millions of disciples of Jesus worldwide who will remember and seek to be transformed by a fresh experience of the meaning of Jesus' suffering and death on the Cross. For those who believe, he is the slain Lamb of God who takes the world's sin away (John 1.29), our glorious Conqueror who leads us in his triumph (2 Cor. 2.14), and the scorned Messiah who bore the curse for us on the Tree (Gal. 3.13). We seek to die daily with him in order that his life might be manifested in us (2 Cor. 4.10-11). He is Lord of all.

Come with us, and kneel at the Cross of him who alone can transform the lives of the millions languishing in oppression and poverty in the inner cities of America. He bids you to come.

A fellow traveler on the way,
Rev. Dr. Don L. Davis

Palm Sunday

Sixth Sunday in Lent • March 20 - 26, 2016

Holy Week recalls the events of our Lord's suffering and death. We recall his triumphant entry into Jerusalem on Palm Sunday, his giving of the commandments on Maundy Thursday, his crucifixion and burial on Good Friday, and the solemn vigil of Saturday night before Easter Sunday.

THIS WEEK'S THEME
When Stones Cry Out, Luke 19.28-40

As Jesus journeyed to Jerusalem for the final time, he went on ahead of his disciples, going up to the city. When he drew near to Bethphage and Bethany, to Mount Olivet, he sent two of his disciples into the village. He told them that on entering the place, they would find a colt tied on which no one had ever ridden. He told them to untie it, and bring it back to him. He further instructed that if anyone asked them why, they were to tell them that "The Lord has need of it."

So, the two went ahead into the village, found it as the Lord said, and as they were untying the colt, its owners asked them why. They replied as the Lord said, and finally brought the colt to the Lord. The disciples threw their cloaks on the colt, and they set Jesus upon it. As Jesus rode along, others spread their cloaks on the road. As the Lord Jesus was drawing near – already on his way down the Mount of Olives – the entire multitude of his disciples began to rejoice and praise God with a loud voice for all the mighty works that they had seen. They cried out, saying, "Blessed is the King who comes in the name of the Lord! Peace in heaven and glory in the highest!"

Some of the Pharisees who were in the crowd witnessing this display asked Jesus to rebuke his disciples. Jesus answered them, "I tell you, if these were silent, the very stones would cry out."

This remarkable episode of Jesus' triumphal, final entry into Jerusalem is the fulfillment of prophecy and a clear witness of his true identity as Israel's Messiah, and the King of glory. This moment, awaited by prophets, saints, and believers for centuries, would have its due. If the disciples present had hushed their praises, the very rocks themselves would have cried out! Israel's King and God's Chosen Son is entering into the place of his glory. Let us all cry out with the worshiping disciples: "Blessed is the King who comes in the name of the Lord! Peace in heaven and glory in the highest!"

Daily Devotional Guide

PREPARING OUR HEARTS

Invocation: Our Prayer of Acclamation
Lamb of God, who takes away the sin of the world, look on us and have mercy on us, you who are both victim and priest, reward and redeemer; keep safe from all evils those whom you have redeemed, O Savior of the world. Amen.

~ Old Gallican Missal (Oden, p. 105)

Call to Worship
Blessed are you, O God: Father, Son, and Holy Spirit. And blessed is your Kingdom, both now and forever, amen.

PRAISING OUR GOD

Te Deum Laudamus
You are God: we praise you; you are the Lord; we acclaim you; you are the eternal Father: All creation worships you. To you all angels, all the powers of heaven, Cherubim and Seraphim, sing in endless praise:

Holy, holy, holy Lord, God of power and might, heaven and earth are full of your glory.

The glorious company of apostles praise you. The noble fellowship of prophets praise you. The white-robed army of martyrs praise you. Throughout the world the holy Church acclaims you; Father, of majesty unbounded, your true and only Son, worthy of all worship, and the Holy Spirit, advocate and guide.

You, Christ, are the king of glory, the eternal Son of the Father. When you became man to set us free you did not shun the Virgin's womb. You overcame the sting of death and opened the kingdom of heaven to all believers. You are seated at God's right hand in glory. We believe that you will come and be our judge. Come then, Lord, and help your people, bought with the price of your own blood, and bring us with your saints to glory everlasting.

Praise and Thanksgiving (Songs and Prayers)

Gloria Patri
Glory be to the Father,
And to the Son and to the Holy Spirit:
As it was in the beginning,
Is now, and ever shall be,
World without end. Amen, amen.

LISTENING TO HIS VOICE

Chronological Reading for the Day
Sunday: 2 Sam. 6.12-23; 1 Chron. 15-16
Monday: 2 Sam. 7-8; 1 Chron. 17-18; Ps. 60
Tuesday: 2 Sam. 9-10; 1 Chron. 6.16-48, vv.50-53; ch.19
Wednesday: 1 Chron. 3.5-9; 14.3-7; 20.1-3; 2 Sam. 11.1-12.25; 5.14-16; Ps. 51
Thursday: 2 Sam. 12.26-14.33

Friday: 2 Sam. 15-17
Saturday: 2 Sam. 18-19; Pss. 3; 63

Chronological Holy Week Readings
Palm Sunday: Matt. 21.1-17; Mark 11.1-11; Luke 19.28-48;
John 12.12-50

Lectionary Readings for *Liturgy of the Palms*

Psalm: Ps. 118.1-2, 19-29   *OT:* Isa. 50.4-9
Gospel: Mark 11.1-11   *NT:* Phil. 2.5-11

Reflection: Silence and/or Journaling

RESPONDING IN FAITH

The Apostles' Creed
*I believe in God, the Father Almighty, Maker of heaven and earth;
and in Jesus Christ, his only Son, our Lord, who was conceived by the
Holy Spirit, born of the Virgin Mary, suffered under Pontius Pilate,
was crucified, dead, and buried; he descended into hell; the third day
he arose again from the dead; he ascended into heaven and sits on
the right hand of God the Father Almighty; from thence he shall come
to judge the quick and the dead.*

I believe in the Holy Spirit, the holy catholic church, the communion
of saints, the forgiveness of sins, the resurrection of the body, and the
life everlasting. Amen.*

* In the Apostles' and Nicene Creeds, the term catholic refers to the Church's
universality, through all ages and times, of all languages and peoples. It refers to no
particular tradition or denominational expression (e.g., as in Roman Catholic).

Prayers of Confession
Let us now confess our sins to God and receive mercy and
grace to help in our time of need.

Assurance of Pardon

Having faithfully confessed and renounced your sin, Christ also has been faithful to forgive your sins and to purify you from all unrighteousness. It is certain, that there is One who has spoken to the Father in your defense, Jesus Christ, the Righteous One who is the atoning sacrifice for our sins and for the sins of the whole world. His grace and peace are with you now. Amen.

Petitions and Supplications, Ending with the Lord's Prayer

Our Father which art in heaven, Hallowed be thy name. Thy kingdom come, Thy will be done in earth, as it is in heaven. Give us this day our daily bread. And forgive us our debts, as we forgive our debtors. And lead us not into temptation, but deliver us from evil: For thine is the kingdom, and the power, and the glory, for ever. Amen.

~ Matthew 6.9-13 (KJV)

Doxology (and/or closing song)

Praise God from whom all blessings flow;
Praise Him all creatures here below;
Praise Him above ye heavenly host;
Praise Father, Son and Holy Ghost. Amen.

DEPARTING TO SERVE

Benediction

Merciful God, as we enter Holy Week and gather at your house of prayer, turn our hearts again to Jerusalem, to the life, death and resurrection of Jesus Christ, that united with Christ and all the faithful we may one day enter in triumph the city not made by human hands, the new Jerusalem, eternal in the heavens, where with you and the Holy Spirit, Christ lives in glory forever. Amen.

~ *Book of Worship United Church of Christ*
(The Theological and Worship Ministry Unit, p. 253)

Affirmation from the Psalms

The stone that the builders rejected has become the cornerstone. [23] This is the Lord's doing; it is marvelous in our eyes. [24] This is the day that the Lord has made; let us rejoice and be glad in it. [25] Save us, we pray, O Lord! O Lord, we pray, give us success! [26] Blessed is he who comes in the name of the Lord! We bless you from the house of the Lord. [27] The Lord is God, and he has made his light to shine upon us. Bind the festal sacrifice with cords, up to the horns of the altar!

~ Psalm 118.22-27

Pray without Ceasing – Flash Prayer for the Day

Lord Jesus Christ, we cry out to you, "Blessed is he who comes in the name of the Lord! We bless you from the house of the Lord."

For Your Weekly Journey

Let God Arise! Seasonal Focus

The Blood of Christ, Hebrews 9.11-15

Book Reading

Hamilton, *The Call, the Life and Message of the Apostle Paul*

Special Church Year Services

Maundy Thursday: Thursday, March 24, 2016
Good Friday: Friday, March 25, 2016
Holy Saturday: Saturday, March 26, 2016

Monday of Holy Week

March 21, 2016

Holy Week recalls the events of our Lord's suffering and death. We recall his triumphant entry into Jerusalem on Palm Sunday, his giving of the commandments on Maundy Thursday, his crucifixion and burial on Good Friday, and the solemn vigil of Saturday night before Easter Sunday.

TODAY'S THEME

The Blood of Christ, Hebrews 9.11-15

The writer of Hebrews speaks of Jesus of Nazareth as the true high priest of God, of which Aaron and subsequent priests were but a shadow. He declares that Christ appeared before the Lord as a high priest of the good things that have come. When he appeared through "the greater and more perfect tent" (not the one made with hands, that is, not of the stuff of this creation), the Lord Jesus entered once for all into the holy places. He entered that tent not by means of the blood of goats and calves but by means of his very own blood, and thus secured for us an eternal redemption.

The writer then argues that the blood of goats and bulls, and the sprinkling of defiled persons with the ashes of a heifer, could actually sanctify for the purification of the flesh. If that be true, then how much more will the blood of Christ, who offered himself without blemish to God through the eternal Spirit, purify our conscience from dead works to serve the living God. Jesus Christ is the mediator of a new covenant, so that those who are called may receive the promised eternal inheritance. This is now true, since a death has occurred that redeems them from the transgressions committed under the first covenant.

The blood of Jesus Christ, offered by him in the tabernacle above to God through the Spirit, now saves us; through it we are forgiven, justified, and purified from our own dead works to serve the living God alone. We overcome the devil through blood, that which washes and redeems us from our sin.

Daily Devotional Guide

PREPARING OUR HEARTS

Invocation: Our Prayer of Acclamation
Holy Father, blessed be your name, for in the gift of your Son he has liberated us from the futility of our own efforts to make ourselves acceptable to you. Thank you for Christ, who offered himself up to you without blemish, the perfect Sacrifice through the eternal Spirit, who has made us acceptable in your presence. We approach you in his name and because of his blood. Thank you for this unspeakable gift of love – the blood of Christ, your only Son. In his name we pray, amen.

Call to Worship
Blessed are you, O God: Father, Son, and Holy Spirit. And blessed is your Kingdom, both now and forever, amen.

PRAISING OUR GOD

Te Deum Laudamus
You are God: we praise you; you are the Lord; we acclaim you; you are the eternal Father: All creation worships you. To you all angels, all the powers of heaven, Cherubim and Seraphim, sing in endless praise: Holy, holy, holy Lord, God of power and might, heaven and earth are full of your glory.

The glorious company of apostles praise you. The noble fellowship of prophets praise you. The white-robed army of martyrs praise you. Throughout the world the holy Church acclaims you; Father, of majesty unbounded, your true and only Son, worthy of all worship, and the Holy Spirit, advocate and guide.

You, Christ, are the king of glory, the eternal Son of the Father. When you became man to set us free you did not shun the Virgin's womb. You overcame the sting of death and opened the kingdom of heaven to all believers. You are seated at God's right hand in glory. We believe that you will come and be our judge. Come then, Lord, and help your people, bought with the price of your own blood, and bring us with your saints to glory everlasting.

Praise and Thanksgiving (Songs and Prayers)

Gloria Patri
Glory be to the Father,
And to the Son and to the Holy Spirit:
As it was in the beginning,
Is now, and ever shall be,
World without end. Amen, amen.

LISTENING TO HIS VOICE

Chronological Reading for the Day
2 Sam. 7-8; 1 Chron. 17-18; Ps. 60

Chronological Holy Week Readings
Monday of Holy Week: Matt. 21.18-19; Mark 11.12-19

Lectionary Readings
Psalm: Ps. 36.5-11 *OT:* Isa. 42.1-9
Gospel: John 12.1-11 *NT:* Heb. 9.11-15

Reflection: Silence and/or Journaling

RESPONDING IN FAITH

The Apostles' Creed
*I believe in God, the Father Almighty, Maker of heaven and earth;
and in Jesus Christ, his only Son, our Lord, who was conceived by the
Holy Spirit, born of the Virgin Mary, suffered under Pontius Pilate,
was crucified, dead, and buried; he descended into hell; the third day
he arose again from the dead; he ascended into heaven and sits on
the right hand of God the Father Almighty; from thence he shall come
to judge the quick and the dead.*

I believe in the Holy Spirit, the holy catholic church, the communion
of saints, the forgiveness of sins, the resurrection of the body, and the
life everlasting. Amen.*

* In the Apostles' and Nicene Creeds, the term catholic refers to the Church's
universality, through all ages and times, of all languages and peoples. It refers to no
particular tradition or denominational expression (e.g., as in Roman Catholic).

Prayers of Confession
Let us now confess our sins to God and receive mercy and
grace to help in our time of need.

Assurance of Pardon
Having faithfully confessed and renounced your sin, Christ
also has been faithful to forgive your sins and to purify you
from all unrighteousness. It is certain, that there is One who
has spoken to the Father in your defense, Jesus Christ, the
Righteous One who is the atoning sacrifice for our sins and
for the sins of the whole world. His grace and peace are with
you now. Amen.

Petitions and Supplications, Ending with the Lord's Prayer
Our Father which art in heaven, Hallowed be thy name. Thy kingdom come, Thy will be done in earth, as it is in heaven. Give us this day our daily bread. And forgive us our debts, as we forgive our debtors. And lead us not into temptation, but deliver us from evil: For thine is the kingdom, and the power, and the glory, for ever. Amen.

~ Matthew 6.9-13 (KJV)

Doxology (and/or closing song)
Praise God from whom all blessings flow;
Praise Him all creatures here below;
Praise Him above ye heavenly host;
Praise Father, Son and Holy Ghost. Amen.

DEPARTING TO SERVE

Benediction
Lord Jesus Christ, our great high priest, who offered yourself without blemish to God in the great tabernacle above, thank you for your cleansing and healing blood. Through that blood the new covenant has come to us, and we are transformed through it, justified before God because of it, and will never come under wrath by its great sanctifying power. Your precious blood has set us free. May all praise be to you, dear Priest of God, for you have offered yourself to God for us, and now we are whole. In your name we offer you thanks, amen.

Affirmation from the Psalms
As for man, his days are like grass; he flourishes like a flower of the field; [16] for the wind passes over it, and it is gone, and its place knows it no more. [17] But the steadfast love of the Lord is from everlasting to everlasting on those who fear him, and his righteousness to children's children, [18] to those who keep his covenant and remember to do his commandments. [19] The Lord has established his throne in the heavens, and his kingdom rules over all.

~ Psalm 103.15-19

Pray without Ceasing – Flash Prayer for the Day
Lord Jesus Christ, Your blood is the cleansing stream that has brought me back to God.

For Your Weekly Journey

Let God Arise! Seasonal Focus
The Blood of Christ, Hebrews 9.11-15

Book Reading
Hamilton, *The Call, the Life and Message of the Apostle Paul*

Tuesday of Holy Week
March 22, 2016

Holy Week recalls the events of our Lord's suffering and death. We recall his triumphant entry into Jerusalem on Palm Sunday, his giving of the commandments on Maundy Thursday, his crucifixion and burial on Good Friday, and the solemn vigil of Saturday night before Easter Sunday.

TODAY'S THEME
But If It Dies, John 12.20-36

On the occasion of Jesus' final Passover visit to Jerusalem, some Greeks also went up to worship at the feast. These came to Philip, a disciple from Bethsaida in Galilee, asking him if they could see Jesus. Philip told Andrew and both of them went and told Jesus.

Jesus' answer to them expresses the heart of his suffering and sacrifice for the world. He said, "The hour has come for the Son of Man to be glorified. Truly, truly, I say to you, unless a grain of wheat falls into the earth and dies, it remains alone; but if it dies, it bears much fruit. Whoever loves his life loses it, and whoever hates his life in this world will keep it for eternal life. If anyone serves me, he must follow me; and where I am, there will my servant be also. If anyone serves me, the Father will honor him."

Jesus gave this word when his soul was deeply troubled. He did not seek deliverance from this fateful hour, but affirmed that it was for this very purpose, for this very hour, that he came into the world. His one desire was that the Father would glorify his name. Indeed, Jesus is the grain of wheat that fell into the earth and died, that refused to save himself, to remain alone. Because he was willing to die, to give up his life for the world, God was able to bear much fruit. Now, those who love their lives will lose them, and those who hate their lives in this world will keep them for eternal life.

Let us all now acknowledge and be shaped by the pattern of the risen Lord. Only in death can there be life. Only if we die can we live. Only if we sacrifice ourselves can others live. Let us never forget: if anyone serves the Lord, the Father himself will bestow honor upon him/her.

Daily Devotional Guide

PREPARING OUR HEARTS

Invocation: Our Prayer of Acclamation
Eternal God, you have so determined that unless a grain of wheat falls into the earth and dies, it will remain alone. However, if the grain dies, it will bear much fruit. Thank you, Father, that you allowed your Son to be that grain on behalf of the world. Through his death, a remnant of humankind will live forever. Make that pattern come alive in our lives in order that as we die, so others might live.

Call to Worship
Blessed are you, O God: Father, Son, and Holy Spirit. And blessed is your Kingdom, both now and forever, amen.

PRAISING OUR GOD

Te Deum Laudamus
You are God: we praise you; you are the Lord; we acclaim you; you are the eternal Father: All creation worships you. To you all angels, all the powers of heaven, Cherubim and Seraphim, sing in endless praise: Holy, holy, holy Lord, God of power and might, heaven and earth are full of your glory.

The glorious company of apostles praise you. The noble fellowship of prophets praise you. The white-robed army of martyrs praise you. Throughout the world the holy Church acclaims you; Father, of majesty unbounded, your true and only Son, worthy of all worship, and the Holy Spirit, advocate and guide.

You, Christ, are the king of glory, the eternal Son of the Father. When you became man to set us free you did not shun the Virgin's womb. You overcame the sting of death and opened the kingdom of heaven to all believers. You are seated at God's right hand in glory. We believe that you will come and be our judge. Come then, Lord, and help your people, bought with the price of your own blood, and bring us with your saints to glory everlasting.

Praise and Thanksgiving (Songs and Prayers)

Gloria Patri
Glory be to the Father,
And to the Son and to the Holy Spirit:
As it was in the beginning,
Is now, and ever shall be,
World without end. Amen, amen.

LISTENING TO HIS VOICE

Chronological Reading for the Day
2 Sam. 9-10; 1 Chron. 6.16-48, vv.50-53; ch.19

Chronological Holy Week Readings
Tuesday of Holy Week: Matt. 21.20-26.13; Mark 11.20-13.37; Luke 20-21

Lectionary Readings
Psalm: Ps. 71.1-14   *OT:* Isa. 49.1-7
Gospel: John 12.20-36   *NT:* 1 Cor. 1.18-31

Reflection: Silence and/or Journaling

RESPONDING IN FAITH

The Apostles' Creed
*I believe in God, the Father Almighty, Maker of heaven and earth;
and in Jesus Christ, his only Son, our Lord, who was conceived by the
Holy Spirit, born of the Virgin Mary, suffered under Pontius Pilate,
was crucified, dead, and buried; he descended into hell; the third day
he arose again from the dead; he ascended into heaven and sits on
the right hand of God the Father Almighty; from thence he shall come
to judge the quick and the dead.*

I believe in the Holy Spirit, the holy catholic church, the communion
of saints, the forgiveness of sins, the resurrection of the body, and the
life everlasting. Amen.*

* In the Apostles' and Nicene Creeds, the term catholic refers to the Church's
universality, through all ages and times, of all languages and peoples. It refers to no
particular tradition or denominational expression (e.g., as in Roman Catholic).

Prayers of Confession
Let us now confess our sins to God and receive mercy and
grace to help in our time of need.

Assurance of Pardon
Having faithfully confessed and renounced your sin, Christ
also has been faithful to forgive your sins and to purify you
from all unrighteousness. It is certain, that there is One who
has spoken to the Father in your defense, Jesus Christ, the
Righteous One who is the atoning sacrifice for our sins and
for the sins of the whole world. His grace and peace are with
you now. Amen.

Petitions and Supplications, Ending with the Lord's Prayer
Our Father which art in heaven, Hallowed be thy name. Thy kingdom come, Thy will be done in earth, as it is in heaven. Give us this day our daily bread. And forgive us our debts, as we forgive our debtors. And lead us not into temptation, but deliver us from evil: For thine is the kingdom, and the power, and the glory, for ever. Amen.

~ Matthew 6.9-13 (KJV)

Doxology (and/or closing song)
Praise God from whom all blessings flow;
Praise Him all creatures here below;
Praise Him above ye heavenly host;
Praise Father, Son and Holy Ghost. Amen.

Departing to Serve

Benediction
Lord Jesus Christ, in your hour of suffering and trouble, you affirmed the truth that only through death can life be given. Thank you, dear Savior, for the wondrous grace and love you displayed in your willingness to lay down your life for the world. For the sake of the Father's glory, for the rescue of your people, you laid it all down. Now, form that heart in us, that we might lose our lives to gain them, and hate our lives in this world to keep them for eternal life. In your name we pray, amen.

Affirmation from the Psalms
O Lord, make me know my end and what is the measure of my days; let me know how fleeting I am! [5] Behold, you have made my days a few handbreadths, and my lifetime is as nothing before you. Surely all mankind stands as a mere breath! Selah [6] Surely a man goes about as a shadow! Surely for nothing they are in turmoil; man heaps up wealth and does not know who will gather! [7] And now, O Lord, for what do I wait? My hope is in you.

~ Psalm 39.4-7

Pray without Ceasing – Flash Prayer for the Day
Lord Jesus Christ, make us the grain of wheat that falls into the earth and dies – bear much fruit through us as we follow your pattern of sacrifice and love.

For Your Weekly Journey

Let God Arise! Seasonal Focus
The Blood of Christ, Hebrews 9.11-15

Book Reading
Hamilton, *The Call, the Life and Message of the Apostle Paul*

Wednesday of Holy Week

March 23, 2016

Holy Week recalls the events of our Lord's suffering and death. We recall his triumphant entry into Jerusalem on Palm Sunday, his giving of the commandments on Maundy Thursday, his crucifixion and burial on Good Friday, and the solemn vigil of Saturday night before Easter Sunday.

TODAY'S THEME
The Lord Has Opened My Ear, Isaiah 50.4-9a

During this Passion week, we recall that the suffering of Messiah was foretold in the prophetic Scriptures. Isaiah 50 provides a powerful sketch of the Messiah's openness to God in the midst of suffering and persecution. Through this text, we come to better understand what our Lord Jesus would endure before his betrayers and accusers.

In Isaiah's prophecy, the Messiah declares that the Lord God has given him the tongue of those who are taught, that he might know how to sustain with a word the one who is weary. Morning by morning the Lord awakens him, awakening his ear to hear as those who are taught. The Messiah says that the Lord God opened his ear, and he was not rebellious; he did not turn backward. He gave his back to those who strike, and his cheeks to those who pull out the beard; he hid not his face from disgrace and spitting.

However, through it all the Messiah says that the Lord God helps him; therefore he has not been disgraced; therefore he, the Christ, has set his face like a flint, and he knows that he will not be put to shame. The Lord who vindicates him is near. Who then, he says, will contend with me? Let us stand up together. Who is my adversary? Let him come near to me. In final affirmation, the Messiah says "Behold, the Lord God helps me; who will declare me guilty? Behold, all of them will wear out like a garment; the moth will eat them up." The Messiah followed the prompting of the Lord till the end. In the face of opposition, persecution, and shame, our Messiah was obedient till death. May his followers do the same.

Daily Devotional Guide

PREPARING OUR HEARTS

Invocation: Our Prayer of Acclamation
Eternal Father, thank you that you provided our Messiah, the Lord Jesus Christ, with the "tongue of those who are taught;" he knew precisely what to say, to whom, about what subject, as you led him. You awakened him morning by morning and caused him to hear. His ear was opened and not rebellious. He obeyed your Word and never turned back. Reproduce that life and spirit in us, his followers, and cause us to glorify you, even as he did while on earth. In his name, amen.

Call to Worship
Blessed are you, O God: Father, Son, and Holy Spirit. And blessed is your Kingdom, both now and forever, amen.

PRAISING OUR GOD

Te Deum Laudamus
You are God: we praise you; you are the Lord; we acclaim you; you are the eternal Father: All creation worships you. To you all angels, all the powers of heaven, Cherubim and Seraphim, sing in endless praise: Holy, holy, holy Lord, God of power and might, heaven and earth are full of your glory.

The glorious company of apostles praise you. The noble fellowship of prophets praise you. The white-robed army of martyrs praise you. Throughout the world the holy Church acclaims you; Father, of majesty unbounded, your true and only Son, worthy of all worship, and the Holy Spirit, advocate and guide.

You, Christ, are the king of glory, the eternal Son of the Father. When you became man to set us free you did not shun the Virgin's womb. You overcame the sting of death and opened the kingdom of heaven to all believers. You are seated at God's right hand in glory. We believe that you will come and be our judge. Come then, Lord, and help your people, bought with the price of your own blood, and bring us with your saints to glory everlasting.

Praise and Thanksgiving (Songs and Prayers)

Gloria Patri
Glory be to the Father,
And to the Son and to the Holy Spirit:
As it was in the beginning,
Is now, and ever shall be,
World without end. Amen, amen.

LISTENING TO HIS VOICE

Chronological Reading for the Day
1 Chron. 3.5-9; 14.3-7; 20.1-3; 2 Sam. 11.1-12.25; 5.14-16; Ps. 51

Chronological Holy Week Readings
Wednesday of Holy Week: Matt. 26.1-16; Mark 14.1-2, 10-11; Luke 22.1-6

Lectionary Readings
Psalm: Ps. 70   OT: Isa. 50.4-9a
Gospel: John 13.21-32   NT: Heb. 12.1-3

Reflection: Silence and/or Journaling

RESPONDING IN FAITH

The Apostles' Creed
I believe in God, the Father Almighty, Maker of heaven and earth; and in Jesus Christ, his only Son, our Lord, who was conceived by the Holy Spirit, born of the Virgin Mary, suffered under Pontius Pilate, was crucified, dead, and buried; he descended into hell; the third day he arose again from the dead; he ascended into heaven and sits on the right hand of God the Father Almighty; from thence he shall come to judge the quick and the dead.

I believe in the Holy Spirit, the holy catholic* church, the communion of saints, the forgiveness of sins, the resurrection of the body, and the life everlasting. Amen.

* In the Apostles' and Nicene Creeds, the term catholic refers to the Church's universality, through all ages and times, of all languages and peoples. It refers to no particular tradition or denominational expression (e.g., as in Roman Catholic).

Prayers of Confession
Let us now confess our sins to God and receive mercy and grace to help in our time of need.

Assurance of Pardon
Having faithfully confessed and renounced your sin, Christ also has been faithful to forgive your sins and to purify you from all unrighteousness. It is certain, that there is One who has spoken to the Father in your defense, Jesus Christ, the Righteous One who is the atoning sacrifice for our sins and for the sins of the whole world. His grace and peace are with you now. Amen.

Petitions and Supplications, Ending with the Lord's Prayer
Our Father which art in heaven, Hallowed be thy name. Thy kingdom
come, Thy will be done in earth, as it is in heaven. Give us this day our
daily bread. And forgive us our debts, as we forgive our debtors. And
lead us not into temptation, but deliver us from evil: For thine is the
kingdom, and the power, and the glory, for ever. Amen.

~ Matthew 6.9-13 (KJV)

Doxology (and/or closing song)
Praise God from whom all blessings flow;
Praise Him all creatures here below;
Praise Him above ye heavenly host;
Praise Father, Son and Holy Ghost. Amen.

DEPARTING TO SERVE

Benediction
Lord Jesus Christ, whose ear was opened, whose heart was
free, and whose will was given to the Father, you obeyed his
Word in all things. You never turned backward or resisted
his will; you were your Father's Son, our Champion who
completed his will in all things. Now, through your Spirit
form your great heart in ours, making us submissive and
open to your will and way in all we do and say. For your
sake, amen.

Affirmation from the Psalms
O God, you are my God; earnestly I seek you; my soul thirsts for you;
my flesh faints for you, as in a dry and weary land where there is no
water. [2] So I have looked upon you in the sanctuary, beholding your
power and glory. [3] Because your steadfast love is better than life,
my lips will praise you. [4] So I will bless you as long as I live; in your
name I will lift up my hands.

~ Psalm 63.1-4

Pray without Ceasing – Flash Prayer for the Day
Lord Jesus Christ, open our ears, and help us to never rebel against your will; cause us to walk in your way, and never turn backward.

For Your Weekly Journey

Let God Arise! Seasonal Focus
The Blood of Christ, Hebrews 9.11-15

Book Reading
Hamilton, *The Call, the Life and Message of the Apostle Paul*

Maundy Thursday
March 24, 2016

Holy Week recalls the events of our Lord's suffering and death. We recall his triumphant entry into Jerusalem on Palm Sunday, his giving of the commandments on Maundy Thursday, his crucifixion and burial on Good Friday, and the solemn vigil of Saturday night before Easter Sunday.

TODAY'S THEME
A Servant Is Not Greater than His Master, John 13.1-17, 31b-35
Soon before the hour of our Lord's death, before the Feast of the Passover, Jesus knew that his hour had come to depart out of this world to the Father. He loved his own who were in the world, and he loved them to the end. During their last supper together, the devil had put it into Judas Iscariot's heart to betray him. Our Lord Jesus then knew fully that the Father had given all things into his hands, that he had come from God and was going back to God.

At this moment of understanding, Jesus arose from supper, laid aside his outer garments, took a towel, and tied it around his waist. He then poured water into a basin and began to wash the disciples' feet and to wipe them with the towel that was wrapped around him.

When he came to Simon Peter, Simon asked if the Lord would wash his feet. Jesus replied, that although he did not understand now what he did, he would afterwards. Peter then said, "You shall never wash my feet!" to which Jesus answered, "If I do not wash you, you have no share with me." On hearing this, Simon said not only his feet but also his hands and head! Jesus told him, "The one who has bathed does not need to wash, except for his feet, but is completely clean. And you are clean, but not every one of you." (In saying this, Jesus indicated that he knew who would betray him.)

After Jesus had washed their feet and put on his outer garments, he resumed his place. He then explained his actions. "Do you understand what I have done to you? You call me Teacher and Lord, and you are right, for so I am. If I then, your Lord and Teacher, have washed your feet, you also ought to wash one another's feet. For I have given you an example, that you also should do just as I have done to you. Truly, truly, I say to you, a servant is not greater than his master, nor is a messenger greater than the one who sent him. If you know these things, blessed are you if you do them."

A servant is not greater than his master. Our Lord has sacrificed for us; now, we must sacrifice for one another.

Daily Devotional Guide

PREPARING OUR HEARTS

Invocation: Our Prayer of Acclamation
Almighty Father, whose dear Son on the night before he suffered did institute the Sacrament of his Body and Blood: Mercifully grant that we may thankfully receive the same, in remembrance of him who in these holy mysteries giveth us a pledge of life eternal, the same thy Son Jesus Christ our Lord; who now liveth and reigneth with thee and the Holy Spirit, ever one God world without end. Amen.

~ *United States Prayer Book* (Suter, p. 18)

Call to Worship
Blessed are you, O God: Father, Son, and Holy Spirit. And blessed is your Kingdom, both now and forever, amen.

PRAISING OUR GOD

Te Deum Laudamus

You are God: we praise you; you are the Lord; we acclaim you; you are the eternal Father: All creation worships you. To you all angels, all the powers of heaven, Cherubim and Seraphim, sing in endless praise: Holy, holy, holy Lord, God of power and might, heaven and earth are full of your glory.

The glorious company of apostles praise you. The noble fellowship of prophets praise you. The white-robed army of martyrs praise you. Throughout the world the holy Church acclaims you; Father, of majesty unbounded, your true and only Son, worthy of all worship, and the Holy Spirit, advocate and guide.

You, Christ, are the king of glory, the eternal Son of the Father. When you became man to set us free you did not shun the Virgin's womb. You overcame the sting of death and opened the kingdom of heaven to all believers. You are seated at God's right hand in glory. We believe that you will come and be our judge. Come then, Lord, and help your people, bought with the price of your own blood, and bring us with your saints to glory everlasting.

Praise and Thanksgiving (Songs and Prayers)

Gloria Patri

Glory be to the Father,
And to the Son and to the Holy Spirit:
As it was in the beginning,
Is now, and ever shall be,
World without end. Amen, amen.

LISTENING TO HIS VOICE

Chronological Reading for the Day
2 Sam. 12.26-14.33

Chronological Holy Week Readings
Maundy Thursday: Matt. 26.17-75; Mark 14.12-42; Luke 22.7-65; John 13.1-18.27

Lectionary Readings
Psalm: Ps. 116.1-2, 12-19   *OT:* Exod. 12.1-14
Gospel: John 13.1-17, 31b-35   *NT:* 1 Cor. 11.23-26

Reflection: Silence and/or Journaling

RESPONDING IN FAITH

The Apostles' Creed
I believe in God, the Father Almighty, Maker of heaven and earth; and in Jesus Christ, his only Son, our Lord, who was conceived by the Holy Spirit, born of the Virgin Mary, suffered under Pontius Pilate, was crucified, dead, and buried; he descended into hell; the third day he arose again from the dead; he ascended into heaven and sits on the right hand of God the Father Almighty; from thence he shall come to judge the quick and the dead.

I believe in the Holy Spirit, the holy catholic* church, the communion of saints, the forgiveness of sins, the resurrection of the body, and the life everlasting. Amen.

* In the Apostles' and Nicene Creeds, the term catholic refers to the Church's universality, through all ages and times, of all languages and peoples. It refers to no particular tradition or denominational expression (e.g., as in Roman Catholic).

Prayers of Confession

Let us now confess our sins to God and receive mercy and grace to help in our time of need.

Assurance of Pardon

Having faithfully confessed and renounced your sin, Christ also has been faithful to forgive your sins and to purify you from all unrighteousness. It is certain, that there is One who has spoken to the Father in your defense, Jesus Christ, the Righteous One who is the atoning sacrifice for our sins and for the sins of the whole world. His grace and peace are with you now. Amen.

Petitions and Supplications, Ending with the Lord's Prayer

Our Father which art in heaven, Hallowed be thy name. Thy kingdom come, Thy will be done in earth, as it is in heaven. Give us this day our daily bread. And forgive us our debts, as we forgive our debtors. And lead us not into temptation, but deliver us from evil: For thine is the kingdom, and the power, and the glory, for ever. Amen.

~ Matthew 6.9-13 (KJV)

Doxology (and/or closing song)

Praise God from whom all blessings flow;
Praise Him all creatures here below;
Praise Him above ye heavenly host;
Praise Father, Son and Holy Ghost. Amen.

DEPARTING TO SERVE

Benediction

O LORD Jesus Christ, who in a wonderful Sacrament hast left unto us a memorial of thy passion: Grant us, we beseech thee, so to venerate the sacred mysteries of thy Body and Blood, that we may ever perceive within ourselves the fruit of thy redemption; who livest and reignest with the Father in the unity of the Holy Spirit, God forever and ever. Amen.

~ Scotland Prayer Book (Suter, p. 18)

Affirmation from the Psalms

But you, O Lord, do not be far off! O you my help, come quickly to my aid! [20] Deliver my soul from the sword, my precious life from the power of the dog! [21] Save me from the mouth of the lion! You have rescued me from the horns of the wild oxen! [22] I will tell of your name to my brothers; in the midst of the congregation I will praise you: [23] You who fear the Lord, praise him! All you offspring of Jacob, glorify him, and stand in awe of him, all you offspring of Israel!

~ Psalm 22.19-23

Pray without Ceasing – Flash Prayer for the Day

Lord Jesus Christ, the servant is not greater than the master. Cause us to wash the feet of our fellow disciples, even as you washed your apostles' feet.

For Your Weekly Journey

Let God Arise! Seasonal Focus

The Blood of Christ, Hebrews 9.11-15

Book Reading

Hamilton, *The Call, the Life and Message of the Apostle Paul*

Good Friday

March 25, 2016

Holy Week recalls the events of our Lord's suffering and death. We recall his triumphant entry into Jerusalem on Palm Sunday, his giving of the commandments on Maundy Thursday, his crucifixion and burial on Good Friday, and the solemn vigil of Saturday night before Easter Sunday.

TODAY'S THEME

Crushed for Our Iniquities, Isaiah 52.13-53.12

On this remembrance of the day of our Lord's death on the Cross, we recall the Isaiah prophecy in Isaiah 52-53 of Messiah's sacrifice for the nation. The picture of the Messiah in Isaiah is both graphic and terribly tragic, showing an innocent figure who would give us his life on behalf of God's people, and for humankind. The servant of Yahweh would act wisely, be high and lifted up, and exalted. Though through his suffering his appearance would be marred beyond human semblance, still his work would touch many nations.

This Savior would grow up like a young plant, and like a root out of dry ground. He would have no form or majesty that we should look at him, and possess no beauty that we should desire him. He would be despised and rejected by men, and be called a man of sorrows, being acquainted with grief. He would live as one from whom men hide their faces, he would be despised, and we would not esteem him. Surely he will bear our griefs and carry our sorrows, says the prophet, yet we would still esteem him stricken, smitten by God, and afflicted. This Savior would be pierced for our transgressions; he would be crushed for our iniquities; upon him would be the chastisement that brought us peace, and with his wounds we would be healed. All we like sheep have gone astray; we have turned – every one – to his own way; and the Lord has laid on this dear Savior, the iniquity of us all.

In his death on the tree, Jesus of Nazareth fulfilled the saying of Isaiah and the prophets regarding the redemption of Israel and the race of Adam. Although he would be mistreated, lied upon, and falsely accused, he would not open his mouth, as like a lamb that is led to the slaughter, or like a sheep that is before its shearers. Jesus, the Son of God, became a curse for us on the tree, in order that we might be redeemed through him.

Daily Devotional Guide

PREPARING OUR HEARTS

Invocation: Our Prayer of Acclamation
Merciful and Everlasting God, who hast not spared thine only Son, but delivered him up for us all that he might bear our sins upon the Cross, grant that our hearts may be so fixed with steadfast faith in him that we may not fear the power of any adversaries; through the same Jesus Christ our Lord. Amen.

~ The Book of English Collects, 1549 (Geffen, p. 81)

Call to Worship
Blessed are you, O God: Father, Son, and Holy Spirit. And blessed is your Kingdom, both now and forever, amen.

PRAISING OUR GOD

Te Deum Laudamus
You are God: we praise you; you are the Lord; we acclaim you; you are the eternal Father: All creation worships you. To you all angels, all the powers of heaven, Cherubim and Seraphim, sing in endless praise: Holy, holy, holy Lord, God of power and might, heaven and earth are full of your glory.

The glorious company of apostles praise you. The noble fellowship of prophets praise you. The white-robed army of martyrs praise you.

Throughout the world the holy Church acclaims you; Father, of majesty unbounded, your true and only Son, worthy of all worship, and the Holy Spirit, advocate and guide.

You, Christ, are the king of glory, the eternal Son of the Father. When you became man to set us free you did not shun the Virgin's womb. You overcame the sting of death and opened the kingdom of heaven to all believers. You are seated at God's right hand in glory. We believe that you will come and be our judge. Come then, Lord, and help your people, bought with the price of your own blood, and bring us with your saints to glory everlasting.

Praise and Thanksgiving (Songs and Prayers)

Gloria Patri
Glory be to the Father,
And to the Son and to the Holy Spirit:
As it was in the beginning,
Is now, and ever shall be,
World without end. Amen, amen.

LISTENING TO HIS VOICE

Chronological Reading for the Day
2 Sam. 15-17

Chronological Holy Week Readings
Good Friday: Matt. 27.1-61; Mark 15.1-47; Luke 22.66-23.56a; John 18.28-19.42

Lectionary Readings
Psalm: Ps. 22
Gospel: John 18.1-19.42

OT: Isa. 52.13-53.12
NT: Heb. 10.16-25

Reflection: Silence and/or Journaling

RESPONDING IN FAITH

The Apostles' Creed
I believe in God, the Father Almighty, Maker of heaven and earth;
and in Jesus Christ, his only Son, our Lord, who was conceived by the
Holy Spirit, born of the Virgin Mary, suffered under Pontius Pilate,
was crucified, dead, and buried; he descended into hell; the third day
he arose again from the dead; he ascended into heaven and sits on
the right hand of God the Father Almighty; from thence he shall come
to judge the quick and the dead.

I believe in the Holy Spirit, the holy catholic* church, the communion
of saints, the forgiveness of sins, the resurrection of the body, and the
life everlasting. Amen.

* In the Apostles' and Nicene Creeds, the term catholic refers to the Church's
universality, through all ages and times, of all languages and peoples. It refers to no
particular tradition or denominational expression (e.g., as in Roman Catholic).

Prayers of Confession
Let us now confess our sins to God and receive mercy and
grace to help in our time of need.

Assurance of Pardon
Having faithfully confessed and renounced your sin, Christ
also has been faithful to forgive your sins and to purify you
from all unrighteousness. It is certain, that there is One who
has spoken to the Father in your defense, Jesus Christ, the
Righteous One who is the atoning sacrifice for our sins and
for the sins of the whole world. His grace and peace are with
you now. Amen.

Petitions and Supplications, Ending with the Lord's Prayer

Our Father which art in heaven, Hallowed be thy name. Thy kingdom come, Thy will be done in earth, as it is in heaven. Give us this day our daily bread. And forgive us our debts, as we forgive our debtors. And lead us not into temptation, but deliver us from evil: For thine is the kingdom, and the power, and the glory, for ever. Amen.

~ Matthew 6.9-13 (KJV)

Doxology (and/or closing song)

Praise God from whom all blessings flow;
Praise Him all creatures here below;
Praise Him above ye heavenly host;
Praise Father, Son and Holy Ghost. Amen.

DEPARTING TO SERVE

Benediction

Almighty and everlasting God, by whose Spirit the whole body of the Church is governed and sanctified: Receive our supplications and prayers which we offer before thee for all estates of men in thy holy Church, that every member of the same, in his vocation and ministry, may truly and godly serve thee; through our Lord and Saviour Jesus Christ. Amen.

~ *England Prayer Book* (Suter, p. 19)

Affirmation from the Psalms

My God, my God, why have you forsaken me? Why are you so far from saving me, from the words of my groaning? [2] O my God, I cry by day, but you do not answer, and by night, but I find no rest. [3] Yet you are holy, enthroned on the praises of Israel. [4] In you our fathers trusted; they trusted, and you delivered them. [5] To you they cried and were rescued; in you they trusted and were not put to shame. [6] But I am a worm and not a man, scorned by mankind and despised by the people. [7] All who see me mock me; they make mouths at me; they wag their heads; [8] "He trusts in the Lord; let him deliver him; let him rescue him, for he delights in him!"

~ Psalm 22.1-8

Pray without Ceasing – Flash Prayer for the Day
Lord Jesus Christ, Savior of the world, all of us like sheep
have gone astray, every one of us has turned to his own way,
and the Father laid on you the iniquity of us all.

For Your Weekly Journey

Let God Arise! Seasonal Focus
The Blood of Christ, Hebrews 9.11-15

Book Reading
Hamilton, *The Call, the Life and Message of the Apostle Paul*

Holy Saturday

March 26, 2016

Holy Week recalls the events of our Lord's suffering and death. We recall his triumphant entry into Jerusalem on Palm Sunday, his giving of the commandments on Maundy Thursday, his crucifixion and burial on Good Friday, and the solemn vigil of Saturday night before Easter Sunday.

TODAY'S THEME

The Burial of Jesus, John 19.38-42

The evidence and biblical testimony regarding the death and burial of our Lord is clear. After the events of our Lord's trial, crucifixion, and death, Joseph of Arimathea, a secret disciple of Jesus because of the threat of Jewish persecution, went to Pilate and asked that he might take away the body of Jesus. Pilate granted Joseph permission to go and take Jesus' body. Nicodemus, the very one who had earlier come to Jesus by night, also came, and brought a mixture of myrrh and aloes, weighing around seventy-five pounds. Together, Joseph and Nicodemus came and took Jesus' body, and bound it in linen cloths with the spices, as is the manner of Jewish burial customs.

There was a garden in the place where Jesus was crucified, and in the garden a new tomb which had not been used yet. In light of the nearness of the Jewish day of Preparation, they laid Jesus in that tomb close by.

Daily Devotional Guide

PREPARING OUR HEARTS

Invocation: Our Prayer of Acclamation
Grant, O Lord, that as we are baptized into the death of thy blessed Son our Saviour Jesus Christ, so by continual mortifying our corrupt affections we may be buried with him; and that through the grave, and gate of death, we may pass to our joyful resurrection; for his merits who died, and was buried, and rose again for us, the same thy Son Jesus Christ our Lord. Amen.

~ United States Prayer Book (Suter, p. 20)

Call to Worship
Blessed are you, O God: Father, Son, and Holy Spirit. And blessed is your Kingdom, both now and forever, amen.

PRAISING OUR GOD

Te Deum Laudamus
You are God: we praise you; you are the Lord; we acclaim you; you are the eternal Father: All creation worships you. To you all angels, all the powers of heaven, Cherubim and Seraphim, sing in endless praise: Holy, holy, holy Lord, God of power and might, heaven and earth are full of your glory.

The glorious company of apostles praise you. The noble fellowship of prophets praise you. The white-robed army of martyrs praise you. Throughout the world the holy Church acclaims you; Father, of majesty unbounded, your true and only Son, worthy of all worship, and the Holy Spirit, advocate and guide.

You, Christ, are the king of glory, the eternal Son of the Father. When you became man to set us free you did not shun the Virgin's womb. You overcame the sting of death and opened the kingdom of heaven to all believers. You are seated at God's right hand in glory. We believe that you will come and be our judge. Come then, Lord, and help your people, bought with the price of your own blood, and bring us with your saints to glory everlasting.

Praise and Thanksgiving (Songs and Prayers)

Gloria Patri
Glory be to the Father,
And to the Son and to the Holy Spirit:
As it was in the beginning,
Is now, and ever shall be,
World without end. Amen, amen.

LISTENING TO HIS VOICE

Chronological Reading for the Day
2 Sam. 18-19; Pss. 3; 63

Chronological Holy Week Readings
Holy Saturday: Matt. 27.62-66; Luke 23.56b

Lectionary Readings
Psalm: Ps. 31.1-4, 15-16   *OT:* Lam. 3.1-9, 19-24
Gospel: John 19.38-42   *NT:* 1 Pet. 4.1-8

Easter Vigil Readings
- Gen. 1.1-2.4a; Ps. 136.1-9, 23-26
- Gen. 7.1-5, 11-18; 8.6-18; 9.8-13; Ps. 46
- Gen. 22.1-18; Ps. 16
- Exod. 14.10-31; 15.20-21; 15.1b-13, 17-18
- Isa. 55.1-11; 12.2-6
- Prov. 8.1-8, 19-21; 9.4b-6; Ps. 19
- Ezek. 36.24-28; Ps. 42, 43

- Ezek. 37.1-14; Ps. 143
- Zeph. 3.14-20; Ps. 98
- Rom. 6.3-11; Ps. 114
- Luke 24.1-12

Reflection: Silence and/or Journaling

RESPONDING IN FAITH

The Apostles' Creed
I believe in God, the Father Almighty, Maker of heaven and earth; and in Jesus Christ, his only Son, our Lord, who was conceived by the Holy Spirit, born of the Virgin Mary, suffered under Pontius Pilate, was crucified, dead, and buried; he descended into hell; the third day he arose again from the dead; he ascended into heaven and sits on the right hand of God the Father Almighty; from thence he shall come to judge the quick and the dead.

I believe in the Holy Spirit, the holy catholic* church, the communion of saints, the forgiveness of sins, the resurrection of the body, and the life everlasting. Amen.

* In the Apostles' and Nicene Creeds, the term catholic refers to the Church's universality, through all ages and times, of all languages and peoples. It refers to no particular tradition or denominational expression (e.g., as in Roman Catholic).

Prayers of Confession
Let us now confess our sins to God and receive mercy and grace to help in our time of need.

Assurance of Pardon
Having faithfully confessed and renounced your sin, Christ also has been faithful to forgive your sins and to purify you from all unrighteousness. It is certain, that there is One who has spoken to the Father in your defense, Jesus Christ, the Righteous One who is the atoning sacrifice for our sins and for the sins of the whole world. His grace and peace are with you now. Amen.

Petitions and Supplications, Ending with the Lord's Prayer

Our Father which art in heaven, Hallowed be thy name. Thy kingdom come, Thy will be done in earth, as it is in heaven. Give us this day our daily bread. And forgive us our debts, as we forgive our debtors. And lead us not into temptation, but deliver us from evil: For thine is the kingdom, and the power, and the glory, for ever. Amen.

~ Matthew 6.9-13 (KJV)

Doxology (and/or closing song)

Praise God from whom all blessings flow;
Praise Him all creatures here below;
Praise Him above ye heavenly host;
Praise Father, Son and Holy Ghost. Amen.

DEPARTING TO SERVE

Benediction

Almighty God, Who, of Thy great love to man, didst give Thy dearly beloved Son to die for us upon the cross as at this time, grant us grace ever to bear in mind His most precious sufferings and death, and to deny ourselves and to take up our cross and follow Him. May we die unto sin, and crucify the flesh in our Redeemer and a thankful remembrance of His death. Help us to love Him better for His exceeding love to us, and grant that our sins may be put away, and nailed to the cross, and buried in His grave, that they may be remembered no more against us; through the same, Thy Son, Jesus Christ our Lord. Amen.

~ Bishop Walsham How, 1823 (Fox, p. 225)

Affirmation from the Psalms

Man in his pomp will not remain; he is like the beasts that perish. [13] This is the path of those who have foolish confidence; yet after them people approve of their boasts. Selah [14] Like sheep they are appointed for Sheol; death shall be their shepherd, and the upright shall rule over them in the morning. Their form shall be consumed in Sheol, with no place to dwell. [15] But God will ransom my soul from the power of Sheol, for he will receive me. Selah.

~ Psalm 49.12-15

Pray without Ceasing – Flash Prayer for the Day
Lord Jesus Christ, you have conquered death and will ransom my soul from the power of Sheol, for you will receive me.

For Your Weekly Journey

Let God Arise! Seasonal Focus
The Blood of Christ, Hebrews 9.11-15

Book Reading
Hamilton, *The Call, the Life and Message of the Apostle Paul*

The Season from Easter to Pentecost

THE RESURRECTION OF CHRIST

And we all, with unveiled face,
beholding the glory of the Lord,
are being transformed into the same image
from one degree of glory to another.
For this comes from the Lord
who is the Spirit.

2 CORINTHIANS 3.18

The Tomb Is Empty, and the Lord Lives!

The exclamation "Christ is risen! He is risen, indeed!" is as old as the Church itself. It testifies to the central, controlling belief of believers in Jesus of Nazareth worldwide as they celebrate his victory over the grave in his bodily resurrection from the dead. As was prophesied in Scripture, and foreseen by our Lord himself, he suffered on the Tree bearing our sins in his body and overcoming the guilt and power of the grave and the curse. Yet, on the third day down he rose triumphant from the grave, and is alive now forevermore! His resurrection serves as the pinnacle of all Christian belief, and is itself the ground for all biblical revelation on the redemption won for us through the Father's love.

The apostles taught that the resurrection of Jesus represents the central doctrine in all Christian faith and belief. Paul told the Corinthians that if the resurrection did not occur, then not even Christ has been raised, their apostolic preaching was worthless, and their faith would be futile. The apostles themselves would be found to be misrepresenting God, having borne witness that Christ has risen, when he did not (1 Cor. 15.12-15).

The Resurrection as the Centerpiece of Our Doctrine and the Heart of Christian Faith

The fact is, however, that Jesus did not simply teach the resurrection; he claimed to be, in fact, the Resurrection and the Life itself (John 11.25-26)! As such, his rising confirms God's veracity and truthfulness, authenticating the testimony of the Scriptures. From its earliest worship, the Church made the resurrection the centerpiece of its worship and community. As the living Savior he is with us to the end of this age (Matt. 28.20). Even his "going away" (in suffering and death) did not prevent him from coming to us again in his resurrected glory, leading to his gift of the Holy Spirit to all believers (John 14.28). By faith we died with him, have been made alive together with him, are raised with him through baptism, and even have ascended and sit with him in heavenly places (Rom. 6.1-4; Eph. 2.5).

Clearly, it is in Jesus' resurrection that *Christus Victor* becomes most convincing (Gal. 1.4; Col. 2.15; 1 John 4.40). In the person of Jesus Christ, and through his resurrection, the Age to Come has broken into this present age, with our Lord becoming the firstfruits of those who sleep. Christ is the first fruits of the eschatological harvest of souls destined to live in the fully consummated Age to come (1 Cor. 15.20). Moreover, he is the "firstborn" from among the dead, i.e., the primary one, the preeminent one, and the pattern of all who with him will rise from the dead and inherit eternal life in the new heavens and earth (Col. 1.18; Rev. 1.5-6). By the power of his resurrection, God has birthed us to a living hope, rooted in God's mercy and an inheritance that will never perish or fade away (1 Pet. 1.3-5).

Surely then, it makes sense that the early Church chose *Easter* as the singular event to welcome new converts into the Church, to restore backsliders and penitents, and to convocate in joyous gatherings of remembrance and worship. Christ's resurrection does not merely guarantee the life of the Age to Come for a future time; rather, it provides us with hope, power, and confidence to live a new life today, right here, right now in him. Truly, if anyone is in Christ, s/he is a new creation. The old has passed away; behold, the new has come (2 Cor. 5.17).

He Is Risen, Indeed!

Come, celebrate this Easter season with glad shouts of victory and honor to Jesus, our risen Lord! His resurrection serves as the absolute proof of the coming consummation of the plan of God, the coming resurrection of the dead, the gift of the Holy Spirit, and the promise of eternal life for those who believe. Let us gladly stir up pure longings for his return, and the end of this present fleeting age of darkness and sin. Join us in confessing that Jesus is Lord, and that God has raised him from the dead. This same Jesus of Nazareth, who was crucified and killed by lawless men is no longer dead. God has raised him up as victorious conqueror, and being loosed from the chains of death, he can secure all who believe by the same power. Because he lives, we can live today and face tomorrow.

"Christ is risen! He is risen, indeed!"

Rev. Dr. Don L. Davis

Easter Sunday, Resurrection of the Lord

WEEK 18

March 27 - April 2, 2016

On Easter Sunday we celebrate the bodily resurrection of Jesus. The same lowly Nazarene – he who was betrayed by his own disciple, who suffered under Pilate's cruel gaze, who was crucified on a Roman cross, and who was buried in a borrowed tomb – the same Lord rose triumphantly on the third day. Jesus has risen from death to life through the power of God. "Christ is risen! He is risen, indeed!"

THIS WEEK'S THEME
"I Have Seen the Lord," John 20.1-18

On the first day of the week, Mary Magdalene came to the tomb early, while it was still dark, and saw that the stone had been taken from the tomb. Mary ran and told Simon Peter and John that someone had taken the Lord from the tomb, and "we do not know where he is laid." They ran to the tomb, saw the linen cloths lying there and the face cloths, and returned to their homes, not yet understanding the Scriptures regarding Jesus' resurrection.

Mary, however, stood weeping outside the tomb. As she cried, she stooped to look into the tomb, and saw two angels in white, sitting where Jesus' body lay, one at the head and the other at the feet. They asked her why she wept, and she replied that they have taken away her Lord and she did not know where they laid him. On saying this, she turned around and saw Jesus standing there. He asked her why she wept, and supposing him to be the gardener, she said "if you have carried him away, tell me where he is now and I will take him away."

At that moment, Jesus said to her, "Mary." Mary turned and said to the Lord in Aramaic, "Rabboni!" (which means Teacher). Jesus said to her, "Do not cling to me, for I have not yet ascended to the Father; but go to my brothers and say to them, 'I am ascending to my Father and your Father, to my God and your God.'"

On hearing this from Jesus, Mary went and announced to the disciples, "I have seen the Lord" – and that he had said these things to her. In the simplest language possible, Mary Magdalene testified to the disciples the foundational truth of Christian belief. As an eyewitness of the risen Christ, her statement, along with the apostles' witness, would form the heart of Christian confession and standard of Christian faith – "I have seen the Lord." Christ is risen, he is risen, indeed!

Daily Devotional Guide

PREPARING OUR HEARTS

Invocation: Our Prayer of Acclamation
O God, you gave your only Son to suffer death on the cross for our redemption, and by his glorious resurrection you delivered us from the power of death. Make us die every day to sin, that we may live with him forever in the joy of the resurrection, through your Son, Jesus Christ our Lord, who lives and reigns with you and the Holy Spirit, one God, now and forever. Amen.

~ Evangelical Lutheran Worship
(Conference of Bishops, Evangelical Lutheran Church in America, p. 91)

Call to Worship
Blessed are you, O God: Father, Son, and Holy Spirit. And blessed is your Kingdom, both now and forever, amen.

PRAISING OUR GOD

Te Deum Laudamus
You are God: we praise you; you are the Lord; we acclaim you; you are the eternal Father: All creation worships you. To you all angels, all the powers of heaven, Cherubim and Seraphim, sing in endless praise:

Holy, holy, holy Lord, God of power and might, heaven and earth are full of your glory.

The glorious company of apostles praise you. The noble fellowship of prophets praise you. The white-robed army of martyrs praise you. Throughout the world the holy Church acclaims you; Father, of majesty unbounded, your true and only Son, worthy of all worship, and the Holy Spirit, advocate and guide.

You, Christ, are the king of glory, the eternal Son of the Father. When you became man to set us free you did not shun the Virgin's womb. You overcame the sting of death and opened the kingdom of heaven to all believers. You are seated at God's right hand in glory. We believe that you will come and be our judge. Come then, Lord, and help your people, bought with the price of your own blood, and bring us with your saints to glory everlasting.

Praise and Thanksgiving (Songs and Prayers)

Gloria Patri
Glory be to the Father,
And to the Son and to the Holy Spirit:
As it was in the beginning,
Is now, and ever shall be,
World without end. Amen, amen.

LISTENING TO HIS VOICE

Chronological Reading for the Day
Sunday: 2 Sam. 20-21; Ps. 7; 1 Chron. 20.4-8
Monday: 2 Sam. 22; Ps. 18
Tuesday: 2 Sam. 24; 1 Chron. 21-22
Wednesday: 1 Chron. 23-25
Thursday: 1 Chron. 26-28
Friday: 1 Chron. 29.1-22; 1 Kings 1
Saturday: 1 Kings 2.1-12; 2 Sam. 23.1-7; 1 Chron. 29.26-30; Pss. 4-6; 8; 9; 11

Chronological Holy Week Readings

Easter Sunday: Mark 16.1-20; Luke 24.1-53; John 20.1-25

Lectionary Readings for *Easter Morning*

Psalm: Ps. 118.1-2, 14-24 *OT:* *Acts 10.34-43
Gospel: John 20.1-18 *NT:* 1 Cor. 15.19-26

* During Eastertide, a reading from Acts is often sustituted for the lesson from the Hebrew Bible.

Lectionary Readings for *Easter Evening*

Psalm: Ps. 114 *OT:* Isa. 25.6-9
Gospel: Luke 24.13-49 *NT:* 1 Cor. 5.6b-8

Reflection: Silence and/or Journaling

RESPONDING IN FAITH

The Apostles' Creed

I believe in God, the Father Almighty, Maker of heaven and earth; and in Jesus Christ, his only Son, our Lord, who was conceived by the Holy Spirit, born of the Virgin Mary, suffered under Pontius Pilate, was crucified, dead, and buried; he descended into hell; the third day he arose again from the dead; he ascended into heaven and sits on the right hand of God the Father Almighty; from thence he shall come to judge the quick and the dead.

I believe in the Holy Spirit, the holy catholic* church, the communion of saints, the forgiveness of sins, the resurrection of the body, and the life everlasting. Amen.

* In the Apostles' and Nicene Creeds, the term catholic refers to the Church's universality, through all ages and times, of all languages and peoples. It refers to no particular tradition or denominational expression (e.g., as in Roman Catholic).

Prayers of Confession

Let us now confess our sins to God and receive mercy and grace to help in our time of need.

Assurance of Pardon
Having faithfully confessed and renounced your sin, Christ also has been faithful to forgive your sins and to purify you from all unrighteousness. It is certain, that there is One who has spoken to the Father in your defense, Jesus Christ, the Righteous One who is the atoning sacrifice for our sins and for the sins of the whole world. His grace and peace are with you now. Amen.

Petitions and Supplications, Ending with the Lord's Prayer
Our Father which art in heaven, Hallowed be thy name. Thy kingdom come, Thy will be done in earth, as it is in heaven. Give us this day our daily bread. And forgive us our debts, as we forgive our debtors. And lead us not into temptation, but deliver us from evil: For thine is the kingdom, and the power, and the glory, for ever. Amen.

~ Matthew 6.9-13 (KJV)

Doxology (and/or closing song)
Praise God from whom all blessings flow;
Praise Him all creatures here below;
Praise Him above ye heavenly host;
Praise Father, Son and Holy Ghost. Amen.

DEPARTING TO SERVE

Benediction
Almighty God, who through thine only-begotten Son, Jesus Christ, hast overcome death and opened unto us the gate of everlasting life, we humbly beseech thee that, as thou dost put into our minds good desires, so by thy continual help we may bring the same to good effect; through the same Jesus Christ our Lord. Amen.

~ *The Sermon and the Propers*, Vol. 2 (Geffen, p. 82)

Affirmation from the Psalms

I bless the Lord who gives me counsel; in the night also my heart instructs me. [8] I have set the Lord always before me; because he is at my right hand, I shall not be shaken. [9] Therefore my heart is glad, and my whole being rejoices; my flesh also dwells secure. [10] For you will not abandon my soul to Sheol, or let your holy one see corruption. [11] You make known to me the path of life; in your presence there is fullness of joy; at your right hand are pleasures forevermore.

~ Psalm 16.7-11

Pray without Ceasing – Flash Prayer for the Day

Lord Jesus Christ, you are risen, back from the dead, alive evermore. You are risen! You are risen, indeed!

For Your Weekly Journey

Let God Arise! Seasonal Focus

Salvation Belongs to Our God, Revelation 7.9-17

Book Reading

Hamilton, *The Call, the Life and Message of the Apostle Paul*

Our Corporate Disciplines

Book Discussion: Monday, March 28, 2016

Second Sunday of Easter
April 3 - 9, 2016

On Easter Sunday we celebrate the bodily resurrection of Jesus. The same lowly Nazarene – he who was betrayed by his own disciple, who suffered under Pilate's cruel gaze, who was crucified on a Roman cross, and who was buried in a borrowed tomb – the same Lord rose triumphantly on the third day. Jesus has risen from death to life through the power of God. "Christ is risen! He is risen, indeed!"

THIS WEEK'S THEME
Jesus Christ, the Faithful Witness, Revelation 1.4-8

On the isle of Patmos, the apostle John wrote to the seven churches that were then in the region referred to as "Asia." His mission would be to tell the churches of the events and conditions of the coming of the Lord. In his opening of his book, he saluted them with prayers of grace and peace from the Father, "the one who is and who was and who is to come." He also greeted them from the Holy Spirit, to whom he referred to as "the seven spirits who are before his throne." Finally, he referred to our Master and Lord, greeting them "Jesus Christ the faithful witness, the firstborn of the dead, and the ruler of kings on earth." This simple greeting provides great insight into the persons of the Trinity, and foreshadows how each member would be depicted in the book, as the revelation is unveiled.

In a doxological statement of praise, John gives honor "to him who loves us and has freed us from our sins by his blood and made us a kingdom, priests to his God and Father, to him be glory and dominion forever and ever. Amen." John then declares plainly the hope and glory of every Christian's heart: the coming of the Lord Jesus to earth. "Behold, he is coming with the clouds, and every eye will see him, even those who pierced him, and all tribes of the earth will wail on account of him. Even so. Amen."

Finally in this paragraph, John quotes the Lord's own affirmation of himself, the Source of our lives and all things. "I am the Alpha and the Omega," says the Lord God, "who is and who was and who is to come, the Almighty."

In such a theologically rich section, it is not surprising the intriguing picture we receive of our Lord Jesus. He is the Faithful Witness, the firstborn (head, highest) of the dead, and the ruler of the kings on earth. His Word is inviolate for he is the one person who has absolute firsthand knowledge of the Father himself. His witness regarding all things is true in the fullest and most comprehensive sense; nothing that he has spoken to can be altered or changed. His testimony regarding all things is foundational, reliable, and unchanging. You can trust him for his witness is true, and it is good.

Daily Devotional Guide

PREPARING OUR HEARTS

Invocation: Our Prayer of Acclamation
God and Father of our Lord Jesus Christ, thank you for the gift of your Son, who is the Faithful Witness, he who cannot lie, whose Word is absolutely reliable, and whose wisdom has neither bounds nor errors. Your supply of Jesus to us reveals your own love for the truth, and your gift of the Spirit shows us your desire that we live in the truth. Jesus of Nazareth is the Truth, and his Word is true. Reveal to us his heart of truth, and teach us to depend on his faithful testimony, he who reigns with you and the Holy Spirit, one God, in Jesus' name.

Call to Worship
Blessed are you, O God: Father, Son, and Holy Spirit. And blessed is your Kingdom, both now and forever, amen.

PRAISING OUR GOD

Te Deum Laudamus

You are God: we praise you; you are the Lord; we acclaim you; you are the eternal Father: All creation worships you. To you all angels, all the powers of heaven, Cherubim and Seraphim, sing in endless praise: Holy, holy, holy Lord, God of power and might, heaven and earth are full of your glory.

The glorious company of apostles praise you. The noble fellowship of prophets praise you. The white-robed army of martyrs praise you. Throughout the world the holy Church acclaims you; Father, of majesty unbounded, your true and only Son, worthy of all worship, and the Holy Spirit, advocate and guide.

You, Christ, are the king of glory, the eternal Son of the Father. When you became man to set us free you did not shun the Virgin's womb. You overcame the sting of death and opened the kingdom of heaven to all believers. You are seated at God's right hand in glory. We believe that you will come and be our judge. Come then, Lord, and help your people, bought with the price of your own blood, and bring us with your saints to glory everlasting.

Praise and Thanksgiving (Songs and Prayers)

Gloria Patri

Glory be to the Father,
And to the Son and to the Holy Spirit:
As it was in the beginning,
Is now, and ever shall be,
World without end. Amen, amen.

LISTENING TO HIS VOICE

Chronological Reading for the Day
Sunday: Pss. 12-17; 19-21
Monday: Pss. 22-26

Tuesday: Pss. 27-32
Wednesday: Pss. 35-38
Thursday: Pss. 39-41; 53; 55; 58
Friday: Pss. 61-62; 64-67
Saturday: Pss. 68-70; 86; 101

Lectionary Readings

Psalm: Ps. 150
Gospel: John 20.19-31

Acts*: Acts 5.27-32
NT: Rev. 1.4-8

* During Eastertide, a reading from Acts is often sustituted for the lesson from the Hebrew Bible.

Reflection: Silence and/or Journaling

RESPONDING IN FAITH

The Apostles' Creed

I believe in God, the Father Almighty, Maker of heaven and earth; and in Jesus Christ, his only Son, our Lord, who was conceived by the Holy Spirit, born of the Virgin Mary, suffered under Pontius Pilate, was crucified, dead, and buried; he descended into hell; the third day he arose again from the dead; he ascended into heaven and sits on the right hand of God the Father Almighty; from thence he shall come to judge the quick and the dead.

I believe in the Holy Spirit, the holy catholic* church, the communion of saints, the forgiveness of sins, the resurrection of the body, and the life everlasting. Amen.

* In the Apostles' and Nicene Creeds, the term catholic refers to the Church's universality, through all ages and times, of all languages and peoples. It refers to no particular tradition or denominational expression (e.g., as in Roman Catholic).

Prayers of Confession

Let us now confess our sins to God and receive mercy and grace to help in our time of need.

Assurance of Pardon

Having faithfully confessed and renounced your sin, Christ also has been faithful to forgive your sins and to purify you from all unrighteousness. It is certain, that there is One who has spoken to the Father in your defense, Jesus Christ, the Righteous One who is the atoning sacrifice for our sins and for the sins of the whole world. His grace and peace are with you now. Amen.

Petitions and Supplications, Ending with the Lord's Prayer

Our Father which art in heaven, Hallowed be thy name. Thy kingdom come, Thy will be done in earth, as it is in heaven. Give us this day our daily bread. And forgive us our debts, as we forgive our debtors. And lead us not into temptation, but deliver us from evil: For thine is the kingdom, and the power, and the glory, for ever. Amen.

~ Matthew 6.9-13 (KJV)

Doxology (and/or closing song)

Praise God from whom all blessings flow;
Praise Him all creatures here below;
Praise Him above ye heavenly host;
Praise Father, Son and Holy Ghost. Amen.

Departing to Serve

Benediction

Lord Jesus Christ, we affirm you as the Faithful Witness, the one whose testimony regarding your Father and eternal life has become our foundation and our hope. We trust your Word, for you cannot lie, and your testimony is faithful and accurate. Show us more and more how we can walk by faith in your witness, and share your witness of truth with those who do no yet know that you are the Faithful Witness for the world. In your name we pray, amen.

Affirmation from the Psalms

The Lord upholds all who are falling and raises up all who are bowed down. [15] The eyes of all look to you, and you give them their food in due season. [16] You open your hand; you satisfy the desire of every living thing. [17] The Lord is righteous in all his ways and kind in all his works. [18] The Lord is near to all who call on him, to all who call on him in truth.

~ Psalm 145.14-18

Pray without Ceasing – Flash Prayer for the Day

Lord Jesus Christ, we are continuing in your Word and are coming to know the truth, and the truth is setting us free.

For Your Weekly Journey

Let God Arise! Seasonal Focus

Salvation Belongs to Our God, Revelation 7.9-17

Book Reading

Hamilton, *The Call, the Life and Message of the Apostle Paul*

Our Corporate Disciplines

Concert of Prayer: Wednesday, April 6, 2016

WEEK 20

Third Sunday of Easter
April 10 - 16, 2016

On Easter Sunday we celebrate the bodily resurrection of Jesus. The same lowly Nazarene – he who was betrayed by his own disciple, who suffered under Pilate's cruel gaze, who was crucified on a Roman cross, and who was buried in a borrowed tomb – the same Lord rose triumphantly on the third day. Jesus has risen from death to life through the power of God. "Christ is risen! He is risen, indeed!"

THIS WEEK'S THEME
Follow Me, John 21.1-19

After Jesus had revealed himself alive to the disciples twice, he again showed himself to the disciples by the Sea of Tiberias (i.e., the Sea of Galilee). This occurred when Simon Peter, Thomas (called the Twin), Nathanael of Cana in Galilee, the sons of Zebedee, and two others of his disciples were together, and Simon suggested that they go fishing. They fished all night (catching very little), and at daybreak were greeted by a man on the shore, who told them to cast their nets on the right side of the boat. On doing this, they hauled in a huge quantity of fish, and John recognized that the man was the Lord. They came to shore and when they got to land, they saw a charcoal fire, with fish laid out on it, and bread. Jesus invited them to bring some of the fish they had caught, and to come and have breakfast.

Although the disciples knew this was the Lord (this was the third appearance of him being alive after his resurrection), they did not ask him any questions. After breakfast, Jesus said to Simon, Peter, "Simon, son of John, do you love me more than these?" Peter replied to the Lord, "Yes, Lord; you know that I love you." Jesus then said to him, "Feed my lambs."

Jesus asked Simon a second time, "Simon, son of John, do you love me?" Again, Peter replied, "Yes, Lord; you know that I love you." Jesus again said, "Tend my sheep." Again, a third time, Jesus asked the same question. This time, though, Peter was grieved because Jesus had asked him three times of his love, and Peter said, "Lord, you know everything; you know that I love you." Again, the Lord said to him, "Feed my sheep."

Then Jesus spoke to Simon of his future, saying that when he was young, he used to dress himself and walk wherever he wished, but, when he becomes old, he would stretch out his hands, and another person would dress him, and carry him where he will not want to go. (In saying this Jesus actually revealed the kind of death Peter would have, the kind that would glorify God). After sharing this, the Lord Jesus said to Peter, "Follow me."

After everything Peter went through (from betrayal of the Lord before his passion, to the revelation of Christ to him after the resurrection), Jesus' final word to Peter was the very same word he gave him when he began his journey with him. Jesus requires that his followers do the obvious thing: "Follow me." When in doubt or indecision or depression or struggle, the solution is always the same. Christ's command is constant and clear: let all disciples follow him. The next step of obedience is the best direction to take.

Daily Devotional Guide

PREPARING OUR HEARTS

Invocation: Our Prayer of Acclamation
Holy Father, we acknowledge that you raised Jesus from the dead. He revealed himself alive to his disciples, and restored Peter to his side with the simple command of "Follow me." Make our one desire, regardless of what we face or where we are or what challenges lie ahead, to simply follow Jesus, your Son and our Savior. Make us like him, for your sake, amen.

Call to Worship

Blessed are you, O God: Father, Son, and Holy Spirit. And blessed is your Kingdom, both now and forever, amen.

PRAISING OUR GOD

Te Deum Laudamus

You are God: we praise you; you are the Lord; we acclaim you; you are the eternal Father: All creation worships you. To you all angels, all the powers of heaven, Cherubim and Seraphim, sing in endless praise: Holy, holy, holy Lord, God of power and might, heaven and earth are full of your glory.

The glorious company of apostles praise you. The noble fellowship of prophets praise you. The white-robed army of martyrs praise you. Throughout the world the holy Church acclaims you; Father, of majesty unbounded, your true and only Son, worthy of all worship, and the Holy Spirit, advocate and guide.

You, Christ, are the king of glory, the eternal Son of the Father. When you became man to set us free you did not shun the Virgin's womb. You overcame the sting of death and opened the kingdom of heaven to all believers. You are seated at God's right hand in glory. We believe that you will come and be our judge. Come then, Lord, and help your people, bought with the price of your own blood, and bring us with your saints to glory everlasting.

Praise and Thanksgiving (Songs and Prayers)

Gloria Patri

Glory be to the Father,
And to the Son and to the Holy Spirit:
As it was in the beginning,
Is now, and ever shall be,
World without end. Amen, amen.

LISTENING TO HIS VOICE

Chronological Reading for the Day
Sunday: Pss. 103; 108-110; 122; 124
Monday: Pss. 131; 133; 138-141; 143
Tuesday: Pss. 144-145; 88-89
Wednesday: Pss. 50; 73-74
Thursday: Pss. 75-78
Friday: Pss. 79-82
Saturday: Ps. 83; 1 Chron. 29.23-25; 2 Chron. 1.1-13;
    1 Kings 2.13-3.28

Lectionary Readings
Psalm: Ps. 30
Gospel: John 21.1-19

Acts*: Acts 9.1-20
NT: Rev. 5.11-14

* During Eastertide, a reading from Acts is often sustituted for the lesson from the Hebrew Bible.

Reflection: Silence and/or Journaling

RESPONDING IN FAITH

The Apostles' Creed
I believe in God, the Father Almighty, Maker of heaven and earth; and in Jesus Christ, his only Son, our Lord, who was conceived by the Holy Spirit, born of the Virgin Mary, suffered under Pontius Pilate, was crucified, dead, and buried; he descended into hell; the third day he arose again from the dead; he ascended into heaven and sits on the right hand of God the Father Almighty; from thence he shall come to judge the quick and the dead.

I believe in the Holy Spirit, the holy catholic* church, the communion of saints, the forgiveness of sins, the resurrection of the body, and the life everlasting. Amen.

* In the Apostles' and Nicene Creeds, the term catholic refers to the Church's universality, through all ages and times, of all languages and peoples. It refers to no particular tradition or denominational expression (e.g., as in Roman Catholic).

Prayers of Confession

Let us now confess our sins to God and receive mercy and grace to help in our time of need.

Assurance of Pardon

Having faithfully confessed and renounced your sin, Christ also has been faithful to forgive your sins and to purify you from all unrighteousness. It is certain, that there is One who has spoken to the Father in your defense, Jesus Christ, the Righteous One who is the atoning sacrifice for our sins and for the sins of the whole world. His grace and peace are with you now. Amen

Petitions and Supplications, Ending with the Lord's Prayer

Our Father which art in heaven, Hallowed be thy name. Thy kingdom come, Thy will be done in earth, as it is in heaven. Give us this day our daily bread. And forgive us our debts, as we forgive our debtors. And lead us not into temptation, but deliver us from evil: For thine is the kingdom, and the power, and the glory, for ever. Amen.

~ Matthew 6.9-13 (KJV)

Doxology (and/or closing song)

Praise God from whom all blessings flow;
Praise Him all creatures here below;
Praise Him above ye heavenly host;
Praise Father, Son and Holy Ghost. Amen.

DEPARTING TO SERVE

Benediction

Lord Jesus, you so gently restored Peter to your side, after all the doubt and betrayal and confusion. You brought him back with love and grace, exhorting him to feed your lambs and tend your sheep, and summarized your good will with the command to follow you. Help us to remember that your will is simple, elegant, and–exhaustive. You want all of us, you want everything, and you want us to follow you. Give us grace to obey your command. Where you lead us, we will go. In your name, amen.

Affirmation from the Psalms

Praise the Lord! I will give thanks to the Lord with my whole heart, in the company of the upright, in the congregation. [2] Great are the works of the Lord, studied by all who delight in them. [3] Full of splendor and majesty is his work, and his righteousness endures forever. [4] He has caused his wondrous works to be remembered; [5] He provides food for those who fear him; he remembers his covenant forever. [6] He has shown his people the power of his works, in giving them the inheritance of the nations. [7] The works of his hands are faithful and just; all his precepts are trustworthy; [8] they are established forever and ever, to be performed with faithfulness and uprightness. [9] He sent redemption to his people; he has commanded his covenant forever. Holy and awesome is his name! [1]0 The fear of the Lord is the beginning of wisdom; all those who practice it have a good understanding. His praise endures forever!

~ Psalm 111.1-10

Pray without Ceasing – Flash Prayer for the Day

Lord Jesus Christ, in the midst of confusion and doubt, teach us to follow you; where you lead us, through your grace, there we will go. In your name we pray, amen.

For Your Weekly Journey

Let God Arise! Seasonal Focus
Salvation Belongs to Our God, Revelation 7.9-17

Book Reading
Hamilton, *The Call, the Life and Message of the Apostle Paul*

Our Corporate Disciplines
Book Discussion: Monday, April 11, 2016

Fourth Sunday of Easter
April 17 - 23, 2016

*On Easter Sunday we celebrate the bodily resurrection of Jesus.
The same lowly Nazarene – he who was betrayed by his own disciple,
who suffered under Pilate's cruel gaze, who was crucified on a Roman
cross, and who was buried in a borrowed tomb – the same Lord rose
triumphantly on the third day. Jesus has risen from death to life
through the power of God. "Christ is risen! He is risen, indeed!"*

THIS WEEK'S THEME
Salvation Belongs to Our God, Revelation 7.9-17

In one of many heavenly scenes witnessed to in his
revelation, John looked and saw an incredibly populated
people, "a great multitude that no one could number,"
who were from all the various tribes, peoples, and language
groupings on earth. These people were standing before
God's throne and before the Lamb, and they were clothed
in white robes, and had palm branches in their hands.

This amazing company cried out with a loud voice before the
throne saying, "Salvation belongs to our God who sits on the
throne, and to the Lamb!" And John also saw that all the
angels that were standing around the throne, as well as the
elders and the four living creatures, fell on their faces before
the throne, worshiping God. They cried out "Amen! Blessing
and glory and wisdom and thanksgiving and honor and
power and might be to our God forever and ever! Amen."

Upon this, one of the elders asked John, "Who are these,
clothed in white robes, and from where have they come?"
with John replying "Sir, you know." The elder then gave the
explanation of this multitude's origin and place. He told
John, "These are the ones coming out of the great tribulation.
They have washed their robes and made them white in the
blood of the Lamb. Therefore they are before the throne of

God, and serve him day and night in his temple; and he who sits on the throne will shelter them with his presence. They shall hunger no more, neither thirst anymore; the sun shall not strike them, nor any scorching heat. For the Lamb in the midst of the throne will be their shepherd, and he will guide them to springs of living water, and God will wipe away every tear from their eyes."

This amazing company cried out before the throne the great truth regarding the rescue of humankind and all creation: "Salvation belongs to our God who sits on the throne, and to the Lamb!" In simple, direct, and final worshiping affirmation, this group gathers up the truth regarding God's salvation in Christ. Salvation belongs to God; he designed it, executed it, and will himself consummate it in his own time and method. Salvation is under God's sovereign oversight, and he will guarantee our deliverance. Praise be to his name!

Daily Devotional Guide

PREPARING OUR HEARTS

Invocation: Our Prayer of Acclamation

God and Father of our Lord Jesus Christ, the great multitude from all nations and peoples in John's vision perfectly summarizes your great rescue of creation and humankind. To you and you alone, O God, does salvation belong, to you and to the Lamb, our Lord Jesus. Thank you for your amazing grace, the same grace that offered Jesus for our sins and raised him from the dead by your power and love. Reveal your heart to us, in Jesus' name, amen.

Call to Worship

Blessed are you, O God: Father, Son, and Holy Spirit. And blessed is your Kingdom, both now and forever, amen.

PRAISING OUR GOD

Te Deum Laudamus

You are God: we praise you; you are the Lord; we acclaim you; you are the eternal Father: All creation worships you. To you all angels, all the powers of heaven, Cherubim and Seraphim, sing in endless praise: Holy, holy, holy Lord, God of power and might, heaven and earth are full of your glory.

The glorious company of apostles praise you. The noble fellowship of prophets praise you. The white-robed army of martyrs praise you. Throughout the world the holy Church acclaims you: Father, of majesty unbounded, your true and only Son, worthy of all worship, and the Holy Spirit, advocate and guide.

You, Christ, are the king of glory, the eternal Son of the Father. When you became man to set us free you did not shun the Virgin's womb. You overcame the sting of death and opened the kingdom of heaven to all believers. You are seated at God's right hand in glory. We believe that you will come and be our judge. Come then, Lord, and help your people, bought with the price of your own blood, and bring us with your saints to glory everlasting.

Praise and Thanksgiving (Songs and Prayers)

Gloria Patri

Glory be to the Father,
And to the Son and to the Holy Spirit:
As it was in the beginning,
Is now, and ever shall be,
World without end. Amen, amen.

LISTENING TO HIS VOICE

Chronological Reading for the Day

Sunday: 1 Kings 5-6; 2 Chron. 2.1-3.14
Monday: 1 Kings 7; 2 Chron. 3.15-4.22

Tuesday: 1 Kings 8; 2 Chron. 5-6
Wednesday: 2 Chron. 7; 1 Kings 9.1-14
Thursday: 2 Chron. 1.14-17; 8.1-9.28; 1 Kings 9.15-10.29
Friday: 1 Kings 4; Pss. 72; 127
Saturday: Prov. 1-4

Lectionary Readings

Psalm: Ps. 23
Gospel: John 10.22-30

Acts*: Acts 9.36-43
NT: Rev. 7.9-17

* During Eastertide, a reading from Acts is often sustituted for the lesson from the Hebrew Bible.

Reflection: Silence and/or Journaling

Responding in Faith

The Apostles' Creed

I believe in God, the Father Almighty, Maker of heaven and earth; and in Jesus Christ, his only Son, our Lord, who was conceived by the Holy Spirit, born of the Virgin Mary, suffered under Pontius Pilate, was crucified, dead, and buried; he descended into hell; the third day he arose again from the dead; he ascended into heaven and sits on the right hand of God the Father Almighty; from thence he shall come to judge the quick and the dead.

I believe in the Holy Spirit, the holy catholic* church, the communion of saints, the forgiveness of sins, the resurrection of the body, and the life everlasting. Amen.

* In the Apostles' and Nicene Creeds, the term catholic refers to the Church's universality, through all ages and times, of all languages and peoples. It refers to no particular tradition or denominational expression (e.g., as in Roman Catholic).

Prayers of Confession

Let us now confess our sins to God and receive mercy and grace to help in our time of need.

Assurance of Pardon

Having faithfully confessed and renounced your sin, Christ also has been faithful to forgive your sins and to purify you from all unrighteousness. It is certain, that there is One who has spoken to the Father in your defense, Jesus Christ, the Righteous One who is the atoning sacrifice for our sins and for the sins of the whole world. His grace and peace are with you now. Amen.

Petitions and Supplications, Ending with the Lord's Prayer

Our Father which art in heaven, Hallowed be thy name. Thy kingdom come, Thy will be done in earth, as it is in heaven. Give us this day our daily bread. And forgive us our debts, as we forgive our debtors. And lead us not into temptation, but deliver us from evil: For thine is the kingdom, and the power, and the glory, for ever. Amen.

~ Matthew 6.9-13 (KJV)

Doxology (and/or closing song)

Praise God from whom all blessings flow;
Praise Him all creatures here below;
Praise Him above ye heavenly host;
Praise Father, Son and Holy Ghost. Amen.

DEPARTING TO SERVE

Benediction

Lord Jesus Christ, the great multitude in John's vision reveals that salvation belongs to God and to you, Lamb of God who takes away the sins of the world. Apart from your mercy and love, there would be no rescue, no hope, no redemption from the powers that have ravaged this world for so long. You alone are the Savior, and to you alone belong all the praise and the honor. We worship you, who reigns with the Father and the Spirit, one great triune Lord, our God, in your name we pray, amen.

Affirmation from the Psalms

Consider and answer me, O Lord my God; light up my eyes, lest I sleep the sleep of death, [4] lest my enemy say, "I have prevailed over him," lest my foes rejoice because I am shaken. [5] But I have trusted in your steadfast love; my heart shall rejoice in your salvation. [6] I will sing to the Lord, because he has dealt bountifully with me.

~ Psalm 13.3-6

Pray without Ceasing – Flash Prayer for the Day

Salvation belongs to you Father, and to You, dear Lord Jesus, Lamb of God and our Savior.

For Your Weekly Journey

Let God Arise! Seasonal Focus

Salvation Belongs to Our God, Revelation 7.9-17

Book Reading

Hamilton, *The Call, the Life and Message of the Apostle Paul*

The Season from Easter to Pentecost

THE ASCENSION OF CHRIST

The chariots of God are twice ten thousand,
thousands upon thousands; the Lord is among them;
Sinai is now in the sanctuary.
You ascended on high, leading a host of captives in your train
and receiving gifts among men, even among the rebellious,
that the LORD God may dwell there.

PSALM 68.17-18

The Risen Lord Has Ascended to the Right Hand of God

The Ascension of Christ to heaven refers to that event where the risen Jesus, after forty days of confirming his resurrection to his disciples, ascended to the Father. On his arrival, God "seated him at his right hand in the heavenly realms, far above all rule and authority, power and dominion, and every title that can be given, not only in the present age but also in the one to come" (Eph. 1.20b-21; 1 Pet. 3.22; Luke 24.17-53). On Thursday, May 5, we celebrate with Christians all over the world the Ascension of our Lord to God's right hand. Glorified by the Father as Head of the Church (cf. Eph. 1.15-23), our Lord has sent his Spirit into the world, intercedes for his own before God, and reigns above in a position of glory and power awaiting the coming judgment.

As one commentator put it, there is "no incident in the life of Jesus at one and the same time so beset with difficulties and so essential as the Ascension" (William Barclay as quoted in Norman Gulley, "The Ascension of Christ" in *The Anchor Bible Dictionary*, Vol. 1, p. 472). Others have referred to this important doctrine of the Church and Creed as the "most neglected doctrine of the church." Still, the Ascension of Jesus is one of the New Testament's central themes. Without it, we cannot understand the sending of the Spirit into the world, Jesus' high priestly ministry for the Church, the harvesting of souls during this age "between the times," or the blessed hope of Jesus' return. The claim of God's exaltation of Jesus to his right hand was a staple in the apostles' preaching and teaching, and it must become a central theme in our worship and mission if we are to be true witnesses of the Gospel.

Proofs of the Resurrection, Promises of the Spirit's Coming

For forty days following his resurrection from the dead, the risen Jesus provided the apostles with a number of convincing proofs of his return from death, and taught them concerning the Kingdom of God (Acts 1.3). He commanded them to stay in Jerusalem until the promise of the Father (i.e., the Holy Spirit) would be granted to them (cf. Acts 1.5; John 14.16; 15.26; 16.7). They questioned him concerning the timing of God's restoration of the Kingdom, revealing the close connection in their minds of the promised outpouring of the Holy Spirit and the end of the age, climaxed with the coming of the promised Kingdom of the Father (cf. Isa. 32.15-20; 44.3-5; Ezek. 39.28-29; Joel 2.28-3.1; Zech. 12.8-10).

After commanding his apostles to share the Good News to the ends of the earth, starting at Jerusalem, Jesus ascended as they looked on, and was lifted up with a cloud taking him out of their sight (Acts 1.9). As firsthand witnesses, the apostles saw the risen Christ ascend. According to Luke's account, "two men in white robes" [i.e., angels of God] made the following affirmation: "Men of Galilee, why do you stand looking into heaven? This Jesus, who was taken up from you into heaven, will come in the same way as you saw him go into heaven" (Acts 1.10-11).

This doctrine is critical for Christian worship, spiritual warfare, and fruitful mission. Christ ascended to the Father's right hand in order to fulfill his promise of his return to the Father (John 6.62; 14.2, 12; 16.5, 10, 28; 20.17), to vindicate his messiahship and sonship, and to pour out the Holy Spirit upon the Church for worship and witness (cf. John 16.7 with Acts 1.8; Acts 2.33). As conquering Lord, Christ now spreads abroad the "spoils" of his divine triumph over the devil and the forces of evil (Eph. 4.8-10), and he now prepares a place (i.e., the New Jerusalem) for his redeemed company and body, the Church (John 14.2-3; Acts 3.21). Because he has ascended, he can now empower all members of his Church with his divine presence through the Spirit (Matt. 28.20, cf. John 16.7-15), and ensure that soon and very soon, he will return and restore creation under his reign (Acts 1.9-11). This central doctrine calls for our shouts of praise, affirmations of faith, and acts of courage in witness. Jesus is risen and ascended to the Father for his own glory, and for us!

Because Jesus our Lord is ascended, exalted, and glorified at the Father's right hand, let us affirm him to be the Head of the Church, the Lord of the Harvest, and the High Priest of the Lord. Let us acknowledge him to be *Christus Victor*, supreme sovereign to whom all authority has been entrusted.

Truly, let us submit our wills to him as our exalted Head, and bear bold witness of his saving work to the world. Above all, let us stir up our hearts in anticipation of his return as the coming Judge of all and our coming King. With all believers, we affirm together the great anthem of the Church: "All hail the power of Jesus' name, let angels prostrate fall! Bring forth the royal diadem, and crown him Lord of all!"

Bring Forth the Royal Diadem, and Crown Jesus Lord of All!
Come, let us continue our Easter celebration with praise and thanksgiving as we remember the Ascension of Jesus Christ. With Christians around the world, let us glory in the exalted status of our Champion and Victor. Having destroyed death, defeated evil and the powers, rescinded the curse, and established the future recreation of all things, he has been enthroned at the Father's right hand as Lord. The crucified One has indeed been given all power, and he must reign until all his enemies are subdued and conquered under his feet. Let us glory in our Lord Jesus, whom the Father has made both Lord and Christ, who has ascended to the Father's presence to intercede on our behalf. From the Father's side, we await the coming of our Savior and Lord. Jesus Christ is Lord, to the glory of God the Father!

Celebrating the exaltation of the Master,
Rev. Dr. Don L. Davis

WEEK
22

Fifth Sunday of Easter
April 24 - 30, 2016

For forty days after his resurrection, Jesus revealed himself alive to his disciples. On the fortieth day, he ascended to heaven to take his place as Lord and Christ at God's right hand. Ten days after this, on the fiftieth day after his resurrection, he would send to us the promise of the Father – the Holy Spirit, the pledge of our salvation. Here we ponder the wonder of God's working, from Easter Sunday to the Spirit's descent at Pentecost.

THIS WEEK'S THEME
Praise the Name of the Lord, Psalm 148

In this song of praise, the psalmist praises God for Israel's creator and for Israel's God. After the exclamation to praise the Lord, he exhorts creation to praise the Lord from the heavens and in the heights! Angels are exhorted to praise him, and all the Lord's hosts, along with the sun and moon, the shining stars, and even the highest heavens, and the waters above the heavens! These all should praise the name of the Lord, because he was the one who commanded, and, as a result, they all were created. And by his sovereign will, these and all creation are established forever and ever. The Lord himself has given a decree, and creation shall not pass away.

In the middle of the song, the psalmist enjoins the inhabitants and creatures from the earth to join the chorus of creation's praise to the Lord. He summons praise for the Lord from the earth, including the great sea creatures and all deeps, the hail, the snow and mist, and the stormy wind that fulfills his word! With them, let the mountains and all hills join the praise, along with the fruit trees and all cedars, the beasts and all livestock, the creeping things and the flying birds!

He then moves to humankind, and exhorts all peoples to come along! He solicits praise from the kings of the earth and all peoples, from princes and all rulers of the earth! He calls for young men and maidens together to join in, with the old men and children! All of these – from the starry heavens to the little child – to praise the name of the Lord, "for his name alone is exalted; his majesty is above earth and heaven."

Finally, the psalmist recognizes that the creator of the universe is also Israel's God! "He has raised up a horn for his people, praise for all his saints, for the people of Israel who are near to him. Praise the Lord!" In the wake of our Lord's recreation of all things through the Lord Jesus Christ, the psalmist binds and gathers all things together under the sovereign grace and care of the one true creator God, the God and Father of our Lord Jesus Christ. From creation to promise to recreation, only one source is to be recognized and adored. Praise the Lord!

Daily Devotional Guide

PREPARING OUR HEARTS

Invocation: Our Prayer of Acclamation

Father, in the light of your Son's resurrection from the dead, it is proper and good to offer you praise. This season beckons for, even demands our heartfelt, joyous, and continuous praise. That which was a statute in Israel, the very law of God, ordained by you, now spontaneously flows from our hearts because of your work in Christ on our behalf. Let us never be silent, but always ready to magnify your name for the glorious work you have done for us in Christ. In his name, amen.

Call to Worship

Blessed are you, O God: Father, Son, and Holy Spirit. And blessed is your Kingdom, both now and forever, amen.

PRAISING OUR GOD

Te Deum Laudamus

You are God: we praise you; you are the Lord; we acclaim you; you are the eternal Father: All creation worships you. To you all angels, all the powers of heaven, Cherubim and Seraphim, sing in endless praise: Holy, holy, holy Lord, God of power and might, heaven and earth are full of your glory.

The glorious company of apostles praise you. The noble fellowship of prophets praise you. The white-robed army of martyrs praise you. Throughout the world the holy Church acclaims you; Father, of majesty unbounded, your true and only Son, worthy of all worship, and the Holy Spirit, advocate and guide.

You, Christ, are the king of glory, the eternal Son of the Father. When you became man to set us free you did not shun the Virgin's womb. You overcame the sting of death and opened the kingdom of heaven to all believers. You are seated at God's right hand in glory. We believe that you will come and be our judge. Come then, Lord, and help your people, bought with the price of your own blood, and bring us with your saints to glory everlasting.

Praise and Thanksgiving (Songs and Prayers)

Gloria Patri

Glory be to the Father,
And to the Son and to the Holy Spirit:
As it was in the beginning,
Is now, and ever shall be,
World without end. Amen, amen.

LISTENING TO HIS VOICE

Chronological Reading for the Day

Sunday: Prov. 5-7
Monday: Prov. 8-10
Tuesday: Prov. 11-13
Wednesday: Prov. 14-16

Thursday: Prov. 17-19
Friday: Prov. 20.1-22.16
Saturday: Prov. 22.17-24.34

Lectionary Readings

Psalm: Ps. 148
Gospel: John 13.31-35

Acts*: Acts 11.1-18
NT: Rev. 21.1-6

* During Eastertide, a reading from Acts is often sustituted for the lesson from the Hebrew Bible.

Reflection: Silence and/or Journaling

RESPONDING IN FAITH

The Apostles' Creed

I believe in God, the Father Almighty, Maker of heaven and earth; and in Jesus Christ, his only Son, our Lord, who was conceived by the Holy Spirit, born of the Virgin Mary, suffered under Pontius Pilate, was crucified, dead, and buried; he descended into hell; the third day he arose again from the dead; he ascended into heaven and sits on the right hand of God the Father Almighty; from thence he shall come to judge the quick and the dead.

I believe in the Holy Spirit, the holy catholic* church, the communion of saints, the forgiveness of sins, the resurrection of the body, and the life everlasting. Amen.

* In the Apostles' and Nicene Creeds, the term catholic refers to the Church's universality, through all ages and times, of all languages and peoples. It refers to no particular tradition or denominational expression (e.g., as in Roman Catholic).

Prayers of Confession

Let us now confess our sins to God and receive mercy and grace to help in our time of need.

Assurance of Pardon

Having faithfully confessed and renounced your sin, Christ also has been faithful to forgive your sins and to purify you from all unrighteousness. It is certain, that there is One who has spoken to the Father in your defense, Jesus Christ, the Righteous One who is the atoning sacrifice for our sins and for the sins of the whole world. His grace and peace are with you now. Amen

Petitions and Supplications, Ending with the Lord's Prayer

Our Father which art in heaven, Hallowed be thy name. Thy kingdom come, Thy will be done in earth, as it is in heaven. Give us this day our daily bread. And forgive us our debts, as we forgive our debtors. And lead us not into temptation, but deliver us from evil: For thine is the kingdom, and the power, and the glory, for ever. Amen.

~ Matthew 6.9-13 (KJV)

Doxology (and/or closing song)

Praise God from whom all blessings flow;
Praise Him all creatures here below;
Praise Him above ye heavenly host;
Praise Father, Son and Holy Ghost. Amen.

Departing to Serve

Benediction

Lord Jesus Christ, you have delivered us, your people from the snare and venom of the enemy. You have answered our prayers for rescue, and set our feet on higher ground. Now, through your grace, we can even approach the very throne room of the Father, and be welcomed as his very own children. And, all this, because of your great love for us.

Receive our praise, dear Savior, and grant us hearts of joy and praise as we remember your mighty acts on our behalf. For your glory's sake we pray, amen.

Affirmation from the Psalms
Praise the Lord! Praise the Lord from the heavens; praise him in the heights! [2] Praise him, all his angels; praise him, all his hosts! [3] Praise him, sun and moon, praise him, all you shining stars! [4] Praise him, you highest heavens, and you waters above the heavens! [5] Let them praise the name of the Lord! For he commanded and they were created. [6] And he established them forever and ever; he gave a decree, and it shall not pass away.

~ Psalm 148.1-6

Pray without Ceasing – Flash Prayer for the Day
Lord Jesus, we praise you, and glorify your name for you are good and your steadfast love and grace will never end.

For Your Weekly Journey

Let God Arise! Seasonal Focus
You Will Be My Witnesses, Acts 1.1-11

Book Reading
Hamilton, *The Call, the Life and Message of the Apostle Paul*

Our Corporate Disciplines
Book Discussion: Monday, April 25, 2016

For forty days after his resurrection, Jesus revealed himself alive to his disciples. On the fortieth day, he ascended to heaven to take his place as Lord and Christ at God's right hand. Ten days after this, on the fiftieth day after his resurrection, he would send to us the promise of the Father – the Holy Spirit, the pledge of our salvation. Here we ponder the wonder of God's working, from Easter Sunday to the Spirit's descent at Pentecost.

THIS WEEK'S THEME
The River of Life, Revelation 21.10; 21.22-22.5

One of the highlights of John's apocalyptic vision was his vision of the holy city, New Jerusalem. John was carried away in the Spirit to a great, high mountain where he was shown the holy city Jerusalem coming down out of heaven from God. John observed that there was no temple in the city, "for its temple is the Lord God the Almighty and the Lamb." Likewise, he noted that city had no need "of sun or moon to shine on it, for the glory of God gives it light, and its lamp is the Lamb."

By the light of the city the nations will themselves walk, and the earth's kings will bring their glory into it. The gates of the New Jerusalem will never be shut by day, and there will be no night there. The kings of the earth will bring the glory and the honor of the nations into it. However, John noted that "nothing unclean will ever enter it, nor anyone who does what is detestable or false, but only those who are written in the Lamb's book of life."

The angel that escorted John in the vision showed him "the river of the water of life," a majestic river bright as crystal, flowing from God's throne and the Lamb through the middle of the street of the city. On either side of the river, also, there was the tree of life with its twelve kinds of fruit, yielding its fruit each month, with its leaves employed for the healing of the nations. John noted that "No longer will there be anything accursed, but the throne of God and of the Lamb will be in it, and his servants will worship him. They will see his face, and his name will be on their foreheads. And night will be no more. They will need no light of lamp or sun, for the Lord God will be their light, and they will reign forever and ever."

This vision of a majestic river bright as crystal flowing from God's throne and the Lamb in the middle of the street of the city – reveals a vision of life, refreshment, blessing, and provision. The entire picture of John's vision reveals a vision of transformation, redemption, and perhaps, above all, joyous life. No longer despoiled by sin or curse, the city is where God's throne and the Lamb reside, with those who look upon the face of God, with his name on their foreheads, without night, or darkness, or suffering, or sin. The river of life–what an amazing picture of God's provision and blessing. This vision awaits all who trust in Christ as Lord – it is the inheritance which is to come.

Daily Devotional Guide

PREPARING OUR HEARTS

Invocation: Our Prayer of Acclamation
Holy Father, thank you for your gracious provision to John of the holy city, the New Jerusalem, the place which we as saints long to reside. There we will see your face, hear your voice, know your presence, and bask in the light and love of your Son, Jesus Christ. We seek this city with all our hearts. Oh, to walk with you in that place! Grant to us that we might, through faith in your Son, be counted worthy to dwell in that place and drink from that river, the river of life in the Jerusalem above. In Jesus' name, amen.

Call to Worship
Blessed are you, O God: Father, Son, and Holy Spirit. And blessed is your Kingdom, both now and forever, amen.

PRAISING OUR GOD

Te Deum Laudamus
You are God: we praise you; you are the Lord; we acclaim you; you are the eternal Father: All creation worships you. To you all angels, all the powers of heaven, Cherubim and Seraphim, sing in endless praise: Holy, holy, holy Lord, God of power and might, heaven and earth are full of your glory.

The glorious company of apostles praise you. The noble fellowship of prophets praise you. The white-robed army of martyrs praise you. Throughout the world the holy Church acclaims you; Father, of majesty unbounded, your true and only Son, worthy of all worship, and the Holy Spirit, advocate and guide.

You, Christ, are the king of glory, the eternal Son of the Father. When you became man to set us free you did not shun the Virgin's womb. You overcame the sting of death and opened the kingdom of heaven to all believers. You are seated at God's right hand in glory. We believe that you will come and be our judge. Come then, Lord, and help your people, bought with the price of your own blood, and bring us with your saints to glory everlasting.

Praise and Thanksgiving (Songs and Prayers)

Gloria Patri
Glory be to the Father,
And to the Son and to the Holy Spirit:
As it was in the beginning,
Is now, and ever shall be,
World without end. Amen, amen.

LISTENING TO HIS VOICE

Chronological Reading for the Day
Sunday: Song of Sol. 1-8
Monday: 1 Kings 11; 2 Chron. 9.29-31
Tuesday: Eccles. 1-6
Wednesday: Eccles. 7-12
Thursday: 1 Kings 12; 2 Chron. 10.1-11.17
Friday: 1 Kings 13.1-15.15, vv.25-34; 2 Chron. 11.18-15.19
Saturday: 1 Kings 15.16-24; 16.1-17.7; 2 Chron. 16-17

Lectionary Readings
Psalm: Ps. 67
Gospel: John 5.1-9

Acts*: Acts 16.9-15
NT: Rev. 21.10; 21.22-22.5

* During Eastertide, a reading from Acts is often sustituted for the lesson from the Hebrew Bible.

Reflection: Silence and/or Journaling

RESPONDING IN FAITH

The Apostles' Creed
I believe in God, the Father Almighty, Maker of heaven and earth; and in Jesus Christ, his only Son, our Lord, who was conceived by the Holy Spirit, born of the Virgin Mary, suffered under Pontius Pilate, was crucified, dead, and buried; he descended into hell; the third day he arose again from the dead; he ascended into heaven and sits on the right hand of God the Father Almighty; from thence he shall come to judge the quick and the dead.

I believe in the Holy Spirit, the holy catholic* church, the communion of saints, the forgiveness of sins, the resurrection of the body, and the life everlasting. Amen.

* In the Apostles' and Nicene Creeds, the term catholic refers to the Church's universality, through all ages and times, of all languages and peoples. It refers to no particular tradition or denominational expression (e.g., as in Roman Catholic).

Prayers of Confession

Let us now confess our sins to God and receive mercy and grace to help in our time of need.

Assurance of Pardon

Having faithfully confessed and renounced your sin, Christ also has been faithful to forgive your sins and to purify you from all unrighteousness. It is certain, that there is One who has spoken to the Father in your defense, Jesus Christ, the Righteous One who is the atoning sacrifice for our sins and for the sins of the whole world. His grace and peace are with you now. Amen.

Petitions and Supplications, Ending with the Lord's Prayer

Our Father which art in heaven, Hallowed be thy name. Thy kingdom come, Thy will be done in earth, as it is in heaven. Give us this day our daily bread. And forgive us our debts, as we forgive our debtors. And lead us not into temptation, but deliver us from evil: For thine is the kingdom, and the power, and the glory, for ever. Amen.

~ Matthew 6.9-13 (KJV)

Doxology (and/or closing song)

Praise God from whom all blessings flow;
Praise Him all creatures here below;
Praise Him above ye heavenly host;
Praise Father, Son and Holy Ghost. Amen.

DEPARTING TO SERVE

Benediction

Lord Jesus Christ, you revealed to your servant and our brother John "the river of the water of life," that holy stream bright as crystal that flows from you and the throne of God in the middle of the street of the city. We long to dwell with you in our true homeland, the place where your honor dwells, the place of our inheritance. Cleanse and prepare us, that we might be found ready to dwell in the place where the throne of God and you, O Lamb, will dwell. There we desire to worship you. Bless your name, and prepare us, your people, for that great Day. In your name, amen.

Affirmation from the Psalms

God is our refuge and strength, a very present help in trouble. [2] Therefore we will not fear though the earth gives way, though the mountains be moved into the heart of the sea, [3] though its waters roar and foam, though the mountains tremble at its swelling. Selah [4] There is a river whose streams make glad the city of God, the holy habitation of the Most High. [5] God is in the midst of her; she shall not be moved; God will help her when morning dawns. [6] The nations rage, the kingdoms totter; he utters his voice, the earth melts. [7] The Lord of hosts is with us; the God of Jacob is our fortress.

~ Psalm 46.1-7

Pray without Ceasing – Flash Prayer for the Day

Come Lord Jesus, Master and Lord, and reign over your people today.

For Your Weekly Journey

Let God Arise! Seasonal Focus
You Will Be My Witnesses, Acts 1.1-11

Book Reading
Hamilton, *The Call, the Life and Message of the Apostle Paul*

Special Church Year Service
Ascension of the Lord: Thursday, May 5, 2016

Ascension of the Lord

May 5, 2016

For forty days after his resurrection, Jesus revealed himself alive to his disciples. On the fortieth day, he ascended to heaven to take his place as Lord and Christ at God's right hand. Ten days after this, on the fiftieth day after his resurrection, he would send to us the promise of the Father – the Holy Spirit, the pledge of our salvation. Here we ponder the wonder of God's working, from Easter Sunday to the Spirit's descent at Pentecost.

TODAY'S THEME

You Will Be My Witnesses, Acts 1.1-11

Luke explains to Theophilus in the prolegomena (opening words) of Acts that the books of Luke and Acts are meant to be viewed as a two-volume work. Luke details the work that Jesus began to do and teach, until the day when he was taken up, i.e., he ascended to the Father's right hand. After our Lord had given commands through the Holy Spirit to his chosen apostles, he presented himself alive to them after his suffering by many proofs. He appeared to the apostolic company during forty days after the resurrection, speaking to them about the Kingdom of God.

The Lord Jesus when he was with them had ordered them not to depart from Jerusalem, but to wait for the Father's promise, which before he had spoken of, saying "you heard from me; for John baptized with water, but you will be baptized with the Holy Spirit not many days from now."

When they all had come together, the apostles asked him, "Lord, will you at this time restore the kingdom to Israel?" Jesus replied, "It is not for you to know times or seasons that the Father has fixed by his own authority. But you will receive power when the Holy Spirit has come upon you, and you will be my witnesses in Jerusalem and in all Judea and

Samaria, and to the end of the earth." And, after Jesus had made these statements, as the apostles were looking on at him, the Lord was lifted up. A cloud took the Lord out of the apostles' sight, and as they gazed into heaven as he went, there were two men standing by in white robes. They said, "Men of Galilee, why do you stand looking into heaven? This Jesus, who was taken up from you into heaven, will come in the same way as you saw him go into heaven."

Jesus' strict order for the apostles to remain in Jerusalem to await the "promise of the Father" is at the heart of their provision for their apostolic witness to the world. Even with the eyewitness testimony and experience of being with our Lord did not, apart from the enabling of the Spirit, prepare them to be his witnesses. Importantly, the "receiving power" statement of Jesus precedes the "you will be my witnesses" statement. The mission of witness demands the empowerment of the Holy Spirit.

Daily Devotional Guide

PREPARING OUR HEARTS

Invocation: Our Prayer of Acclamation
Hear us. O merciful God, and grant our minds to be lifted up, whither our Redeemer hath ascended; that at the second coming of the Mediator we may receive from Thy manifested bounty what we now venture to hope for as a promised gift; through the same Jesus Christ our Lord. Amen.

~ *Leonine Sacramentary* (Bright, p. 60)

Call to Worship
Blessed are you, O God: Father, Son, and Holy Spirit. And blessed is your Kingdom, both now and forever, amen.

PRAISING OUR GOD

Te Deum Laudamus

You are God: we praise you; you are the Lord; we acclaim you; you are the eternal Father: All creation worships you. To you all angels, all the powers of heaven, Cherubim and Seraphim, sing in endless praise: Holy, holy, holy Lord, God of power and might, heaven and earth are full of your glory.

The glorious company of apostles praise you. The noble fellowship of prophets praise you. The white-robed army of martyrs praise you. Throughout the world the holy Church acclaims you; Father, of majesty unbounded, your true and only Son, worthy of all worship, and the Holy Spirit, advocate and guide.

You, Christ, are the king of glory, the eternal Son of the Father. When you became man to set us free you did not shun the Virgin's womb. You overcame the sting of death and opened the kingdom of heaven to all believers. You are seated at God's right hand in glory. We believe that you will come and be our judge. Come then, Lord, and help your people, bought with the price of your own blood, and bring us with your saints to glory everlasting.

Praise and Thanksgiving (Songs and Prayers)

Gloria Patri

Glory be to the Father,
And to the Son and to the Holy Spirit:
As it was in the beginning,
Is now, and ever shall be,
World without end. Amen, amen.

LISTENING TO HIS VOICE

Chronological Reading for the Day
1 Kings 12; 2 Chron. 10.1-11.17

Lectionary Readings

Psalm: Ps. 47

Gospel: Luke 24.44-53

Acts*: Acts 1.1-11

NT: Eph. 1.15-23

* During Eastertide, a reading from Acts is often sustituted for the lesson from the Hebrew Bible.

Reflection: Silence and/or Journaling

RESPONDING IN FAITH

The Apostles' Creed

I believe in God, the Father Almighty, Maker of heaven and earth; and in Jesus Christ, his only Son, our Lord, who was conceived by the Holy Spirit, born of the Virgin Mary, suffered under Pontius Pilate, was crucified, dead, and buried; he descended into hell; the third day he arose again from the dead; he ascended into heaven and sits on the right hand of God the Father Almighty; from thence he shall come to judge the quick and the dead.

I believe in the Holy Spirit, the holy catholic* church, the communion of saints, the forgiveness of sins, the resurrection of the body, and the life everlasting. Amen.

* In the Apostles' and Nicene Creeds, the term catholic refers to the Church's universality, through all ages and times, of all languages and peoples. It refers to no particular tradition or denominational expression (e.g., as in Roman Catholic).

Prayers of Confession

Let us now confess our sins to God and receive mercy and grace to help in our time of need.

Assurance of Pardon

Having faithfully confessed and renounced your sin, Christ also has been faithful to forgive your sins and to purify you from all unrighteousness. It is certain, that there is One who has spoken to the Father in your defense, Jesus Christ, the

Righteous One who is the atoning sacrifice for our sins and for the sins of the whole world. His grace and peace are with you now. Amen.

Petitions and Supplications, Ending with the Lord's Prayer
Our Father which art in heaven, Hallowed be thy name. Thy kingdom come, Thy will be done in earth, as it is in heaven. Give us this day our daily bread. And forgive us our debts, as we forgive our debtors. And lead us not into temptation, but deliver us from evil: For thine is the kingdom, and the power, and the glory, for ever. Amen.

~ Matthew 6.9-13 (KJV)

Doxology (and/or closing song)
Praise God from whom all blessings flow;
Praise Him all creatures here below;
Praise Him above ye heavenly host;
Praise Father, Son and Holy Ghost. Amen.

DEPARTING TO SERVE

Benediction
O God, Who, to show forth the wonders of Thy Majesty, didst after Thy Resurrection from the dead ascend this day into heaven, in the presence of Thine Apostles, grant us the aid of Thy loving-kindness; that according to Thy promise thou mayest ever dwell with us on earth, and we with Thee in heaven; where with the Father, through the same Jesus our Lord. Amen.

~ *Gelasian Sacramentary* (Bright, p. 60)

Affirmation from the Psalms
O mountain of God, mountain of Bashan; O many-peaked mountain, mountain of Bashan! [16] Why do you look with hatred, O many-peaked mountain, at the mount that God desired for his abode, yes, where the Lord will dwell forever? [17] The chariots of God are twice ten thousand, thousands upon thousands; the Lord is among them; Sinai is now in the sanctuary. [18] You ascended on high, leading a host of captives in your train and receiving gifts among men, even

among the rebellious, that the Lord God may dwell there. [19] Blessed be the Lord, who daily bears us up; God is our salvation. Selah [20] Our God is a God of salvation, and to God, the Lord, belong deliverances from death.

~ Psalm 68.15-20

Pray without Ceasing – Flash Prayer for the Day
Lord Jesus Christ, who commanded the apostles to wait for the promise of the Father, we look to you for the same power of the Holy Spirit today.

For Your Weekly Journey

Let God Arise! Seasonal Focus
You Will Be My Witnesses, Acts 1.1-11

Book Reading
Hamilton, *The Call, the Life and Message of the Apostle Paul*

Seventh Sunday of Easter

May 8 - 14, 2016

For forty days after his resurrection, Jesus revealed himself alive to his disciples. On the fortieth day, he ascended to heaven to take his place as Lord and Christ at God's right hand. Ten days after this, on the fiftieth day after his resurrection, he would send to us the promise of the Father – the Holy Spirit, the pledge of our salvation. Here we ponder the wonder of God's working, from Easter Sunday to the Spirit's descent at Pentecost.

THIS WEEK'S THEME
That They May All Be One, John 17.20-26

In John chapter 17, our Lord prayed a high priestly prayer of petition to the Father on behalf of the apostles, and all those who would believe on him through their word. Jesus asked that the Father keep the apostles, not taking them out of the world, but keeping them from the evil within it. He prayed for their sanctification and protection, and assured the Father that they had received his Word, and believed on him.

He told the Father that he did not make his requests only for the apostolic band, but also for those who would believe in him through their word. He prayed that these believers might be one, all of us, just as the Father was in him, and he in the Father, that believers might also be in the Father and the Son, in order that the world might come to believe that the Father sent Jesus into the world.

Jesus prayed to the Father that the glory he had given him was now given to the apostles. He asked that all who would come to believe in him through their word might be one as he and the Father are one – he, Jesus, in them, and the Father in Jesus, perfectly one. Through this unity, Jesus said that the world would know that the Father sent him, and that he loved his followers as his own even as the Father loved him.

Jesus ended his petition with a plea to the Father that those whom he had given to him might "be with me where I am, to see my glory that you have given me because you loved me before the foundation of the world. O righteous Father, even though the world does not know you, I know you, and these know that you have sent me. I made known to them your name, and I will continue to make it known, that the love with which you have loved me may be in them, and I in them."

This amazing prayer reveals the heart of the Savior – his devotion to the Father, his love for the apostles, his acknowledgment of all believers, and his desire for their unity and connection with him and the Father. The burning desire of the Savior is that all those who belong to him be one – with one another, with the Father and Jesus – that the world could comprehend that Jesus came from the Father. Our unity is prime evidence to the world of God's mission to send Jesus into the world.

Daily Devotional Guide

PREPARING OUR HEARTS

Invocation: Our Prayer of Acclamation
Father, your beautiful Son prayed for us during his days on earth, for our provision, protection, and blessing. He asked you to make us one in you and in him, that we who believe in the apostles' word might possess a unity so deep and defining that the world itself would know that you sent him to earth. Forgive us for our pettiness and selfishness; instill in us the unity the Savior prayed for, and make us worthy to bear the name of Jesus of Nazareth. For his name's sake, amen.

Call to Worship
Blessed are you, O God: Father, Son, and Holy Spirit. And blessed is your Kingdom, both now and forever, amen.

PRAISING OUR GOD

Te Deum Laudamus

You are God: we praise you; you are the Lord; we acclaim you; you are the eternal Father: All creation worships you. To you all angels, all the powers of heaven, Cherubim and Seraphim, sing in endless praise: Holy, holy, holy Lord, God of power and might, heaven and earth are full of your glory.

The glorious company of apostles praise you. The noble fellowship of prophets praise you. The white-robed army of martyrs praise you. Throughout the world the holy Church acclaims you; Father, of majesty unbounded, your true and only Son, worthy of all worship, and the Holy Spirit, advocate and guide.

You, Christ, are the king of glory, the eternal Son of the Father. When you became man to set us free you did not shun the Virgin's womb. You overcame the sting of death and opened the kingdom of heaven to all believers. You are seated at God's right hand in glory. We believe that you will come and be our judge. Come then, Lord, and help your people, bought with the price of your own blood, and bring us with your saints to glory everlasting.

Praise and Thanksgiving (Songs and Prayers)

Gloria Patri

Glory be to the Father,
And to the Son and to the Holy Spirit:
As it was in the beginning,
Is now, and ever shall be,
World without end. Amen, amen.

LISTENING TO HIS VOICE

Chronological Reading for the Day

Sunday: 1 Kings 17.8-20.22
Monday: 1 Kings 20.23-22.9; 2 Chron. 18.1-8

Tuesday: 1 Kings 22.10-40, vv.51-53; 2 Chron. 18.9-20.37
Wednesday: 2 Kings 1; 3; 8.16-22; 1 Kings 22.41-50;
    2 Chron. 21.1-7
Thursday: 2 Kings 2; ch.4
Friday: 2 Kings 5.1-8.15
Saturday: 2 Chron. 21.8-22.9; 2 Kings 8.23-10.31

Lectionary Readings

Psalm: Ps. 97

Gospel: John 17.20-26

Acts*: Acts 16.16-34

NT: Rev. 22.12-14, 16-17, 20-21

* During Eastertide, a reading from Acts is often sustituted for the lesson from the Hebrew Bible.

Reflection: Silence and/or Journaling

RESPONDING IN FAITH

The Apostles' Creed

I believe in God, the Father Almighty, Maker of heaven and earth; and in Jesus Christ, his only Son, our Lord, who was conceived by the Holy Spirit, born of the Virgin Mary, suffered under Pontius Pilate, was crucified, dead, and buried; he descended into hell; the third day he arose again from the dead; he ascended into heaven and sits on the right hand of God the Father Almighty; from thence he shall come to judge the quick and the dead.

I believe in the Holy Spirit, the holy catholic* church, the communion of saints, the forgiveness of sins, the resurrection of the body, and the life everlasting. Amen.

* In the Apostles' and Nicene Creeds, the term catholic refers to the Church's universality, through all ages and times, of all languages and peoples. It refers to no particular tradition or denominational expression (e.g., as in Roman Catholic).

Prayers of Confession

Let us now confess our sins to God and receive mercy and grace to help in our time of need.

Assurance of Pardon

Having faithfully confessed and renounced your sin, Christ also has been faithful to forgive your sins and to purify you from all unrighteousness. It is certain, that there is One who has spoken to the Father in your defense, Jesus Christ, the Righteous One who is the atoning sacrifice for our sins and for the sins of the whole world. His grace and peace are with you now. Amen.

Petitions and Supplications, Ending with the Lord's Prayer

Our Father which art in heaven, Hallowed be thy name. Thy kingdom come, Thy will be done in earth, as it is in heaven. Give us this day our daily bread. And forgive us our debts, as we forgive our debtors. And lead us not into temptation, but deliver us from evil: For thine is the kingdom, and the power, and the glory, for ever. Amen.

~ Matthew 6.9-13 (KJV)

Doxology (and/or closing song)

Praise God from whom all blessings flow;
Praise Him all creatures here below;
Praise Him above ye heavenly host;
Praise Father, Son and Holy Ghost. Amen.

Departing to Serve

Benediction

Lord Jesus Christ, who as our Advocate and High Priest prayed to the Father that we might be one and with you where you are, fulfill your Word and prepare us. We long to be with you in your presence, to see your glory, to honor you in all that we are, and to bring pleasure and joy to your great heart. Forgive us for embracing lesser aims. Cleanse, heal, and strengthen us, to be yours, to be holy, to be one. In your name we pray, amen.

Affirmation from the Psalms
Behold, how good and pleasant it is when brothers dwell in unity!
[2] It is like the precious oil on the head, running down on the beard,
on the beard of Aaron, running down on the collar of his robes! [3] It
is like the dew of Hermon, which falls on the mountains of Zion! For
there the Lord has commanded the blessing, life forevermore.

~ Psalm 133.1-3

Pray without Ceasing – Flash Prayer for the Day
Lord Jesus Christ, make us one in you and the Father, that the
world might know that the Father sent you into the world.

For Your Weekly Journey

Let God Arise! Seasonal Focus
You Will Be My Witnesses, Acts 1.1-11

Book Reading
Hamilton, *The Call, the Life and Message of the Apostle Paul*

Our Corporate Disciplines
National Day of Prayer: Monday, May 9, 2016

For forty days after his resurrection, Jesus revealed himself alive to his disciples. On the fortieth day, he ascended to heaven to take his place as Lord and Christ at God's right hand. Ten days after this, on the fiftieth day after his resurrection, he would send to us the promise of the Father – the Holy Spirit, the pledge of our salvation. Here we ponder the wonder of God's working, from Easter Sunday to the Spirit's descent at Pentecost.

THIS WEEK'S THEME
The Coming of the Holy Spirit, Acts. 2.1-21

After the ascension of Jesus, the apostolic company were all together in one place when the day of Pentecost arrived. As they were present, there came suddenly from heaven a sound like a mighty rushing wind, and it filled the entire house where they were. And at that moment divided tongues as of fire appeared to them and rested on each one of them. All the company was filled with the Holy Spirit, and each one began to speak in other tongues, as the Spirit moved.

At that time of the feast, devout Jews from every nation under heaven were there dwelling in Jerusalem. At the sound the multitude came together, being astonished and bewildered, for each one heard the apostolic company speaking in his own language. The crowd said, "Are not all these who are speaking Galileans? And how is it that we hear, each of us in his own native language? Parthians and Medes and Elamites and residents of Mesopotamia, Judea and Cappadocia, Pontus and Asia, Phrygia and Pamphylia, Egypt and the parts of Libya belonging to Cyrene, and visitors from Rome, both Jews and proselytes, Cretans and

Arabians – we hear them telling in our own tongues the mighty works of God." They were amazed and perplexed, questioning what this event meant.

Some folk in the crowd mocked them, saying, "They are filled with new wine." Peter, standing with the eleven, lifted up his voice and addressed the multitude, saying "Men of Judea and all who dwell in Jerusalem, let this be known to you, and give ear to my words. For these people are not drunk, as you suppose, since it is only the third hour of the day [around 9:00 am in the morning]."

Peter then connected this episode with a prophecy given through the prophet Joel, which he quoted: "'And in the last days it shall be', God declares, 'that I will pour out my Spirit on all flesh, and your sons and your daughters shall prophesy, and your young men shall see visions, and your old men shall dream dreams; even on my male servants and female servants in those days I will pour out my Spirit, and they shall prophesy. And I will show wonders in the heavens above and signs on the earth below, blood, and fire, and vapor of smoke; the sun shall be turned to darkness and the moon to blood, before the day of the Lord comes, the great and magnificent day. And it shall come to pass that everyone who calls upon the name of the Lord shall be saved.'"

Peter reveals that the event of Pentecost, the Holy Spirit falling on the apostolic company, was a fulfillment of the end-time prophecy of God's promise to pour his Spirit on "all flesh," i.e., those who believe in Christ. A new dimension of God's blessing, anointing, and revelation is upon us: through the redemption of Jesus the gift of God's Holy Spirit is now granted to every one who believes. The life of God is among us in the indwelling of the Spirit of God in the church.

Daily Devotional Guide

PREPARING OUR HEARTS

Invocation: Our Prayer of Acclamation

God of fire and light, on the first Pentecost you formed the hearts of those who believed in you by the indwelling of the Holy Spirit: Under the inspiration of that same Spirit, give us a taste for what is right and true and a continuing sense of his joy-bringing presence and power. We ask this through Christ our Lord. Amen.

~ A Prayer Book of Catholic Devotions (Storey, p. 183-184)

Call to Worship

Blessed are you, O God: Father, Son, and Holy Spirit. And blessed is your Kingdom, both now and forever, amen.

PRAISING OUR GOD

Te Deum Laudamus

You are God: we praise you; you are the Lord; we acclaim you; you are the eternal Father: All creation worships you. To you all angels, all the powers of heaven, Cherubim and Seraphim, sing in endless praise: Holy, holy, holy Lord, God of power and might, heaven and earth are full of your glory.

The glorious company of apostles praise you. The noble fellowship of prophets praise you. The white-robed army of martyrs praise you. Throughout the world the holy Church acclaims you; Father, of majesty unbounded, your true and only Son, worthy of all worship, and the Holy Spirit, advocate and guide.

You, Christ, are the king of glory, the eternal Son of the Father. When you became man to set us free you did not shun the Virgin's womb. You overcame the sting of death and opened the kingdom of heaven to all believers. You are seated at God's right hand in glory. We believe

that you will come and be our judge. Come then, Lord, and help your people, bought with the price of your own blood, and bring us with your saints to glory everlasting.

Praise and Thanksgiving (Songs and Prayers)

Gloria Patri
Glory be to the Father,
And to the Son and to the Holy Spirit:
As it was in the beginning,
Is now, and ever shall be,
World without end. Amen, amen.

LISTENING TO HIS VOICE

Chronological Reading for the Day
Sunday: 2 Kings 10.32-12.16; 2 Chron. 22.10-24.22
Monday: 2 Chron. 24.23-27; 2 Kings 12.17-13.25
Tuesday: 2 Kings 14.1-27; 15.1-5; 2 Chron. 25.1-26.21; Jon. 1-4
Wednesday: Amos 1-6
Thursday: Amos 7-9; 2 Kings 14.28-29; 15.6-29; 2 Chron. 26.22-23; Isa. 6
Friday: 2 Kings 15.32-16.9; 2 Chron. 27.1-28.15; Mic. 1; Isa. 7
Saturday: Isa. 8-11

Lectionary Readings
Psalm: Ps. 104.24-34, 35b   *Acts*:* Acts 2.1-21
Gospel: John 14.8-17, 25-27   *NT:* Rom. 8.14-17

* During Eastertide, a reading from Acts is often sustituted for the lesson from the Hebrew Bible.

Reflection: Silence and/or Journaling

RESPONDING IN FAITH

The Apostles' Creed
I believe in God, the Father Almighty, Maker of heaven and earth; and in Jesus Christ, his only Son, our Lord, who was conceived by the Holy Spirit, born of the Virgin Mary, suffered under Pontius Pilate, was crucified, dead, and buried; he descended into hell; the third day he arose again from the dead; he ascended into heaven and sits on the right hand of God the Father Almighty; from thence he shall come to judge the quick and the dead.

I believe in the Holy Spirit, the holy catholic* church, the communion of saints, the forgiveness of sins, the resurrection of the body, and the life everlasting. Amen.

* In the Apostles' and Nicene Creeds, the term catholic refers to the Church's universality, through all ages and times, of all languages and peoples. It refers to no particular tradition or denominational expression (e.g., as in Roman Catholic).

Prayers of Confession
Let us now confess our sins to God and receive mercy and grace to help in our time of need.

Assurance of Pardon
Having faithfully confessed and renounced your sin, Christ also has been faithful to forgive your sins and to purify you from all unrighteousness. It is certain, that there is One who has spoken to the Father in your defense, Jesus Christ, the Righteous One who is the atoning sacrifice for our sins and for the sins of the whole world. His grace and peace are with you now. Amen.

Petitions and Supplications, Ending with the Lord's Prayer
Our Father which art in heaven, Hallowed be thy name. Thy kingdom come, Thy will be done in earth, as it is in heaven. Give us this day our daily bread. And forgive us our debts, as we forgive our debtors. And

*lead us not into temptation, but deliver us from evil: For thine is the
kingdom, and the power, and the glory, for ever. Amen.*

~ Matthew 6.9-13 (KJV)

Doxology (and/or closing song)

*Praise God from whom all blessings flow;
Praise Him all creatures here below;
Praise Him above ye heavenly host;
Praise Father, Son and Holy Ghost. Amen.*

DEPARTING TO SERVE

Benediction

*Almighty Saviour, who, being exalted by the right hand of God, didst
receive gifts for men: Send down the grace of thy Holy Spirit upon thy
people, and grant that they may give cheerfully of their substance for
the evangelizing of the world. Bless all those who are banded together
for the spread of the Gospel; make them faithful and true witnesses in
proclaiming thy glorious Name; and prosper the work of their hands
upon them, that the light of thy truth may shine into the darkest corners
of the earth. Hear us, O merciful Saviour, who with the Father and the
Holy Spirit, livest and reignest ever, one God world without end. Amen.*

~ *Canada Prayer Book* (Suter 180)

Affirmation from the Psalms

*Create in me a clean heart, O God, and renew a right spirit within
me. [11] Cast me not away from your presence, and take not your
Holy Spirit from me. [12] Restore to me the joy of your salvation, and
uphold me with a willing spirit. [13] Then I will teach transgressors
your ways, and sinners will return to you.*

~ Psalm 51.10-13

Pray without Ceasing – Flash Prayer for the Day
Come, Holy Spirit, fill us, transform us, and lead us into the fullness of God, for Jesus' sake.

For Your Weekly Journey

Let God Arise! Seasonal Focus
You Will Be My Witnesses, Acts 1.1-11

Book Reading
Hamilton, *The Call, the Life and Message of the Apostle Paul*

Our Corporate Disciplines
Book Discussion: Monday, May 16, 2016
TUMI Retreat: Friday, May 20, 2016

The Season after Pentecost

THE COMING OF THE HOLY SPIRIT

On the last day of the feast, the great day,
Jesus stood up and cried out,
"If anyone thirsts, let him come to me and drink.
Whoever believes in me, as the Scripture has said,
'Out of his heart will flow rivers of living water.'"
Now this he said about the Spirit, whom
those who believed in him were to receive.

JOHN 7.37-39A

The Holy Spirit Has Come to God's People

On *Pentecost* we commemorate the coming of the Holy
Spirit to the people of God, the Church. Jesus Christ, the
risen Lord, is now present with his people in the person
of the Spirit of God in the midst of the assemblies of faith.
Now during this season after Pentecost, we affirm the
work of the holy Trinity on behalf of humankind. The love
of the Father elects us to salvation, the grace of the Lord
Jesus Christ has won us to God through his blood, and the
Holy Spirit indwells the Church, helping and empowering
us to represent and advance the Kingdom in the earth. On
Trinity Sunday, we worship our Triune God: Father, Son,
and Holy Spirit, and celebrate the mystery of God's revealed
nature in three persons, expressed in their unity, equality,
and diversity.

The Season after Pentecost is called *Ordinary Time* or
Kingdomtide. During this time the Church considers the
overarching theme of salvation history, the need for
diligence in Christian discipleship, and focuses on the
advance of the Kingdom to the ends of the earth. This
is the longest season in the Church's calendar, having from
twenty-three to twenty-eight Sundays, and lasting until
Advent. During this time we, as believers and congregations,
focus on the Church's maturity and multiplication and
emphasize Christ's headship and the power of the Holy
Spirit in the ministry of the apostles and through the
body of Christ.

The phrase *Ordinary Time* ought not to be interpreted as
"unimportant time." Rather, it should be understood in the
sense of "counted or numbered days," i.e., like "ordinal"

numbers – first, second, third. This has to do with the numbered Sundays of the year outside of the special seasons in the two cycles. These "ordinary" Sundays tend to emphasize Jesus' earthly life and ministry (in the first group of Ordinary Time between *Epiphany* and *Lent*), and his headship, harvest, and vigilance in light of Christ as our hope (in the larger group of Sundays in the second).

In a real sense, the Season after Pentecost emphasizes the most significant sign of the Kingdom's presence in this world: the coming of the Holy Spirit. As Peter recounted in his sermon so many years ago, God promised that in the last time the Spirit of God would be poured out on humankind, with all of the people of God prophesying, seeing visions, and dreaming dreams, both male and female. God's wonders would be seen in the earth, and the witness to God's salvation in Christ would be taken to the ends of the earth. Glory to God, we live in that age, the time of the presence of the heavenly dove and entrance of the Spirit into our world!

O, Heavenly Dove, Fill Your People with Your Power and Light
During this Season after Pentecost, we join with congregations worldwide to seek the power of the Spirit for our own transformation and the fruitfulness of our mission to the inner cities of America. Let us depend on the Holy Spirit, the One who has sealed us for the day of redemption, who indwells us and fills us with the presence and power of God for mission. Let us neither grieve nor quench him, but yield ourselves afresh to him for strength, grace, and wisdom. Only through the power of the Spirit can the cities of America be reached with the Gospel. Truly, if the cities of the world are won to Christ, it will not be by power nor by might, but by the Spirit of the Living God.

We desire to do all we can to help you fulfill the purpose of the Lord as you display Christ's love in the inner cities of America. May God grant you grace and strength as you exalt Christ in the city where you live!

Refreshed by the living waters of the Spirit,
Rev. Dr. Don L. Davis

WEEK 26

Trinity Sunday
First Sunday after Pentecost • May 22 - 28, 2016

On Pentecost we commemorate the descent of the Holy Spirit to earth on Christ's believers, his infilling of the people of God, the Church. Through him, the third person of the Trinity, Jesus our Lord is now present with his people. The Spirit is the guarantee of the promised inheritance to come. We ponder the fullness and mystery of our God's person and work in our celebration on Trinity Sunday.

THIS WEEK'S THEME
The Working of the Triune God, John 16.12-15

The great rescue and redemption of creation, and of all humankind, was designed and executed by the triune God, the Father, Son, and Holy Spirit. Although the doctrine is not explicitly taught in the Scriptures, the evidence of this truth is clearly asserted. Each member of the Trinity is a person, endowed with all the attributes of God, and all share in the fundamental workings of creation, redemption, the resurrection, and the saving works of the one God.

In the Upper Room discourse, Jesus repeatedly taught the apostles on the prospect of the coming of the Holy Spirit. Although sorrow and pain filled their hearts, making it difficult to take in all that he was saying, he promised to send to them the Spirit of truth. Jesus said that when the "Spirit of truth" appeared, he would guide them into all the truth, for the Holy Spirit would not speak on his own authority, but whatever he heard (whatever was given to him) he would speak, and would declare to the apostles the things that were to come.

Jesus promised the apostles that the Holy Spirit would glorify him, because the Spirit would take what belonged to Jesus and declare it to the apostles. Jesus asserted that everything that the Father possessed was his, and therefore, the Holy Spirit would take what belonged to him and declare it to them.

In every facet of our great and grand salvation, each member has a distinct and necessary working and role. The saving work of God in Christ is truly triune in nature – the love of the Father is executed by the grace of the Son and made real through the communion of the Holy Spirit.

Daily Devotional Guide

PREPARING OUR HEARTS

Invocation: Our Prayer of Acclamation
Almighty God, you have revealed to your Church your eternal Being of glorious majesty and perfect love as one God in Trinity of Persons: Give us grace to continue steadfast in the confession of this faith, and constant in our worship of you, Father, Son, and Holy Spirit; for you live and reign, one God now and for ever. Amen.

~ *The Episcopal Church in the United States of America*
(The Episcopal Church, p. 251)

Call to Worship
Blessed are you, O God: Father, Son, and Holy Spirit. And blessed is your Kingdom, both now and forever, amen.

PRAISING OUR GOD

Te Deum Laudamus
You are God: we praise you; you are the Lord; we acclaim you; you are the eternal Father: All creation worships you. To you all angels, all the powers of heaven, Cherubim and Seraphim, sing in endless praise: Holy, holy, holy Lord, God of power and might, heaven and earth are full of your glory.

*The glorious company of apostles praise you. The noble fellowship
of prophets praise you. The white-robed army of martyrs praise you.
Throughout the world the holy Church acclaims you; Father, of
majesty unbounded, your true and only Son, worthy of all worship,
and the Holy Spirit, advocate and guide.*

*You, Christ, are the king of glory, the eternal Son of the Father. When
you became man to set us free you did not shun the Virgin's womb.
You overcame the sting of death and opened the kingdom of heaven
to all believers. You are seated at God's right hand in glory. We believe
that you will come and be our judge. Come then, Lord, and help your
people, bought with the price of your own blood, and bring us with
your saints to glory everlasting.*

Praise and Thanksgiving (Songs and Prayers)

Gloria Patri
*Glory be to the Father,
And to the Son and to the Holy Spirit:
As it was in the beginning,
Is now, and ever shall be,
World without end. Amen, amen.*

Listening to His Voice

Chronological Reading for the Day
Sunday: Isa. 12; 17; 2 Chron. 28.16-25; 29.1-2; 2 Kings
    15.30-31; 16.10-18; 17.1-4; 18.1-8
Monday: Hos. 1-7
Tuesday: Hos. 8-14
Wednesday: Isa. 28; 1.1-20; 2 Kings 17.5-41; 18.9-12
Thursday: Isa. 1.21-5.30
Friday: 2 Kings 16.19-20; 2 Chron. 28.26-27; Isa. 13-16
Saturday: 2 Chron. 29.3-31.21

Lectionary Readings

Psalm: Ps. 8

OT: Prov. 8.1-4, 22-31

Gospel: John 16.12-15

NT: Rom. 5.1-5

Reflection: Silence and/or Journaling

RESPONDING IN FAITH

The Apostles' Creed

I believe in God, the Father Almighty, Maker of heaven and earth; and in Jesus Christ, his only Son, our Lord, who was conceived by the Holy Spirit, born of the Virgin Mary, suffered under Pontius Pilate, was crucified, dead, and buried; he descended into hell; the third day he arose again from the dead; he ascended into heaven and sits on the right hand of God the Father Almighty; from thence he shall come to judge the quick and the dead.

I believe in the Holy Spirit, the holy catholic* church, the communion of saints, the forgiveness of sins, the resurrection of the body, and the life everlasting. Amen.

* In the Apostles' and Nicene Creeds, the term catholic refers to the Church's universality, through all ages and times, of all languages and peoples. It refers to no particular tradition or denominational expression (e.g., as in Roman Catholic).

Prayers of Confession

Let us now confess our sins to God and receive mercy and grace to help in our time of need.

Assurance of Pardon

Having faithfully confessed and renounced your sin, Christ also has been faithful to forgive your sins and to purify you from all unrighteousness. It is certain, that there is One who has spoken to the Father in your defense, Jesus Christ, the Righteous One who is the atoning sacrifice for our sins and for the sins of the whole world. His grace and peace are with you now. Amen.

Petitions and Supplications, Ending with the Lord's Prayer

Our Father which art in heaven, Hallowed be thy name. Thy kingdom come, Thy will be done in earth, as it is in heaven. Give us this day our daily bread. And forgive us our debts, as we forgive our debtors. And lead us not into temptation, but deliver us from evil: For thine is the kingdom, and the power, and the glory, for ever. Amen.

~ Matthew 6.9-13 (KJV)

Doxology (and/or closing song)

Praise God from whom all blessings flow;
Praise Him all creatures here below;
Praise Him above ye heavenly host;
Praise Father, Son and Holy Ghost. Amen.

DEPARTING TO SERVE

Benediction

Almighty God, Creator of the heavens and the earth, and Lord over all: we bless thee that thy power and wisdom are plainly seen in the things thou hast made. We thank thee that in Jesus Christ thou hast come near to us in our weakness and need. We bless thee that he hath conquered sin and death, and hath bestowed upon us the Holy Spirit, by whom we have passed from death into life. And we pray thee to increase and perfect in us the life thou hast given, that we may ever be to the praise of thy great and holy name; through Jesus Christ our Lord. Amen.

~ Desiderius Erasmus, *Great Souls at Prayer* (Ferguson, p. 72)

Affirmation from the Psalms

Bless the Lord, O my soul! O Lord my God, you are very great! You are clothed with splendor and majesty, [2] covering yourself with light as with a garment, stretching out the heavens like a tent. [3] He lays the beams of his chambers on the waters; he makes the clouds his chariot; he rides on the wings of the wind; [4] he makes his messengers winds, his ministers a flaming fire.

~ Psalm 104.1-4

Pray without Ceasing – Flash Prayer for the Day
Lord Jesus Christ, we worship you, dear Savior, who reigns
with the Father and Holy Spirit, one God, forever.

For Your Weekly Journey

Let God Arise! Seasonal Focus
An Ambassador in Chains, Ephesians 6.19-20

Book Reading
Bruce, *Paul: Apostle of the Heart Set Free*

Our Corporate Disciplines
Book Discussion: Monday, May 23, 2016

Second Sunday after Pentecost
May 29 - June 4 • Proper 4

On Pentecost we commemorate the descent of the Holy Spirit to earth on Christ's believers, his infilling of the people of God, the Church. Through him, the third person of the Trinity, Jesus our Lord is now present with his people. The Spirit is the guarantee of the promised inheritance to come. We ponder the fullness and mystery of our God's person and work in our celebration on Trinity Sunday.

THIS WEEK'S THEME
An Ambassador in Chains, Ephesians 6.19-20

In writing to the Ephesians (traditionally referred to as one of the "Prison epistles," including Ephesians, Philippians, Colossians, and Philemon), Paul highlights the immeasurable riches of the believer's union with Christ. He ends his grand letter with a call to diligent spiritual warfare in the strength of the Lord, commenting on the armor that each believer must daily embrace in his/her battle with the enemy. He states that in every circumstance we must take up the shield of faith which extinguishes the evil one's flaming darts, the helmet of salvation, and the Spirit's sword, the Word of God. He exhorts us to continue in prayer at all times in the Spirit, with all prayer and supplication, keeping alert and persevering, making supplication for all the saints.

At the end of his discussion, Paul asked the Ephesians to pray for him, that God would grant to him words of grace "in the opening of his mouth" to boldly proclaim the mystery of the Gospel, for which he was "an ambassador in chains." He wanted God's grace that he might declare that Gospel with boldness, which was the way he said he "ought to speak it."

In this simple phrase, "ambassador in chains," Paul summarizes that amazingly fruitful season of his ministry which involved imprisonment. As a result of the false accusation of legalists who plagued his ministry from the start, Paul was imprisoned for his witness to Jesus of Nazareth, and the Gospel of salvation by grace through faith. Scholars generally agree that Paul went through perhaps several imprisonments before he was finally imprisoned and beheaded under emperor Nero.

Paul referred to himself as an "ambassador in chains," and so the analogy fits perfectly. As Christ's ambassador, he stood in God's stead, a trained, deputized agent of the Kingdom of God, representing the citizenship of Christ's rule with integrity and honor.

His faith, perseverance, and devotion to Christ are an amazing example of what it means to represent Christ with honor, even in the midst of terrible persecution, false accusation, and even abandonment from colleagues and co-workers. Regardless of what he endured, Paul remained faithful to Christ throughout the terms of his imprisonment, writing letters which have become the staple of spiritual nourishment for believers down through the ages. His heart for Christ and the lost shine as a present-day model of what it means to be sold out to Christ. May God grant to us the grace of his fierce heart and deep devotion to Christ, and to the Great Commission.

Daily Devotional Guide

PREPARING OUR HEARTS

Invocation: Our Prayer of Acclamation

God and Father of our Lord Jesus Christ, we thank you for your servant Paul, of whom the Lord promised even at his conversion that he indeed would suffer much on account of the Gospel. Paul loved your Son and his Gospel, and paid the extreme price of persecution, suffering, and martyrdom because of Jesus and his Kingdom. Our desire is to learn from you through meditation on this servant – his teaching, his example, and his life. Anoint us with your Holy Spirit, that he might do in us as he did in your servant Paul. For Christ's sake, amen.

Call to Worship

Blessed are you, O God: Father, Son, and Holy Spirit. And blessed is your Kingdom, both now and forever, amen.

PRAISING OUR GOD

Te Deum Laudamus

You are God: we praise you; you are the Lord; we acclaim you; you are the eternal Father: All creation worships you. To you all angels, all the powers of heaven, Cherubim and Seraphim, sing in endless praise: Holy, holy, holy Lord, God of power and might, heaven and earth are full of your glory.

The glorious company of apostles praise you. The noble fellowship of prophets praise you. The white-robed army of martyrs praise you. Throughout the world the holy Church acclaims you; Father, of majesty unbounded, your true and only Son, worthy of all worship, and the Holy Spirit, advocate and guide.

You, Christ, are the king of glory, the eternal Son of the Father. When you became man to set us free you did not shun the Virgin's womb. You overcame the sting of death and opened the kingdom of heaven to all believers. You are seated at God's right hand in glory. We believe that you will come and be our judge. Come then, Lord, and help your people, bought with the price of your own blood, and bring us with your saints to glory everlasting.

Praise and Thanksgiving (Songs and Prayers)

Gloria Patri

Glory be to the Father,
And to the Son and to the Holy Spirit:
As it was in the beginning,
Is now, and ever shall be,
World without end. Amen, amen.

LISTENING TO HIS VOICE

Chronological Reading for the Day

Sunday: Prov. 25-29
Monday: Prov. 30-31
Tuesday: Pss. 42-46
Wednesday: Pss. 47-49; 84-85; 87
Thursday: Pss. 1-2; 10; 33; 71; 91
Friday: Pss. 92-97
Saturday: Pss. 98-100; 102; 104

Lectionary Readings

Psalm: Ps. 96

Gospel: Luke 7.1-10

OT: 1 Kings 18.20-39

NT: Gal. 1.1-12

Reflection: Silence and/or Journaling

RESPONDING IN FAITH

The Apostles' Creed

I believe in God, the Father Almighty, Maker of heaven and earth;
and in Jesus Christ, his only Son, our Lord, who was conceived by the
Holy Spirit, born of the Virgin Mary, suffered under Pontius Pilate,
was crucified, dead, and buried; he descended into hell; the third day
he arose again from the dead; he ascended into heaven and sits on
the right hand of God the Father Almighty; from thence he shall come
to judge the quick and the dead.

I believe in the Holy Spirit, the holy catholic* church, the communion of saints, the forgiveness of sins, the resurrection of the body, and the life everlasting. Amen.

* In the Apostles' and Nicene Creeds, the term catholic refers to the Church's universality, through all ages and times, of all languages and peoples. It refers to no particular tradition or denominational expression (e.g., as in Roman Catholic).

Prayers of Confession

Let us now confess our sins to God and receive mercy and grace to help in our time of need.

Assurance of Pardon

Having faithfully confessed and renounced your sin, Christ also has been faithful to forgive your sins and to purify you from all unrighteousness. It is certain, that there is One who has spoken to the Father in your defense, Jesus Christ, the Righteous One who is the atoning sacrifice for our sins and for the sins of the whole world. His grace and peace are with you now. Amen.

Petitions and Supplications, Ending with the Lord's Prayer

Our Father which art in heaven, Hallowed be thy name. Thy kingdom come, Thy will be done in earth, as it is in heaven. Give us this day our daily bread. And forgive us our debts, as we forgive our debtors. And lead us not into temptation, but deliver us from evil: For thine is the kingdom, and the power, and the glory, for ever. Amen.

~ Matthew 6.9-13 (KJV)

Doxology (and/or closing song)

Praise God from whom all blessings flow;
Praise Him all creatures here below;
Praise Him above ye heavenly host;
Praise Father, Son and Holy Ghost. Amen.

DEPARTING TO SERVE

Benediction

Lord Jesus, our heart's desire is to become an ambassador for you – one who stands in your stead, representing our citizenship with integrity and honor, fulfilling our King's mandate, with a willingness to pay the extreme price for that representation. Make us your agents – outfit us with the mind and will to represent you with honor in all that we are and do, in order that you might be glorified, and the Father through you, for your sake, amen.

Affirmation from the Psalms

I waited patiently for the Lord; he inclined to me and heard my cry. [2] He drew me up from the pit of destruction, out of the miry bog, and set my feet upon a rock, making my steps secure. [3] He put a new song in my mouth, a song of praise to our God. Many will see and fear, and put their trust in the Lord. [4] Blessed is the man who makes the Lord his trust, who does not turn to the proud, to those who go astray after a lie! [5] You have multiplied, O Lord my God, your wondrous deeds and your thoughts toward us; none can compare with you! I will proclaim and tell of them, yet they are more than can be told.

~ Psalm 40.1-5

Pray without Ceasing – Flash Prayer for the Day

Lord Jesus Christ, our Lord and King, make us the kind of ambassadors who prove worthy to represent you and your kingdom rule.

For Your Weekly Journey

Let God Arise! Seasonal Focus
An Ambassador in Chains, Ephesians 6.19-20

Book Reading
Bruce, *Paul: Apostle of the Heart Set Free*

Third Sunday after Pentecost

June 5 - 11, 2016 • Proper 5

WEEK
28

On Pentecost we commemorate the descent of the Holy Spirit to earth on Christ's believers, his infilling of the people of God, the Church. Through him, the third person of the Trinity, Jesus our Lord is now present with his people. The Spirit is the guarantee of the promised inheritance to come. We ponder the fullness and mystery of our God's person and work in our celebration on Trinity Sunday.

THIS WEEK'S THEME
Life in Christ, Ephesians 1.1-2

In the first of the prison epistles, we begin with a very important theme. Location matters. Where you are has a great deal of significance for who you are. In this letter, Paul begins with three chapters describing our position "in Christ," and he then spends three chapters working out the implications of our position "in Christ." In this short letter, Paul describes the believer's position as "in Christ" or "in the Lord" some thirty times.

There is some debate as to whether or not Paul actually sent this letter to the city of Ephesus, or rather to a group of churches in the larger region. Whatever the case, the issues addressed in this letter are issues that must be addressed in a particular geographical and social context. Once we as believers begin to understand that we are "in Christ," it changes everything.

Daily Devotional Guide

PREPARING OUR HEARTS

Invocation: Our Prayer of Acclamation

Blessed be the God and Father of our Lord Jesus Christ who has chosen us to be united to his Son. Thank you Father for placing us in Christ. In Him we have adoption, we have grace, we have wisdom, we have every spiritual blessing. Help us to comprehend the truth about where we are in you. Help us today to live in correspondence with the true location of our souls, a location secure and safe in you. In the name of the Father, the Son, and the Holy Spirit, amen.

Call to Worship

Blessed are you, O God: Father, Son, and Holy Spirit. And blessed is your Kingdom, both now and forever, amen.

PRAISING OUR GOD

Te Deum Laudamus

You are God: we praise you; you are the Lord; we acclaim you; you are the eternal Father: All creation worships you. To you all angels, all the powers of heaven, Cherubim and Seraphim, sing in endless praise: Holy, holy, holy Lord, God of power and might, heaven and earth are full of your glory.

The glorious company of apostles praise you. The noble fellowship of prophets praise you. The white-robed army of martyrs praise you. Throughout the world the holy Church acclaims you; Father, of majesty unbounded, your true and only Son, worthy of all worship, and the Holy Spirit, advocate and guide.

You, Christ, are the king of glory, the eternal Son of the Father. When you became man to set us free you did not shun the Virgin's womb. You overcame the sting of death and opened the kingdom of heaven to all believers. You are seated at God's right hand in glory. We believe that you will come and be our judge. Come then, Lord, and help your people, bought with the price of your own blood, and bring us with your saints to glory everlasting.

Praise and Thanksgiving (Songs and Prayers)

Gloria Patri
Glory be to the Father,
And to the Son and to the Holy Spirit:
As it was in the beginning,
Is now, and ever shall be,
World without end. Amen, amen.

LISTENING TO HIS VOICE

Chronological Reading for the Day
Sunday: Pss. 105-106
Monday: Pss. 107; 111-114
Tuesday: Pss. 115-118
Wednesday: Ps. 119
Thursday: Pss. 120-121; 123; 125-126
Friday: Pss. 128-130; 132; 134-135
Saturday: Pss. 136; 146-150

Lectionary Readings
Psalm: Ps. 146   *OT:* 1 Kings 17.8-24
Gospel: Luke 7.11-17   *NT:* Gal. 1.11-24

Reflection: Silence and/or Journaling

Responding in Faith

The Apostles' Creed
*I believe in God, the Father Almighty, Maker of heaven and earth;
and in Jesus Christ, his only Son, our Lord, who was conceived by the
Holy Spirit, born of the Virgin Mary, suffered under Pontius Pilate,
was crucified, dead, and buried; he descended into hell; the third day
he arose again from the dead; he ascended into heaven and sits on
the right hand of God the Father Almighty; from thence he shall come
to judge the quick and the dead.*

I believe in the Holy Spirit, the holy catholic church, the communion
of saints, the forgiveness of sins, the resurrection of the body, and the
life everlasting. Amen.*

* In the Apostles' and Nicene Creeds, the term catholic refers to the Church's
universality, through all ages and times, of all languages and peoples. It refers to no
particular tradition or denominational expression (e.g., as in Roman Catholic).

Prayers of Confession
Let us now confess our sins to God and receive mercy and
grace to help in our time of need.

Assurance of Pardon
Having faithfully confessed and renounced your sin, Christ
also has been faithful to forgive your sins and to purify you
from all unrighteousness. It is certain, that there is One who
has spoken to the Father in your defense, Jesus Christ, the
Righteous One who is the atoning sacrifice for our sins and
for the sins of the whole world. His grace and peace are with
you now. Amen.

Petitions and Supplications, Ending with the Lord's Prayer
Our Father which art in heaven, Hallowed be thy name. Thy kingdom come, Thy will be done in earth, as it is in heaven. Give us this day our daily bread. And forgive us our debts, as we forgive our debtors. And lead us not into temptation, but deliver us from evil: For thine is the kingdom, and the power, and the glory, for ever. Amen.

~ Matthew 6.9-13 (KJV)

Doxology (and/or closing song)
Praise God from whom all blessings flow;
Praise Him all creatures here below;
Praise Him above ye heavenly host;
Praise Father, Son and Holy Ghost. Amen.

DEPARTING TO SERVE

Benediction
Lord Jesus Christ, you commissioned and sent Paul to be your representative. In the same way you send us forth today to walk in the grace and peace of the Father through the power of the Holy Spirit. Help us today as we work, witness, and worship. Remind us that we live and breathe in you. In the name of the Father, the Son, and the Holy Spirit, amen.

Affirmation from the Psalms
Praise the Lord! Praise the Lord, O my soul! [2] I will praise the Lord as long as I live; I will sing praises to my God while I have my being.

~ Psalm 146.1-2

Pray without Ceasing – Flash Prayer for the Day
Lord Jesus Christ, my life is in you.

For Your Weekly Journey

Let God Arise! Seasonal Focus
An Ambassador in Chains, Ephesians 6.19-20

Book Reading
Bruce, *Paul, Apostle of the Heart Set Free*

Our Corporate Disciplines
Book Discussion: Monday, June 6, 2016
Day of Solitude: Thursday, June 9, 2016

Fourth Sunday after Pentecost

June 12 - 18, 2016 • Proper 6

WEEK
29

On Pentecost we commemorate the descent of the Holy Spirit to earth on Christ's believers, his infilling of the people of God, the Church. Through him, the third person of the Trinity, Jesus our Lord is now present with his people. The Spirit is the guarantee of the promised inheritance to come. We ponder the fullness and mystery of our God's person and work in our celebration on Trinity Sunday.

THIS WEEK'S THEME

The Purpose of the Church, Ephesians 1.3-14

Paul begins his letter to the Ephesians with a single sentence of praise – a sentence 202 words long in the Greek. We are to bless the Father for his incredible plan of salvation. We praise him for his choice to adopt us into his family as his own children. We praise him for the redemption and forgiveness we have received through the blood of Christ. We praise him because he has revealed the mystery of his salvation plan to us in the fullness of time. We praise him because we have been chosen to live for the praise of God's glory. We praise him because we have received and been sealed with the promised Holy Spirit.

In the midst of this exuberant praise, Paul repeats a phrase three times. He explains that we have been called to live "to the praise of his grace/glory." Father, Son, and Holy Spirit each receive glory in Paul's song of praise. Here is the purpose of the church, we are a redeemed people who have received life so that we may live for the praise of his glory.

Daily Devotional Guide

PREPARING OUR HEARTS

Invocation: Our Prayer of Acclamation

Our Father, we join Paul in blessing your name. In Christ you have blessed us with every spiritual blessing. You chose us to live for the praise of your glory. Thank you for the love which destined us to be adopted as your children. Thank you for the cross, and for sending your Son at the fulness of time to purchase our salvation. Thank you that you have sealed us with the long awaited outpouring of your Holy Spirit. Help us to understand these mysteries. Help us to believe and receive the gifts you have poured down on us. Amen.

Call to Worship

Blessed are you, O God: Father, Son, and Holy Spirit. And blessed is your Kingdom, both now and forever, amen.

PRAISING OUR GOD

Te Deum Laudamus

You are God: we praise you; you are the Lord; we acclaim you; you are the eternal Father: All creation worships you. To you all angels, all the powers of heaven, Cherubim and Seraphim, sing in endless praise: Holy, holy, holy Lord, God of power and might, heaven and earth are full of your glory.

The glorious company of apostles praise you. The noble fellowship of prophets praise you. The white-robed army of martyrs praise you. Throughout the world the holy Church acclaims you; Father, of majesty unbounded, your true and only Son, worthy of all worship, and the Holy Spirit, advocate and guide.

You, Christ, are the king of glory, the eternal Son of the Father. When you became man to set us free you did not shun the Virgin's womb. You overcame the sting of death and opened the kingdom of heaven to all believers. You are seated at God's right hand in glory. We believe that you will come and be our judge. Come then, Lord, and help your people, bought with the price of your own blood, and bring us with your saints to glory everlasting.

Praise and Thanksgiving (Songs and Prayers)

Gloria Patri
Glory be to the Father,
And to the Son and to the Holy Spirit:
As it was in the beginning,
Is now, and ever shall be,
World without end. Amen, amen.

LISTENING TO HIS VOICE

Chronological Reading for the Day
Sunday: Isa. 18-23
Monday: Isa. 24-27; ch.29
Tuesday: Isa. 30-33
Wednesday: Isa. 34-35; Mic. 2-5
Thursday: Mic. 6-7; 2 Chron. 32.1-8; 2 Kings 18.13-37; Isa. 36
Friday: 2 Kings 19; Isa. 37; 2 Chron. 32.9-23
Saturday: 2 Kings 20.1-19; Isa. 38-39; 2 Chron. 32.24-31

Lectionary Readings
Psalm: Ps. 32   *OT:* 2 Sam. 11.26-12.10, 13-15
Gospel: Luke 7.36-8.3   *NT:* Gal. 2.15-21

Reflection: Silence and/or Journaling

RESPONDING IN FAITH

The Apostles' Creed

I believe in God, the Father Almighty, Maker of heaven and earth; and in Jesus Christ, his only Son, our Lord, who was conceived by the Holy Spirit, born of the Virgin Mary, suffered under Pontius Pilate, was crucified, dead, and buried; he descended into hell; the third day he arose again from the dead; he ascended into heaven and sits on the right hand of God the Father Almighty; from thence he shall come to judge the quick and the dead.

I believe in the Holy Spirit, the holy catholic* church, the communion of saints, the forgiveness of sins, the resurrection of the body, and the life everlasting. Amen.

* In the Apostles' and Nicene Creeds, the term catholic refers to the Church's universality, through all ages and times, of all languages and peoples. It refers to no particular tradition or denominational expression (e.g., as in Roman Catholic).

Prayers of Confession

Let us now confess our sins to God and receive mercy and grace to help in our time of need.

Assurance of Pardon

Having faithfully confessed and renounced your sin, Christ also has been faithful to forgive your sins and to purify you from all unrighteousness. It is certain, that there is One who has spoken to the Father in your defense, Jesus Christ, the Righteous One who is the atoning sacrifice for our sins and for the sins of the whole world. His grace and peace are with you now. Amen.

Petitions and Supplications, Ending with the Lord's Prayer
Our Father which art in heaven, Hallowed be thy name. Thy kingdom come, Thy will be done in earth, as it is in heaven. Give us this day our daily bread. And forgive us our debts, as we forgive our debtors. And lead us not into temptation, but deliver us from evil: For thine is the kingdom, and the power, and the glory, for ever. Amen.

~ Matthew 6.9-13 (KJV)

Doxology (and/or closing song)
Praise God from whom all blessings flow;
Praise Him all creatures here below;
Praise Him above ye heavenly host;
Praise Father, Son and Holy Ghost. Amen.

Departing to Serve

Benediction
Lord Jesus Christ, teach us to bless you at all times. Teach us to begin our thoughts and talk about the church with the kind of praise that begins Paul's letter to the Ephesians. Help our actions on behalf of the church to be an outflow of our praise to you for your love for your bride. Fill us with awe at the sovereign plan of your Father. Fill us with power as we receive the Holy Spirit's wisdom and counsel for the tasks you have called us to today. May you receive the praise and the glory. Amen.

Affirmation from the Psalms
Blessed is the one whose transgression is forgiven, whose sin is covered. [11] Be glad in the Lord, and rejoice, O righteous, and shout for joy, all you upright in heart!

~ Psalm 32.1, 11

Pray without Ceasing – Flash Prayer for the Day
Lord Jesus Christ, today I live for the praise of your glory.

For Your Weekly Journey

Let God Arise! Seasonal Focus
An Ambassador in Chains, Ephesians 6.19-20

Book Reading
Bruce, *Paul, Apostle of the Heart Set Free*

Fifth Sunday after Pentecost

June 19 - 25, 2016 • Proper 7

WEEK
30

On Pentecost we commemorate the descent of the Holy Spirit to earth on Christ's believers, his infilling of the people of God, the Church. Through him, the third person of the Trinity, Jesus our Lord is now present with his people. The Spirit is the guarantee of the promised inheritance to come. We ponder the fullness and mystery of our God's person and work in our celebration on Trinity Sunday.

THIS WEEK'S THEME
God's Poetry, Ephesians 2.8-10

Grace. Paul uses the word "grace" one hundred times in his letters. In Ephesians 2.8, "For by grace you have been saved through faith," we find the sixth of twelve uses of "grace" in Ephesians. What is so amazing about this grace? It is grace which we have received as a gift; grace we have received from God without any strings; grace that comes to us in such a way that none of us can boast of anything to deserve it.

This grace marks us. It shapes us and makes us. We are God's workmanship. The Greek word behind "workmanship" is poiema – a word some claim lies behind the English word for poem. Poiema was used to refer to something that a craftsman would shape, for example, a crown or a piece of art. God's grace in our lives produces his masterpieces, his works of art, his poetry. Together the mosaic of redeemed lives reflects the absolute beauty of our great God.

The beauty of God's work is seen in the good works of his new creation. Each believer has specific good works which God has prepared before the foundation of the world to perform. As we walk in the good works which God has prepared each day, we find his beauty revealed through us.

Daily Devotional Guide

PREPARING OUR HEARTS

Invocation: Our Prayer of Acclamation

Eternal Father, you have given us amazing grace. What better gift could you have given than your own Son? Thank you for the grace of Christ. Thank you for your Holy Spirit who is now pouring out your grace on us. As we have received, so help us to give. Teach us now what it means to know and receive your grace. In the name of the Father, the Son, and the Holy Spirit, amen.

Call to Worship

Blessed are you, O God: Father, Son, and Holy Spirit. And blessed is your Kingdom, both now and forever, amen.

PRAISING OUR GOD

Te Deum Laudamus

You are God: we praise you; you are the Lord; we acclaim you; you are the eternal Father: All creation worships you. To you all angels, all the powers of heaven, Cherubim and Seraphim, sing in endless praise: Holy, holy, holy Lord, God of power and might, heaven and earth are full of your glory.

The glorious company of apostles praise you. The noble fellowship of prophets praise you. The white-robed army of martyrs praise you. Throughout the world the holy Church acclaims you; Father, of majesty unbounded, your true and only Son, worthy of all worship, and the Holy Spirit, advocate and guide.

You, Christ, are the king of glory, the eternal Son of the Father. When you became man to set us free you did not shun the Virgin's womb. You overcame the sting of death and opened the kingdom of heaven

to all believers. You are seated at God's right hand in glory. We believe
that you will come and be our judge. Come then, Lord, and help your
people, bought with the price of your own blood, and bring us with
your saints to glory everlasting.

Praise and Thanksgiving (Songs and Prayers)

Gloria Patri
Glory be to the Father,
And to the Son and to the Holy Spirit:
As it was in the beginning,
Is now, and ever shall be,
World without end. Amen, amen.

LISTENING TO HIS VOICE

Chronological Reading for the Day
Sunday: Isa. 40-43
Monday: Isa. 44-48
Tuesday: Isa. 49-53
Wednesday: Isa. 54-57
Thursday: Isa. 58-62
Friday: Isa. 63-66; 2 Kings 20.20-21; 2 Chron. 32.32-33
Saturday: 2 Kings 21.1-22.2; 2 Chron. 33.1-34.7

Lectionary Readings
Psalm: Pss. 42-43   *OT:* 1 Kings 19.1-15a
Gospel: Luke 8.26-39   *NT:* Gal. 3.23-29

Reflection: Silence and/or Journaling

RESPONDING IN FAITH

The Apostles' Creed
I believe in God, the Father Almighty, Maker of heaven and earth;
and in Jesus Christ, his only Son, our Lord, who was conceived by the

Holy Spirit, born of the Virgin Mary, suffered under Pontius Pilate, was crucified, dead, and buried; he descended into hell; the third day he arose again from the dead; he ascended into heaven and sits on the right hand of God the Father Almighty; from thence he shall come to judge the quick and the dead.

I believe in the Holy Spirit, the holy catholic* church, the communion of saints, the forgiveness of sins, the resurrection of the body, and the life everlasting. Amen.

* In the Apostles' and Nicene Creeds, the term catholic refers to the Church's universality, through all ages and times, of all languages and peoples. It refers to no particular tradition or denominational expression (e.g., as in Roman Catholic).

Prayers of Confession

Let us now confess our sins to God and receive mercy and grace to help in our time of need.

Assurance of Pardon

Having faithfully confessed and renounced your sin, Christ also has been faithful to forgive your sins and to purify you from all unrighteousness. It is certain, that there is One who has spoken to the Father in your defense, Jesus Christ, the Righteous One who is the atoning sacrifice for our sins and for the sins of the whole world. His grace and peace are with you now. Amen.

Petitions and Supplications, Ending with the Lord's Prayer

Our Father which art in heaven, Hallowed be thy name. Thy kingdom come, Thy will be done in earth, as it is in heaven. Give us this day our daily bread. And forgive us our debts, as we forgive our debtors. And lead us not into temptation, but deliver us from evil: For thine is the kingdom, and the power, and the glory, for ever. Amen.

~ Matthew 6.9-13 (KJV)

Doxology (and/or closing song)
Praise God from whom all blessings flow;
Praise Him all creatures here below;
Praise Him above ye heavenly host;
Praise Father, Son and Holy Ghost. Amen.

DEPARTING TO SERVE

Benediction
Dear Jesus, thank you for the work you did on the cross. Thank you for conquering sin, death, and the Devil. Thank you for the grace you have given freely. Help me today to be marked by the grace I have received. As one who has been forgiven much, will you help me to love much? I pray this in the name of the Father, the Son, and the Holy Spirit, amen.

Affirmation from the Psalms
Why are you cast down, O my soul, and why are you in turmoil within me? Hope in God; for I shall again praise him, my salvation and my God.

~ Psalm 42.11

Pray without Ceasing – Flash Prayer for the Day
Lord Jesus Christ, help me to freely share the grace I have received.

For Your Weekly Journey

Let God Arise! Seasonal Focus
An Ambassador in Chains, Ephesians 6.19-20

Book Reading
Bruce, *Paul, Apostle of the Heart Set Free*

Our Corporate Disciplines
Book Discussion: Monday, June 20, 2016

The Season after Pentecost

A SEASON OF CHRIST'S HEADSHIP

For he will deliver you
from the snare of the fowler
and from the deadly pestilence.
He will cover you with his pinions,
and under his wings you will find refuge;
his faithfulness is a shield and buckler.

PSALM 91.3-4

The Name above Every Name That Is Named

The Season after Pentecost is a season of recognition and affirmation of the headship and lordship of Jesus Christ. According to the Apostle Paul in his letter to the Ephesians, God the Father has displayed his immeasurable power to the world in raising his Son Jesus Christ from the dead. The same Jesus who was humiliated and abused in a sham Roman trial and Jewish Sanhedrin council proceeding has now been vindicated. Through his death and resurrection, Jesus the Nazarene has proven himself to be the one, true Son of God, the Christ and Lord of all.

Now, because of his obedience and sacrifice, God has highly magnified him and through his ascension has seated Jesus at his right hand in the heavenly places. This exalted status is unique and singular; he has been raised "far above all rule and authority and power and dominion, and above every name that is named, not only in this age but also in the one to come" (Eph. 1.21, ESV). In honor of his work as God's servant, the Father has put all things under his feet, and given Jesus Christ to be head over all things to his body, the Church, which is called "the fullness of him who fills all in all" (Eph. 1.23). The exaltation of Jesus Christ is appropriate and right; his is the only name under heaven given to humankind whereby they can be reconciled to God and forgiven of their sins (Acts 4.12).

The Already/Not Yet Kingdom: The Exaltation of Jesus Christ

During this unique season, we reflect and act in real time. We both ponder and live in that amazing "already/not yet" moment of Christ's reign between the sending of the Holy Spirit and his return at the Second Coming. During this season of God's calendar, we acknowledge and recognize Jesus' place in the universe. Given all authority in heaven and on earth, he now commands his people to go and make disciples of all nations (Matt. 28.18-19). Because our Lord is alive and exalted, we are empowered to accomplish his mandate of world evangelization, and serve as his ambassadors around the globe where people and nations still do not know him to be the Lord and Savior of the world. During this Season after Pentecost we extol him who has been given a name above every name, the same name that all tongues one day will confess and all knees one day will be made to bow to. Truly, Jesus Christ is Lord to the glory of God, the Father (Phil. 2.9-11).

According to Paul in 1 Corinthians 15, Jesus Christ must reign until God has put all of his enemies under his feet (cf. 15.25). As he whom God has exalted, Christ ever lives now to make intercession for his own (Heb. 7.25). As he whom God has honored, he alone is the head over all things to his people, leading and directing them as the Shepherd of their souls (1 Pet. 2.25). As he whom God has granted authority over all things, Jesus alone can provide for us the grace and strength to endure all that this world and its prince may do to thwart God's will (1 John 4.4).

Those of us committed to advancing the Kingdom of God in the cities of the world need to remind ourselves that things are not as they appear. On every hand God seems to be ignorant of the chaos around us, or worse, impotent to change the affairs in a world that seems to daily spin more and more out of control. Evil taunts righteousness in numerous societies that flail and wobble towards corruption, coasting without bearing or compass. In the face of such tragedies, let us worship God during this Season after Pentecost, and remember his holy Word: Jesus our Lord has been exalted at the Father's right hand, given a name above all names, and is the head of his people, directing his Church's affairs as we both show and tell the lost of the Good News of the Kingdom.

In the midst of despair and difficulty, we need never abandon our hope that, in spite of it all, God in Christ Jesus still commands the universe, and reigns in all the corridors of history. In all things, our Lord Christ alone will have the final say. The Ascension is our opportunity to confess that Christ is risen and exalted, and that God is still on the throne. This is the key to ministry, and this is the key to life.

He Must Reign until All His Enemies Are under His Feet
It turns out then that our remembrance during Ordinary Time is not that ordinary after all. During this Kingdomtide, let us affirm the truth that spans the centuries and binds all epochs of salvation history together. In Jesus Christ, God intends to rule and reign, and our Lord must now reign until all his enemies are under his feet. As we continue to worship and serve our Lord during this the longest season in the Church's calendar, let's remember as believers and congregations that the next season to follow is Advent: the return of the exalted Lord to the earth to complete the work he started on the Cross. Let us strive on toward maturity and multiplication in power of the Holy Spirit as the body of Christ in the world.

Join us as believers in Jesus Christ in giving glory to the Father for his exaltation of Christ, and let us strive in all our worship and service to give him the honor and praise he deserves. There is no other name under heaven given for us to be saved, and no other Lord in the universe who will reign and rule as God's sovereign King forever.

Let our knees gladly bow and our tongues joyfully confess that Jesus Christ is Lord, to the glory of God the Father. May we advance his kingdom reign in all that we are and say and do during this Season after Pentecost.

Standing in awe of the Risen and Exalted Lord,
Rev. Dr. Don L. Davis

WEEK
31

Sixth Sunday after Pentecost
June 26 - July 2, 2016 • Proper 8

During "Ordinary Time" (Kingdomtide), we consider God's saving acts through the unfolding of our days. As Christus Victor, Jesus is exalted at God's right hand, and he must reign until his enemies are put under his feet. He is the head of the body, the Church, and now he empowers his people to bear witness of his saving grace in the world.

THIS WEEK'S THEME
A Prisoner's Prayer, Ephesians 3.14-21

Paul is a man of prayer, and Ephesians includes several of his prayers. In our passage Paul prays to the Father as the supreme Lord over all of humanity. He prays that the Father will strengthen believers through his Spirit in our hearts.

He prays that Christ will dwell in us through faith, and that his love will grow deep roots in our hearts. He prays that we will know the breadth and length and height and depth of God's love as it has been revealed in Christ. This love surpasses all human knowledge, and it results in the fulness of God's presence.

The power of God that is working in us is more powerful than we could ask or think. The Father who has this power reveals it through the Spirit and the Son so that he might receive glory in all generations forever and ever.

Daily Devotional Guide

PREPARING OUR HEARTS

Invocation: Our Prayer of Acclamation

Our Father in heaven, it is a mystery why you would choose the church to reveal your love to the world. We are weak and full of faults. But you have chosen us so that you might receive glory. You have called us beloved, for we rest in your beloved Son. Teach us to know the power of your love. Help us to receive that which we cannot apart from your great grace. In the name of the Father, the Son, and the Holy Spirit, amen.

Call to Worship

Blessed are you, O God: Father, Son, and Holy Spirit. And blessed is your Kingdom, both now and forever, amen.

PRAISING OUR GOD

Te Deum Laudamus

You are God: we praise you; you are the Lord; we acclaim you; you are the eternal Father: All creation worships you. To you all angels, all the powers of heaven, Cherubim and Seraphim, sing in endless praise: Holy, holy, holy Lord, God of power and might, heaven and earth are full of your glory.

The glorious company of apostles praise you. The noble fellowship of prophets praise you. The white-robed army of martyrs praise you. Throughout the world the holy Church acclaims you; Father, of majesty unbounded, your true and only Son, worthy of all worship, and the Holy Spirit, advocate and guide.

You, Christ, are the king of glory, the eternal Son of the Father. When you became man to set us free you did not shun the Virgin's womb. You overcame the sting of death and opened the kingdom of heaven to all believers. You are seated at God's right hand in glory. We believe that you will come and be our judge. Come then, Lord, and help your people, bought with the price of your own blood, and bring us with your saints to glory everlasting.

Praise and Thanksgiving (Songs and Prayers)

Gloria Patri
Glory be to the Father,
And to the Son and to the Holy Spirit:
As it was in the beginning,
Is now, and ever shall be,
World without end. Amen, amen.

LISTENING TO HIS VOICE

Chronological Reading for the Day
Sunday: Jer. 1-4
Monday: Jer. 5-6; 2 Kings 22.3-20; 2 Chron. 34.8-28
Tuesday: 2 Kings 23.1-28; 2 Chron. 34.29-35.19; Nah. 1-3
Wednesday: Hab. 1-3
Thursday: Zeph. 1-3; 2 Chron. 35.20-27; 2 Kings 23.29-30;
    Jer. 47-48
Friday: 2 Chron. 36.1-5; 2 Kings 23.31-24.4; Jer. 22.1-23; ch.26
Saturday: Jer. 25; 36; 45-46

Lectionary Readings
Psalm: Ps. 16   *OT:* 1 Kings 19.15-16, 19-21
Gospel: Luke 9.51-62   *NT:* Gal. 5.1, 13-25

Reflection: Silence and/or Journaling

RESPONDING IN FAITH

The Apostles' Creed
I believe in God, the Father Almighty, Maker of heaven and earth;
and in Jesus Christ, his only Son, our Lord, who was conceived by the
Holy Spirit, born of the Virgin Mary, suffered under Pontius Pilate,
was crucified, dead, and buried; he descended into hell; the third day
he arose again from the dead; he ascended into heaven and sits on
the right hand of God the Father Almighty; from thence he shall come
to judge the quick and the dead.

I believe in the Holy Spirit, the holy catholic* church, the communion of saints, the forgiveness of sins, the resurrection of the body, and the life everlasting. Amen.

* In the Apostles' and Nicene Creeds, the term catholic refers to the Church's universality, through all ages and times, of all languages and peoples. It refers to no particular tradition or denominational expression (e.g., as in Roman Catholic).

Prayers of Confession

Let us now confess our sins to God and receive mercy and grace to help in our time of need.

Assurance of Pardon

Having faithfully confessed and renounced your sin, Christ also has been faithful to forgive your sins and to purify you from all unrighteousness. It is certain, that there is One who has spoken to the Father in your defense, Jesus Christ, the Righteous One who is the atoning sacrifice for our sins and for the sins of the whole world. His grace and peace are with you now. Amen.

Petitions and Supplications, Ending with the Lord's Prayer

Our Father which art in heaven, Hallowed be thy name. Thy kingdom come, Thy will be done in earth, as it is in heaven. Give us this day our daily bread. And forgive us our debts, as we forgive our debtors. And lead us not into temptation, but deliver us from evil: For thine is the kingdom, and the power, and the glory, for ever. Amen.

~ Matthew 6.9-13 (KJV)

Doxology (and/or closing song)

Praise God from whom all blessings flow;
Praise Him all creatures here below;
Praise Him above ye heavenly host;
Praise Father, Son and Holy Ghost. Amen.

DEPARTING TO SERVE

Benediction

Lord Jesus your love is greater than the ocean, wider than the sea. Help us to come to you today resting in this deep, deep, love. May our prayers to you echo back the love we have received. Fill us with the power of your Spirit so that you, Christ, may reign supreme in our hearts through faith. To you be all glory and power, now, and in the church for eternity, amen.

Affirmation from the Psalms

You make known to me the path of life; in your presence there is fullness of joy; at your right hand are pleasures forevermore.

~ Psalm 42.11

Pray without Ceasing – Flash Prayer for the Day

Lord Jesus Christ, grant me power to know and show your love.

For Your Weekly Journey

Let God Arise! Seasonal Focus

Stand Firm in Christ, Ephesians 6.19-20

Book Reading

Bruce, *Paul, Apostle of the Heart Set Free*

Seventh Sunday after Pentecost

July 3 - 9, 2016 • Proper 9

WEEK
32

During "Ordinary Time" (Kingdomtide), we consider God's saving acts through the unfolding of our days. As Christus Victor, Jesus is exalted at God's right hand, and he must reign until his enemies are put under his feet. He is the head of the body, the Church, and now he empowers his people to bear witness of his saving grace in the world.

THIS WEEK'S THEME

The Constitution of the Church, Ephesians 4.1-6

A prison cell focuses your attention. Paul begins the second half of this letter with a reminder that he is a prisoner of the Lord. From his prison cell he emphasizes four times the importance of calling. A called life is marked by humility, meekness, patience, and forbearing with other believers in love. It is a life eager for the unity of the Holy Spirit and lived in submission to the Father. Those who are called share one Lord, one faith, one baptism.

Yes, the church is a people called. We are a community that finds our origin in a specific call. Jesus said "follow me," and the church grows in faithfulness and fruitfulness as we learn to live a life worthy of this call we have received. A life centered on the call of Christ is mere Christianity; it is the essence of discipleship. The call to follow Jesus is the same today as it was 2000 years ago. Jesus still speaks to his disciples, "You, follow me!"

Daily Devotional Guide

PREPARING OUR HEARTS

Invocation: Our Prayer of Acclamation

Our Father in heaven, your voice spoke the universe into existence. On earth, your Son, our Lord Jesus, spoke your words of truth and light. Today, your Spirit speaks to our hearts as we listen for your voice in Holy Scripture. Thank you for the call to be your people. Help us today to live in a manner worthy of the call we have received. In the name of the Father, the Son, and the Holy Spirit, amen.

Call to Worship

Blessed are you, O God: Father, Son, and Holy Spirit. And blessed is your Kingdom, both now and forever, amen.

PRAISING OUR GOD

Te Deum Laudamus

You are God: we praise you; you are the Lord; we acclaim you; you are the eternal Father: All creation worships you. To you all angels, all the powers of heaven, Cherubim and Seraphim, sing in endless praise: Holy, holy, holy Lord, God of power and might, heaven and earth are full of your glory.

The glorious company of apostles praise you. The noble fellowship of prophets praise you. The white-robed army of martyrs praise you. Throughout the world the holy Church acclaims you; Father, of majesty unbounded, your true and only Son, worthy of all worship, and the Holy Spirit, advocate and guide.

You, Christ, are the king of glory, the eternal Son of the Father. When you became man to set us free you did not shun the Virgin's womb. You overcame the sting of death and opened the kingdom of heaven to all believers. You are seated at God's right hand in glory. We believe that you will come and be our judge. Come then, Lord, and help your people, bought with the price of your own blood, and bring us with your saints to glory everlasting.

Praise and Thanksgiving (Songs and Prayers)

Gloria Patri
Glory be to the Father,
And to the Son and to the Holy Spirit:
As it was in the beginning,
Is now, and ever shall be,
World without end. Amen, amen.

LISTENING TO HIS VOICE

Chronological Reading for the Day
Sunday: Jer. 19-20; Dan. 1
Monday: Dan. 2-3; Jer. 7.1-8.3
Tuesday: Jer. 8.4-11.23
Wednesday: Jer. 12-15
Thursday: Jer. 16-18; ch.35
Friday: Jer. 49.1-33; 22.24-23.32; 2 Kings 24.5-9; 2 Chron. 36.6-9
Saturday: Jer. 23.33-24.10; 29.1-31.14

Lectionary Readings
Psalm: Ps. 66.1-9   *OT:* Isa. 66.10-14
Gospel: Luke 10.1-11, 16-20   *NT:* Gal. 6.1-16

Reflection: Silence and/or Journaling

RESPONDING IN FAITH

The Apostles' Creed
I believe in God, the Father Almighty, Maker of heaven and earth; and in Jesus Christ, his only Son, our Lord, who was conceived by the Holy Spirit, born of the Virgin Mary, suffered under Pontius Pilate, was crucified, dead, and buried; he descended into hell; the third day

he arose again from the dead; he ascended into heaven and sits on the right hand of God the Father Almighty; from thence he shall come to judge the quick and the dead.

I believe in the Holy Spirit, the holy catholic* church, the communion of saints, the forgiveness of sins, the resurrection of the body, and the life everlasting. Amen.

* In the Apostles' and Nicene Creeds, the term catholic refers to the Church's universality, through all ages and times, of all languages and peoples. It refers to no particular tradition or denominational expression (e.g., as in Roman Catholic).

Prayers of Confession

Let us now confess our sins to God and receive mercy and grace to help in our time of need.

Assurance of Pardon

Having faithfully confessed and renounced your sin, Christ also has been faithful to forgive your sins and to purify you from all unrighteousness. It is certain, that there is One who has spoken to the Father in your defense, Jesus Christ, the Righteous One who is the atoning sacrifice for our sins and for the sins of the whole world. His grace and peace are with you now. Amen.

Petitions and Supplications, Ending with the Lord's Prayer

Our Father which art in heaven, Hallowed be thy name. Thy kingdom come, Thy will be done in earth, as it is in heaven. Give us this day our daily bread. And forgive us our debts, as we forgive our debtors. And lead us not into temptation, but deliver us from evil: For thine is the kingdom, and the power, and the glory, for ever. Amen.

~ Matthew 6.9-13 (KJV)

Doxology (and/or closing song)
Praise God from whom all blessings flow;
Praise Him all creatures here below;
Praise Him above ye heavenly host;
Praise Father, Son and Holy Ghost. Amen.

DEPARTING TO SERVE

Benediction
Lord Jesus Christ, like Paul, you were once a prisoner. As you waited for your captors, you prayed to your Father with the words, "not my will but yours be done." As we obey the call you have placed on our lives and follow you in joyful obedience, make us eager to live worthy of the calling we have been given. Lead us into unity with your people all around the world and help us to pursue the things that will lead to peace today. In the name of the Father, the Son, and the Holy Spirit, amen.

Affirmation from the Psalms
Shout for joy to God, all the earth; [2] sing the glory of his name; give to him glorious praise! [3] Say to God, "How awesome are your deeds!

~ Psalm 66.1-3a

Pray without Ceasing – Flash Prayer for the Day
Lord Jesus Christ, help me to live worthy of the calling with which I have been called.

For Your Weekly Journey

Let God Arise! Seasonal Focus
Stand Firm in Christ, Ephesians 6.19-20

Book Reading
Bruce, *Paul, Apostle of the Heart Set Free*

Eighth Sunday after Pentecost
July 10 - 16, 2016 • Proper 10

During "Ordinary Time" (Kingdomtide), we consider God's saving acts through the unfolding of our days. As Christus Victor, Jesus is exalted at God's right hand, and he must reign until his enemies are put under his feet. He is the head of the body, the Church, and now he empowers his people to bear witness of his saving grace in the world.

THIS WEEK'S THEME
The Fulness of Christ, Ephesians 4.11-16

Paul is working out the implications of being "in Christ" throughout the last three chapters of Ephesians. First he emphasized the unity to which the body of Christ is called, a unity modeled on the oneness found in the Trinity. He then emphasizes the exalted place of our ascended Lord Jesus Christ. As King of kings and Lord of lords, Jesus has provided a way for his people to grow into maturity.

The risen Lord has given his church the gift of leaders, apostles, prophets, evangelists, shepherds and teachers. These leaders are given to equip the saints so that the saints might perform their work of service with the result that the body of Christ is built up into maturity. As each member of the body does his or her work, the whole body grows into maturity. Paul describes this state of maturity as "the fulness of Christ."

The fulness of Christ carries with it specific fruit. Christ's mature body will not be swayed by the winds of false doctrine or the deceitful schemes of the world system that so often stands opposed to the way of the Kingdom. The body will be characterized by truth speaking–but this truth will always be spoken in love. It is this love of Christ which joins the body together, and which empowers each member to perform its specific function. As each member performs its specific work, the body grows in health and maturity. We grow into the fulness of Christ.

Daily Devotional Guide

PREPARING OUR HEARTS

Invocation: Our Prayer of Acclamation

Our Father in heaven, through your Son you have sent the gift of leaders to your church. Thank you for the way these leaders equip your saints to do the work of ministry. Thank you for the specific ministries you have given to each of us. Thank you that you have chosen to place us in your family and to use us for the praise of your glory. Help us today to see how you wish to use us to build up Christ's body. In the name of the Father, the Son, and the Holy Spirit, amen.

Call to Worship

Blessed are you, O God: Father, Son, and Holy Spirit. And blessed is your Kingdom, both now and forever, amen.

PRAISING OUR GOD

Te Deum Laudamus

You are God: we praise you; you are the Lord; we acclaim you; you are the eternal Father: All creation worships you. To you all angels, all the powers of heaven, Cherubim and Seraphim, sing in endless praise: Holy, holy, holy Lord, God of power and might, heaven and earth are full of your glory.

The glorious company of apostles praise you. The noble fellowship of prophets praise you. The white-robed army of martyrs praise you. Throughout the world the holy Church acclaims you; Father, of majesty unbounded, your true and only Son, worthy of all worship, and the Holy Spirit, advocate and guide.

You, Christ, are the king of glory, the eternal Son of the Father. When you became man to set us free you did not shun the Virgin's womb. You overcame the sting of death and opened the kingdom of heaven to all believers. You are seated at God's right hand in glory. We believe

that you will come and be our judge. Come then, Lord, and help your people, bought with the price of your own blood, and bring us with your saints to glory everlasting.

Praise and Thanksgiving (Songs and Prayers)

Gloria Patri
Glory be to the Father,
And to the Son and to the Holy Spirit:
As it was in the beginning,
Is now, and ever shall be,
World without end. Amen, amen.

LISTENING TO HIS VOICE

Chronological Reading for the Day
Sunday: Jer. 31.15-40; 49.34-51.14
Monday: Jer. 51.15-58; 52.1-3a; 37.1-10; 2 Kings 24.10-20a; 2 Chron. 36.10-14; 1 Chron. 3.10-16
Tuesday: Jer. 37.11-38.28; Ezek. 1.1-3.15
Wednesday: Ezek. 3.16-4.17; Jer. 27.1-28.17; 51.59-64
Thursday: Ezek. 5-9
Friday: Ezek. 10-13
Saturday: Ezek. 14-16

Lectionary Readings
Psalm: Ps. 25.1-10

Gospel: Luke 10.25-37

OT: Deut. 30.9-14

NT: Col. 1.1-14

Reflection: Silence and/or Journaling

RESPONDING IN FAITH

The Apostles' Creed
I believe in God, the Father Almighty, Maker of heaven and earth; and in Jesus Christ, his only Son, our Lord, who was conceived by the

Holy Spirit, born of the Virgin Mary, suffered under Pontius Pilate, was crucified, dead, and buried; he descended into hell; the third day he arose again from the dead; he ascended into heaven and sits on the right hand of God the Father Almighty; from thence he shall come to judge the quick and the dead.

I believe in the Holy Spirit, the holy catholic* church, the communion of saints, the forgiveness of sins, the resurrection of the body, and the life everlasting. Amen.

* In the Apostles' and Nicene Creeds, the term catholic refers to the Church's universality, through all ages and times, of all languages and peoples. It refers to no particular tradition or denominational expression (e.g., as in Roman Catholic).

Prayers of Confession
Let us now confess our sins to God and receive mercy and grace to help in our time of need.

Assurance of Pardon
Having faithfully confessed and renounced your sin, Christ also has been faithful to forgive your sins and to purify you from all unrighteousness. It is certain, that there is One who has spoken to the Father in your defense, Jesus Christ, the Righteous One who is the atoning sacrifice for our sins and for the sins of the whole world. His grace and peace are with you now. Amen.

Petitions and Supplications, Ending with the Lord's Prayer
Our Father which art in heaven, Hallowed be thy name. Thy kingdom come, Thy will be done in earth, as it is in heaven. Give us this day our daily bread. And forgive us our debts, as we forgive our debtors. And lead us not into temptation, but deliver us from evil: For thine is the kingdom, and the power, and the glory, for ever. Amen.

~ Matthew 6.9-13 (KJV)

Doxology (and/or closing song)

Praise God from whom all blessings flow;
Praise Him all creatures here below;
Praise Him above ye heavenly host;
Praise Father, Son and Holy Ghost. Amen.

DEPARTING TO SERVE

Benediction

Blessed be you, our Lord Jesus Christ. You are risen and ascended in glory. You reign over all. We praise you for the plan you have had from before the world began. Use us today to bring you glory in unique and specific ways. Use all that we have, our gifts and talents, our weaknesses and even our faults. Use us to build up your body, and fill us with your love that we might grow into the fulness to which we are called. We pray this in your holy name, amen.

Affirmation from the Psalms

Good and upright is the Lord; therefore he instructs sinners in the way. [9] He leads the humble in what is right, and teaches the humble his way. [10] All the paths of the Lord are steadfast love and faithfulness, for those who keep his covenant and his testimonies.

~ Psalm 25.8-10

Pray without Ceasing – Flash Prayer for the Day

Lord Jesus Christ, do your work through me, that we might reach maturity.

For Your Weekly Journey

Let God Arise! Seasonal Focus
Stand Firm in Christ, Ephesians 6.19-20

Book Reading
Bruce, *Paul, Apostle of the Heart Set Free*

Our Corporate Disciplines
Book Discussion: Monday, July 11, 2016
Day of Prayer and Fasting: Thursday, July 14, 2016

Ninth Sunday after Pentecost

July 17 - 23, 2016 • Proper 11

During "Ordinary Time" (Kingdomtide), we consider God's saving acts through the unfolding of our days. As Christus Victor, Jesus is exalted at God's right hand, and he must reign until his enemies are put under his feet. He is the head of the body, the Church, and now he empowers his people to bear witness of his saving grace in the world.

THIS WEEK'S THEME

The Wisdom of Christ, Ephesians 5.15-21

Life in Christ leads to the way of Christ. The way of Christ is the way of wisdom. Some 1,900 years ago a pastor wrote, "there are two ways, one of life and one of death, and there is a great difference between these two ways" (Didache 1:1). Life in Christ is the way of life and this way is marked by specific characteristics.

Jesus' way of wisdom leads us to redeem the time. As good stewards, we seek to make the most of the hours, days, and years we are given for the praise of his glory. We seek to understand what the Lord's will is for us and our community. By grace we desire to be filled with the Spirit and to walk minute by minute in his mighty power. We sing and pray from Jesus' prayerbook, the book of Psalms. We sing the spirituals of the saints who have gone before, and we sing with all of our heart. In all things, we give thanks in the name of our Lord Jesus Christ to the Father. Finally, we submit to one another in the fear of Christ, recognizing our Lord's sovereign presence in our midst.

Daily Devotional Guide

PREPARING OUR HEARTS

Invocation: Our Prayer of Acclamation

Almighty Father, you have revealed your own wisdom to us in giving us your Son, our Lord Jesus Christ. Truly your thoughts are not our thoughts, nor your ways our ways. We need your grace today to walk in your way. Teach us to hear your Spirit's voice as he directs us today. Help us to understand your will, and to faithfully steward the minutes and hours of this day for the specific work you have called us to do. Fill our hearts with songs of praise to you, who reign in unspeakable glory. In the name of the Father, the Son, and the Holy Spirit, amen.

Call to Worship

Blessed are you, O God: Father, Son, and Holy Spirit. And blessed is your Kingdom, both now and forever, amen.

PRAISING OUR GOD

Te Deum Laudamus

You are God: we praise you; you are the Lord; we acclaim you; you are the eternal Father: All creation worships you. To you all angels, all the powers of heaven, Cherubim and Seraphim, sing in endless praise: Holy, holy, holy Lord, God of power and might, heaven and earth are full of your glory.

The glorious company of apostles praise you. The noble fellowship of prophets praise you. The white-robed army of martyrs praise you. Throughout the world the holy Church acclaims you; Father, of majesty unbounded, your true and only Son, worthy of all worship, and the Holy Spirit, advocate and guide.

You, Christ, are the king of glory, the eternal Son of the Father. When you became man to set us free you did not shun the Virgin's womb. You overcame the sting of death and opened the kingdom of heaven to all believers. You are seated at God's right hand in glory. We believe that you will come and be our judge. Come then, Lord, and help your people, bought with the price of your own blood, and bring us with your saints to glory everlasting.

Praise and Thanksgiving (Songs and Prayers)

Gloria Patri
Glory be to the Father,
And to the Son and to the Holy Spirit:
As it was in the beginning,
Is now, and ever shall be,
World without end. Amen, amen.

LISTENING TO HIS VOICE

Chronological Reading for the Day
Sunday: Ezek. 17-19
Monday: Ezek. 20.1-22.16
Tuesday: Ezek. 22.17-24.14; 2 Kings 24.20b-25.2;
    Jer. 52.3b-5; 39.1
Wednesday: Ezek. 24.15-25.17; 29.1-16; 30.20-31.18;
    Jer. 34; ch.21
Thursday: Jer. 32-33; Ezek. 26
Friday: Ezek. 27-28; 2 Kings 25.3-7; Jer. 52.6-11; 39.2-10
Saturday: Jer. 39.11-18; 40.1-6; 52.12-27; 2 Kings 25.8-21;
    2 Chron. 36.15-21

Lectionary Readings
Psalm: Ps. 52   *OT:* Amos 8.1-12
Gospel: Luke 10.38-42   *NT:* Col. 1.15-28

Reflection: Silence and/or Journaling

RESPONDING IN FAITH

The Apostles' Creed
I believe in God, the Father Almighty, Maker of heaven and earth; and in Jesus Christ, his only Son, our Lord, who was conceived by the Holy Spirit, born of the Virgin Mary, suffered under Pontius Pilate, was crucified, dead, and buried; he descended into hell; the third day he arose again from the dead; he ascended into heaven and sits on the right hand of God the Father Almighty; from thence he shall come to judge the quick and the dead.

I believe in the Holy Spirit, the holy catholic* church, the communion of saints, the forgiveness of sins, the resurrection of the body, and the life everlasting. Amen.

* In the Apostles' and Nicene Creeds, the term catholic refers to the Church's universality, through all ages and times, of all languages and peoples. It refers to no particular tradition or denominational expression (e.g., as in Roman Catholic).

Prayers of Confession
Let us now confess our sins to God and receive mercy and grace to help in our time of need.

Assurance of Pardon
Having faithfully confessed and renounced your sin, Christ also has been faithful to forgive your sins and to purify you from all unrighteousness. It is certain, that there is One who has spoken to the Father in your defense, Jesus Christ, the Righteous One who is the atoning sacrifice for our sins and for the sins of the whole world. His grace and peace are with you now. Amen.

Petitions and Supplications, Ending with the Lord's Prayer
Our Father which art in heaven, Hallowed be thy name. Thy kingdom come, Thy will be done in earth, as it is in heaven. Give us this day our daily bread. And forgive us our debts, as we forgive our debtors. And lead us not into temptation, but deliver us from evil: For thine is the kingdom, and the power, and the glory, for ever. Amen.

~ Matthew 6.9-13 (KJV)

Doxology (and/or closing song)
Praise God from whom all blessings flow;
Praise Him all creatures here below;
Praise Him above ye heavenly host;
Praise Father, Son and Holy Ghost. Amen.

DEPARTING TO SERVE

Benediction
Lord Jesus Christ, your way is the beginning of wisdom. To know you, fear you, love you–this is the path of life. Lead us in your way today. Fill us with your Holy Spirit. Fill our hearts with thanksgiving. Bring glory to your Father and lead us deeper into the mystery of your love. We ask this in your holy name, amen.

Affirmation from the Psalms
But I am like a green olive tree in the house of God. I trust in the steadfast love of God forever and ever. [9] I will thank you forever, because you have done it. I will wait for your name, for it is good, in the presence of the godly.

~ Psalm 52.8-9

Pray without Ceasing – Flash Prayer for the Day
Lord Jesus Christ, teach us your way, that we might walk in wisdom.

For Your Weekly Journey

Let God Arise! Seasonal Focus
Stand Firm in Christ, Ephesians 6.19-20

Book Reading
Bruce, *Paul, Apostle of the Heart Set Free*

Our Corporate Disciplines
Book Discussion: Monday, July 18, 2016

Tenth Sunday after Pentecost
July 24 - 30, 2016 • Proper 12

During "Ordinary Time" (Kingdomtide), we consider God's saving acts through the unfolding of our days. As Christus Victor, Jesus is exalted at God's right hand, and he must reign until his enemies are put under his feet. He is the head of the body, the Church, and now he empowers his people to bear witness of his saving grace in the world.

THIS WEEK'S THEME
Stand Firm in Christ, Ephesians 6.10-20

Some years ago, the artist Tim Ladwig painted a picture entitled, "We Will Not Bow." The picture shows the three Hebrew boys standing in the fire of Nebuchadnezzer's furnace. This image of defiance against the flesh, the world, and the devil provides a helpful picture of what it means to stand firm in Christ.

Four times in our passage Paul describes the need for believers to stand. Walking in the wisdom of the Lord is not something that takes place in a vacuum. There are powerful spiritual beings who are opposed to the way of Christ. The Devil, principalities, powers, and spiritual forces in high places seek to rob, to kill, and to destroy the members of Christ's body.

To be "in Christ" is to follow his example of standing firm against every temptation. It is to pursue obedience to the Father's will above all else, even when this means taking up a cross as did our Lord. But in this battle we are not left without defense. We have been given the armor of God: truth and the righteousness of Christ, the gospel of peace and the shield of faith, salvation and the Word of God.

Above all, we have been granted access to the Holy of Holies through our new position "in Christ." By means of the Spirit we can pray at all times and in all places with all perseverance for all the saints. We pray especially for those apostolic warriors who carry the gospel into new places, planting churches and proclaiming the mystery of the Gospel. We pray for peace, love, and grace upon all who love our Lord Jesus Christ with an undying love.

Daily Devotional Guide

PREPARING OUR HEARTS

Invocation: Our Prayer of Acclamation
Almighty Father, like Elisha's servant, we need you to open our eyes. Open them not only to the spiritual forces which stand behind the fleshly obstacles of your will in this world, but open them to the infinite power of your mighty arms. Help us to see that the battle has already been won by our great King Jesus. Today, fill us anew with faith, truth, righteousness, peace, and the saving power of your Word. We pray this for the glory of your name, amen.

Call to Worship
Blessed are you, O God: Father, Son, and Holy Spirit. And blessed is your Kingdom, both now and forever, amen.

PRAISING OUR GOD

Te Deum Laudamus
You are God: we praise you; you are the Lord; we acclaim you; you are the eternal Father: All creation worships you. To you all angels, all the powers of heaven, Cherubim and Seraphim, sing in endless praise: Holy, holy, holy Lord, God of power and might, heaven and earth are full of your glory.

The glorious company of apostles praise you. The noble fellowship of prophets praise you. The white-robed army of martyrs praise you. Throughout the world the holy Church acclaims you; Father, of majesty unbounded, your true and only Son, worthy of all worship, and the Holy Spirit, advocate and guide.

You, Christ, are the king of glory, the eternal Son of the Father. When you became man to set us free you did not shun the Virgin's womb. You overcame the sting of death and opened the kingdom of heaven to all believers. You are seated at God's right hand in glory. We believe that you will come and be our judge. Come then, Lord, and help your people, bought with the price of your own blood, and bring us with your saints to glory everlasting.

Praise and Thanksgiving (Songs and Prayers)

Gloria Patri
Glory be to the Father,
And to the Son and to the Holy Spirit:
As it was in the beginning,
Is now, and ever shall be,
World without end. Amen, amen.

LISTENING TO HIS VOICE

Chronological Reading for the Day
Sunday: Lam. 1-3
Monday: Lam. 4-5; Obad.; 2 Kings 25.22-26; Jer. 40.7-41.18
Tuesday: Jer. 42-44; Ezek. 33.21-33
Wednesday: Ezek. 34-36
Thursday: Ezek. 37-39; 32.1-16
Friday: Ezek. 32.17-33.20; Jer. 52.28-30; Ps. 137;
    1 Chron. 4.24-5.17
Saturday: 1 Chron. 5.18-26; 6.3b-15, v.49; 7.1-8.28

Lectionary Readings
Psalm: Ps. 85   *OT:* Hos. 1.2-10
Gospel: Luke 11.1-13   *NT:* Col. 2.6-19

Reflection: Silence and/or Journaling

RESPONDING IN FAITH
_____

The Apostles' Creed
*I believe in God, the Father Almighty, Maker of heaven and earth;
and in Jesus Christ, his only Son, our Lord, who was conceived by the
Holy Spirit, born of the Virgin Mary, suffered under Pontius Pilate,
was crucified, dead, and buried; he descended into hell; the third day
he arose again from the dead; he ascended into heaven and sits on
the right hand of God the Father Almighty; from thence he shall come
to judge the quick and the dead.*

I believe in the Holy Spirit, the holy catholic church, the communion
of saints, the forgiveness of sins, the resurrection of the body, and the
life everlasting. Amen.*

* In the Apostles' and Nicene Creeds, the term catholic refers to the Church's
universality, through all ages and times, of all languages and peoples. It refers to no
particular tradition or denominational expression (e.g., as in Roman Catholic).

Prayers of Confession
Let us now confess our sins to God and receive mercy and
grace to help in our time of need.

Assurance of Pardon
Having faithfully confessed and renounced your sin, Christ
also has been faithful to forgive your sins and to purify you
from all unrighteousness. It is certain, that there is One who
has spoken to the Father in your defense, Jesus Christ, the
Righteous One who is the atoning sacrifice for our sins and
for the sins of the whole world. His grace and peace are with
you now. Amen.

Petitions and Supplications, Ending with the Lord's Prayer
*Our Father which art in heaven, Hallowed be thy name. Thy kingdom
come, Thy will be done in earth, as it is in heaven. Give us this day our
daily bread. And forgive us our debts, as we forgive our debtors. And
lead us not into temptation, but deliver us from evil: For thine is the
kingdom, and the power, and the glory, for ever. Amen.*

~ Matthew 6.9-13 (KJV)

Doxology (and/or closing song)
Praise God from whom all blessings flow;
Praise Him all creatures here below;
Praise Him above ye heavenly host;
Praise Father, Son and Holy Ghost. Amen.

DEPARTING TO SERVE

Benediction
Lord Jesus Christ, we leave this place in your mighty power.
We go forth from this time, but not from your presence. We
live and breathe and have our being in you through the power
of your Holy Spirit. We will not bow to the spiritual forces
of this world, to the lies or the pressure which seeks to burn
us alive in a furnace of fear. Be glorified in our stand on
this day, and by your grace preserve us that we may wake
tomorrow to serve and to stand in your holy presence with
all joy. In the name of the Father, the Son, and the Holy
Spirit, amen.

Affirmation from the Psalms
*Let me hear what God the Lord will speak, for he will speak peace to
his people, to his saints; but let them not turn back to folly. [9] Surely
his salvation is near to those who fear him, that glory may dwell in
our land.*

~ Psalm 85.8-9

Pray without Ceasing – Flash Prayer for the Day
Lord Jesus Christ, we bow to you, and stand against the enemy.

For Your Weekly Journey

Let God Arise! Seasonal Focus
Stand Firm in Christ, Ephesians 6.19-20

Book Reading
Bruce, *Paul, Apostle of the Heart Set Free*

The Season after Pentecost

A SEASON OF CHRIST'S HARVEST

Do you not say,
'There are yet four months, then comes the harvest'?
Look, I tell you, lift up your eyes,
and see that the fields are white for harvest.

JOHN 4.35

The Harvest Is Great, but the Laborers Are Few

During the Season after Pentecost we engage in mission to
the world. The risen and exalted Christ has given his people
the commission to make disciples of all nations, to spread
the Gospel of salvation to the ends of the earth. In Matthew
9.37-38 Jesus said to his disciples, "The harvest is plentiful,
but the workers are few. Therefore beseech the Lord of the
harvest to send out workers into his harvest." He exhorted
them to lift up their eyes and simply look to the fields of
harvest, the teeming millions of the nations who need to
know of God's grace in the Son of God. The harvest is ripe,
and the fields are white; the peoples of the world are truly
ready for harvest (John 4.34-35).

The call to mission is a call to obedience and perseverance.
We are called to share the apostolic heart, its clarity, passion,
and vision. Christ has revealed to us that the harvest of souls
is vast, the judgment that the lost face is inevitable, and the
time is urgent. The opportunity for millions to hear of God's
love in Christ has been given to God's messengers. They are
called to proclaim to the very ends of the earth, to cross the
barriers of race, culture, and class in order to prophesy
deliverance in Christ, new hope of eternal salvation, and
the certainty of divine judgment. These truths, when embraced and believed, produced a kind of internal urgency in
the heart of the apostles, and can do the same in us.

The Season after Pentecost, therefore, is a time of urgency
and readiness. No time can be wasted, no opportunity should
be ignored, and no prospect overlooked. Our understanding
of the harvest's fullness and ripeness, when combined with a
deep sense of the shortage of workers, should produce in us
an overwhelming burden to share the Gospel with the lost,

and to hazard our lives to go to the ends of the earth in order to tell those who have not heard the good news of salvation. This is a season of preparation, of mobilization, of engagement, and of courage. If we truly come to see and understand what the apostles saw and understood, then we, like them, will be moved to share and go even as they did.

Pray to the Lord of the Harvest to Send Forth Laborers into His Harvest

Even though the workers are few, the harvest is great, and the time is short, we can be hopeful during this season of the Church Year. Jesus asserts that the harvest is his own, he who is called the "Lord of the harvest." It is neither ours to possess nor ours alone to superintend. Neither the enemy nor God's workers are possessors of the harvest. It belongs to Christ alone.

The breadth of the harvest and its Gospel is mind boggling, indeed: It is universal, including the "entire creation" (Mark 16.15-16). It involves every person, with offers to be made to every man, woman, boy, and girl who does not know the Lord Jesus as their personal Savior (Col. 1.27-29). It crosses all barriers of race and clan, the Gospel itself being a dynamic power to be proclaimed to every person and which can save all who hear and believe, not only the Jew but also the Gentile (Rom. 1.16-17). The Gospel is to be proclaimed to every single person beginning from Jerusalem, to Judea, in Samaria, and to the very ends of the earth (Acts 1.8), covering all nations, kindreds, peoples, and tongues who will one day worship Christ (Rev. 7.9-11). Every one of Adam's condemned race, all who are currently under the power of the prince of the air, can hear, believe, and be delivered by faith in the Gospel (Rom. 5; Eph. 2.2; Col. 1.13; 3.5-7).

During this season, therefore, let us exalt the risen Christ as Head of the Church, and the Holy Spirit as the anointing power who is given to us in order to fulfill his commission in the world. Let us, during this season, pray for courage to share the Gospel with our family and friends, and let us strive to be used of God in order to do all we can to help God's messengers cross barriers of culture and class with the message of reconciliation. Let us contribute our time and treasure to persuade as many people as we can to become obedient disciples of Jesus of Nazareth, now the exalted Lord of all. Let us pray that all who believe will too become joyful members of his Church, living in community with the saints, and fleshing out in their lives God's kingdom power.

The next season we celebrate is Advent, the coming of the Lord. Let us labor with all the strength he gives us, declaring unashamedly that Jesus Christ is the Victor over all sin and the forces of evil. He alone is the true King who will return in power and reign as Lord in his Kingdom. Then the ancient words will be fulfilled: the knowledge of the Lord will cover the earth even as the waters cover the sea. Until then, let us proclaim Jesus as both Lord and Christ. To him be glory evermore!

Praying for laborers for the Lord's harvest,
Rev. Dr. Don L. Davis

As Lord of the harvest, Jesus has commissioned his Church during this age to go and make disciples of all nations. During this season after Pentecost, let us obey Christ's command and share the Gospel to the ends of the earth, gathering in the harvest of souls so ripe for reaping. As Christ's hands and feet in the world, let us both show and tell of his salvation to a dying and hurting world. This is a season of harvest.

THIS WEEK'S THEME
Imprisoned with Purpose, Philippians 1.1-30

Paul wrote to the Philippians to thank them and encourage them in their work of the Gospel. He assured them that he held them in his heart and thanked the Lord for them. He encouraged them in their walk with Christ and assured them that Christ would continue his good work in them. Paul prayed for their maturity, fruitfulness and keeping in Christ until the day of Christ.

Recognizing their concern for him and his situation, Paul encouraged the church at Philippi by assuring them that what was happening to him served to advance the gospel and that his imprisonment was for Christ. This had even been recognized by the entire imperial guard. Through this, many of the brothers had become more bold to speak the Word without fear.

While some preached Christ out of good will, there were those who were preaching Christ out of envy and rivalry to afflict Paul during his imprisonment. However, Paul had refused to allow their selfish ambition to bring him discouragement. He celebrated that, whether in pretense or in truth, Christ was proclaimed.

While Paul was sitting in a prison, not serving the Lord and spreading the Gospel as he had in mind to do, he had the ability to look past his personal interests and his own plans and see that God had a purpose in this . . . it is for Christ. Paul knew he was representing Christ to his captors. Paul knew of the concern on the hearts and minds of the church at Philippi and he represented Christ to them, assuring them that what has happened to him was serving the purpose of advancing the Kingdom. Even in response to those who were taking advantage of his imprisonment, Paul holds true to what is most important, that Christ is proclaimed. Even when considering if his imprisonment would lead to his death, or result in his release, Paul's focus was on the value of fruitful labor for the glory of Christ.

Daily Devotional Guide

PREPARING OUR HEARTS

Invocation: Our Prayer of Acclamation
Great and Mighty God, who gave Paul the vision to see through his circumstance and see you at work, open our eyes to see you and the work of your Spirit. Teach our hearts to trust in you and our eyes to see your hand at work. Lord Jesus, teach us what it means to represent you no matter what we face. In the name of our Lord and Savior, Jesus Christ, amen.

Call to Worship
Blessed are you, O God: Father, Son, and Holy Spirit. And blessed is your Kingdom, both now and forever, amen.

PRAISING OUR GOD

Te Deum Laudamus
You are God: we praise you; you are the Lord; we acclaim you; you are the eternal Father: All creation worships you. To you all angels, all the

powers of heaven, Cherubim and Seraphim, sing in endless praise: Holy, holy, holy Lord, God of power and might, heaven and earth are full of your glory.

The glorious company of apostles praise you. The noble fellowship of prophets praise you. The white-robed army of martyrs praise you. Throughout the world the holy Church acclaims you; Father, of majesty unbounded, your true and only Son, worthy of all worship, and the Holy Spirit, advocate and guide.

You, Christ, are the king of glory, the eternal Son of the Father. When you became man to set us free you did not shun the Virgin's womb. You overcame the sting of death and opened the kingdom of heaven to all believers. You are seated at God's right hand in glory. We believe that you will come and be our judge. Come then, Lord, and help your people, bought with the price of your own blood, and bring us with your saints to glory everlasting.

Praise and Thanksgiving (Songs and Prayers)

Gloria Patri
Glory be to the Father,
And to the Son and to the Holy Spirit:
As it was in the beginning,
Is now, and ever shall be,
World without end. Amen, amen.

LISTENING TO HIS VOICE

Chronological Reading for the Day
Sunday: 1 Chron. 8.29-9.1a; Dan. 4; Ezek. 40
Monday: Ezek. 41-43
Tuesday: Ezek. 44-46
Wednesday: Ezek. 47-48; 29.17-30.19; 2 Kings 25.27-30;
     Jer. 52.31-34
Thursday: Dan. 7-8; ch.5

Friday: Dan. 6; 9; 2 Chron. 36.22-23; Ezra 1; 1 Chron. 3.17-19a
Saturday: Ezra 2.1-4.5; 1 Chron. 3.19b-24

Lectionary Readings

Psalm: Ps. 107.1-9, 43   *OT:* Hos. 11.1-11
Gospel: Luke 12.13-21   *NT:* Col. 3.1-11

Reflection: Silence and/or Journaling

RESPONDING IN FAITH

The Apostles' Creed

*I believe in God, the Father Almighty, Maker of heaven and earth;
and in Jesus Christ, his only Son, our Lord, who was conceived by the
Holy Spirit, born of the Virgin Mary, suffered under Pontius Pilate,
was crucified, dead, and buried; he descended into hell; the third day
he arose again from the dead; he ascended into heaven and sits on
the right hand of God the Father Almighty; from thence he shall come
to judge the quick and the dead.*

I believe in the Holy Spirit, the holy catholic church, the communion
of saints, the forgiveness of sins, the resurrection of the body, and the
life everlasting. Amen.*

* In the Apostles' and Nicene Creeds, the term catholic refers to the Church's
universality, through all ages and times, of all languages and peoples. It refers to no
particular tradition or denominational expression (e.g., as in Roman Catholic).

Prayers of Confession

Let us now confess our sins to God and receive mercy and
grace to help in our time of need.

Assurance of Pardon

Having faithfully confessed and renounced your sin, Christ
also has been faithful to forgive your sins and to purify you
from all unrighteousness. It is certain, that there is One who
has spoken to the Father in your defense, Jesus Christ, the

Righteous One who is the atoning sacrifice for our sins and for the sins of the whole world. His grace and peace are with you now. Amen.

Petitions and Supplications, Ending with the Lord's Prayer

Our Father which art in heaven, Hallowed be thy name. Thy kingdom come, Thy will be done in earth, as it is in heaven. Give us this day our daily bread. And forgive us our debts, as we forgive our debtors. And lead us not into temptation, but deliver us from evil: For thine is the kingdom, and the power, and the glory, for ever. Amen.

~ Matthew 6.9-13 (KJV)

Doxology (and/or closing song)

Praise God from whom all blessings flow;
Praise Him all creatures here below;
Praise Him above ye heavenly host;
Praise Father, Son and Holy Ghost. Amen.

DEPARTING TO SERVE

Benediction

Our Father in Heaven, who gave Paul purpose while he was imprisoned, turn our eyes and our focus away from ourselves and our circumstances so that we may fulfill your purpose. Help us to trust you and your will and to represent you and the Gospel in all situations. Help us at all times to be thankful for our brothers and sisters in Christ and to pray for them. Through the name of our Lord Jesus, amen.

Affirmation from the Psalms

Though I walk in the midst of trouble, you preserve my life; you stretch out your hand against the wrath of my enemies, and your right hand delivers me. [8] The Lord will fulfill his purpose for me; your steadfast love, O Lord, endures forever. Do not forsake the work of your hands.

~ Psalm 138.7-8

Pray without Ceasing – Flash Prayer for the Day
Lord Jesus, we choose to represent you and the Gospel
throughout this day.

For Your Weekly Journey

Let God Arise! Seasonal Focus
The Lord Is at Hand, Philippians 4.1-9

Book Reading
Bruce, *Paul, Apostle of the Heart Set Free*

Our Corporate Disciplines
Book Discussion: Monday, August 1, 2016
Fallow Day: Friday, August 5, 2016

As Lord of the harvest, Jesus has commissioned his Church during this age to go and make disciples of all nations. During this season after Pentecost, let us obey Christ's command and share the Gospel to the ends of the earth, gathering in the harvest of souls so ripe for reaping. As Christ's hands and feet in the world, let us both show and tell of his salvation to a dying and hurting world. This is a season of harvest.

THIS WEEK'S THEME
Every Knee will Bow, Every Tongue Confess, Philippians 2.1-18

As Paul did not allow his circumstances to overcome him, but kept a perspective of the furtherance of the Gospel, he instructed the Philippians to live their lives with the same encouragement, comfort, participation with the Spirit and compassion as seen in Christ. He admonished them to do nothing out of selfish ambition, but to live in humility, holding others as more significant than themselves. Paul exhorted them to not only look out for their own interests, but to also look out for the interests of others.

Paul shows the example we have in Christ of humility and putting others and the Gospel ahead of self. He instructs them to have the same mind as Christ Jesus, who did not hold on to his position in the Godhead, but emptied himself, took on the form of a servant, and was born in the likeness of men. Jesus made himself nothing. In Christ's humility, even to the point of a torturous death on a cross, Paul finds the purpose for his own life and even the purpose for his own suffering. He tells this to the Philippians so they too will draw courage from this purpose and be able to stand strong in all situations.

God has highly exalted Jesus and bestowed on him the name that is above every name. And here we find the purpose that gives Paul the ability to keep focus and endure such great hardship: so that at the name of Jesus every knee will bow, in heaven and on earth and under the earth, and every tongue confess that Jesus Christ is Lord, to the glory of God the Father!

This was God's purpose in sending Jesus, this was Jesus' purpose in his lowliness, this was Paul's purpose in enduring suffering under the imperial guard, and this is our purpose in walking with the Lord through all that life might bring: that Jesus Christ is proclaimed Lord, to the glory of God the Father.

Daily Devotional Guide

PREPARING OUR HEARTS

Invocation: Our Prayer of Acclamation
Father of our Lord Jesus Christ, you are eternal, holy and all powerful. You sent your son into this world with purpose. Jesus, you willingly laid down your glory, left your rightful place, entered this world as a helpless baby out of obedience and out of desire for the greater glory. You suffered and died that at your name every knee will bow and every tongue confess that Jesus Christ is Lord, to the glory of God the Father. Teach us, Lord, to be obedient, to humble ourselves and to endure as ambassadors of your Kingdom, confessing that Jesus Christ is Lord, to the glory of the Father. Amen.

Call to Worship
Blessed are you, O God: Father, Son, and Holy Spirit. And blessed is your Kingdom, both now and forever, amen.

PRAISING OUR GOD

Te Deum Laudamus

You are God: we praise you; you are the Lord; we acclaim you; you are the eternal Father: All creation worships you. To you all angels, all the powers of heaven, Cherubim and Seraphim, sing in endless praise: Holy, holy, holy Lord, God of power and might, heaven and earth are full of your glory.

The glorious company of apostles praise you. The noble fellowship of prophets praise you. The white-robed army of martyrs praise you. Throughout the world the holy Church acclaims you: Father, of majesty unbounded, your true and only Son, worthy of all worship, and the Holy Spirit, advocate and guide.

You, Christ, are the king of glory, the eternal Son of the Father. When you became man to set us free you did not shun the Virgin's womb. You overcame the sting of death and opened the kingdom of heaven to all believers. You are seated at God's right hand in glory. We believe that you will come and be our judge. Come then, Lord, and help your people, bought with the price of your own blood, and bring us with your saints to glory everlasting.

Praise and Thanksgiving (Songs and Prayers)

Gloria Patri

Glory be to the Father,
And to the Son and to the Holy Spirit:
As it was in the beginning,
Is now, and ever shall be,
World without end. Amen, amen.

LISTENING TO HIS VOICE

Chronological Reading for the Day

Sunday: Dan. 10-12; Ezra 4.24-5.1
Monday: Hag. 1-2; Zech. 1-5; Ezra 5.2

Tuesday: Zech. 6-8; Ezra 5.3-6.14a
Wednesday: Zech. 9-14
Thursday: Ezra 6.14b-22; 4.6; Esther 1-4
Friday: Esther 5-10
Saturday: Ezra 4.7-23; ch.7-8

Lectionary Readings

Psalm: Ps. 50.1-8, 22-23   *OT:* Gen. 15.1-6
Gospel: Luke 12.32-40   *NT:* Heb. 11.1-3, 8-16

Reflection: Silence and/or Journaling

RESPONDING IN FAITH

The Apostles' Creed

*I believe in God, the Father Almighty, Maker of heaven and earth;
and in Jesus Christ, his only Son, our Lord, who was conceived by the
Holy Spirit, born of the Virgin Mary, suffered under Pontius Pilate,
was crucified, dead, and buried; he descended into hell; the third day
he arose again from the dead; he ascended into heaven and sits on
the right hand of God the Father Almighty; from thence he shall come
to judge the quick and the dead.*

I believe in the Holy Spirit, the holy catholic church, the communion
of saints, the forgiveness of sins, the resurrection of the body, and the
life everlasting. Amen.*

* In the Apostles' and Nicene Creeds, the term catholic refers to the Church's
universality, through all ages and times, of all languages and peoples. It refers to no
particular tradition or denominational expression (e.g., as in Roman Catholic).

Prayers of Confession

Let us now confess our sins to God and receive mercy and
grace to help in our time of need.

Assurance of Pardon

Having faithfully confessed and renounced your sin, Christ
also has been faithful to forgive your sins and to purify you

from all unrighteousness. It is certain, that there is One who has spoken to the Father in your defense, Jesus Christ, the Righteous One who is the atoning sacrifice for our sins and for the sins of the whole world. His grace and peace are with you now. Amen.

Petitions and Supplications, Ending with the Lord's Prayer

Our Father which art in heaven, Hallowed be thy name. Thy kingdom come, Thy will be done in earth, as it is in heaven. Give us this day our daily bread. And forgive us our debts, as we forgive our debtors. And lead us not into temptation, but deliver us from evil: For thine is the kingdom, and the power, and the glory, for ever. Amen.

~ Matthew 6.9-13 (KJV)

Doxology (and/or closing song)

Praise God from whom all blessings flow;
Praise Him all creatures here below;
Praise Him above ye heavenly host;
Praise Father, Son and Holy Ghost. Amen.

DEPARTING TO SERVE

Benediction

Our great and mighty God, help us to walk by your Spirit, having the mind which is ours in Christ Jesus. Thank you that it is you, and not our own brilliance or ability, that works in us to both will and to work for your good pleasure. Guide us as we work out our salvation with fear and trembling, and do all things without grumbling or questioning. Lord, we hold fast to the Word of Life. We bow our knee at the name of Jesus and confess with our tongue that Jesus Christ is Lord, to the glory of God the Father. In the mighty name of Jesus, amen.

Affirmation from the Psalms

Shout for joy to God, all the earth; [2] sing the glory of his name; give to him glorious praise! [3] Say to God, "How awesome are your deeds! So great is your power that your enemies come cringing to you. [4] All the earth worships you and sings praises to you; they sing praises to your name."

~ Psalm 66.1-4

Pray without Ceasing – Flash Prayer for the Day

At the name of Jesus Christ every knee will bow, in heaven and in earth and under the earth, and every tongue confess that Jesus Christ is Lord, to the glory of God the Father.

For Your Weekly Journey

Let God Arise! Seasonal Focus

The Lord Is at Hand, Philippians 4.1-9

Book Reading

Bruce, *Paul, Apostle of the Heart Set Free*

WEEK 38

Thirteenth Sunday after Pentecost
August 14 - 20, 2016 • Proper 15

As Lord of the harvest, Jesus has commissioned his Church during this age to go and make disciples of all nations. During this season after Pentecost, let us obey Christ's command and share the Gospel to the ends of the earth, gathering in the harvest of souls so ripe for reaping. As Christ's hands and feet in the world, let us both show and tell of his salvation to a dying and hurting world. This is a season of harvest.

THIS WEEK'S THEME
For the Work of Christ, Philippians 2.19-30

The life of the body of Christ, our fellowship and shared service, is a strength to us and should be highly valued. Yet, we do not live together for our own interests and elevation. We do it for the work of Christ.

Paul drew much encouragement from the Philippians' partnership in the Gospel. He looked forward to hearing further reports of their faithful service and devotion to the Lord. He applauded Timothy for his faithfulness to him and to the Gospel of Jesus Christ. Paul hoped to one day soon go visit Philippi himself.

Paul wrote about Epaphroditus, a brother, fellow worker and fellow soldier. He updated them on Epaphroditus' recent illness and miraculous recovery through the mercy of the Lord. Paul is sending him back to Philippi so the church can see him, receive him back home and rejoice. In Paul's words to the Philippians we see that we should honor those who are faithful in the service of the Lord, those who serve with honor as brothers and sisters, faithful workers and soldiers who have given their lives, even at great personal risk, for the work of Christ.

This should be our focus in life and ministry, the reason we get out of bed each day and live as fellow soldiers and workers; for the work of Christ, even if this means risking our lives to serve him and serve one another.

Daily Devotional Guide

PREPARING OUR HEARTS

Invocation: Our Prayer of Acclamation

Jesus, head of your body and Lord of all, thank you for the Church. Thank you for the fellowship and shared service that we have in you. May we be truly delighted in news of your work in and through others. Teach us to seek your interests and not our own. Strengthen us in our service to you and to one another. Strengthen us for the work of Christ. Be glorified among us that your name will be lifted up in all the earth. Amen.

Call to Worship

Blessed are you, O God: Father, Son, and Holy Spirit. And blessed is your Kingdom, both now and forever, amen.

PRAISING OUR GOD

Te Deum Laudamus

You are God: we praise you; you are the Lord; we acclaim you; you are the eternal Father: All creation worships you. To you all angels, all the powers of heaven, Cherubim and Seraphim, sing in endless praise: Holy, holy, holy Lord, God of power and might, heaven and earth are full of your glory.

The glorious company of apostles praise you. The noble fellowship of prophets praise you. The white-robed army of martyrs praise you.

Throughout the world the holy Church acclaims you; Father, of majesty unbounded, your true and only Son, worthy of all worship, and the Holy Spirit, advocate and guide.

You, Christ, are the king of glory, the eternal Son of the Father. When you became man to set us free you did not shun the Virgin's womb. You overcame the sting of death and opened the kingdom of heaven to all believers. You are seated at God's right hand in glory. We believe that you will come and be our judge. Come then, Lord, and help your people, bought with the price of your own blood, and bring us with your saints to glory everlasting.

Praise and Thanksgiving (Songs and Prayers)

Gloria Patri
Glory be to the Father,
And to the Son and to the Holy Spirit:
As it was in the beginning,
Is now, and ever shall be,
World without end. Amen, amen.

LISTENING TO HIS VOICE

Chronological Reading for the Day
Sunday: Ezra 9-10; Neh. 1-2
Monday: Neh. 3.1-5.13; 6.1-7.3
Tuesday: Neh. 7.4-8.18
Wednesday: Neh. 9-10
Thursday: 1 Chron. 9.1b-34; Neh. 11-12
Friday: Neh. 13; 5.14-19; Mal. 1-4
Saturday: Joel 1-3

Lectionary Readings
Psalm: Ps. 82
Gospel: Luke 12.49-56

OT: Jer. 23.23-29
NT: Heb. 11.29-12.2

Reflection: Silence and/or Journaling

Responding in Faith

The Apostles' Creed

I believe in God, the Father Almighty, Maker of heaven and earth; and in Jesus Christ, his only Son, our Lord, who was conceived by the Holy Spirit, born of the Virgin Mary, suffered under Pontius Pilate, was crucified, dead, and buried; he descended into hell; the third day he arose again from the dead; he ascended into heaven and sits on the right hand of God the Father Almighty; from thence he shall come to judge the quick and the dead.

I believe in the Holy Spirit, the holy catholic* church, the communion of saints, the forgiveness of sins, the resurrection of the body, and the life everlasting. Amen.

* In the Apostles' and Nicene Creeds, the term catholic refers to the Church's universality, through all ages and times, of all languages and peoples. It refers to no particular tradition or denominational expression (e.g., as in Roman Catholic).

Prayers of Confession

Let us now confess our sins to God and receive mercy and grace to help in our time of need.

Assurance of Pardon

Having faithfully confessed and renounced your sin, Christ also has been faithful to forgive your sins and to purify you from all unrighteousness. It is certain, that there is One who has spoken to the Father in your defense, Jesus Christ, the Righteous One who is the atoning sacrifice for our sins and for the sins of the whole world. His grace and peace are with you now. Amen.

Petitions and Supplications, Ending with the Lord's Prayer
Our Father which art in heaven, Hallowed be thy name. Thy kingdom come, Thy will be done in earth, as it is in heaven. Give us this day our daily bread. And forgive us our debts, as we forgive our debtors. And lead us not into temptation, but deliver us from evil: For thine is the kingdom, and the power, and the glory, for ever. Amen.

~ Matthew 6.9-13 (KJV)

Doxology (and/or closing song)
Praise God from whom all blessings flow;
Praise Him all creatures here below;
Praise Him above ye heavenly host;
Praise Father, Son and Holy Ghost. Amen.

Departing to Serve

Benediction
Father of our Lord and Savior Jesus Christ, lead us to serve as faithful workers and soldiers, giving our lives for the work of Christ. May your life be lived out through us and may your name be honored and glorified through our praise, worship, unity and service. May we receive our brothers and sisters with all joy, honoring those who serve you and minister in your name. May your church bring you glory and honor throughout the world. Amen.

Affirmation from the Psalms
Oh sing to the Lord a new song; sing to the Lord all the earth! [2] Sing to the Lord, bless his name; tell of his salvation from day to day. [3] Declare his glory among the nations, his marvelous works among all the peoples! [4] For great is the Lord, and greatly to be praised; he is to be feared above all Gods. [5] For all the gods of the peoples are worthless idols, but the Lord made the heavens. [6] Splendor and majesty are before him; strength and beauty are his sanctuary.

~ Psalm 96.1-6

Pray without Ceasing – Flash Prayer for the Day
Lord Jesus, we live for the work of Christ, telling of your salvation from day to day.

For Your Weekly Journey

Let God Arise! Seasonal Focus
The Lord Is at Hand, Philippians 4.1-9

Book Reading
Bruce, *Paul, Apostle of the Heart Set Free*

Our Corporate Disciplines
Book Discussion: Monday, August 15, 2016

WEEK 39

Fourteenth Sunday after Pentecost
August 21 - 27, 2016 • Proper 16

As Lord of the harvest, Jesus has commissioned his Church during this age to go and make disciples of all nations. During this season after Pentecost, let us obey Christ's command and share the Gospel to the ends of the earth, gathering in the harvest of souls so ripe for reaping. As Christ's hands and feet in the world, let us both show and tell of his salvation to a dying and hurting world. This is a season of harvest.

THIS WEEK'S THEME
True Citizenship, Philippians 3.1-21

Though Paul was under arrest and imprisoned, he looked beyond himself and even went so far as to tell his readers to rejoice in the Lord. While he had been physically overtaken, he did not allow his imprisonment to overtake him. He continued to focus on Christ and encouraged fellow believers by making it clear that he knew his citizenship was in heaven.

Paul warned the believers in Philippi to watch out for evildoers, those who seek to distract them from the true gospel, the true circumcision. There are those who place their trust in outward things and in the accomplishments and accolades of men. Paul made the case that if this was the real purpose in life, he could play that game and be quite competitive at it. He outlined his heritage, his training, his accomplishments and his dedication. Yet he said that whatever he has gained by all this, he counts it all as loss, a liability, for the sake of Christ. All the traditions, training and dedication are worth nothing in comparison to the value of knowing Jesus Christ his Lord. In fact, Paul said that for Christ he had lost all position and stature that was previously gained, and now considers it all garbage. He had willingly left that behind and suffered loss to gain Christ and be found in him. Paul understood that righteousness does not come from the law and ones own actions. True righteousness comes from God through faith in Christ.

Paul went on to explain how he could lay aside all the honors and accomplishments of this world. He knew that in Christ he and all who believed on him were no longer citizens of this world and its systems and structures. In Christ our citizenship is in heaven. We don't look to this world for our value, rescue or future. We look toward heaven, awaiting a Savior, the Lord Jesus Christ. We know he will transform our lowly body to be like his glorious body by his own power.

Daily Devotional Guide

PREPARING OUR HEARTS

Invocation: Our Prayer of Acclamation

Our Father in heaven, you sent your Son to live, suffer and die that we might live as your children, citizens of your Kingdom. Lord, we willingly lay down all the trophies, scars, diplomas and names we have gathered in this life. We release them to you and find our value, rescue and future in you. We thank you for the place we have gained in the Kingdom of God through Jesus your Son. Prepare us, Lord, for that day when we will enter your glory and be transformed to be like your glorious body, by your power. In the mighty name of Jesus our Lord, amen.

Call to Worship

Blessed are you, O God: Father, Son, and Holy Spirit. And blessed is your Kingdom, both now and forever, amen.

PRAISING OUR GOD

Te Deum Laudamus

You are God: we praise you; you are the Lord; we acclaim you; you are the eternal Father: All creation worships you. To you all angels, all the powers of heaven, Cherubim and Seraphim, sing in endless praise: Holy, holy, holy Lord, God of power and might, heaven and earth are full of your glory.

The glorious company of apostles praise you. The noble fellowship of prophets praise you. The white-robed army of martyrs praise you. Throughout the world the holy Church acclaims you; Father, of majesty unbounded, your true and only Son, worthy of all worship, and the Holy Spirit, advocate and guide.

You, Christ, are the king of glory, the eternal Son of the Father. When you became man to set us free you did not shun the Virgin's womb. You overcame the sting of death and opened the kingdom of heaven to all believers. You are seated at God's right hand in glory. We believe that you will come and be our judge. Come then, Lord, and help your people, bought with the price of your own blood, and bring us with your saints to glory everlasting.

Praise and Thanksgiving (Songs and Prayers)

Gloria Patri

Glory be to the Father,
And to the Son and to the Holy Spirit:
As it was in the beginning,
Is now, and ever shall be,
World without end. Amen, amen.

LISTENING TO HIS VOICE

Chronological Reading for the Day

Sunday: Mark 1.1; Luke 1.1-38; 3.23b-38; John 1.1-18; Matt. 1.1-17

Monday: Luke 1.39-2.40; Matt. 1.18-25

Tuesday: Matt. 2-3; Luke 2.41-3.18; 3.21-22; Mark 1.2-11
Wednesday: Mark 1.12-13; Matt. 4.1-11; Luke 4.1-15;
    John 1.19-2.25
Thursday: John 3.1-4.45; Luke 3.19-20
Friday: Mark 1.14-39; Matt. 4.12-25; 8.14-17; Luke 3.23a;
    4.16-44; John 4.46-54
Saturday: Luke 5; Mark 1.40-2.22; Matt. 8.1-4; 9.1-17

Lectionary Readings

Psalm: Ps. 71.1-6   *OT:* Jer. 1.4-10
Gospel: Luke 13.10-17   *NT:* Heb. 12.18-29

Reflection: Silence and/or Journaling

RESPONDING IN FAITH

The Apostles' Creed

*I believe in God, the Father Almighty, Maker of heaven and earth;
and in Jesus Christ, his only Son, our Lord, who was conceived by the
Holy Spirit, born of the Virgin Mary, suffered under Pontius Pilate,
was crucified, dead, and buried; he descended into hell; the third day
he arose again from the dead; he ascended into heaven and sits on
the right hand of God the Father Almighty; from thence he shall come
to judge the quick and the dead.*

I believe in the Holy Spirit, the holy catholic church, the communion
of saints, the forgiveness of sins, the resurrection of the body, and the
life everlasting. Amen.*

* In the Apostles' and Nicene Creeds, the term catholic refers to the Church's
universality, through all ages and times, of all languages and peoples. It refers to no
particular tradition or denominational expression (e.g., as in Roman Catholic).

Prayers of Confession

Let us now confess our sins to God and receive mercy and
grace to help in our time of need.

Assurance of Pardon

Having faithfully confessed and renounced your sin, Christ also has been faithful to forgive your sins and to purify you from all unrighteousness. It is certain, that there is One who has spoken to the Father in your defense, Jesus Christ, the Righteous One who is the atoning sacrifice for our sins and for the sins of the whole world. His grace and peace are with you now. Amen.

Petitions and Supplications, Ending with the Lord's Prayer

Our Father which art in heaven, Hallowed be thy name. Thy kingdom come, Thy will be done in earth, as it is in heaven. Give us this day our daily bread. And forgive us our debts, as we forgive our debtors. And lead us not into temptation, but deliver us from evil: For thine is the kingdom, and the power, and the glory, for ever. Amen.

~ Matthew 6.9-13 (KJV)

Doxology (and/or closing song)

Praise God from whom all blessings flow;
Praise Him all creatures here below;
Praise Him above ye heavenly host;
Praise Father, Son and Holy Ghost. Amen.

Departing to Serve

Benediction

Jesus, our Lord and life giver, who gives us life and breath, we thank you for giving us life eternal. Help us to live our life here in this time, on this earth, worshiping you and placing no confidence in the flesh. For the sake of Christ, may we suffer all things and count all we have gained in this world as rubbish, in order that we might gain Christ and be found in him, in his righteousness that comes through faith in Christ. Amen.

Affirmation from the Psalms
Out of the depths I cry to you, O Lord! [2] O Lord, hear my voice! Let your ears be attentive to the voice of my pleas for mercy! [3] If you, O Lord, should mark iniquities, O Lord, who could stand? [4] But with you there is forgiveness, that you may be feared. [5] I wait for the Lord, my soul waits, and in his word I hope; [6] my soul waits for the Lord more than watchmen for the morning, more than watchmen for the morning.

~ Psalm 130.1-6

Pray without Ceasing – Flash Prayer for the Day
Lord Jesus, may we be ever mindful of our citizenship in your Kingdom, representing our king, as we await our Savior, the Lord Jesus Christ.

For Your Weekly Journey

Let God Arise! Seasonal Focus
The Lord Is at Hand, Philippians 4.1-9

Book Reading
Bruce, *Paul, Apostle of the Heart Set Free*

Our Corporate Disciplines
Book Discussion: Monday, August 22, 1016

Fifteenth Sunday after Pentecost
August 28 - September 3, 2016 • Proper 17

As Lord of the harvest, Jesus has commissioned his Church during this age to go and make disciples of all nations. During this season after Pentecost, let us obey Christ's command and share the Gospel to the ends of the earth, gathering in the harvest of souls so ripe for reaping. As Christ's hands and feet in the world, let us both show and tell of his salvation to a dying and hurting world. This is a season of harvest.

THIS WEEK'S THEME
The Lord Is at Hand, Phillippians 4.1-9

As Paul begins to wrap up his letter to the church at Philippi he told them, in light of all he has instructed them in, to stand firm in the Lord. Paul's deep care and shepherding heart toward the church is evident.

He even spoke about strife within the body of the local church which had come to his attention, calling them to set differences aside and agree in the Lord. He instructed his readers to help them work things out. Unity within the body of Christ is important to being able to stand strong in the Lord.

Paul called his readers to rejoice in the Lord always. He repeated it again, rejoice. In all situations they should let their reasonableness be known as they live and work together as the body of Christ. He told them to not be anxious about anything and in everything by prayer and supplication with thanksgiving let their requests be known to God. And through this the peace of God which is greater than all understanding, will guard their hearts and minds in Christ Jesus.

Hidden in the middle of this challenge we find the words, "the Lord is at hand." This is the key to being able to live the life of believers, as his church. We must at all times remember that the Lord is at hand. He is near, he is with us, he will return in glory, he is on the throne. The Kingdom has come and the Lord Jesus Christ is at hand.

Therefore we can set our minds on whatever is true, honorable, just, pure, lovely, commendable, excellent, and praiseworthy, knowing that the God of peace will be with us. The Lord is at hand.

Daily Devotional Guide

PREPARING OUR HEARTS

Invocation: Our Prayer of Acclamation
Our Father in heaven, all time and activity is in your hands. Help us to learn to rest in you and not be anxious. Teach us to rejoice in you always, in thanksgiving making our concerns known to you. Teach us to be reasonable with one another. Lord, teach us to live in the knowledge that the Lord is most certainly at hand. In Christ's name, amen.

Call to Worship
Blessed are you, O God: Father, Son, and Holy Spirit. And blessed is your Kingdom, both now and forever, amen.

PRAISING OUR GOD

Te Deum Laudamus
You are God: we praise you; you are the Lord; we acclaim you; you are the eternal Father: All creation worships you. To you all angels, all the powers of heaven, Cherubim and Seraphim, sing in endless praise: Holy, holy, holy Lord, God of power and might, heaven and earth are full of your glory.

The glorious company of apostles praise you. The noble fellowship of prophets praise you. The white-robed army of martyrs praise you.

Throughout the world the holy Church acclaims you; Father, of majesty unbounded, your true and only Son, worthy of all worship, and the Holy Spirit, advocate and guide.

You, Christ, are the king of glory, the eternal Son of the Father. When you became man to set us free you did not shun the Virgin's womb. You overcame the sting of death and opened the kingdom of heaven to all believers. You are seated at God's right hand in glory. We believe that you will come and be our judge. Come then, Lord, and help your people, bought with the price of your own blood, and bring us with your saints to glory everlasting.

Praise and Thanksgiving (Songs and Prayers)

Gloria Patri
Glory be to the Father,
And to the Son and to the Holy Spirit:
As it was in the beginning,
Is now, and ever shall be,
World without end. Amen, amen.

LISTENING TO HIS VOICE

Chronological Reading for the Day
Sunday: John 5; Mark 2.23-3.6; Matt. 12.1-21; Luke 6.1-11
Monday: Mark 3.7-19; Luke 6.12-36; Matt. 5.1-6.4
Tuesday: Matt. 6.5-7.29; Luke 6.37-49
Wednesday: Matt. 8.5-13; ch.11; Luke 7
Thursday: Luke 8.1-8, vv.19-21; Mark 3.20-4.20; Matt. 12.22-13.9
Friday: Matt. 13.10-52; 8.23-27; Luke 8.9-18, vv.22-25;
    Mark 4.21-41
Saturday: Mark 5; Matt. 8.28-34; 9.18-26; Luke 8.26-56

Lectionary Readings
Psalm: Ps. 112   *OT:* Prov. 25.6-7
Gospel: Luke 14.1, 7-14   *NT:* Heb. 13.1-8, 15-16

Reflection: Silence and/or Journaling

RESPONDING IN FAITH

The Apostles' Creed
I believe in God, the Father Almighty, Maker of heaven and earth; and in Jesus Christ, his only Son, our Lord, who was conceived by the Holy Spirit, born of the Virgin Mary, suffered under Pontius Pilate, was crucified, dead, and buried; he descended into hell; the third day he arose again from the dead; he ascended into heaven and sits on the right hand of God the Father Almighty; from thence he shall come to judge the quick and the dead.

I believe in the Holy Spirit, the holy catholic* church, the communion of saints, the forgiveness of sins, the resurrection of the body, and the life everlasting. Amen.

* In the Apostles' and Nicene Creeds, the term catholic refers to the Church's universality, through all ages and times, of all languages and peoples. It refers to no particular tradition or denominational expression (e.g., as in Roman Catholic).

Prayers of Confession
Let us now confess our sins to God and receive mercy and grace to help in our time of need.

Assurance of Pardon
Having faithfully confessed and renounced your sin, Christ also has been faithful to forgive your sins and to purify you from all unrighteousness. It is certain, that there is One who has spoken to the Father in your defense, Jesus Christ, the Righteous One who is the atoning sacrifice for our sins and for the sins of the whole world. His grace and peace are with you now. Amen.

Petitions and Supplications, Ending with the Lord's Prayer
Our Father which art in heaven, Hallowed be thy name. Thy kingdom come, Thy will be done in earth, as it is in heaven. Give us this day our daily bread. And forgive us our debts, as we forgive our debtors. And

lead us not into temptation, but deliver us from evil: For thine is the
kingdom, and the power, and the glory, for ever. Amen.

~ Matthew 6.9-13 (KJV)

Doxology (and/or closing song)
Praise God from whom all blessings flow;
Praise Him all creatures here below;
Praise Him above ye heavenly host;
Praise Father, Son and Holy Ghost. Amen.

DEPARTING TO SERVE

Benediction
Father God, thank you for the confidence we have in the fact
that the Lord is at hand. In light of this truth, help us to rejoice
always, to let our reasonableness be known to everyone and to
be anxious for nothing. Help us to make our requests known
to you with thanksgiving. Lord, may the peace of God, which
surpasses all understanding, guard our hearts and our minds
in Christ Jesus. Amen.

Affirmation from the Psalms
I lift up my eyes to the hills. From where does my help come from?
[2] My help comes from the Lord, who made heaven and earth. [3] He
will not let your foot be moved; he who keeps you will not slumber.
[4] Behold, he who keeps Israel will neither slumber nor sleep. [5] The
Lord is your keeper; the Lord is your shade on your right hand. [6] The
sun shall not strike you by day, nor the moon by night. [7] The Lord will
keep you from all evil; he will keep your life. [8] The Lord will keep your
going out and your coming in from this time forth and forevermore.

~ Psalm 121.1-8

Pray without Ceasing – Flash Prayer for the Day
Jesus, we rejoice today, walking in you, anxious for nothing, with the peace of God guarding our hearts and minds because the Lord is at hand.

For Your Weekly Journey

Let God Arise! Seasonal Focus
The Lord Is at Hand, Philippians 4.1-9

Book Reading
Bruce, *Paul, Apostle of the Heart Set Free*

The Season after Pentecost

A SEASON OF CHRIST'S HOPE

Sing, O heavens, for the LORD has done it;
shout, O depths of the earth;
break forth into singing, O mountains,
O forest, and every tree in it!
For the LORD has redeemed Jacob,
and will be glorified in Israel.

ISAIAH 44.23

Ordinary Time in the Church Year
Is Anything But Ordinary Time

As the dawn follows night, so our Lord will surely appear in power and glory to gather his own to himself, to make an end of war and sin, and to restore creation under God's will. This is a season of the hope of Christ's soon return.

The Season after Pentecost (Kingdomtide) is a season of celebration, recognizing Christ's headship; a season of soul winning, affirming our role as laborers in Christ's harvest; and a season of expectation, grounded in the hope of Christ's return. In one sense, this Season after Pentecost is anything but what it is usually referred to in Church-Year-celebrating circles: "Ordinary Time."

Dan Connors in his wonderful little book, *The Liturgical Year*, explains the meaning of "ordinary" in this designation of the Church Year's final season.

> *The word 'ordinary' in Ordinary Time doesn't mean ordinary in the usual sense. Remember "ordinal" numbers – first, second, third? That's what 'ordinary' refers to here. The numbered Sundays of the year outside of the special seasons. Yet ordinary time does seem rather ordinary, it doesn't bring any strong images to mind the way the other seasons do. In fact, the Sundays of Ordinary Time don't all fall during the same time of the year. To understand Ordinary Time, we need to understand the Church Year as a whole. We need to remember the essential meaning of all the other seasons and then think about the rhythms of time.*

> ~ Dan Connors. *The Liturgical Year.*
> Mystic, CT: Twenty-Third Publications, 2005, p. 39.

At the Coming of Christ, God Will Make an End of War and Sin, and Restore His Creation to Himself

The rhythms of time, of all time, will consummate with the coming of Jesus Christ at his return. Christians throughout the ages have yearned for the time when God will consummate his plan of salvation with the revelation of his Son at the end of this age. The darkness and shadow of this tragic human story, the Fall's dread and ugly curse, the costly punishment for our original foreparents' and our own willful disobedience – death – will finally be overcome. The glory of God is destined to fill all heaven and earth, and God's own dear warrior-Son will put all enemies of the Father under his feet. This is our hope and our future!

Nothing could be more encouraging to us in the midst of a dark, foreboding, and confused world system than knowing that God the Father has set a time in his own sovereign will to shine his light into every dark crack of this world, and bring an end to this long, hard night of sin and sorrow and death. Truly, as the dawn follows night, so our Lord will surely appear in power and glory to gather his own to himself, to make an end of war and sin, and to restore creation under God's will. The Season after Pentecost is a season of hope, the hope of a restored earth, a new humanity, and a consummated Kingdom. Only Christ can restore this creation, and we recall and remember this during this season, the season of hope of Christ's soon return.

At the end of this remarkable time of expectation, we celebrate two feast days which underscore the remarkable character of our hope in the soon return of Christ. *All Saints Day* is our time as believers to remember those martyrs and saints, those heroes of the faith who came before us. It is also a time to especially recall and remember those who gave up their lives for the sake of Christ and the Gospel. We affirm that the Church is the body of Christ, and that the living

Savior now lives and is seen in the world through the words and deeds of his people (John 14.12; Heb. 11; Rev. 17.6).

The second feast day at the end of this season, the *Feast of Christ the King* (also called the *Feast of the Reign of Christ*), is the last Sunday of this season, and the last one before Advent. According to Scripture, our Lord Jesus Christ will return and finish the work he began on the Cross, to judge the world and save his own. The *Feast of Christ the King* points to that day when the kingdom of this world will become the kingdom of our Lord and of his Christ, who will reign forever and ever (Rev. 11.15ff.). How appropriate to end the season after the coming of the Holy Spirit with a feast which honors the future reign of our risen Savior, the true Lord who one day will reign alone and supreme!

May our hearts' cry resound with the prayers of the saints of the ages in saying, "Maranatha!" Even so, Lord Jesus, come soon!

Awaiting that Great Day,
Rev. Dr. Don L. Davis

The Season after Pentecost is likewise the season before Advent – it is a season of the blessed hope. As we declare Jesus' return in every Communion celebration, so we confess that he will assuredly appear in power and glory to complete God's salvation for the world. He will come in power to rescue his own, to make an end of war and sin, and to restore creation under God's will.

THIS WEEK'S THEME

Trust in God, Philippians 4.10-23

In thanking the Philippians for their concern for him, Paul makes it clear that his focus is not on his need. Paul showed that in all situations, whether brought low or abounding, in plenty and in hunger, in abundance and in need he had learned to be content. He could face all situations the Lord allowed in his life through Jesus Christ who strengthened him.

Paul understood that God supplied his needs through the Philippians and their generosity. He knew that in all situations, it was God who gave him strength and provided all that he needed. Paul encouraged them, knowing that God would supply every need they had according to his riches in glory in Christ Jesus.

Living in this truth, Paul could suffer. He could handle imprisonment and even death with a joyful heart, praising the Lord. Through it all he could give testimony to the goodness of the Lord and the hope of the gospel. Paul closed with greetings from the brothers who were with him, all the saints, especially those of Caesar's household. Paul walked with the Lord through his suffering and imprisonment in such a way as to have influenced members of Caesar's household. The testimony of Paul and his fellow believers led to the spread of the gospel. Paul never stopped representing

Jesus Christ and the Good News of salvation in the name of the Lord.

Paul knew the great and open secret to living this life is to trust in the one who supplies all we need, in the one who gives us strength. We are not citizens of this world, our citizenship is in heaven, and it is our honor, privilege and duty to represent him, giving testimony to his goodness and grace. As we serve with one another, as we live content in our situation, representing our Lord Jesus Christ, it is our God and Father that receives all the glory forever and ever. Amen.

Daily Devotional Guide

PREPARING OUR HEARTS

Invocation: Our Prayer of Acclamation
Our great God and Father of our Lord Jesus Christ, who was near to Paul and gave him strength to face his situation, the confidence to share the gospel with his captors, and the grace to encourage and teach the church at Philippi. Shape and mold our hearts through your Word that you delivered through your servant, Paul. Grow our trust in you ever deeper that we will rejoice in you in all circumstances. Amen.

Call to Worship
Blessed are you, O God: Father, Son, and Holy Spirit. And blessed is your Kingdom, both now and forever, amen.

PRAISING OUR GOD

Te Deum Laudamus
You are God: we praise you; you are the Lord; we acclaim you; you are the eternal Father: All creation worships you. To you all angels, all the powers of heaven, Cherubim and Seraphim, sing in endless praise:

Holy, holy, holy Lord, God of power and might, heaven and earth are full of your glory.

The glorious company of apostles praise you. The noble fellowship of prophets praise you. The white-robed army of martyrs praise you. Throughout the world the holy Church acclaims you; Father, of majesty unbounded, your true and only Son, worthy of all worship, and the Holy Spirit, advocate and guide.

You, Christ, are the king of glory, the eternal Son of the Father. When you became man to set us free you did not shun the Virgin's womb. You overcame the sting of death and opened the kingdom of heaven to all believers. You are seated at God's right hand in glory. We believe that you will come and be our judge. Come then, Lord, and help your people, bought with the price of your own blood, and bring us with your saints to glory everlasting.

Praise and Thanksgiving (Songs and Prayers)

Gloria Patri
Glory be to the Father,
And to the Son and to the Holy Spirit:
As it was in the beginning,
Is now, and ever shall be,
World without end. Amen, amen.

LISTENING TO HIS VOICE

Chronological Reading for the Day
Sunday: Matt. 9.27-10.42; 13.53-58; Mark 6.1-13; Luke 9.1-6
Monday: Luke 9.7-17; Mark 6.14-56; Matt. 14; John 6.1-21
Tuesday: John 6.22-71; Mark 7.1-23; Matt. 15.1-20
Wednesday: Mark 7.24-8.21; Matt. 15.21-16.12
Thursday: Mark 8.22-9.13; Matt. 16.13-17.13; Luke 9.18-36
Friday: Mark 9.14-50; Matt. 17.14-18.35; Luke 9.37-50
Saturday: John 7.1-8.20; Luke 9.51-62; Matt. 8.18-22

Lectionary Readings
Psalm: Ps. 139.1-6, 13-18   *OT:* Jer. 18.1-11
Gospel: Luke 14.25-33   *NT:* Philem. 1.1-21

Reflection: Silence and/or Journaling

RESPONDING IN FAITH

The Apostles' Creed
*I believe in God, the Father Almighty, Maker of heaven and earth;
and in Jesus Christ, his only Son, our Lord, who was conceived by the
Holy Spirit, born of the Virgin Mary, suffered under Pontius Pilate,
was crucified, dead, and buried; he descended into hell; the third day
he arose again from the dead; he ascended into heaven and sits on
the right hand of God the Father Almighty; from thence he shall come
to judge the quick and the dead.*

I believe in the Holy Spirit, the holy catholic church, the communion
of saints, the forgiveness of sins, the resurrection of the body, and the
life everlasting. Amen.*

* In the Apostles' and Nicene Creeds, the term catholic refers to the Church's
universality, through all ages and times, of all languages and peoples. It refers to no
particular tradition or denominational expression (e.g., as in Roman Catholic).

Prayers of Confession
Let us now confess our sins to God and receive mercy and
grace to help in our time of need.

Assurance of Pardon
Having faithfully confessed and renounced your sin, Christ
also has been faithful to forgive your sins and to purify you
from all unrighteousness. It is certain, that there is One who
has spoken to the Father in your defense, Jesus Christ, the
Righteous One who is the atoning sacrifice for our sins and
for the sins of the whole world. His grace and peace are with
you now. Amen.

Petitions and Supplications, Ending with the Lord's Prayer
Our Father which art in heaven, Hallowed be thy name. Thy kingdom come, Thy will be done in earth, as it is in heaven. Give us this day our daily bread. And forgive us our debts, as we forgive our debtors. And lead us not into temptation, but deliver us from evil: For thine is the kingdom, and the power, and the glory, for ever. Amen.

~ Matthew 6.9-13 (KJV)

Doxology (and/or closing song)
Praise God from whom all blessings flow;
Praise Him all creatures here below;
Praise Him above ye heavenly host;
Praise Father, Son and Holy Ghost. Amen.

DEPARTING TO SERVE

Benediction
Lord Jesus, guard our hearts and minds with your peace and the truth that you are our provider and protector. Help us to honor you in how we live this life together as your servants, your body, your family. Help us to trust you in all things at all times. Give us the confidence to give testimony to the faithfulness and goodness of the Lord, and to share the Good News of the gospel with those who have not yet believed, for your glory and honor. Amen.

Affirmation from the Psalms
For a day in your courts is better than a thousand elsewhere. I would rather be a door keeper in the house of my God than dwell in the tents of wickedness. [11] For the Lord God is a sun and a shield; the Lord bestows favor and honor. No good thing does he withhold from those who walk uprightly. [12] O Lord of hosts, blessed is the one who trusts in you.

~ Psalm 84.10-12

Pray without Ceasing – Flash Prayer for the Day

Lord, you are a sun and a shield. We trust in you. Make yourself known today, in and through us, your people.

For Your Weekly Journey

Let God Arise! Seasonal Focus

The Shadow and the Substance, Colossians 2.8-23

Book Reading

Ramsay and Wilson, *St. Paul: the Traveler and Roman Citizen*

Seventeenth Sunday after Pentecost

September 11 - 17, 2016 • Proper 19

The Season after Pentecost is likewise the season before Advent – it is a season of the blessed hope. As we declare Jesus' return in every Communion celebration, so we confess that he will assuredly appear in power and glory to complete God's salvation for the world. He will come in power to rescue his own, to make an end of war and sin, and to restore creation under God's will.

THIS WEEK'S THEME
The Preeminence of Christ, Colossians 1.15-23

During Paul's imprisonment he wrote a circulating letter meant for the believers in Colossae, to be shared with those in Laodicea. A short letter, Paul establishes the supremacy and glory of Jesus, the Christ. Throughout the book, Paul argues that Jesus is superior in all respects to all things, since the Father's desire was that he own the highest place in creation and redemption.

In this rich hymn of praise and revelation, Paul clearly provides seven reasons for the preeminence of Christ Jesus over all things. First, he is the image of the invisible God, the exact representation and manifestation of God Godself, in human form. Second, he is the the firstborn of all creation (not the first created thing). This term implies sovereignty, exalted one (cf. Ps. 89.27). Third, by him all things were created, including all things in both heaven and on earth, things that are both visible and invisible, whether they be thrones, dominions, rulers or authorities. Paul asserts that all things were created through Christ, and for Christ. He is before all things, and in him all things are sustained and hold together.

Fourth, Jesus' superiority is seen in his headship of the body, the church of God. Fifth, he is the beginning and the firstborn from the dead, having triumphed over death through his resurrection, and now lives in the power of indestructible life (cf. Heb. 7.16). All this is so in order that he might have the supremacy in everything, the highest place, the name above every name.

Sixth, in the risen Christ all the fullness of God (i.e., completeness) dwells in him, which Paul will tell us this fullness "dwells" permanently in Jesus in "bodily form" (2.9), a clear assertion of his divine nature. The seventh and final claim of Christ's supremacy is that he is the reconciler of all things to himself, whether they be things on earth or in heaven. Jesus now makes peace with the entire creation by the blood of his cross.

These amazing claims are revealed to us, who once were alienated and hostile in our minds, doing deeds of un-righteousness, and yet now he has reconciled us to God in his body of flesh by his death. Now, Jesus is working in us in order to present us holy and blameless and above reproach before him. We should therefore then continue in the faith, stable and steadfast, and never shift from this Gospel hope. Christ is supreme, the Lord over all.

Daily Devotional Guide

PREPARING OUR HEARTS

Invocation: Our Prayer of Acclamation

Holy Father, thank you that it has been your intent to exalt Christ and make him supreme in your creation. He is beautiful beyond description, our Lord, the Creator, Reconciler, Head of the Church, and Sustainer of all things. Our desire is to glorify you as we cling to him, and represent his Kingdom in the earth. Grant us the mind and heart of the apostle Paul to see Jesus as he is, and serve him as he deserves. In Christ's name we pray, amen.

Call to Worship
Blessed are you, O God: Father, Son, and Holy Spirit. And blessed is your Kingdom, both now and forever, amen.

PRAISING OUR GOD

Te Deum Laudamus
You are God: we praise you; you are the Lord; we acclaim you; you are the eternal Father: All creation worships you. To you all angels, all the powers of heaven, Cherubim and Seraphim, sing in endless praise: Holy, holy, holy Lord, God of power and might, heaven and earth are full of your glory.

The glorious company of apostles praise you. The noble fellowship of prophets praise you. The white-robed army of martyrs praise you. Throughout the world the holy Church acclaims you; Father, of majesty unbounded, your true and only Son, worthy of all worship, and the Holy Spirit, advocate and guide.

You, Christ, are the king of glory, the eternal Son of the Father. When you became man to set us free you did not shun the Virgin's womb. You overcame the sting of death and opened the kingdom of heaven to all believers. You are seated at God's right hand in glory. We believe that you will come and be our judge. Come then, Lord, and help your people, bought with the price of your own blood, and bring us with your saints to glory everlasting.

Praise and Thanksgiving (Songs and Prayers)

Gloria Patri
Glory be to the Father,
And to the Son and to the Holy Spirit:
As it was in the beginning,
Is now, and ever shall be,
World without end. Amen, amen.

LISTENING TO HIS VOICE

Chronological Reading for the Day
Sunday: John 8.21-59; Luke 10.1-11.13
Monday: Luke 11.14-12.34
Tuesday: Luke 12.35-13.21; John 9
Wednesday: John 10; Luke 13.22-14.24
Thursday: Luke 14.25-17.10; John 11.1-37
Friday: John 11.38-57; Luke 17.11-18.8
Saturday: Luke 18.9-30; Mark 10.1-31; Matt. 19

Lectionary Readings
Psalm: Ps. 51.1-10   *OT:* Exod. 32.7-14
Gospel: Luke 15.1-10   *NT:* 1 Tim. 1.12-17

Reflection: Silence and/or Journaling

RESPONDING IN FAITH

The Apostles' Creed
I believe in God, the Father Almighty, Maker of heaven and earth; and in Jesus Christ, his only Son, our Lord, who was conceived by the Holy Spirit, born of the Virgin Mary, suffered under Pontius Pilate, was crucified, dead, and buried; he descended into hell; the third day he arose again from the dead; he ascended into heaven and sits on the right hand of God the Father Almighty; from thence he shall come to judge the quick and the dead.

I believe in the Holy Spirit, the holy catholic* church, the communion of saints, the forgiveness of sins, the resurrection of the body, and the life everlasting. Amen.

* In the Apostles' and Nicene Creeds, the term catholic refers to the Church's universality, through all ages and times, of all languages and peoples. It refers to no particular tradition or denominational expression (e.g., as in Roman Catholic).

Prayers of Confession

Let us now confess our sins to God and receive mercy and grace to help in our time of need.

Assurance of Pardon

Having faithfully confessed and renounced your sin, Christ also has been faithful to forgive your sins and to purify you from all unrighteousness. It is certain, that there is One who has spoken to the Father in your defense, Jesus Christ, the Righteous One who is the atoning sacrifice for our sins and for the sins of the whole world. His grace and peace are with you now. Amen.

Petitions and Supplications, Ending with the Lord's Prayer

Our Father which art in heaven, Hallowed be thy name. Thy kingdom come, Thy will be done in earth, as it is in heaven. Give us this day our daily bread. And forgive us our debts, as we forgive our debtors. And lead us not into temptation, but deliver us from evil: For thine is the kingdom, and the power, and the glory, for ever. Amen.

~ Matthew 6.9-13 (KJV)

Doxology (and/or closing song)

Praise God from whom all blessings flow;
Praise Him all creatures here below;
Praise Him above ye heavenly host;
Praise Father, Son and Holy Ghost. Amen.

DEPARTING TO SERVE

Benediction

Lord Jesus Christ, firstborn of creation and firstborn from the dead, we acknowledge you. You are the perfect representation of God, sharing his fullness in your person, working his will in your actions. Our ambition is to represent as we ought, and yet, apart from your grace, we could never honor you as you deserve. Fill us with your Holy Spirit in order that whatever you call us to do and be, where we are, we can honor you as we ought. You are the Lord, and our Savior. In your name we pray, amen.

Affirmation from the Psalms

I love the Lord, because he has heard my voice and my pleas for mercy. [2] Because he inclined his ear to me, therefore I will call on him as long as I live. [3] The snares of death encompassed me; the pangs of Sheol laid hold on me; I suffered distress and anguish. [4] Then I called on the name of the Lord: "O Lord, I pray, deliver my soul!" [5] Gracious is the Lord, and righteous; our God is merciful. [6] The Lord preserves the simple; when I was brought low, he saved me. [7] Return, O my soul, to your rest; for the Lord has dealt bountifully with you.

~ Psalm 116.1-7

Pray without Ceasing – Flash Prayer for the Day

Lord Jesus Christ, reign supreme in my heart today.

For Your Weekly Journey

Let God Arise! Seasonal Focus

The Shadow and the Substance, Colossians 2.8-23

Book Reading

Ramsay and Wilson, *St. Paul: the Traveler and Roman Citizen*

Our Corporate Disciplines

Book Discussion: Monday, September 12, 2016
Concert of Prayer: Thursday, September 15, 2016

Eighteenth Sunday after Pentecost
September 18 - 24, 2016 • Proper 20

The Season after Pentecost is likewise the season before Advent – it is a season of the blessed hope. As we declare Jesus' return in every Communion celebration, so we confess that he will assuredly appear in power and glory to complete God's salvation for the world. He will come in power to rescue his own, to make an end of war and sin, and to restore creation under God's will.

THIS WEEK'S THEME
So Walk in Him, Colossians 2.1-7

Paul possessed a shepherd's heart, a desire to strengthen and protect those who belonged to the Lord Jesus. He commented to the Colossian believers that he owned a great struggle for them as well as for those at Laodicea, who at the time of this letter had not actually seen him face to face. This may be clear firsthand testimony that he, Paul, was not the one who planted these churches, and their wrestling with the place and position of Christ was the beginning of false teaching in that area.

Paul's burning desire was that in seeing him their hearts might be encouraged, as he says, "being knit together in love, to reach all the riches of full assurance of understanding and the knowledge of God's mystery, which is Christ, in whom are hidden all the treasures of wisdom and knowledge." Paul exhorts the believers that authentic Christian unity enables us to come to a full assurance of God's revealed truth, the person of Jesus Christ, in who alone was God's knowledge (the apprehension of the truth) and God's wisdom (the appropriation of the truth).

This Christ-centered focus on truth is different from a worldly, philosophical approach or stance, even if they might be couched in plausible arguments that delude the gullible.

Paul reminds the believers that although he is not present with them in his body, he is fully present with them in spirit, and is rejoicing in their "good order and the firmness of your faith in Christ."

The heart of the matter regarding issues of the Christian pursuit of wisdom and knowledge is this: "as you received Christ Jesus the Lord, so walk in him, rooted and built up in him and established in the faith, just as you were taught, abounding in thanksgiving." If truly all the treasures of wisdom and knowledge are hidden in Christ, the most logical thing we can do is to focus on Christ. As we received him (as Lord and Savior, the King of glory), so let us to continue to walk in him – learning of and from him, as we were originally instructed, filled with thanksgiving to God for the gift of his Son to us.

Daily Devotional Guide

PREPARING OUR HEARTS

Invocation: Our Prayer of Acclamation
Eternal God our Father, giver of the treasure of all wisdom and knowledge, who is your Son, Jesus Christ, open up our eyes to see how supreme and glorious your Son truly is. Protect us from worldly philosophical arguments, which appear plausible, but only delude since they do not anchor themselves in Christ. Rather, as we received our Lord as our life, teach us by the Spirit to so walk in him. Fill us with thanksgiving and wisdom as we rely on Christ Jesus alone as our strength and hope. In his name we pray, amen.

Call to Worship
Blessed are you, O God: Father, Son, and Holy Spirit. And blessed is your Kingdom, both now and forever, amen.

PRAISING OUR GOD

Te Deum Laudamus

You are God: we praise you; you are the Lord; we acclaim you; you are the eternal Father: All creation worships you. To you all angels, all the powers of heaven, Cherubim and Seraphim, sing in endless praise: Holy, holy, holy Lord, God of power and might, heaven and earth are full of your glory.

The glorious company of apostles praise you. The noble fellowship of prophets praise you. The white-robed army of martyrs praise you. Throughout the world the holy Church acclaims you; Father, of majesty unbounded, your true and only Son, worthy of all worship, and the Holy Spirit, advocate and guide.

You, Christ, are the king of glory, the eternal Son of the Father. When you became man to set us free you did not shun the Virgin's womb. You overcame the sting of death and opened the kingdom of heaven to all believers. You are seated at God's right hand in glory. We believe that you will come and be our judge. Come then, Lord, and help your people, bought with the price of your own blood, and bring us with your saints to glory everlasting.

Praise and Thanksgiving (Songs and Prayers)

Gloria Patri

Glory be to the Father,
And to the Son and to the Holy Spirit:
As it was in the beginning,
Is now, and ever shall be,
World without end. Amen, amen.

LISTENING TO HIS VOICE

Chronological Reading for the Day
Sunday: Matt. 20; Mark 10.32-52; Luke 18.31-19.27

Monday: Mark 14.3-9; 11.1-11; Matt. 26.6-13; 21.1-11;
    John 12.1-36; Luke 19.28-44
Tuesday: John 12.37-50; Mark 11.12-33; Matt. 21.12-27;
    Luke 19.45-20.8
Wednesday: Matt. 21.28-22.33; Mark 12.1-27; Luke 20.9-40
Thursday: Mark 12.28-44; Matt. 22.34-23.39; Luke 20.41-21.4
Friday: Mark 13.1-31; Matt. 24.1-35; Luke 21.5-33
Saturday: Mark 13.32-37; Matt. 24.36-25.46; Luke 21.34-38

Lectionary Readings

Psalm: Ps. 113   *OT:* Amos 8.4-7
Gospel: Luke 16.1-13   *NT:* 1 Tim. 2.1-7

Reflection: Silence and/or Journaling

RESPONDING IN FAITH

The Apostles' Creed
*I believe in God, the Father Almighty, Maker of heaven and earth;
and in Jesus Christ, his only Son, our Lord, who was conceived by the
Holy Spirit, born of the Virgin Mary, suffered under Pontius Pilate,
was crucified, dead, and buried; he descended into hell; the third day
he arose again from the dead; he ascended into heaven and sits on
the right hand of God the Father Almighty; from thence he shall come
to judge the quick and the dead.*

I believe in the Holy Spirit, the holy catholic church, the communion
of saints, the forgiveness of sins, the resurrection of the body, and the
life everlasting. Amen.*

* In the Apostles' and Nicene Creeds, the term catholic refers to the Church's
universality, through all ages and times, of all languages and peoples. It refers to no
particular tradition or denominational expression (e.g., as in Roman Catholic).

Prayers of Confession
Let us now confess our sins to God and receive mercy and
grace to help in our time of need.

Assurance of Pardon

Having faithfully confessed and renounced your sin, Christ also has been faithful to forgive your sins and to purify you from all unrighteousness. It is certain, that there is One who has spoken to the Father in your defense, Jesus Christ, the Righteous One who is the atoning sacrifice for our sins and for the sins of the whole world. His grace and peace are with you now. Amen.

Petitions and Supplications, Ending with the Lord's Prayer

Our Father which art in heaven, Hallowed be thy name. Thy kingdom come, Thy will be done in earth, as it is in heaven. Give us this day our daily bread. And forgive us our debts, as we forgive our debtors. And lead us not into temptation, but deliver us from evil: For thine is the kingdom, and the power, and the glory, for ever. Amen.

~ Matthew 6.9-13 (KJV)

Doxology (and/or closing song)

Praise God from whom all blessings flow;
Praise Him all creatures here below;
Praise Him above ye heavenly host;
Praise Father, Son and Holy Ghost. Amen.

DEPARTING TO SERVE

Benediction

Lord Jesus Christ, Paul your servant revealed to us that in you are hidden all the treasures of God's wisdom and knowledge. You are the mystery of God revealed, the source of life and hope of the world. Now, through your Holy Spirit, instruct us in the truth we understood when we first believed in you. Teach us to walk in you, to grow in you, to delight in you, and so, dear Master, to become like you. In your name we pray, amen.

Affirmation from the Psalms

Nevertheless, I am continually with you; you hold my right hand. [24] You guide me with your counsel, and afterward you will receive me to glory. [25] Whom have I in heaven but you? And there is nothing on earth that I desire besides you. [26] My flesh and my heart may fail, but God is the strength of my heart and my portion forever. [27] For behold, those who are far from you shall perish; you put an end to everyone who is unfaithful to you. [28] But for me it is good to be near God; I have made the Lord God my refuge, that I may tell of all your works.

~ Psalm 73.23-28

Pray without Ceasing – Flash Prayer for the Day

Lord Jesus Christ, as we have received you, so enable us to walk in you, filled with your presence and with grateful hearts.

For Your Weekly Journey

Let God Arise! Seasonal Focus

The Shadow and the Substance, Colossians 2.8-23

Book Reading

Ramsay and Wilson, *St. Paul: the Traveler and Roman Citizen*

Nineteenth Sunday after Pentecost
September 25 - October 1, 2016 • Proper 21

The Season after Pentecost is likewise the season before Advent – it is a season of the blessed hope. As we declare Jesus' return in every Communion celebration, so we confess that he will assuredly appear in power and glory to complete God's salvation for the world. He will come in power to rescue his own, to make an end of war and sin, and to restore creation under God's will.

THIS WEEK'S THEME
The Shadow and the Substance, Colossians 2.8-23

Paul held in great contempt any doctrine or argument which failed to recognize the supremacy and preeminence of Jesus Christ. He strongly ordered those in Colossae to be on guard, especially those who were tempted to become captive by philosophy and empty deceit, based on human tradition and bizarre notions of spirituality, and not according to Christ. Christ is supreme; in him the whole fullness of deity dwells in bodily form. There is no need for some other system or viewpoint, for we have been filled in him, the one who himself is the head of all rule and authority.

Paul argues that in Christ the Colossians were circumcised with a circumcision made without hands, by the circumcision of Christ. They had been buried with him in baptism, and raised with Christ through faith in God's powerful working, who also raised Jesus from the dead. Before we were dead in our trespasses and the uncircumcision of our flesh, yet God by grace made us alive together with Christ, forgave all our trespasses, and canceled the record of debt that the Law made upon us. This debt God set aside, nailing it to Christ's cross. Christ disarmed the rulers and authorities, and put them to open shame, by triumphing over them in his cross.

In light of this amazing work, Paul tells the Colossians to let no one pass judgment on them in matters of the Law, in questions such as of food and drink, or festivals or new moons or Sabbaths. These things of the Law were a shadow of the things to come, but Jesus Christ himself is the substance they pointed towards. Christ is the purpose and end of all spiritual things.

No one is legitimate, therefore, who seeks to disqualify another believer on the basis of strict adherence to asceticism or novel spiritualities. No model of spirituality is valid that fails to hold on to Christ, who himself is the Head of the Church. From him alone the entire body of believers is nourished and knit together through its joints and ligaments, and grows with a growth that is from God. Strict adherence to legalistic religious regulations such as "Do not handle, Do not taste, Do not touch," while they appear to be wise in promoting outward self-denial and asceticism, do nothing at all in stopping the indulgence of the flesh. In Christ alone there is authentic relationship with God, and genuine spirituality.

Daily Devotional Guide

PREPARING OUR HEARTS

Invocation: Our Prayer of Acclamation

Eternal God our Father, thank you for the total sufficiency of faith in Jesus. You receive us on the basis of him, who is the substance of the things referred to and pictured in the feasts, festivals, and activities of the Law. Thank you for freeing us from the Law's condemnation and judgment against us; in the Cross you have set us free, defeated our enemies, and rescued us from our enemies. We believe in Christ, and in him alone do we find a right relationship with you. In him your fullness dwells in bodily form. In his name we pray, amen.

Call to Worship
Blessed are you, O God: Father, Son, and Holy Spirit. And
blessed is your Kingdom, both now and forever, amen.

PRAISING OUR GOD

Te Deum Laudamus
*You are God: we praise you; you are the Lord; we acclaim you; you are
the eternal Father: All creation worships you. To you all angels, all the
powers of heaven, Cherubim and Seraphim, sing in endless praise:
Holy, holy, holy Lord, God of power and might, heaven and earth are
full of your glory.*

*The glorious company of apostles praise you. The noble fellowship
of prophets praise you. The white-robed army of martyrs praise you.
Throughout the world the holy Church acclaims you; Father, of
majesty unbounded, your true and only Son, worthy of all worship,
and the Holy Spirit, advocate and guide.*

*You, Christ, are the king of glory, the eternal Son of the Father. When
you became man to set us free you did not shun the Virgin's womb.
You overcame the sting of death and opened the kingdom of heaven
to all believers. You are seated at God's right hand in glory. We believe
that you will come and be our judge. Come then, Lord, and help your
people, bought with the price of your own blood, and bring us with
your saints to glory everlasting.*

Praise and Thanksgiving (Songs and Prayers)

Gloria Patri
*Glory be to the Father,
And to the Son and to the Holy Spirit:
As it was in the beginning,
Is now, and ever shall be,
World without end. Amen, amen.*

LISTENING TO HIS VOICE

Chronological Reading for the Day

Sunday: Mark 14.1-2, vv.10-26; Matt. 26.1-5, vv.14-30;
  Luke 22.1-30; John 13.1-30
Monday: John 13.31-15.17; Mark 14.27-31; Matt. 26.31-35;
  Luke 22.31-38
Tuesday: John 15.18-17.26
Wednesday: John 18.1-24; Mark 14.32-52; Matt. 26.36-56;
  Luke 22.39-53
Thursday: Mark 14.53-15.1; Matt. 26.57-27.10; Luke 22.54-71;
  John 18.25-27
Friday: Mark 15.2-20; Matt. 27.11-31; Luke 23.1-25;
  John 18.28-19.16
Saturday: Mark 15.21-41; Matt. 27.32-56; Luke 23.26-49;
  John 19.17-37

Lectionary Readings

Psalm: Ps. 91.1-6, 14-16   *OT:* Jer. 32.1-3a, 6-15
Gospel: Luke 16.19-31   *NT:* 1 Tim. 6.6-19

Reflection: Silence and/or Journaling

RESPONDING IN FAITH

The Apostles' Creed

*I believe in God, the Father Almighty, Maker of heaven and earth;
and in Jesus Christ, his only Son, our Lord, who was conceived by the
Holy Spirit, born of the Virgin Mary, suffered under Pontius Pilate,
was crucified, dead, and buried; he descended into hell; the third day
he arose again from the dead; he ascended into heaven and sits on
the right hand of God the Father Almighty; from thence he shall come
to judge the quick and the dead.*

I believe in the Holy Spirit, the holy catholic* church, the communion of saints, the forgiveness of sins, the resurrection of the body, and the life everlasting. Amen.

* In the Apostles' and Nicene Creeds, the term catholic refers to the Church's universality, through all ages and times, of all languages and peoples. It refers to no particular tradition or denominational expression (e.g., as in Roman Catholic).

Prayers of Confession

Let us now confess our sins to God and receive mercy and grace to help in our time of need.

Assurance of Pardon

Having faithfully confessed and renounced your sin, Christ also has been faithful to forgive your sins and to purify you from all unrighteousness. It is certain, that there is One who has spoken to the Father in your defense, Jesus Christ, the Righteous One who is the atoning sacrifice for our sins and for the sins of the whole world. His grace and peace are with you now. Amen.

Petitions and Supplications, Ending with the Lord's Prayer

Our Father which art in heaven, Hallowed be thy name. Thy kingdom come, Thy will be done in earth, as it is in heaven. Give us this day our daily bread. And forgive us our debts, as we forgive our debtors. And lead us not into temptation, but deliver us from evil: For thine is the kingdom, and the power, and the glory, for ever. Amen.

~ Matthew 6.9-13 (KJV)

Doxology (and/or closing song)

Praise God from whom all blessings flow;
Praise Him all creatures here below;
Praise Him above ye heavenly host;
Praise Father, Son and Holy Ghost. Amen.

DEPARTING TO SERVE

Benediction

Lord Jesus, deliver us from the ever-present tendency to try to relate to you on the basis of our legalistic regulations. Reveal yourself to us in order that we can truly see how supreme, sufficient, and preeminent you are in all things spiritual. You are enough for us; train us to live in that truth. For your sake we pray, amen.

Affirmation from the Psalms

I will extol you, O Lord, for you have drawn me up and have not let my foes rejoice over me. [2] O Lord my God, I cried to you for help, and you have healed me. [3] O Lord, you have brought up my soul from Sheol; you restored me to life from among those who go down to the pit. [4] Sing praises to the Lord, O you his saints, and give thanks to his holy name.[5] For his anger is but for a moment, and his favor is for a lifetime. Weeping may tarry for the night, but joy comes with the morning.

~ Psalm 30.1-5

Pray without Ceasing – Flash Prayer for the Day

Lord Jesus Christ, through your death on the Cross you disarmed the rulers and authorities, and put them to open shame—you have triumphed over our enemies on your cross.

For Your Weekly Journey

Let God Arise! Seasonal Focus

The Shadow and the Substance, Colossians 2.8-23

Book Reading

Ramsay and Wilson, *St. Paul: the Traveler and Roman Citizen*

Twentieth Sunday after Pentecost
October 2 - 8, 2016 • Proper 22

The Season after Pentecost is likewise the season before Advent – it is a season of the blessed hope. As we declare Jesus' return in every Communion celebration, so we confess that he will assuredly appear in power and glory to complete God's salvation for the world. He will come in power to rescue his own, to make an end of war and sin, and to restore creation under God's will.

THIS WEEK'S THEME
Seek the Things That Are Above, Colossians 3.1-11

Having argued that in Christ is hidden all wisdom and knowledge, and that we should walk in Christ as we received him (2.1-7), Paul made his case against depending on works righteousness or asceticism to relate to God (2.8-23). He now argues concerning the implications of our union with Christ: if we have been raised with Christ, we should seek the things that are above, where Christ is, seated at the right hand of God. We need to set our minds on things above, not on earthly things, for we have died, and our life is hidden with Christ in God. When the Lord Jesus appears, he who is our very life, then we will appear with him in glory.

Our union with Christ then calls for us to put to death all things that are "earthly" in ourselves: sexual immorality, impurity, passion, evil desire, and covetousness (which is idolatry). God's wrath will appear on those engaged in such things, the kind of actions we used to do, when we lived that way. Now, as new creatures, we are to put all of them away, including anger, wrath, malice, slander, obscene talk, and lying to one another. We do this because we have put off the old self with its practices and have put on the new self, which is being renewed in knowledge after God's own image. In our community there is no final designation of human particularities, such as Greek and Jew, circumcised and uncircumcised, barbarian, Scythian, slave and free; rather, in our life together, Christ is all, and in all.

Paul exhorts the Colossians to live into the truth of their position in the Lord, to actually flesh out the meaning of their identity and union with Christ in their conduct and relationships. Being one with Christ, we must seek the things which are above.

Daily Devotional Guide

PREPARING OUR HEARTS

Invocation: Our Prayer of Acclamation
Holy Father, thank you for joining us by faith to our Lord; we died with him, and now live with him. His life through the Spirit flows through us, and therefore we must seek the things above where he is, at your right hand. Lord, show us how to practically make the life of Christ real in our relationships and habits. Change our speech, our thoughts, our longings, our habits to be consistent with what you have made us in him. Do this for your glory, in Christ's name, amen.

Call to Worship
Blessed are you, O God: Father, Son, and Holy Spirit. And blessed is your Kingdom, both now and forever, amen.

PRAISING OUR GOD

Te Deum Laudamus
You are God: we praise you; you are the Lord; we acclaim you; you are the eternal Father: All creation worships you. To you all angels, all the powers of heaven, Cherubim and Seraphim, sing in endless praise: Holy, holy, holy Lord, God of power and might, heaven and earth are full of your glory.

The glorious company of apostles praise you. The noble fellowship of prophets praise you. The white-robed army of martyrs praise you. Throughout the world the holy Church acclaims you; Father, of majesty unbounded, your true and only Son, worthy of all worship, and the Holy Spirit, advocate and guide.

You, Christ, are the king of glory, the eternal Son of the Father. When you became man to set us free you did not shun the Virgin's womb. You overcame the sting of death and opened the kingdom of heaven to all believers. You are seated at God's right hand in glory. We believe that you will come and be our judge. Come then, Lord, and help your people, bought with the price of your own blood, and bring us with your saints to glory everlasting.

Praise and Thanksgiving (Songs and Prayers)

Gloria Patri
Glory be to the Father,
And to the Son and to the Holy Spirit:
As it was in the beginning,
Is now, and ever shall be,
World without end. Amen, amen.

LISTENING TO HIS VOICE

Chronological Reading for the Day
Sunday: Mark 15.42-16.11; Matt. 27.57-28.15; Luke 23.50-24.12; John 19.38-20.18
Monday: Luke 24.13-49; Mark 16.12-18; John 20.19-21.25; Matt. 28.16-20
Tuesday: Mark 16.19-20; Luke 24.50-53; Acts 1-2
Wednesday: Acts 3-5
Thursday: Acts 6.1-8.1a
Friday: Acts 8.1b-9.43
Saturday: Acts 10-12

Lectionary Readings

Psalm: Ps. 37.1-9   *OT:* Hab. 1.1-4; 2.1-4
Gospel: Luke 17.5-10   *NT:* 2 Tim. 1.1-14

Reflection: Silence and/or Journaling

RESPONDING IN FAITH

The Apostles' Creed

I believe in God, the Father Almighty, Maker of heaven and earth; and in Jesus Christ, his only Son, our Lord, who was conceived by the Holy Spirit, born of the Virgin Mary, suffered under Pontius Pilate, was crucified, dead, and buried; he descended into hell; the third day he arose again from the dead; he ascended into heaven and sits on the right hand of God the Father Almighty; from thence he shall come to judge the quick and the dead.

I believe in the Holy Spirit, the holy catholic* church, the communion of saints, the forgiveness of sins, the resurrection of the body, and the life everlasting. Amen.

* In the Apostles' and Nicene Creeds, the term catholic refers to the Church's universality, through all ages and times, of all languages and peoples. It refers to no particular tradition or denominational expression (e.g., as in Roman Catholic).

Prayers of Confession

Let us now confess our sins to God and receive mercy and grace to help in our time of need.

Assurance of Pardon

Having faithfully confessed and renounced your sin, Christ also has been faithful to forgive your sins and to purify you from all unrighteousness. It is certain, that there is One who has spoken to the Father in your defense, Jesus Christ, the Righteous One who is the atoning sacrifice for our sins and for the sins of the whole world. His grace and peace are with you now. Amen.

Petitions and Supplications, Ending with the Lord's Prayer
*Our Father which art in heaven, Hallowed be thy name. Thy kingdom
come, Thy will be done in earth, as it is in heaven. Give us this day our
daily bread. And forgive us our debts, as we forgive our debtors. And
lead us not into temptation, but deliver us from evil: For thine is the
kingdom, and the power, and the glory, for ever. Amen.*

~ Matthew 6.9-13 (KJV)

Doxology (and/or closing song)
*Praise God from whom all blessings flow;
Praise Him all creatures here below;
Praise Him above ye heavenly host;
Praise Father, Son and Holy Ghost. Amen.*

DEPARTING TO SERVE

Benediction
Lord Jesus Christ, we stand in awe of the simple truth Paul
spoke to your church in Colossae: we have died with you, and
now, you are our very life, at the right hand of God. We know
that when you return we will share your very life and nature.
Now, Lord make us like you, so that in all we do and say, we
reflect your beauty and glory to those with whom we relate.
You are our very life, and we love you. Be honored through us,
for your sake, amen.

Affirmation from the Psalms
*How precious is your steadfast love, O God! The children of mankind
take refuge in the shadow of your wings. [8] They feast on the
abundance of your house, and you give them drink from the river
of your delights. [9] For with you is the fountain of life; in your
light do we see light. [10] Oh, continue your steadfast love to those
who know you, and your righteousness to the upright of heart!*

~ Psalm 36.7-10

Pray without Ceasing – Flash Prayer for the Day
Lord Jesus Christ, help us to seek the things above, where you are, at the right hand of God.

For Your Weekly Journey

Let God Arise! Seasonal Focus
The Shadow and the Substance, Colossians 2.8-23

Book Reading
Ramsay and Wilson, *St. Paul: the Traveler and Roman Citizen*

Our Corporate Disciplines
Book Discussion: Monday, October 3, 2106

Twenty-first Sunday after Pentecost
October 9 - 15, 2016 • Proper 23

The Season after Pentecost is likewise the season before Advent – it is a season of the blessed hope. As we declare Jesus' return in every Communion celebration, so we confess that he will assuredly appear in power and glory to complete God's salvation for the world. He will come in power to rescue his own, to make an end of war and sin, and to restore creation under God's will.

THIS WEEK'S THEME
Let the Peace of Christ Rule, Colossians 3.12-4.1

Now joined to Christ's very own life, Paul exhorts the Colossians to clothe themselves in virture, as God's chosen ones, holy and beloved. Now in Christ, their hearts are to be compassionate, showing kindness, humility, meekness, and patience in their relation to others. In regard to complaints against others, they are to bear with and forgive each other, in the same way that the Lord has forgiven them. Above all these virtues, Paul tells them to put on love, that virtue that binds everything together in perfect harmony.

Paul challenges the Colossian believers to let the peace of Christ rule in their hearts, to which they were called in one body, and to be thankful. They were to let the Word of Christ richly dwell in their midst, teaching and admonishing each another in all wisdom. Their hearts were to be full of song, singing psalms and hymns and spiritual songs, with thankfulness in their hearts to God. And, whatever they did, whether in word or deed, they were to do everything in the name of the Lord Jesus, giving thanks to God the Father through him.

As to the "rules of the Christian household," wives were to submit to their husbands, and husbands to love their wives without harshness. Children are called to obey their parents in all they ask, for that pleases the Lord, and fathers are not to provoke their children, lest they become discouraged.

Bondservants are called to obey their earthly masters in everything, not with eye-service as a people-pleaser, but with genuine sincerity of heart, fearing the Lord. Whatever they do, they ought to work heartily, as if working for the Lord and not for people, since the Lord will give them the inheritance as their reward. They serve the Lord Christ. Any wrongdoer, however, will be paid back for his deeds, with no partiality shown. Masters, are called to treat their bondservants justly and with fairness, being mindful that they also have a Master in heaven.

Paul connects the ethics of the Christian life directly to its highest theology. We flesh out in our role relationships the very relationship that we have with Christ. Our relationship to Christ becomes the pattern by which we relate to those in our marriages, families, friends, co-workers, and neighbors. Whatever we do, we do all in the name of the Lord Jesus, letting his peace dwell within our hearts.

Daily Devotional Guide

PREPARING OUR HEARTS

Invocation: Our Prayer of Acclamation

Eternal Father, Paul your servant said that we are to clothe ourselves with the virtues that arise from knowing you, and being in your Son. Each of our relationships is to be informed by and connected to our relationship to you, and to Jesus our Lord. You have created a new image within us; as your own holy, beloved, and dear children, we are to please you from our hearts, not to earn your favor, but to reveal our love for you because of your care and forgiveness. Let the peace of Jesus dwell within us, and let your light shine in every dimension of our lives. Do this for Christ's sake, amen.

Call to Worship

Blessed are you, O God: Father, Son, and Holy Spirit. And blessed is your Kingdom, both now and forever, amen.

PRAISING OUR GOD

Te Deum Laudamus

You are God: we praise you; you are the Lord; we acclaim you; you are the eternal Father: All creation worships you. To you all angels, all the powers of heaven, Cherubim and Seraphim, sing in endless praise: Holy, holy, holy Lord, God of power and might, heaven and earth are full of your glory.

The glorious company of apostles praise you. The noble fellowship of prophets praise you. The white-robed army of martyrs praise you. Throughout the world the holy Church acclaims you; Father, of majesty unbounded, your true and only Son, worthy of all worship, and the Holy Spirit, advocate and guide.

You, Christ, are the king of glory, the eternal Son of the Father. When you became man to set us free you did not shun the Virgin's womb. You overcame the sting of death and opened the kingdom of heaven to all believers. You are seated at God's right hand in glory. We believe that you will come and be our judge. Come then, Lord, and help your people, bought with the price of your own blood, and bring us with your saints to glory everlasting.

Praise and Thanksgiving (Songs and Prayers)

Gloria Patri

Glory be to the Father,
And to the Son and to the Holy Spirit:
As it was in the beginning,
Is now, and ever shall be,
World without end. Amen, amen.

LISTENING TO HIS VOICE

Chronological Reading for the Day
Sunday: Acts 13-14
Monday: Gal. 1.1-4.7
Tuesday: Gal. 4.8-6.18; Acts 15
Wednesday: Acts 16.1-18.3
Thursday: 1 Thess. 1-5
Friday: 2 Thess. 1-3; Acts 18.4-28
Saturday: Acts 19.1-20; 1 Cor. 1-3

Lectionary Readings
Psalm: Ps. 66.1-12
Gospel: Luke 17.11-19

OT: Jer. 29.1, 4-7
NT: 2 Tim. 2.8-15

Reflection: Silence and/or Journaling

RESPONDING IN FAITH

The Apostles' Creed
I believe in God, the Father Almighty, Maker of heaven and earth; and in Jesus Christ, his only Son, our Lord, who was conceived by the Holy Spirit, born of the Virgin Mary, suffered under Pontius Pilate, was crucified, dead, and buried; he descended into hell; the third day he arose again from the dead; he ascended into heaven and sits on the right hand of God the Father Almighty; from thence he shall come to judge the quick and the dead.

I believe in the Holy Spirit, the holy catholic* church, the communion of saints, the forgiveness of sins, the resurrection of the body, and the life everlasting. Amen.

* In the Apostles' and Nicene Creeds, the term catholic refers to the Church's universality, through all ages and times, of all languages and peoples. It refers to no particular tradition or denominational expression (e.g., as in Roman Catholic).

Prayers of Confession

Let us now confess our sins to God and receive mercy and grace to help in our time of need.

Assurance of Pardon

Having faithfully confessed and renounced your sin, Christ also has been faithful to forgive your sins and to purify you from all unrighteousness. It is certain, that there is One who has spoken to the Father in your defense, Jesus Christ, the Righteous One who is the atoning sacrifice for our sins and for the sins of the whole world. His grace and peace are with you now. Amen.

Petitions and Supplications, Ending with the Lord's Prayer

Our Father which art in heaven, Hallowed be thy name. Thy kingdom come, Thy will be done in earth, as it is in heaven. Give us this day our daily bread. And forgive us our debts, as we forgive our debtors. And lead us not into temptation, but deliver us from evil: For thine is the kingdom, and the power, and the glory, for ever. Amen.

~ Matthew 6.9-13 (KJV)

Doxology (and/or closing song)

Praise God from whom all blessings flow;
Praise Him all creatures here below;
Praise Him above ye heavenly host;
Praise Father, Son and Holy Ghost. Amen.

Departing to Serve

Benediction

Lord Jesus, you called us into one body, to be thankful, allowing your peace to rule in our hearts. Enable us to let your Word dwell richly in our lives, and give us hearts to teach and admonish each another in all wisdom. Fill our hearts with psalms, hymns, and spiritual songs, and give us thankful hearts. Let what we say and do be done in your name, to the Father's thanks and glory. We love you; make us like you today. In your name, amen.

Affirmation from the Psalms

Show us your steadfast love, O Lord, and grant us your salvation.
[8] Let me hear what God the Lord will speak, for he will speak peace to his people, to his saints; but let them not turn back to folly.
[9] Surely his salvation is near to those who fear him, that glory may dwell in our land.

~ Psalm 85.7-9

Pray without Ceasing – Flash Prayer for the Day

Lord Jesus Christ, let your peace rule in our hearts – calm us according to your Word, and free our minds of worry and anxiety.

For Your Weekly Journey

Let God Arise! Seasonal Focus

The Shadow and the Substance, Colossians 2.8-23

Book Reading

Ramsay and Wilson, *St. Paul: the Traveler and Roman Citizen*

Our Corporate Disciplines

Book Discussion: Monday, October 10, 2016

The Season after Pentecost

REMEMBERING THE SAINTS, EXALTING THE KING

But for you who fear my name,
the sun of righteousness shall rise
with healing in its wings.

MALACHI 4.2A

After the longest season of the Church Year, our calendar ends with three significant days of remembrance and readiness. On October 31 we commemorate the protestant reformation of the church (*Reformation Day*), and on November 1 we anticipate the gathering of all believers together at his throne, while remembering his martyrs and generations gone by (*All Saints Day*). On the last Sunday before Advent, we celebrate the *Feast of Christ the King* (also called the *Feast of the Reign of Christ*) which points to that day when the kingdom of this world will become the kingdom of our Lord and of his Christ.

Reformation Day *(semper reformanda)*
Reformation Day is the Christian festival day celebrated on October 31 to mark the Reformation, and is observed largely by Protestant mainline churches, and in particular, by both Lutheran and some Reformed churches. During the time of 1516–17, Johann Tetzel, a friar of the Dominican order and official commissioner of the Pope for indulgences, was given the assignment to go to Germany and to raise money through the sale of indulgences to rebuild St. Peter's Basilica in Rome.

On October 31, 1517, Martin Luther, an Augustinian monk, wrote to Albrecht, Archbishop of Mainz and Magdeburg, levying his argument against the scandal surrounding the sale and purchase of indulgences (a Roman Catholic practice to shorten terms of dead loved ones in Purgatory). Luther enclosed in his letter to Archbishop Albrecht a copy of his case entitled "Disputation of Martin Luther on the Power and Efficacy of Indulgences," a document which later came to be referred to as *The 95 Theses*. Luther probably did not intend for his views to be taken as undermining the church; he more probably viewed his letter as a reasoned scholarly, spiritual objection to these kinds of church allowances. Nevertheless, the thrust of Luther's argument came to be seen as a direct challenge to the pope's authority and policies, and this simple act would become the touchstone of sweeping changes in the life of the Church.

Luther's nailing his letter to the door of the Schlosskirche (known as the Castle Church) in Wittenberg has been marked as the initial spark that ignited the movement known as the Reformation. Even a contemporary of Luther, Philip Melanchthon, would write in 1546 that Luther's writing and posting of his arguments against indulgence was a seminal event in the Reformation's start. While this has been debated in some scholarly circles, it is clear that *The 95 Theses* would go on to be published from Latin into German, and copied much throughout Europe, aided remarkably by the dawning of the printing press. It would set in motion a series of events which would effect the Church's faith and practice, even to the present day.

We at TUMI recognize this festival, even though it is not broadly celebrated as the other feast days in the Christian calendar. We are unashamedly Protestant in that, while we affirm the unity of the one, holy, catholic, and apostolic church, we recognize the significance and authority of the prophetic and apostolic testimony of the Scriptures, and reference to the Word of God as ultimate authority in all matters of Christian faith and practice. The church must ever be open to the Holy Spirit-inspired Scriptures, manifesting a willingness to be corrected, directed, and reformed ("*ecclesia semper reformands, semper reformanda*": "the church is always reformed, always reforming"). To be open to Christ is to be ever open to responding to his leadership among us, as Head and Lord of the church.

Bruce Epperly succinctly summarizes the heart of the Reformer's desire for a faith anchored in Scripture, faith, grace, and Christ, all for the glory of God alone. "As they sought to articulate their reforming faith, the Reformers affirmed 'five solas' – *sola scriptura, sola fides, sola gratia, solus Christus, soli Deo Gloria*. These '*solas*' expressed the contours of Reformation faith while not narrowly defining its meaning. To be faithful to the Reformed spirit, each of these must be constantly updated to respond to God's call in a constantly changing universe."[1]

Confessing the Communion of Saints: All Saints Day

The remembrance of *All Saints Day* calls the Church to recognize the singular, universal, and potent communion of saints who have believed in and followed Christ through the ages. With its special remembrance of the martyrs historically and within contemporary society, the focus of *All Saints Day* enables us to never forget the organic unity we share with all believers everywhere throughout all time. We are spiritually, theologically, and eschatologically linked: We sup at the same Table, hold fast to the same Word, preach to the lost the same Gospel, and wait for the same return of the exalted King, the Lord Jesus Christ.

All Saints Day is our time as believers to remember our membership in the one, holy, catholic (universal), and apostolic Church, the same company of which Christ is head, and which awaits his glorious return in power. We share both DNA and destiny with those martyrs and saints, those heroes of the faith who came before us. Of special importance, *All Saints Day* is a time to recall and remember those who gave up their lives for the sake of Christ and the Gospel. In celebrating this feast we gladly affirm that the Church is the body of Christ, and that the living Savior now lives and is seen in the world through the words and deeds

---

[1] Bruce Epperly, "A Church Always Reforming: Reflections on Reformation Day." *http:// www.patheos.com/Resources/Additional-Resources/Church-Always-Reforming-Bruce-Epperly-10-24-2011.html*, Oct. 23, 2011.

of his people (John 14.12; Heb. 11; Rev. 17.6), and through all who through time have clung to him by faith.

To whet your appetite on the riches available to those interested in spending time considering the discipleship of the saints, both ancient and modern, please read a synopsis of some of the heroes and heroines of the faith in our *Saints, Martyrs, and Other Luminaries of the Faith* (located at *www.tumi.org/annual*).

Awaiting the Arrival of our Lord: The Feast of Christ the King

According to the testimony of Scripture, our Lord will return and finish the work he began on the Cross, judging the world, saving his own, and making a final end to evil and sin.

The third feast day at the end of this season, the *Feast of Christ the King* (also called the *Feast of the Reign of Christ*) is the last Sunday of this season, and the final one before Advent. The hope of the saints throughout the ages is that the Lord Jesus will return to rightfully claim this world as his own, to establish in fullness the reign of God, restoring creation to its edenic glory, and putting down evil, once and for all. The *Feast of Christ the King* points to that day when the kingdom of this world will become the kingdom of our Lord and of his Christ, who will reign forever and ever (Rev. 11.15ff.). How appropriate to end the season after the coming of the Holy Spirit with a feast which honors the future reign of our risen Savior, the true Lord who one day will reign alone and supreme!

One, Undivided Church: For All the Saints

William W. How and Ralph Vaughan Williams created a marvelous lyrical poem that summarizes and highlights the glorious communion and unity we share with all true believers in Jesus Christ who hold the hope of the new heavens and earth in their hearts, and who long to see the Lord soon. It is entitled *For All the Saints*, and is considered a classic hymn outlining the amazing perseverance of the martyrs and believers who have held true in their witness to Christ and his Kingdom.

For All the Saints

For all the saints, who from their labors rest,
Who Thee by faith before the world confessed,
Thy Name, O Jesus, be forever blessed. Alleluia, Alleluia!

Thou wast their Rock, their Fortress and their Might;
Thou, Lord, their Captain in the well-fought fight;
Thou, in the darkness drear, their one true Light. Alleluia, Alleluia!

For the Apostles' glorious company,
Who bearing forth the Cross o'er land and sea,
Shook all the mighty world, we sing to Thee: Alleluia, Alleluia!

For the Evangelists, by whose blest word,
Like fourfold streams, the garden of the Lord,
Is fair and fruitful, be Thy Name adored. Alleluia, Alleluia!

For Martyrs, who with rapture-kindled eye,
Saw the bright crown descending from the sky,
And seeing, grasped it, Thee we glorify. Alleluia, Alleluia!

O blest communion, fellowship divine!
We feebly struggle; they in glory shine.
All are one in Thee, for all are Thine. Alleluia, Alleluia!

O may Thy soldiers, faithful, true and bold,
Fight as the saints who nobly fought of old,
And win with them the victor's crown of gold. Alleluia, Alleluia!

And when the strife is fierce, the warfare long,
Steals on the ear the distant triumph song,
And hearts are brave, again, and arms are strong. Alleluia, Alleluia!

The golden evening brightens in the west;
Soon, soon to faithful warriors comes their rest;
Sweet is the calm of paradise the blessed. Alleluia, Alleluia!

But lo! there breaks a yet more glorious day;
The saints triumphant rise in bright array;
The King of glory passes on His way. Alleluia, Alleluia!

From earth's wide bounds, from ocean's farthest coast,
Through gates of pearl streams in the countless host,
And singing to Father, Son and Holy Ghost: Alleluia, Alleluia!

~ Words: William W. How.
Music: Sine Nomine. Ralph Vaughan Williams.
© Public Domain.

As sojourners of the Way, we must ever be open to hear and respond to the living voice of God in the Spirit, the Word of God preached in the Church. It is in this spirit of meekness, lowliness, and humility that we celebrate the dramatic impact of the Reformation on the church, and its ongoing legacy for mission, discipleship, and spiritual formation today. We remember our membership, with all the saints through the ages, in the one, holy, catholic (universal), and apostolic Church of which Christ is the head. And, we share with those saints, the hope throughout the ages that the Lord Jesus will return in power and establish his kingdom reign. To live by faith is to have this hope and do nothing less than be responsive to the risen Christ as he directs his people into his good, perfect, and acceptable will.

Anticipating the reign of the ages,
Rev. Dr. Don L. Davis

Twenty-second Sunday after Pentecost

October 16 - 22, 2016 • Proper 24

WEEK 47

According to God's holy promise, the saints of Christ will dine at the marriage supper of the Lamb, a feast of love and communion with the risen Lord and Savior himself. The Feast of Christ the King, the last Sunday before Advent, anticipates the day when Christ will reign supreme, and the saints of God will never again leave the presence of their Lord.

THIS WEEK'S THEME
The Final Instructions, Colossians 4.2-6

One of the key characteristics of Paul's ministry to believers in prison was his constant, fervent prayers on their behalf. He practiced a rich prayer life (e.g., 1.3-12) for those under his care, but he also exhorted them to do the same. As to their prayer lives, he challenges them to devote themselves steadfastly to prayer, being watchful (alert, aware) in seeking the Lord with thanksgiving. Regardless of what we ask for, the tone of our petition should always be anchored in a recognition of God's grace and goodness. Whatever we need, and however we ask, it should always be done with thankful hearts. Thanksgiving alone places us in the right place to ask anything of the Lord.

Paul also asked the Colossians to remember his status as a prisoner; he asked that they might "pray also for us" (he and his fellow prisoners), that "God may open to us a door for the word, to declare the mystery of Christ, on account of which I am in prison – that I may make it clear, which is how I ought to speak." This is extraordinary; rather than have them pray for his release from or provision in prison, he asks for open doors and clear communication. In everything and at every place, Paul's heart was seeking to share the Good News of God's salvation with others.

As to their public lives, Paul's final instruction was for them to walk in wisdom toward outsiders, making the best use of the time. The way they acted and spoke would make a difference in relating to people who did not know the Lord. Their actions were to be wise, and their speech was always to be gracious, "seasoned with salt," (as one commentator calls it, "pure and penetrating"), in order that they might know just how they ought to answer each person.

Paul's final greetings reveal his parental and shepherding tendencies for the Colossians, the Laodiceans, for Onesimus, Aristarchus, and others. He sent word of his activities by Tychichus, reminding them of the faithful service of Epaphras on their behalf. After sending them greetings from his party (including Luke, Demas, and others), he sent greetings to the churches of the Laodiceans, Nymphas and the church in her house, and he asked the Colossians to read the letter he sent to Laodicea, and vice versa. He closes by exhorting Archippus to fulfill his ministry.

In a tender final phrase, Paul wrote his greeting with his own hand, and asked his dear Christian friends to "remember my chains." "Grace be with you" were his last words to them.

Daily Devotional Guide

PREPARING OUR HEARTS

Invocation: Our Prayer of Acclamation

Father God, the heart of your apostle Paul revealed a deep burden to pray for others, to share the Gospel with the lost, and to provide a compelling testimony before outsiders, those who do not know you. His tenderness and thoughtfulness for these dear Christians moves us; reproduce his burdens and longings within us, especially his ability to pray for opportunities to share the Good News with others, even in the midst of persecution and suffering. We depend on you. In Christ's name, amen.

Call to Worship
Blessed are you, O God: Father, Son, and Holy Spirit. And blessed is your Kingdom, both now and forever, amen.

PRAISING OUR GOD

Te Deum Laudamus
You are God: we praise you; you are the Lord; we acclaim you; you are the eternal Father: All creation worships you. To you all angels, all the powers of heaven, Cherubim and Seraphim, sing in endless praise: Holy, holy, holy Lord, God of power and might, heaven and earth are full of your glory.

The glorious company of apostles praise you. The noble fellowship of prophets praise you. The white-robed army of martyrs praise you. Throughout the world the holy Church acclaims you; Father, of majesty unbounded, your true and only Son, worthy of all worship, and the Holy Spirit, advocate and guide.

You, Christ, are the king of glory, the eternal Son of the Father. When you became man to set us free you did not shun the Virgin's womb. You overcame the sting of death and opened the kingdom of heaven to all believers. You are seated at God's right hand in glory. We believe that you will come and be our judge. Come then, Lord, and help your people, bought with the price of your own blood, and bring us with your saints to glory everlasting.

Praise and Thanksgiving (Songs and Prayers)

Gloria Patri
Glory be to the Father,
And to the Son and to the Holy Spirit:
As it was in the beginning,
Is now, and ever shall be,
World without end. Amen, amen.

LISTENING TO HIS VOICE

Chronological Reading for the Day
Sunday: 1 Cor. 4-7
Monday: 1 Cor. 8.1-11.1
Tuesday: 1 Cor. 11.2-13.13
Wednesday: 1 Cor. 14-15
Thursday: 1 Cor. 16; Acts 19.21-20.6
Friday: Rom. 1-3
Saturday: Rom. 4-6

Lectionary Readings
Psalm: Ps. 119.97-104   *OT:* Jer. 31.27-34
Gospel: Luke 18.1-8   *NT:* 2 Tim. 3.14-4.5

Reflection: Silence and/or Journaling

RESPONDING IN FAITH

The Apostles' Creed
*I believe in God, the Father Almighty, Maker of heaven and earth;
and in Jesus Christ, his only Son, our Lord, who was conceived by the
Holy Spirit, born of the Virgin Mary, suffered under Pontius Pilate,
was crucified, dead, and buried; he descended into hell; the third day
he arose again from the dead; he ascended into heaven and sits on
the right hand of God the Father Almighty; from thence he shall come
to judge the quick and the dead.*

I believe in the Holy Spirit, the holy catholic church, the communion
of saints, the forgiveness of sins, the resurrection of the body, and the
life everlasting. Amen.*

* In the Apostles' and Nicene Creeds, the term catholic refers to the Church's
universality, through all ages and times, of all languages and peoples. It refers to no
particular tradition or denominational expression (e.g., as in Roman Catholic).

Prayers of Confession

Let us now confess our sins to God and receive mercy and grace to help in our time of need.

Assurance of Pardon

Having faithfully confessed and renounced your sin, Christ also has been faithful to forgive your sins and to purify you from all unrighteousness. It is certain, that there is One who has spoken to the Father in your defense, Jesus Christ, the Righteous One who is the atoning sacrifice for our sins and for the sins of the whole world. His grace and peace are with you now. Amen.

Petitions and Supplications, Ending with the Lord's Prayer

Our Father which art in heaven, Hallowed be thy name. Thy kingdom come, Thy will be done in earth, as it is in heaven. Give us this day our daily bread. And forgive us our debts, as we forgive our debtors. And lead us not into temptation, but deliver us from evil: For thine is the kingdom, and the power, and the glory, for ever. Amen.

~ Matthew 6.9-13 (KJV)

Doxology (and/or closing song)

Praise God from whom all blessings flow;
Praise Him all creatures here below;
Praise Him above ye heavenly host;
Praise Father, Son and Holy Ghost. Amen.

DEPARTING TO SERVE

Benediction

Lord Jesus, we stand in awe of your servant, whose final petition to his friends was for them to remember his chains, the bonds of your ambassador who ultimately would give his very life for you. We know that unless a grain of wheat fall into the ground and die, it will abide alone. Yet, Lord, if it die, it will bring forth much fruit. Like Paul, help us to die to ourselves in order that your life might be seen in us. Help us to live for your glory alone, in your name we ask this, amen.

Affirmation from the Psalms

Not to us, O Lord, not to us, but to your name give glory, for the sake of your steadfast love and your faithfulness! [2] Why should the nations say, "Where is their God?" [3] Our God is in the heavens; he does all that he pleases.

~ Psalm 115.1-3

Pray without Ceasing – Flash Prayer for the Day

Lord Jesus Christ, help us to walk in wisdom toward those who are outside, speaking to them words of grace that they may understand who you are.

For Your Weekly Journey

Let God Arise! Seasonal Focus

The Everlasting Dominion to Come, Daniel 7.1-3, 15-18

Book Reading

Ramsay and Wilson, *St. Paul: the Traveler and Roman Citizen*

Twenty-third Sunday after Pentecost
October 23 - 29, 2016 • Proper 25

WEEK
48

According to God's holy promise, the saints of Christ will dine at the marriage supper of the Lamb, a feast of love and communion with the risen Lord and Savior himself. The Feast of Christ the King, the last Sunday before Advent, anticipates the day when Christ will reign supreme, and the saints of God will never again leave the presence of their Lord.

THIS WEEK'S THEME
Paul's Remembrance of Philemon, Philemon 1-7
In the only letter that Paul refers to himself as a "prisoner of Christ," he with Timothy entreats his dear brother and friend, Philemon, making requests regarding a new convert, Onesimus. Philemon was his "fellow worker" (v. 24), suggesting that they labored for Christ together, along with Apphia, perhaps Philemon's wife and Archippus, a "fellow soldier." The epistle written also to the "church that meets in your home" addresses the issue of reconciliation, welcome, and reincorporation into an assembly of Christ. With thankfulness to God Paul always remembered Philemon in his prayers, having heard of his love and faith he had toward the Lord Jesus and for all the people of God. Paul's memories of Philemon were strong, and he joined them with prayer on his behalf, asking God that the sharing of Philemon's faith might become effective "for the full knowledge of every good thing that is in us for the sake of Christ."

Philemon's profound love for the Lord and for the saints resulted in much joy and comfort for Paul, who affectionately refers to him as "my brother," because through that love "the hearts of the saints have been refreshed through you." This is not mere set up for his coming pleas on behalf of Onesimus, but a reinforcement of what God had done in Philemon, and the obvious evidence of his maturity in

Christ. Paul remembered Philemon's kindness, and he testified that he had heard the same about his behavior to others. Philemon was a refreshment to the saints, with a record of compassionate conduct to believers and love to the Lord Jesus. Paul's remembrance of these good works would form the basis of his appeal for his newly converted servant, Onesimus. The testimony of Philemon's gracious spirit would now be tested in his kind reception of his wayward servant.

Daily Devotional Guide

PREPARING OUR HEARTS

Invocation: Our Prayer of Acclamation
Eternal God, whose heart is full of goodness and mercy for the truly penitent, thank you for grace and love, the love of Christ for us all. Your love has brought us home, and now, through faith in Christ, you ask that we demonstrate that same mercy and graciousness to all we relate to today. Refresh us, Father, in order that we might be a refreshment to others, for Christ's sake, amen.

Call to Worship
Blessed are you, O God: Father, Son, and Holy Spirit. And blessed is your Kingdom, both now and forever, amen.

PRAISING OUR GOD

Te Deum Laudamus
You are God: we praise you; you are the Lord; we acclaim you; you are the eternal Father: All creation worships you. To you all angels, all the powers of heaven, Cherubim and Seraphim, sing in endless praise: Holy, holy, holy Lord, God of power and might, heaven and earth are full of your glory.

The glorious company of apostles praise you. The noble fellowship of prophets praise you. The white-robed army of martyrs praise you. Throughout the world the holy Church acclaims you; Father, of majesty unbounded, your true and only Son, worthy of all worship, and the Holy Spirit, advocate and guide.

You, Christ, are the king of glory, the eternal Son of the Father. When you became man to set us free you did not shun the Virgin's womb. You overcame the sting of death and opened the kingdom of heaven to all believers. You are seated at God's right hand in glory. We believe that you will come and be our judge. Come then, Lord, and help your people, bought with the price of your own blood, and bring us with your saints to glory everlasting.

Praise and Thanksgiving (Songs and Prayers)

Gloria Patri
Glory be to the Father,
And to the Son and to the Holy Spirit:
As it was in the beginning,
Is now, and ever shall be,
World without end. Amen, amen.

LISTENING TO HIS VOICE

Chronological Reading for the Day
Sunday: Rom. 7-9
Monday: Rom. 10-13
Tuesday: Rom. 14-16
Wednesday: 2 Cor. 1.1-6.13
Thursday: 2 Cor. 6.14-10.18
Friday: 2 Cor. 11-13
Saturday: Acts 20.7-21.36

Lectionary Readings
Psalm: Ps. 65   *OT:* Joel 2.23-32
Gospel: Luke 18.9-14   *NT:* 2 Tim. 4.6-8, 16-18

Reflection: Silence and/or Journaling

RESPONDING IN FAITH

The Apostles' Creed
*I believe in God, the Father Almighty, Maker of heaven and earth;
and in Jesus Christ, his only Son, our Lord, who was conceived by the
Holy Spirit, born of the Virgin Mary, suffered under Pontius Pilate,
was crucified, dead, and buried; he descended into hell; the third day
he arose again from the dead; he ascended into heaven and sits on
the right hand of God the Father Almighty; from thence he shall come
to judge the quick and the dead.*

I believe in the Holy Spirit, the holy catholic church, the communion
of saints, the forgiveness of sins, the resurrection of the body, and the
life everlasting. Amen.*

* In the Apostles' and Nicene Creeds, the term catholic refers to the Church's
universality, through all ages and times, of all languages and peoples. It refers to no
particular tradition or denominational expression (e.g., as in Roman Catholic).

Prayers of Confession
Let us now confess our sins to God and receive mercy and
grace to help in our time of need.

Assurance of Pardon
Having faithfully confessed and renounced your sin, Christ
also has been faithful to forgive your sins and to purify you
from all unrighteousness. It is certain, that there is One who
has spoken to the Father in your defense, Jesus Christ, the
Righteous One who is the atoning sacrifice for our sins and
for the sins of the whole world. His grace and peace are with
you now. Amen.

Petitions and Supplications, Ending with the Lord's Prayer
*Our Father which art in heaven, Hallowed be thy name. Thy kingdom
come, Thy will be done in earth, as it is in heaven. Give us this day our*

daily bread. And forgive us our debts, as we forgive our debtors. And lead us not into temptation, but deliver us from evil: For thine is the kingdom, and the power, and the glory, for ever. Amen.

~ Matthew 6.9-13 (KJV)

Doxology (and/or closing song)

Praise God from whom all blessings flow;
Praise Him all creatures here below;
Praise Him above ye heavenly host;
Praise Father, Son and Holy Ghost. Amen.

DEPARTING TO SERVE

Benediction

Dear Lord Jesus, whose inner being was moved with compassion for the multitudes, for the grieving, and for the lost, reproduce in us that same tender heart of love. Make us vessels of your grace and kindness, that we might demonstrate your heart for others in practical ways right where we are. Form us to be your channels of blessings for others, in the same way you laid your life down for us. In your name we pray, amen.

Affirmation from the Psalms

Make me to know your ways, O Lord; teach me your paths. [5] Lead me in your truth and teach me, for you are the God of my salvation; for you I wait all the day long. [6] Remember your mercy, O Lord, and your steadfast love, for they have been from of old. [7] Remember not the sins of my youth or my transgressions; according to your steadfast love remember me, for the sake of your goodness, O Lord!

~ Psalm 25.4-7

Pray without Ceasing – Flash Prayer for the Day
Lord Jesus Christ, make us vessels of love and mercy, and use us today to minister grace to all we encounter.

For Your Weekly Journey

Let God Arise! Seasonal Focus
The Everlasting Dominion to Come, Daniel 7.1-3, 15-18

Book Reading
Ramsay and Wilson, *St. Paul: the Traveler and Roman Citizen*

Our Corporate Disciplines
Book Discussion: Monday, October 24, 2016

Twenty-fourth Sunday after Pentecost
October 30 - November 5, 2016 • Proper 26

WEEK
49

According to God's holy promise, the saints of Christ will dine at the marriage supper of the Lamb, a feast of love and communion with the risen Lord and Savior himself. The Feast of Christ the King, the last Sunday before Advent, anticipates the day when Christ will reign supreme, and the saints of God will never again leave the presence of their Lord.

THIS WEEK'S THEME
Paul's Request for Onesimus, Philemon 8-25

Paul's memory of Philemon's gracious spirit and refreshing heart drew him to be bold on behalf of his new child in the faith, Onesimus. Although Paul knew that he could demand that Philemon welcome Onesimus, "yet for love's sake" he appealed to Philemon's heart. He, Paul, made the appeal to Philemon, as he puts it, "I, Paul, an old man and now a prisoner also for Christ Jesus." He asked him on behalf of his "child, Onesimus," whom Paul had won to the Lord during his imprisonment. Paul tells Philemon that while formerly Onesimus was "useless" to him, now truly he was both useful to him and will soon be to Philemon himself.

Paul's tender plea is evident in his appeal for Onesimus (whose name means "useful"). He tells Philemon that in sending Onesimus back to him he was sending his "very heart." Although Paul said it would be great to keep him there to serve his needs during his imprisonment, he thought it prudent not to let Onesimus do anything without Philemon's consent. Paul requested Philemon's joyful consent, not his grudging obedience! Paul suggested that perhaps is why Onesimus was parted temporarily from him in order to get him back forever, this time not as a bond-servant, but rather as a beloved brother, both to Paul as well as to Philemon.

Paul summarizes his request by appealing to Philemon's devotion to himself. Paul told Philemon that if he considered him to be his partner, that he should receive Onesimus even as he would receive himself. If Onesimus owed him, he was to charge whatever it was to his own account. Paul promised with his own handwriting that he would repay it – even though, as Paul said, Philemon owed him his own self! Paul pleaded for Philemon to show graciousness to Onesimus as though offering it to him, Paul, treating Onesimus as he would treat him, refreshing his heart, and benefitting him in the Lord.

This strong appeal was accompanied by Paul's confidence that Philemon would act on his appeal, doing even more than Paul requested. Paul "called in his favors" with Philemon for the sake of his new convert in Christ, Onesimus. Even in chains and in desperate need for care himself, the apostle Paul used every opportunity to make a plea for gracious forgiveness and love for the bondservant now turn brother in Christ.

Daily Devotional Guide

PREPARING OUR HEARTS

Invocation: Our Prayer of Acclamation
Eternal God of grace, God and Father of our Lord Jesus Christ, we thank you for the love and care demonstrated by Paul for his child in the faith Onesimus. Even though he was in prison and in desperate need himself, Paul appealed to Philemon on Onesimus' behalf, asking for and giving grace in all things. Thank you for the mercy you have demonstrated to us. Now, in the spirit of that same mercy, may we be forgiving, gracious, and welcoming to all with whom we relate. For the sake of Jesus we pray these things, amen.

Call to Worship

Blessed are you, O God: Father, Son, and Holy Spirit. And blessed is your Kingdom, both now and forever, amen.

PRAISING OUR GOD

Te Deum Laudamus

You are God: we praise you; you are the Lord; we acclaim you; you are the eternal Father: All creation worships you. To you all angels, all the powers of heaven, Cherubim and Seraphim, sing in endless praise: Holy, holy, holy Lord, God of power and might, heaven and earth are full of your glory.

The glorious company of apostles praise you. The noble fellowship of prophets praise you. The white-robed army of martyrs praise you. Throughout the world the holy Church acclaims you; Father, of majesty unbounded, your true and only Son, worthy of all worship, and the Holy Spirit, advocate and guide.

You, Christ, are the king of glory, the eternal Son of the Father. When you became man to set us free you did not shun the Virgin's womb. You overcame the sting of death and opened the kingdom of heaven to all believers. You are seated at God's right hand in glory. We believe that you will come and be our judge. Come then, Lord, and help your people, bought with the price of your own blood, and bring us with your saints to glory everlasting.

Praise and Thanksgiving (Songs and Prayers)

Gloria Patri

Glory be to the Father,
And to the Son and to the Holy Spirit:
As it was in the beginning,
Is now, and ever shall be,
World without end. Amen, amen.

LISTENING TO HIS VOICE

Chronological Reading for the Day
Sunday: Acts 21.37-23.35
Monday: Acts 24-26
Tuesday: Acts 27-28
Wednesday: Eph. 1-3
Thursday: Eph. 4-6
Friday: Col. 1-2
Saturday: Col. 3-4

Lectionary Readings
Psalm: Ps. 32.1-7   *OT:* Isa. 1.10-18
Gospel: Luke 19.1-10   *NT:* 2 Thess. 1.1-4, 11-12

Reflection: Silence and/or Journaling

RESPONDING IN FAITH

The Apostles' Creed
*I believe in God, the Father Almighty, Maker of heaven and earth;
and in Jesus Christ, his only Son, our Lord, who was conceived by the
Holy Spirit, born of the Virgin Mary, suffered under Pontius Pilate,
was crucified, dead, and buried; he descended into hell; the third day
he arose again from the dead; he ascended into heaven and sits on
the right hand of God the Father Almighty; from thence he shall come
to judge the quick and the dead.*

I believe in the Holy Spirit, the holy catholic church, the communion
of saints, the forgiveness of sins, the resurrection of the body, and the
life everlasting. Amen.*

* In the Apostles' and Nicene Creeds, the term catholic refers to the Church's
universality, through all ages and times, of all languages and peoples. It refers to no
particular tradition or denominational expression (e.g., as in Roman Catholic).

Prayers of Confession

Let us now confess our sins to God and receive mercy and grace to help in our time of need.

Assurance of Pardon

Having faithfully confessed and renounced your sin, Christ also has been faithful to forgive your sins and to purify you from all unrighteousness. It is certain, that there is One who has spoken to the Father in your defense, Jesus Christ, the Righteous One who is the atoning sacrifice for our sins and for the sins of the whole world. His grace and peace are with you now. Amen.

Petitions and Supplications, Ending with the Lord's Prayer

Our Father which art in heaven, Hallowed be thy name. Thy kingdom come, Thy will be done in earth, as it is in heaven. Give us this day our daily bread. And forgive us our debts, as we forgive our debtors. And lead us not into temptation, but deliver us from evil: For thine is the kingdom, and the power, and the glory, for ever. Amen.

~ Matthew 6.9-13 (KJV)

Doxology (and/or closing song)

Praise God from whom all blessings flow;
Praise Him all creatures here below;
Praise Him above ye heavenly host;
Praise Father, Son and Holy Ghost. Amen.

DEPARTING TO SERVE

Benediction

Lord Jesus Christ, we know and depend on your amazing grace, that although you were rich you became poor for our sakes in order that we might through your poverty become rich, indeed. Forgive us for the times when we have forgotten how much you gave for us to belong to the Father. Teach us, show us, work in us that same grace you displayed in your life, and your death. Make us like you. For your sake we pray, amen.

Affirmation from the Psalms

To you I lift up my eyes, O you who are enthroned in the heavens! [2] Behold, as the eyes of servants look to the hand of their master, as the eyes of a maidservant to the hand of her mistress, so our eyes look to the Lord our God, till he has mercy upon us.

~ Psalm 123.1-2

Pray without Ceasing – Flash Prayer for the Day

Lord Jesus Christ, Son of God, let your mercy flow through us to those we meet today, making us a vessel of grace to all.

For Your Weekly Journey

Let God Arise! Seasonal Focus
The Everlasting Dominion to Come, Daniel 7.1-3, 15-18

Book Reading
Ramsay and Wilson, *St. Paul: the Traveler and Roman Citizen*

Special Church Year Services
Reformation Day: Monday, October 31, 2016
All Saints Day: Tuesday, November 1, 2016

Reformation Day

October 31, 2016

According to God's holy promise, the saints of Christ will dine at the marriage supper of the Lamb, a feast of love and communion with the risen Lord and Savior himself. The Feast of Christ the King, the last Sunday before Advent, anticipates the day when Christ will reign supreme, and the saints of God will never again leave the presence of their Lord.

TODAY'S THEME
The Truth Will Set You Free, John 8.31-36
On this Reformation Day celebration we remember the role of true confession and hope in the Lord Jesus. The spirit of the reformers was a fierce, unflagging defense of the truth as they found it in the Lord Jesus Christ. In one of the many tense interactions our Lord had with crowds who heard his Word, it was clear that some of those who listened paid attention to his words and committed themselves personally to him. Jesus recognized their faith and said to those who believed, "If you abide in my word, you are truly my disciples, and you will know the truth, and the truth will set you free." Others answered the Lord's Word, protesting themselves to be the "offspring of Abraham," those who had never been enslaved to anyone. They demanded to know what Jesus meant in saying "You will become free." Jesus replied to them "Truly, truly, I say to you, everyone who practices sin is a slave to sin. The slave does not remain in the house forever; the son remains forever. So if the Son sets you free, you will be free indeed."

Jesus knew that his Word was the key to freedom in God, freedom from sin and freedom in life. Only faith in his Word alone can truly liberate a person from the tyranny of falsehood and the bondage of sin. In him alone can humankind truly be set free from the ages-long deception of the enemy and the horrendous effects of sin. Abiding in his Word is the key to discipleship and to personal liberation.

Daily Devotional Guide

PREPARING OUR HEARTS

Invocation: Our Prayer of Acclamation
Mercifully receive, O Lord, the prayers of Thy Church; that all adversities and errors may be destroyed, and it may serve Thee in quiet freedom; and give Thy peace in our times, through Jesus Christ our Lord. Amen.

~ *Leonine Sacramentary* (Bright, p. 97)

Call to Worship
Blessed are you, O God: Father, Son, and Holy Spirit. And blessed is your Kingdom, both now and forever, amen.

PRAISING OUR GOD

Te Deum Laudamus
You are God: we praise you; you are the Lord; we acclaim you; you are the eternal Father: All creation worships you. To you all angels, all the powers of heaven, Cherubim and Seraphim, sing in endless praise: Holy, holy, holy Lord, God of power and might, heaven and earth are full of your glory.

The glorious company of apostles praise you. The noble fellowship of prophets praise you. The white-robed army of martyrs praise you. Throughout the world the holy Church acclaims you; Father, of majesty unbounded, your true and only Son, worthy of all worship, and the Holy Spirit, advocate and guide.

You, Christ, are the king of glory, the eternal Son of the Father. When you became man to set us free you did not shun the Virgin's womb.

You overcame the sting of death and opened the kingdom of heaven to all believers. You are seated at God's right hand in glory. We believe that you will come and be our judge. Come then, Lord, and help your people, bought with the price of your own blood, and bring us with your saints to glory everlasting.

Praise and Thanksgiving (Songs and Prayers)

Gloria Patri
Glory be to the Father,
And to the Son and to the Holy Spirit:
As it was in the beginning,
Is now, and ever shall be,
World without end. Amen, amen.

LISTENING TO HIS VOICE

Chronological Reading for the Day
Acts 24-26

Lectionary Readings
Psalm: Ps. 46   OT: Jer. 31.31-34
Gospel: John 8.31-36   NT: Rom. 3.19-28

Reflection: Silence and/or Journaling

RESPONDING IN FAITH

The Apostles' Creed
I believe in God, the Father Almighty, Maker of heaven and earth; and in Jesus Christ, his only Son, our Lord, who was conceived by the Holy Spirit, born of the Virgin Mary, suffered under Pontius Pilate, was crucified, dead, and buried; he descended into hell; the third day he arose again from the dead; he ascended into heaven and sits on the right hand of God the Father Almighty; from thence he shall come to judge the quick and the dead.

I believe in the Holy Spirit, the holy catholic* church, the communion of saints, the forgiveness of sins, the resurrection of the body, and the life everlasting. Amen.

* In the Apostles' and Nicene Creeds, the term catholic refers to the Church's universality, through all ages and times, of all languages and peoples. It refers to no particular tradition or denominational expression (e.g., as in Roman Catholic).

Prayers of Confession

Let us now confess our sins to God and receive mercy and grace to help in our time of need.

Assurance of Pardon

Having faithfully confessed and renounced your sin, Christ also has been faithful to forgive your sins and to purify you from all unrighteousness. It is certain, that there is One who has spoken to the Father in your defense, Jesus Christ, the Righteous One who is the atoning sacrifice for our sins and for the sins of the whole world. His grace and peace are with you now. Amen.

Petitions and Supplications, Ending with the Lord's Prayer

Our Father which art in heaven, Hallowed be thy name. Thy kingdom come, Thy will be done in earth, as it is in heaven. Give us this day our daily bread. And forgive us our debts, as we forgive our debtors. And lead us not into temptation, but deliver us from evil: For thine is the kingdom, and the power, and the glory, for ever. Amen.

~ Matthew 6.9-13 (KJV)

Doxology (and/or closing song)

Praise God from whom all blessings flow;
Praise Him all creatures here below;
Praise Him above ye heavenly host;
Praise Father, Son and Holy Ghost. Amen.

DEPARTING TO SERVE

Benediction

Almighty God, gracious Lord, we thank you that your Holy Spirit renews the church in every age. Pour out your Holy Spirit on your faithful people. Keep them steadfast in your word, protect and comfort then in times of trial, defend them against all enemies of the gospel, and bestow on the church your saving peace, through Jesus Christ, our Savior and Lord, who lives and reigns with you and the Holy Spirit, one God, now and forever. Amen.

~ Evangelical Lutheran Worship
(Conference of Bishops, Evangelical Lutheran Church in America, p. 320)

Affirmation from the Psalms

How can a young man keep his way pure? By guarding it according to your word. [10] With my whole heart I seek you; let me not wander from your commandments! [11] I have stored up your word in my heart, that I might not sin against you. [12] Blessed are you, O Lord; teach me your statutes! [13] With my lips I declare all the rules of your mouth. [14] In the way of your testimonies I delight as much as in all riches. [15] I will meditate on your precepts and fix my eyes on your ways. [16] I will delight in your statutes; I will not forget your word.

~ Psalm 119.9-16

Pray without Ceasing – Flash Prayer for the Day

Lord Jesus, fill my heart with your Word, that I may constantly meditate on your truth, and be set free to obey your will.

For Your Weekly Journey

Let God Arise! Seasonal Focus

The Everlasting Dominion to Come, Daniel 7.1-3, 15-18

Book Reading

Ramsay and Wilson, *St. Paul: the Traveler and Roman Citizen*

All Saints Day
November 1, 2016

According to God's holy promise, the saints of Christ will dine at the marriage supper of the Lamb, a feast of love and communion with the risen Lord and Savior himself. The Feast of Christ the King, the last Sunday before Advent, anticipates the day when Christ will reign supreme, and the saints of God will never again leave the presence of their Lord.

TODAY'S THEME

The Everlasting Dominion to Come, Daniel 7.1-3, 15-18

Daniel, the great seer and prophet, during the first year of Belshazzar king of Babylon, saw dreams and visions as he lay in his bed. After the dreams, he wrote them down and summarized the meaning of them. Daniel spoke regarding his visions in the night, an image of the "four winds of heaven" stirring up the great sea, with four beasts coming up out of the sea, all different from each other. After beholding these images, Daniel said that his spirit was anxious, alarmed by the visions he saw. On approaching "one of those who stood there" (perhaps an angelic being?), he was told the truth concerning these visions and their interpretation by this personage. The messenger said, "These four great beasts are four kings who shall arise out of the earth. But the saints of the Most High shall receive the kingdom and possess the kingdom forever, forever and ever."

In the same chapter, Daniel looked and saw thrones placed with the Ancient of Days taking his seat, full of splendor, glory, and majesty. A stream of fire came out from before him, and "a thousand thousands" served him, and ten thousand times ten thousand" stood before. In the night visions, with the clouds of heaven, there came one like a Son of Man before the Ancient of Days and was presented before him. To this Son of Man was given dominion, glory, and a kingdom, that all peoples, nations, and languages should serve him. Daniel said his "dominion is an everlasting dominion which shall not pass away, and his kingdom one that shall not be destroyed." The saints of the Most High shall receive the kingdom and rule with the Son of Man as his co-regents forever. God's ultimate intention is to bring all creation back under his reign, under the rule of the Son of Man, with the saints receiving this reign as an inheritance forever.

Daily Devotional Guide

PREPARING OUR HEARTS

Invocation: Our Prayer of Acclamation
O God of the spirits of all flesh: We praise and magnify thy holy Name for all thy servants who have finished their course in thy faith and fear; for the blessed Virgin Mary, for the holy Patriarchs, Prophets, Apostles, and Martyrs, and for all other thy righteous servants, known to us or unknown; and we beseech thee that, encouraged by their examples and strengthened by their fellowship, we also may be found meet to be partakers of the inheritance of the saints in light; through the merits of thy Son Jesus Christ our Lord. Amen.

~ England Revised Prayer Book (Suten, p. 72)

Call to Worship
Blessed are you, O God: Father, Son, and Holy Spirit. And blessed is your Kingdom, both now and forever, amen.

PRAISING OUR GOD

Te Deum Laudamus
You are God: we praise you; you are the Lord; we acclaim you; you are the eternal Father: All creation worships you. To you all angels, all the powers of heaven, Cherubim and Seraphim, sing in endless praise:

Holy, holy, holy Lord, God of power and might, heaven and earth are full of your glory.

The glorious company of apostles praise you. The noble fellowship of prophets praise you. The white-robed army of martyrs praise you. Throughout the world the holy Church acclaims you; Father, of majesty unbounded, your true and only Son, worthy of all worship, and the Holy Spirit, advocate and guide.

You, Christ, are the king of glory, the eternal Son of the Father. When you became man to set us free you did not shun the Virgin's womb. You overcame the sting of death and opened the kingdom of heaven to all believers. You are seated at God's right hand in glory. We believe that you will come and be our judge. Come then, Lord, and help your people, bought with the price of your own blood, and bring us with your saints to glory everlasting.

Praise and Thanksgiving (Songs and Prayers)

Gloria Patri
Glory be to the Father,
And to the Son and to the Holy Spirit:
As it was in the beginning,
Is now, and ever shall be,
World without end. Amen, amen.

LISTENING TO HIS VOICE

Chronological Reading for the Day
Acts 27-28

Lectionary Readings
Psalm: Ps. 149   *OT:* Dan. 7.1-3, 15-18
Gospel: Luke 6.20-31   *NT:* Eph. 1.11-23

Reflection: Silence and/or Journaling

RESPONDING IN FAITH

The Apostles' Creed
I believe in God, the Father Almighty, Maker of heaven and earth; and in Jesus Christ, his only Son, our Lord, who was conceived by the Holy Spirit, born of the Virgin Mary, suffered under Pontius Pilate, was crucified, dead, and buried; he descended into hell; the third day he arose again from the dead; he ascended into heaven and sits on the right hand of God the Father Almighty; from thence he shall come to judge the quick and the dead.

I believe in the Holy Spirit, the holy catholic* church, the communion of saints, the forgiveness of sins, the resurrection of the body, and the life everlasting. Amen.

* In the Apostles' and Nicene Creeds, the term catholic refers to the Church's universality, through all ages and times, of all languages and peoples. It refers to no particular tradition or denominational expression (e.g., as in Roman Catholic).

Prayers of Confession
Let us now confess our sins to God and receive mercy and grace to help in our time of need.

Assurance of Pardon
Having faithfully confessed and renounced your sin, Christ also has been faithful to forgive your sins and to purify you from all unrighteousness. It is certain, that there is One who has spoken to the Father in your defense, Jesus Christ, the Righteous One who is the atoning sacrifice for our sins and for the sins of the whole world. His grace and peace are with you now. Amen.

Petitions and Supplications, Ending with the Lord's Prayer

Our Father which art in heaven, Hallowed be thy name. Thy kingdom come, Thy will be done in earth, as it is in heaven. Give us this day our daily bread. And forgive us our debts, as we forgive our debtors. And lead us not into temptation, but deliver us from evil: For thine is the kingdom, and the power, and the glory, for ever. Amen.

~ Matthew 6.9-13 (KJV)

Doxology (and/or closing song)

Praise God from whom all blessings flow;
Praise Him all creatures here below;
Praise Him above ye heavenly host;
Praise Father, Son and Holy Ghost. Amen.

DEPARTING TO SERVE

Benediction

O Almighty God, who has knit together thine elect in one communion and fellowship in the mystical body of thy Son Christ our Lord: Grant us grace so to follow thy blessed saints in all virtuous and godly living, that we may come to those ineffable joys which thou hast prepared for those who infeignedly live thee; through the same Jesus Christ our Lord, who with thee and the Holy Spirit liveth and reigneth, one God, now and for ever. Amen.

~ *The Episcopal Church in the United States of America*
(The Episcopal Church, p. 194)

Affirmation from the Psalms

May he have dominion from sea to sea, and from the River to the ends of the earth! [9] May desert tribes bow down before him, and his enemies lick the dust! [10] May the kings of Tarshish and of the coastlands render him tribute; may the kings of Sheba and Seba bring gifts! [11] May all kings fall down before him, all nations serve him!

~ Psalm 72.8-11

Pray without Ceasing – Flash Prayer for the Day
Marantha, Lord Jesus Christ, our King and Lord, come and reign in your glory!

For Your Weekly Journey

Let God Arise! Seasonal Focus
The Everlasting Dominion to Come, Daniel 7.1-3, 15-18

Book Reading
Ramsay and Wilson, *St. Paul: the Traveler and Roman Citizen*

WEEK 50

Twenty-fifth Sunday after Pentecost
November 6 - 12, 2016 • Proper 27

According to God's holy promise, the saints of Christ will dine at the marriage supper of the Lamb, a feast of love and communion with the risen Lord and Savior himself. The Feast of Christ the King, the last Sunday before Advent, anticipates the day when Christ will reign supreme, and the saints of God will never again leave the presence of their Lord.

THIS WEEK'S THEME
Stand Firm, and Hold Fast to the Tradition, 2 Thessalonians 2.1-5, 13-17

One of the most important themes of Paul's preaching and writing was the Second Coming (Parousia) of the Lord Jesus Christ. This was a major emphasis in his letters to those in Thessalonica. He warned them that in regard to the coming of our Lord Jesus Christ and our being gathered together to him, not to be quickly shaken in mind or alarmed by a teaching that affirmed that he had already come. Whether this came from some prophet or spirit or spoken word or a letter, if they claimed to be one of the apostles they were false. He challenged them to allow no one to deceive them in any way as to the Lord's coming. Why? "For that day will not come, unless the rebellion comes first, and the man of lawlessness is revealed, the son of destruction, who opposes and exalts himself against every so-called god or object of worship, so that he takes his seat in the temple of God, proclaiming himself to be God" (2 Thess. 2.3-4). He reminded them that he had mentioned these very truths when he was still with them.

Rather than chasing wild claims about Christ's coming, Paul told them that his company always give thanks to God for them, "brothers beloved by the Lord," for God chose them to be the firstfruits among those being saved "through sanctification by the Spirit and belief in the truth" (v. 13). Through the Gospel which the apostles preached they have been called in order to "obtain the glory of our Lord Jesus Christ" (v. 14). This amazing hope was theirs through the Gospel teaching of the apostles.

In light of this, Paul exhorted the believers to stand firm and hold to the traditions that they were taught by them, whether the oral tradition (by their spoken word) or by their epistles (i.e., their letters). Having the truth announced and embodied by the apostles, they were called to remain in it, defend it, and hold fast to it. And, they will be assured that the Lord Jesus Christ himself, and God the Father, the very one who loved them and gave them eternal comfort and good hope through grace, would work on their behalf. The Father and the Lord Jesus would comfort their hearts and establish them in every good work and word.

Daily Devotional Guide

PREPARING OUR HEARTS

Invocation: Our Prayer of Acclamation
Lord, in the wake of being in constant danger to falsehood, deception, and error, please provide us wisdom in the Holy Spirit to hold on to the teaching of the apostles. Do not allow us to be swept away with the latest teachings of culture and the world, but rather strengthen us as we stand firm on the truth. Teach us that we might never loosen our grip to the teachings of your apostles, and ever defend your truth against the lies of the enemy. We pray this in Christ's name, amen.

Call to Worship
Blessed are you, O God: Father, Son, and Holy Spirit. And blessed is your Kingdom, both now and forever, amen.

PRAISING OUR GOD

Te Deum Laudamus

You are God: we praise you; you are the Lord; we acclaim you; you are the eternal Father: All creation worships you. To you all angels, all the powers of heaven, Cherubim and Seraphim, sing in endless praise: Holy, holy, holy Lord, God of power and might, heaven and earth are full of your glory.

The glorious company of apostles praise you. The noble fellowship of prophets praise you. The white-robed army of martyrs praise you. Throughout the world the holy Church acclaims you; Father, of majesty unbounded, your true and only Son, worthy of all worship, and the Holy Spirit, advocate and guide.

You, Christ, are the king of glory, the eternal Son of the Father. When you became man to set us free you did not shun the Virgin's womb. You overcame the sting of death and opened the kingdom of heaven to all believers. You are seated at God's right hand in glory. We believe that you will come and be our judge. Come then, Lord, and help your people, bought with the price of your own blood, and bring us with your saints to glory everlasting.

Praise and Thanksgiving (Songs and Prayers)

Gloria Patri

Glory be to the Father,
And to the Son and to the Holy Spirit:
As it was in the beginning,
Is now, and ever shall be,
World without end. Amen, amen.

LISTENING TO HIS VOICE

Chronological Reading for the Day
Sunday: Philem.; Phil. 1-4
Monday: James 1-3
Tuesday: James 4-5; 1 Tim. 1-2
Wednesday: 1 Tim. 3-6
Thursday: Titus 1-3
Friday: 2 Tim. 1-4
Saturday: Heb. 1.1-4.13

Lectionary Readings
Psalm: Ps. 98
Gospel: Luke 20.27-38

OT: Hag. 1.15b-2.9
NT: 2 Thess. 2.1-5, 13-17

Reflection: Silence and/or Journaling

RESPONDING IN FAITH

The Apostles' Creed
I believe in God, the Father Almighty, Maker of heaven and earth; and in Jesus Christ, his only Son, our Lord, who was conceived by the Holy Spirit, born of the Virgin Mary, suffered under Pontius Pilate, was crucified, dead, and buried; he descended into hell; the third day he arose again from the dead; he ascended into heaven and sits on the right hand of God the Father Almighty; from thence he shall come to judge the quick and the dead.

I believe in the Holy Spirit, the holy catholic* church, the communion of saints, the forgiveness of sins, the resurrection of the body, and the life everlasting. Amen.

* In the Apostles' and Nicene Creeds, the term catholic refers to the Church's universality, through all ages and times, of all languages and peoples. It refers to no particular tradition or denominational expression (e.g., as in Roman Catholic).

Prayers of Confession

Let us now confess our sins to God and receive mercy and grace to help in our time of need.

Assurance of Pardon

Having faithfully confessed and renounced your sin, Christ also has been faithful to forgive your sins and to purify you from all unrighteousness. It is certain, that there is One who has spoken to the Father in your defense, Jesus Christ, the Righteous One who is the atoning sacrifice for our sins and for the sins of the whole world. His grace and peace are with you now. Amen.

Petitions and Supplications, Ending with the Lord's Prayer

Our Father which art in heaven, Hallowed be thy name. Thy kingdom come, Thy will be done in earth, as it is in heaven. Give us this day our daily bread. And forgive us our debts, as we forgive our debtors. And lead us not into temptation, but deliver us from evil: For thine is the kingdom, and the power, and the glory, for ever. Amen.

~ Matthew 6.9-13 (KJV)

Doxology (and/or closing song)

Praise God from whom all blessings flow;
Praise Him all creatures here below;
Praise Him above ye heavenly host;
Praise Father, Son and Holy Ghost. Amen.

DEPARTING TO SERVE

Benediction

Lord Jesus Christ, thank you for the apostolic tradition that has established us in the sanctification of the Holy Spirit and our belief in your truth. You revealed to us your glory through the testimony of your servants, and we have believed through their word. Now, teach us to stand firm and hold fast to their teaching and life. In your name we pray, amen.

Affirmation from the Psalms

I will remember the deeds of the Lord; yes, I will remember your wonders of old. [12] I will ponder all your work, and meditate on your mighty deeds. [13] Your way, O God, is holy. What god is great like our God? [14] You are the God who works wonders; you have made known your might among the peoples. [15] You with your arm redeemed your people, the children of Jacob and Joseph. Selah [16] When the waters saw you, O God, when the waters saw you, they were afraid; indeed, the deep trembled.

~ Psalm 77.11-16

Pray without Ceasing – Flash Prayer for the Day

Lord Jesus Christ, thank you for the apostles, whose word and example continues to guide us into your truth to this day.

For Your Weekly Journey

Let God Arise! Seasonal Focus

The Everlasting Dominion to Come, Daniel 7.1-3, 15-18

Book Reading

Ramsay and Wilson, *St. Paul: the Traveler and Roman Citizen*

Our Corporate Disciplines

Book Discussion: Monday, November 7, 2016
Fallow Day: Friday, November 11, 2016

Twenty-sixth Sunday after Pentecost
November 13 - 19, 2016 • Proper 28

According to God's holy promise, the saints of Christ will dine at the marriage supper of the Lamb, a feast of love and communion with the risen Lord and Savior himself. The Feast of Christ the King, the last Sunday before Advent, anticipates the day when Christ will reign supreme, and the saints of God will never again leave the presence of their Lord.

THIS WEEK'S THEME
By Your Endurance You Gain Your Life, Luke 21.5-19

On the occasion of being in the temple where people were speaking of its beauty and nobility, its adornment with great noble stones and offerings, Jesus affirmed that the days would come where not a single stone would remain and not be thrown down. His disciples asked him when those things would be, and what would be the sign of those things taking place. Jesus told them that they must be careful not to be led astray. Many would come in his name, claiming to be the Christ and that the Kingdom had come. He warned them not to go after such people. They would hear of wars and conflicts, but they had no need to be terrified, for these things are merely of the beginning things that must happen, but the end would not be all at once.

Rather, Jesus said that nations and kingdoms would rise against one another, and there would be great earthquakes, and famines and pestilences in various places. Those times would be accompanied by terrors and great heavenly signs as well. Yet, before all these things, others would lay their hands on them, persecuting and delivering them up to the synagogues and prisons. For his name's sake, they would be brought before kings and governors, which will become their opportunity to bear witness of the truth. There was no need to meditate beforehand what to say, for he the Lord himself would give them "a mouth and wisdom which none of your adversaries will be able to withstand or contradict."

These times would cause betrayal among dearest family members, and they would be delivered up "even by parents and brothers and relatives and friends." Some of the believers would even be put to death, hated by everyone because of Jesus' own name. Jesus assured them, however, that not even a hair of their heads head would perish. By their endurance during these times, they would in fact gain their lives.

Jesus predicted that the end would truly be a time of persecution, trial, and painful affliction. God's grace, however, will prove sufficient to the faithful, who will gain their very lives as they persevere in the face of that suffering.

Daily Devotional Guide

PREPARING OUR HEARTS

Invocation: Our Prayer of Acclamation

Eternal God and Father of our Lord Jesus Christ, thank you for informing us of the conditions that are bound to accompany the second coming of your Son. He assured us that your grace would be sufficient to maintain us in the midst of horrible affliction and turbulent experiences. We will trust in you, no matter what we face, no matter how long, for only in you can we endure at all. In Jesus name, amen.

Call to Worship

Blessed are you, O God: Father, Son, and Holy Spirit. And blessed is your Kingdom, both now and forever, amen.

PRAISING OUR GOD

Te Deum Laudamus

You are God: we praise you; you are the Lord; we acclaim you; you are the eternal Father: All creation worships you. To you all angels, all the powers of heaven, Cherubim and Seraphim, sing in endless praise: Holy, holy, holy Lord, God of power and might, heaven and earth are full of your glory.

The glorious company of apostles praise you. The noble fellowship of prophets praise you. The white-robed army of martyrs praise you. Throughout the world the holy Church acclaims you; Father, of majesty unbounded, your true and only Son, worthy of all worship, and the Holy Spirit, advocate and guide.

You, Christ, are the king of glory, the eternal Son of the Father. When you became man to set us free you did not shun the Virgin's womb. You overcame the sting of death and opened the kingdom of heaven to all believers. You are seated at God's right hand in glory. We believe that you will come and be our judge. Come then, Lord, and help your people, bought with the price of your own blood, and bring us with your saints to glory everlasting.

Praise and Thanksgiving (Songs and Prayers)

Gloria Patri

Glory be to the Father,
And to the Son and to the Holy Spirit:
As it was in the beginning,
Is now, and ever shall be,
World without end. Amen, amen.

LISTENING TO HIS VOICE

Chronological Reading for the Day

Sunday: Heb. 4.14-7.28 *Thursday:* 1 Pet. 3-5
Monday: Heb. 8-10 *Friday:* 2 Pet. 1-3
Tuesday: Heb. 11-13 *Saturday:* 1 John 1-3
Wednesday: 1 Pet. 1-2

Lectionary Readings

Psalm: Ps. 98 *OT:* Mal. 4.1-2a
Gospel: Luke 21.5-19 *NT:* 2 Thess. 3.6-13

Reflection: Silence and/or Journaling

RESPONDING IN FAITH

The Apostles' Creed

I believe in God, the Father Almighty, Maker of heaven and earth; and in Jesus Christ, his only Son, our Lord, who was conceived by the Holy Spirit, born of the Virgin Mary, suffered under Pontius Pilate, was crucified, dead, and buried; he descended into hell; the third day he arose again from the dead; he ascended into heaven and sits on the right hand of God the Father Almighty; from thence he shall come to judge the quick and the dead.

I believe in the Holy Spirit, the holy catholic* church, the communion of saints, the forgiveness of sins, the resurrection of the body, and the life everlasting. Amen.

* In the Apostles' and Nicene Creeds, the term catholic refers to the Church's universality, through all ages and times, of all languages and peoples. It refers to no particular tradition or denominational expression (e.g., as in Roman Catholic).

Prayers of Confession

Let us now confess our sins to God and receive mercy and grace to help in our time of need.

Assurance of Pardon

Having faithfully confessed and renounced your sin, Christ also has been faithful to forgive your sins and to purify you from all unrighteousness. It is certain, that there is One who has spoken to the Father in your defense, Jesus Christ, the Righteous One who is the atoning sacrifice for our sins and for the sins of the whole world. His grace and peace are with you now. Amen.

Petitions and Supplications, Ending with the Lord's Prayer

Our Father which art in heaven, Hallowed be thy name. Thy kingdom come. Thy will be done in earth, as it is in heaven. Give us this day our daily bread. And forgive us our debts, as we forgive our debtors. And lead us not into temptation, but deliver us from evil: For thine is the kingdom, and the power, and the glory, for ever. Amen.

~ Matthew 6.9-13 (KJV)

Doxology (and/or closing song)

Praise God from whom all blessings flow;
Praise Him all creatures here below;
Praise Him above ye heavenly host;
Praise Father, Son and Holy Ghost. Amen.

DEPARTING TO SERVE

Benediction

Lord Jesus Christ, thank you for your reassuring word that you gave to your disciples about the circumstances that will accompany your coming again. We know that we will not be able to endure apart from your grace and supply by your Spirit. Sustain us, as you did your apostles, in their persecutions and enable us to faithfully persevere through all things, for your name and kingdom's sake. In your name we pray, amen.

Affirmation from the Psalms

But I call to God, and the Lord will save me. [17] Evening and morning and at noon I utter my complaint and moan, and he hears my voice. [18] He redeems my soul in safety from the battle that I wage, for many are arrayed against me. [19] God will give ear and humble them, he who is enthroned from of old, Selah because they do not change and do not fear God.

~ Psalm 55.16-19

Pray without Ceasing – Flash Prayer for the Day

Lord Jesus Christ, help us to endure in the midst of trial for in endurance we will gain our very lives.

For Your Weekly Journey

Let God Arise! Seasonal Focus

The Everlasting Dominion to Come, Daniel 7.1-3, 15-18

Book Reading

Ramsay and Wilson, *St. Paul: the Traveler and Roman Citizen*

Reign of Christ the King
November 20 - 26, 2016 • Proper 29

According to God's holy promise, the saints of Christ will dine at the marriage supper of the Lamb, a feast of love and communion with the risen Lord and Savior himself. The Feast of Christ the King, the last Sunday before Advent, anticipates the day when Christ will reign supreme, and the saints of God will never again leave the presence of their Lord.

THIS WEEK'S THEME
The Righteous Branch, Jeremiah 23.1-6

The LORD God, the good shepherd of his people, pronounced judgment on the unsavory and lazy care provided to his people by the undershepherds of the nation – the kings, priests, and rulers of Israel. Through Jeremiah the Lord declared "Woe to the shepherds who destroy and scatter the sheep of my pasture!" (v.1). To those shepherds he rebuked them for scattering his flock and driving them away, failing to attend them. He promised that he would in fact, however, attend to them for their evil deeds of negligence and scattering. The Lord then promises to gather the remnant of his flock from all the countries where he had driven them. He would bring them back to their fold, and they would then be fruitful and multiply. And, he promised to set shepherds over them who would care for them, and never again would they be afraid, dismayed, or missing.

In the midst of this prophetic declaration, the Lord gave a revelation regarding the coming of the Messiah. "Behold, the days are coming", declares the Lord, "when I will raise up for David a righteous Branch, and he shall reign as king and deal wisely, and shall execute justice and righteousness in the land. In his days Judah will be saved, and Israel will dwell securely. And this is the name by which he will be called: 'The Lord is our righteousness.'" God's intent is, in the proper time and moment, to raise up for his people a Righteous Branch, one of the lineage of Jesse, a King, who would reign in wisdom, executing justice and righteousness throughout the land. Through his rule, Judah would be saved and Israel made secure, and his name would be called, "The Lord is our righteousness."

Now, in this age we have come to know that Jesus of Nazareth is the Messiah, the fulfillment of Jeremiah's prophecy and the soon-and-coming King who will reign in righteousness over the entire earth forever. He is the Priest-King, who shed his blood to make us free, and will reign on God's throne as Lord forever. Indeed, the King will be called "The Lord is our righteousness."

Daily Devotional Guide

PREPARING OUR HEARTS

Invocation: Our Prayer of Acclamation
O ruler of the universe, Lord God, great deeds are they that you have done, surpassing human understanding. Your ways are ways of righteousness and truth, O King of all the ages. Who can gail to do your homage, Lord and sing the praise of your Name? For you only are the Holy One. All nations will draw near and fall down before you, because your just and holy works have been revealed. Amen.

~ Revelation 15.3-4

Call to Worship
Blessed are you, O God: Father, Son, and Holy Spirit. And blessed is your Kingdom, both now and forever, amen.

PRAISING OUR GOD

Te Deum Laudamus

You are God: we praise you; you are the Lord; we acclaim you; you are the eternal Father: All creation worships you. To you all angels, all the powers of heaven, Cherubim and Seraphim, sing in endless praise: Holy, holy, holy Lord, God of power and might, heaven and earth are full of your glory.

The glorious company of apostles praise you. The noble fellowship of prophets praise you. The white-robed army of martyrs praise you. Throughout the world the holy Church acclaims you; Father, of majesty unbounded, your true and only Son, worthy of all worship, and the Holy Spirit, advocate and guide.

You, Christ, are the king of glory, the eternal Son of the Father. When you became man to set us free you did not shun the Virgin's womb. You overcame the sting of death and opened the kingdom of heaven to all believers. You are seated at God's right hand in glory. We believe that you will come and be our judge. Come then, Lord, and help your people, bought with the price of your own blood, and bring us with your saints to glory everlasting.

Praise and Thanksgiving (Songs and Prayers)

Gloria Patri

Glory be to the Father,
And to the Son and to the Holy Spirit:
As it was in the beginning,
Is now, and ever shall be,
World without end. Amen, amen.

LISTENING TO HIS VOICE

Chronological Reading for the Day

Sunday: 1 John 4-5; 2 John 1; 3 John 1
Monday: Jude 1; Rev. 1-2

Tuesday: Rev. 3-6
Wednesday: Rev. 7-10
Thursday: Rev. 11-14
Friday: Rev. 15-18
Saturday: Rev. 19-22

Lectionary Readings

Psalm: Luke 1.68-79   *OT:* Jer. 23.1-6
Gospel: Luke 23.33-43   *NT:* Col. 1.11-20

Reflection: Silence and/or Journaling

RESPONDING IN FAITH

The Apostles' Creed

*I believe in God, the Father Almighty, Maker of heaven and earth;
and in Jesus Christ, his only Son, our Lord, who was conceived by the
Holy Spirit, born of the Virgin Mary, suffered under Pontius Pilate,
was crucified, dead, and buried; he descended into hell; the third day
he arose again from the dead; he ascended into heaven and sits on
the right hand of God the Father Almighty; from thence he shall come
to judge the quick and the dead.*

I believe in the Holy Spirit, the holy catholic church, the communion
of saints, the forgiveness of sins, the resurrection of the body, and the
life everlasting. Amen.*

* In the Apostles' and Nicene Creeds, the term catholic refers to the Church's
universality, through all ages and times, of all languages and peoples. It refers to no
particular tradition or denominational expression (e.g., as in Roman Catholic).

Prayers of Confession

Let us now confess our sins to God and receive mercy and
grace to help in our time of need.

Assurance of Pardon

Having faithfully confessed and renounced your sin, Christ also has been faithful to forgive your sins and to purify you from all unrighteousness. It is certain, that there is One who has spoken to the Father in your defense, Jesus Christ, the Righteous One who is the atoning sacrifice for our sins and for the sins of the whole world. His grace and peace are with you now. Amen.

Petitions and Supplications, Ending with the Lord's Prayer

Our Father which art in heaven, Hallowed be thy name. Thy kingdom come, Thy will be done in earth, as it is in heaven. Give us this day our daily bread. And forgive us our debts, as we forgive our debtors. And lead us not into temptation, but deliver us from evil: For thine is the kingdom, and the power, and the glory, for ever. Amen.

~ Matthew 6.9-13 (KJV)

Doxology (and/or closing song)

Praise God from whom all blessings flow;
Praise Him all creatures here below;
Praise Him above ye heavenly host;
Praise Father, Son and Holy Ghost. Amen.

DEPARTING TO SERVE

Benediction

God of power and love, you raised Jesus from death to life, resplendent on glory to rule over all creation. Free the world to rejoice in his peace, to glory in his justice, and to live in his love. Unite all humankind in Jesus Christ your Son, who lives and reigns with you and the Holy Spirit, one God, forever and ever. Amen.

~ *Supplemental Liturgical Recourse 7*
(The Theological and Worship Ministry Unit, p. 394-395)

Affirmation from the Psalms

The Lord reigns; let the peoples tremble! He sits enthroned upon the cherubim; let the earth quake! [2] The Lord is great in Zion; he is exalted over all the peoples. [3] Let them praise your great and awesome name! Holy is he! [4] The King in his might loves justice. You have established equity; you have executed justice and righteousness in Jacob. [5] Exalt the Lord our God; worship at his footstool! Holy is he!

~ Psalm 99.1-5

Pray without Ceasing – Flash Prayer for the Day

O Righteous Branch, from the lineage of Jesse, Lord Jesus Christ, descend and execute justice and righteousness upon your throne.

For Your Weekly Journey

Let God Arise! Seasonal Focus
The Everlasting Dominion to Come, Daniel 7.1-3, 15-18

Book Reading
Ramsay and Wilson, *St. Paul: the Traveler and Roman Citizen*

Our Corporate Disciplines
Book Discussion: Monday, November 21, 2016

Special Church Year Services
Thanksgiving Day: November 24, 2016

Thanksgiving Day
November 24, 2016

According to God's holy promise, the saints of Christ will dine at the marriage supper of the Lamb, a feast of love and communion with the risen Lord and Savior himself. The Feast of Christ the King, the last Sunday before Advent, anticipates the day when Christ will reign supreme, and the saints of God will never again leave the presence of their Lord.

TODAY'S THEME
His Steadfast Love Endures Forever, Psalm 100

Nothing is more appropriate for human beings than to offer to God the appropriate worship and praise due to his name. Psalm 100's superscription affirms that this song is for giving thanks, with the previous songs affirming his majesty and glory as King of all heaven and earth. It demands that all the earth should make a joyful noise to him, serving him with gladness, and coming into his presence with joyful songs. This exuberant praise is rooted in the recognition that the Lord, the God of Israel, is God, the one who made us. We, indeed, are therefore the sheep of his pasture, the objects of his care, provision, and love.

In light of this, we should enter into his temple gates with thanksgiving, and into his courts with praise! All peoples should offer their thanks to him, blessing his name. And the song gives the reason for this extreme show of praise to the LORD: "For the Lord is good; his steadfast love endures forever, and his faithfulness to all generations." On this Thanksgiving Day let us acknowledge that the LORD has been good to us, that his steadfast love has endured another year, and that his faithfulness has continued through all time, up to our very own generation, demonstrated to us in the days of our lives. His love has never failed us; it will be displayed in all the things he has provided and will never come to an end.

Daily Devotional Guide

PREPARING OUR HEARTS

Invocation: Our Prayer of Acclamation

Almighty and gracious Father, we give thee thanks for the fruits of the earth in their season and for the labors of those who harvest them. Make us, we beseech thee, faithful stewards of thy great bounty, for the provision of our necessities and the relief of all who are in need, to the glory of thy Name; through Jesus Christ our Lord, who liveth and reigneth with thee and the Holy Spirit, one God, now and for ever. Amen.

~ The Episcopal Church in the United States of America
(The Episcopal Church, p. 194)

Call to Worship

Blessed are you, O God: Father, Son, and Holy Spirit. And blessed is your Kingdom, both now and forever, amen.

PRAISING OUR GOD

Te Deum Laudamus

You are God: we praise you; you are the Lord; we acclaim you; you are the eternal Father: All creation worships you. To you all angels, all the powers of heaven, Cherubim and Seraphim, sing in endless praise: Holy, holy, holy Lord, God of power and might, heaven and earth are full of your glory.

The glorious company of apostles praise you. The noble fellowship of prophets praise you. The white-robed army of martyrs praise you. Throughout the world the holy Church acclaims you; Father, of majesty unbounded, your true and only Son, worthy of all worship, and the Holy Spirit, advocate and guide.

You, Christ, are the king of glory, the eternal Son of the Father. When you became man to set us free you did not shun the Virgin's womb. You overcame the sting of death and opened the kingdom of heaven to all believers. You are seated at God's right hand in glory. We believe that you will come and be our judge. Come then, Lord, and help your people, bought with the price of your own blood, and bring us with your saints to glory everlasting.

Praise and Thanksgiving (Songs and Prayers)

Gloria Patri
*Glory be to the Father,
And to the Son and to the Holy Spirit:
As it was in the beginning,
Is now, and ever shall be,
World without end. Amen, amen.*

LISTENING TO HIS VOICE

Chronological Reading for the Day
Rev. 11-14

Lectionary Readings
Psalm: Ps. 100   *OT:* Deut. 26.1-11
Gospel: John 6.25-35   *NT:* Phil. 4.4-9

Reflection: Silence and/or Journaling

RESPONDING IN FAITH

The Apostles' Creed
I believe in God, the Father Almighty, Maker of heaven and earth; and in Jesus Christ, his only Son, our Lord, who was conceived by the Holy Spirit, born of the Virgin Mary, suffered under Pontius Pilate, was crucified, dead, and buried; he descended into hell; the third day he arose again from the dead; he ascended into heaven and sits on

the right hand of God the Father Almighty; from thence he shall come to judge the quick and the dead.

I believe in the Holy Spirit, the holy catholic* church, the communion of saints, the forgiveness of sins, the resurrection of the body, and the life everlasting. Amen.

* In the Apostles' and Nicene Creeds, the term catholic refers to the Church's universality, through all ages and times, of all languages and peoples. It refers to no particular tradition or denominational expression (e.g., as in Roman Catholic).

Prayers of Confession

Let us now confess our sins to God and receive mercy and grace to help in our time of need.

Assurance of Pardon

Having faithfully confessed and renounced your sin, Christ also has been faithful to forgive your sins and to purify you from all unrighteousness. It is certain, that there is One who has spoken to the Father in your defense, Jesus Christ, the Righteous One who is the atoning sacrifice for our sins and for the sins of the whole world. His grace and peace are with you now. Amen.

Petitions and Supplications, Ending with the Lord's Prayer

Our Father which art in heaven, Hallowed be thy name. Thy kingdom come, Thy will be done in earth, as it is in heaven. Give us this day our daily bread. And forgive us our debts, as we forgive our debtors. And lead us not into temptation, but deliver us from evil: For thine is the kingdom, and the power, and the glory, for ever. Amen.

~ Matthew 6.9-13 (KJV)

Doxology (and/or closing song)

Praise God from whom all blessings flow;
Praise Him all creatures here below;
Praise Him above ye heavenly host;
Praise Father, Son and Holy Ghost. Amen.

DEPARTING TO SERVE

Benediction

O most merciful Father, we humbly thank thee for all thy gifts so freely bestowed upon us. For life and health and safety, for all that is beautiful in creation and in the lives of men, we praise and magnify thy holy Name. But above all we thank thee for our spiritual mercies in Christ Jesus our Lord, for the means of grace, and for the hope of glory. Fill our hearts with all joy and peace in believing; through Jesus Christ our Lord. Amen.

~ *Canada Prayer Book* (Suter, p. 283)

Affirmation from the Psalms

Oh give thanks to the Lord; call upon his name; make known his deeds among the peoples! [2] Sing to him, sing praises to him; tell of all his wondrous works! [3] Glory in his holy name; let the hearts of those who seek the Lord rejoice! [4] Seek the Lord and his strength; seek his presence continually! [5] Remember the wondrous works that he has done, his miracles, and the judgments he uttered, [6] O offspring of Abraham, his servant, children of Jacob, his chosen ones!

~ Psalm 105.1-6

Pray without Ceasing – Flash Prayer for the Day

Lord Jesus Christ, we give thanks to you, and call upon your name, for you alone are good and your mercy endures to the end.

For Your Weekly Journey

Let God Arise! Seasonal Focus

The Everlasting Dominion to Come, Daniel 7.1-3, 15-18

Book Reading

Ramsay and Wilson, *St. Paul: the Traveler and Roman Citizen*

Made in the USA
Lexington, KY
13 November 2015